Lewis and Clark among the Indians

James P. Ronda

Lewis and Clark among the Indians

University of Nebraska Press, *Lincoln and London*

First Bison Book printing: 1988

Most recent printing indicated by the first digit below:

3   4   5   6   7   8   9   10

Library of Congress Cataloging in Publication Data

Ronda, James P., 1943–
  Lewis and Clark among the Indians.

  Bibliography p.
  Includes index.
  1. Lewis and Clark Expedition (1804–1806) 2. Lewis,
Meriwether, 1774–1809. 3. Clark, William, 1770–1838.
4. West (U.S.)—Description and travel—To 1848.
5. United States—Exploring expeditions. 6. Indians of
North America—West (U.S.) 7.Indians of North America—
West (U.S.)—First contact with Occidental civilization.
1. Title
F592.7.R66   1984   978′.02′0922   84-3544
ISBN 0-8032-3870-3 (alk. paper)
ISBN 0-8032-8929-4 (pbk.)

For my father,

JAMES R. RONDA.

The West he loved but never saw.

Contents

Illustrations

Preface

The Lewis and Clark expedition has long symbolized the westering impulse in American life. No other exploring party has so fully captured the imagination of ordinary citizens or the attention of scholars. In ways that defy rational explanation, the picture of Lewis and Clark struggling up the Missouri and across the mountains to the great western sea continues to stir our national consciousness. Books, highway markers, museum displays, and a foundation dedicated to preserving the Lewis and Clark trail all bear witness to a fascination that time has only deepened.

Over the generations since the expedition returned from the Pacific, its achievement and significance for America heading west have undergone constant reappraisal. From an early emphasis on the journey as an epic of physical endurance and courage, Lewis and Clark have emerged in this century as pioneer western naturalists, cartographers, and diplomats. Thomas Jefferson, the man William Clark once called "that great Chaructor the Main Spring" of the expedition, would have heartily endorsed an evaluation of the Corps of Discovery that included sharp minds as well as strong bodies. And Jefferson would have reminded us that his explorers were part of that long encounter between Euro-Americans and native Americans. In its daily affairs and official actions, the expedition passed through, changed, and was in turn changed by countless native lives.

In the simplest terms, this book is about what happens when people from different cultural persuasions meet and deal with each other. The Lewis and Clark expedition was an integral and symbolic part of what James Axtell has aptly called "the American encounter." Nearly two and a half years of almost constant contact between explorers and Indians illuminate the larger and longer series of cultural relationships that began centuries before on the margins of the continent. This book is not a retelling of the familiar Lewis and Clark adventure. That story has been told with grace and skill by Bernard DeVoto and in the magnificent photographs of Ingvard Eide and David Muench. But readers will find moments of high drama not previously well known or clearly understood. This book is not an attempt to dress up exploration history with feathers and paint to satisfy current political needs. Nor is it a stitching together of capsule tribal histories and ethnographies. Finally, readers need not expect a catalog of every ethnographic observation recorded in the journals of the expedition.

What this book does offer is something new for the history of exploration in general and Lewis and Clark literature in particular—a full-scale contact study of the official and personal relations between the explorers and the Indians. In 1952, Bernard DeVoto wrote that "a dismaying amount of our history has been written without regard to the Indians." While much has changed since then, the history of exploration remains largely the story of the explorers themselves. *Lewis and Clark among the Indians* is an effort to meet DeVoto's challenge by looking at the very explorers he wrote about with such passion and perception. Lewis and Clark were indeed what William Goetzmann has labeled them, "diplomats in buckskin," but they and their party amounted to something more as well. The Corps of Discovery was a human community living in the midst of other human communities. The word *among* in the title was chosen to suggest that sense of living together. The daily dealings of Indians and explorers touched the full range of action and emotion. What is treated in these pages runs the gamut from high policy to personal liaisons, from the careful collection of ethnographic data to the sharing of food and songs around a blazing fire.

Every historian must first come to terms with his sources. Because the thoughts and actions of men like Weuche, Yelleppit, and Coboway are as central to the story of the expedition as the plans and designs of the explorers themselves, it is important to note the evidence and method used in this study. Donald Jackson once described Lewis and Clark as "the writingest explorers of their time." Lewis, Clark, Sergeants John Ordway, Charles Floyd, and Patrick Gass, and Private Joseph Whitehouse all wrote long, often perceptive passages in their diaries about native people. Despite the kinds of obvious cultural biases that scholars have long since learned to deal with in documentary analysis, the Lewis and Clark records provide a store of information about Indians unequaled in the literature of exploration. When joined to other contemporary evidence produced by the likes of David Thompson, Alexander Henry the Younger, Pierre-Antoine Tabeau, and Prince Maximilian of Wied, the historical record is rich indeed. But by itself that written documentary record cannot fully explain the intricate patterns of encounter that bound Indians and explorers together. To that evidence this study brings the findings of anthropology and archaeology. Site reports and culture element distributions are used here not as fashionable window dressing but as a vital means to give depth and meaning to the behavior of native people. Tribal history is here meant to suggest context in human action. Ethnohistory has been usefully defined by Mildred Wedel and Raymond DeMallie as the critical examination of written evidence in the light of anthropological perspectives. This book is exploration ethnohistory, a deliberate effort to probe the complexity of Indian-white encounters in North America by examining a memorable venture that has come to represent the westward movement.

The Lewis and Clark drama had actors drawn from both sides of the cultural divide. As Lewis and Clark were important players with powerful lines, so too were Black Buffalo, Cameahwait, and the Nez Perce woman Watkuweis. If the expedition was what the western photographer Ingvard Eide called it, "the American odyssey," then all the argonauts—those who ventured to the sea and those who watched in wonder—must have their voices heard. The Lewis and Clark expedition has come to mean something special if indefinable in our national history. All the participants in that odyssey require their measure so that the story of the expedition and the nation not be half-told. This book is about that measure and those voices.

Acknowledgments

Meriwether Lewis once called the expedition "a darling project of mine." This book has been that for me during the past four years. Thanking friends, colleagues, and companions for support, encouragement, and criticism is the most pleasant task any writer can undertake. This book began when I read John Allen's brilliant *Passage through the Garden* and wondered if anyone had made a study of the Corps of Discovery and native peoples. My earliest research on explorers and Indians was aided and abetted by two institutions—the Youngstown State University Research Council and Mike Faklis, gifted bookman and supplier of endlessly delightful volumes. As that research progressed I steadily incurred debts that demand at least interest paid here. I am especially grateful to the staff at the Missouri Historical Society, William Lang at the Montana Historical Society, Joseph Porter at the Joslyn Art Museum, and Stephen Catlett at the American Philosophical Society. John Allen, William Goetzmann, and Alvin Josephy, Jr., provided comments and inspiration in greater measure than hoped for. Five minutes with John Ewers cleared up a whole knot of Blackfeet questions. I owe a special debt to Ray Wood for anthropological services rendered. Gary Moulton, editor of the new Lewis and Clark Journals project, has been both friend and long-distance colleague.

Anyone pursuing Lewis and Clark must eventually encounter the wonderful people who make up the Lewis and Clark Trail Heritage Foundation. Among those in the foundation who gave me support and encouragement were Irving Anderson, E. G. "Frenchy" Chuinard, Robert Lange, and the best guide any greenhorn could want, Wilbur Werner of Cut Bank, Montana. Closer to home, research was made easier by the services of Hildegard Schnuttgen, who heads the Interlibrary Loan Department at Maag Library, Youngstown State University. Mrs. Margaret Carl took drafts filled with strange names and distant places and made sense of them all. Colleagues in the Department of History—especially Fred Blue, Lowell Satre, Agnes Smith, and Martin Berger—have heard more about Lewis and Clark than they ever wanted to know.

If this book did not already have a dedication promised long ago, it would be sent with affection and thanks to three extraordinary people. From the beginning of this

xiv

venture, Donald Jackson has read each chapter with the kind of critical eye for both style and substance that only he has. Don's enthusiasm prodded me on when several chapters got stalled on the wrong side of the Great Divide. Jim Axtell was part of my life long before it was invaded by Lewis and Clark. His patient, perceptive reading of the chapters has meant more than I can tell. That both of us appear in each other's acknowledgments, books, and articles only hints at what more than ten years of conversations and letters have yielded. But no one has lived more with this enterprise than my wife, Jeanne. She braved five weeks of demanding dirt camping in the summer of 1980 as we retraced the Lewis and Clark route. Her faith never wavered; my gratitude is equally unwavering. All of these friends share in what is good between these covers, but not in the shortcomings, which are mine.

Youngstown, Ohio
January 1984

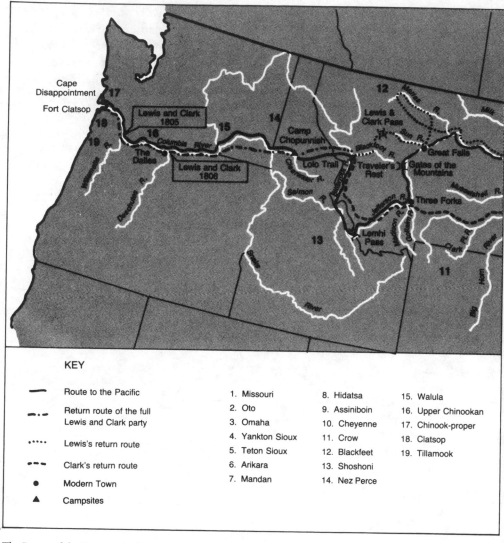

The Route of the Lewis and Clark Expedition 1804–1806

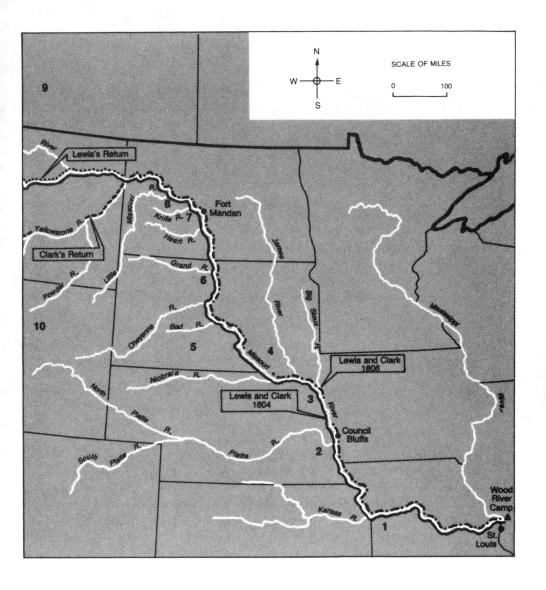

SCALE OF MILES

0   100

9

Lewis's Return

River

Missouri R.

8

7

Fort Mandan

Knife R.

Heart R.

Yellowstone R.

Clark's Return

Powder R.

Little

Grand R.

6

James River

Big Sioux R.

Mississippi River

Cheyenne R.

Bad R.

5

4

Lewis and Clark 1806

10

North

Niobrara R.

Lewis and Clark 1804

3

River

Platte

South Platte R.

Platte R.

Platte R.

2

Council Bluffs

Kansas R.

1

River

Wood River Camp

St. Louis

1

The Voyage Begins

"In all your intercourse with the natives, treat them in the most friendly and
conciliatory manner which their own conduct will permit."
—THOMAS JEFFERSON, "Instructions to Lewis, June, 1803"

The Indian relations of the Lewis and Clark expedition began long before the
explorers nosed their boats into the Missouri current and headed upriver. Thomas
Jefferson knew that as his explorers moved over the visible world of rivers, mountains, and plains, they would also pass through a more important world—a sometimes invisible universe of Indian politics and European rivalries. He grasped what
so often escaped others, that the American West was a crowded wilderness. Although
nudged by reading Alexander Mackenzie, Jefferson did not need the dour Scot to
tell him that lands from St. Louis to the great western sea were neither empty nor
unclaimed. The political and economic face of the land had already been transformed by a generation of intense competition between tribal peoples and agents of
Spain, France, and Great Britain. The president understood at least the outlines and
implications of that struggle and the place of a latecoming American republic in it. If
the Lewis and Clark expedition was to be successful, whether for science, commerce, or statecraft, it would need to navigate through troubled Indian waters.

From the beginning, Jefferson sought to fashion an expedition capable of gathering
valuable information about western Indians while living at peace with them. That
search became plain as he drafted instructions for his young secretary, Meriwether
Lewis. The president loved questionnaires. He used them to explore new areas of
knowledge and then to organize what he had learned. Jefferson's only published
book, *Notes on Virginia,* was written in response to a questionnaire from the French
diplomat and scientist François Barbé-Marbois and retained the question-and-answer
form in its chapters.[1] Jefferson's instructions to Lewis were a series of interlocking
questions ranging from mineralogy to medicine. The ethnographic queries covered
nearly every aspect of Indian life, including languages, customs, occupations,
diseases, and morals.

Where did those very precise questions come from? The traditional answer has
been that the Indian objectives pursued by Lewis and Clark reflected Jefferson's
lifelong fascination with native American cultures. But there was more than one
mind and one set of motives behind the expedition's Indian questions and its general

policy toward native people. Early in 1803 Jefferson began to write friends both in and out of government asking their aid and advice for his western enterprise. In February he wrote three prominent Philadelphia scientists, Caspar Wistar, Dr. Benjamin Smith Barton, and Dr. Benjamin Rush, asking each to prepare some thoughts "in the lines of botany, zoology, or of Indian history which you think most worthy of inquiry and observation."[2]

Even before his consultants submitted their questions, Jefferson began to prepare a preliminary draft of the instructions. By mid-April 1803 he was ready to circulate it among certain cabinet members for their responses. The remarks of Secretary of the Treasury Albert Gallatin focused on western geography and the future expansion of the United States. Later in his career Gallatin made a major contribution in collecting and systematizing Indian material in his "Synopsis of the Indian Tribes." But just how much he had to do with framing the expedition's Indian questions remains unclear.[3] On the other hand, the reply from Attorney General Levi Lincoln clearly influenced Jefferson's thinking. This important member of Jefferson's official family has not received much attention from students of western exploration. Lincoln, an able New England lawyer and a skillful Republican politician, understood that the expedition served many purposes. Lincoln's April 17 letter to Jefferson suggests that the early draft of instructions he saw contained very little about Indians. To remedy this deficiency, Lincoln urged Jefferson to include questions about tribal religions, native legal practice, concepts of property ownership, and Indian medical procedures. Although Jefferson was acquainted with smallpox inoculation, it appears that Lincoln was the first to suggest that Lewis take some cowpox matter along to administer to the Indians. If they were to have extensive contact with whites, they needed to be protected against smallpox. Dead Indians could not participate in an American trade network and dying natives could only blame the explorers for spreading disease. The attorney general's suggestions were of major importance, although he made them more out of political expediency than scientific curiosity. Lincoln was very sensitive to Federalist opposition to the journey, and indeed to any American westward expansion. He realized that the administration would need to justify the expedition on the high ground of science if it failed.[4]

Levi Lincoln's helpful comments sharpened Jefferson's focus on Indians. That focus was further enlarged and refined in May 1803 when Benjamin Rush gave Lewis a detailed list of ethnographic queries. In 1774 Rush had presented a long paper before the American Philosophical Society titled "Natural History of Medicine among the Indians of North America." That discourse presented his thoughts on all physical aspects of Indian life from diet and hygiene to sexual performance and pregnancy.[5] The same wide range of interests was evident in a list Rush prepared for the expedition. That document was divided into three sections, with medical concerns predictably taking first place. Under the heading "Physical history & medicine," Rush proposed twenty separate questions. He asked the explorers to record Indian eating, sleeping, and bathing habits as well as native diseases and remedies. The Philadelphia savant wanted to know when Indians married, how long children were breast fed, and how long they lived. Rush even urged Lewis to find time to check Indian pulse rates morning, noon, and night both before and after they ate.

Rush's interests went well beyond medicine, encompassing Indian customs and values as well. The second part of Rush's list included four questions touching on crime, suicide, and intoxication. His third section probed native American worship practices, sacred objects, and burial rituals. Like so many other European and American scientists, Rush was fascinated by Indian religions. Moreover, he believed, as did many of his contemporaries, that studies of Indian languages and religious ceremonies might prove or disprove a very old and persistent notion about the origin of native people. A widespread academic theory held that Indians might constitute one of the lost tribes of the children of Israel. If the Mandans were misplaced Welshmen, as so many thought, why not see if there were any Jewish Indians in the West?[6]

By June 1803 Jefferson had before him all the suggestions from fellow scientists and government officials. He also had delivered in January the confidential message to Congress that justified the expedition on grounds of extending the Indian trade. He could draw on instructions written for the abortive Michaux expedition a decade before.[7] Sometime during June, Jefferson synthesized these documents into a final draft of instructions for the expedition—instructions that now contained detailed questions in seventeen areas of Indian life and culture. Those questions covered everything from language and law to trade and technology. The explorers were to record what Indians wore, what they ate, how they made a living, and what they believed in. In short, Jefferson told Lewis: "You will therefore endeavor to make yourself acquainted as far as a diligent pursuit of your journey shall admit, with the names of the nations & their numbers."[8]

Jefferson's reasons for converting two army officers and at least some of their companions into ethnographers were central to the many purposes of the journey. One of those aims linked exploration and business enterprise to national expansion. Finding the passage to the Pacific was supposed to yield financial rewards. "The commerce," wrote Jefferson, "which may be carried on with the people inhabiting the line you will pursue, renders a knolege of those people important."[9] The president did not fully understand the complex character of trade systems already functioning on the northern plains and in the Pacific Northwest. But he was intent on expanding American commercial influence. Jefferson knew that fur traders and other eager entrepreneurs needed to know about future markets and sources of supply. He envisioned western America as a vast trade empire to rival a similar system already being forged by agents of the Hudson's Bay Company and the North West Company. If the United States was to compete in the great western space race, Indians needed to be wooed away from John Bull's Canadian traders and written into the ledger books of Uncle Sam's St. Louis merchants.

But there was something else behind Jefferson's requirement that the Lewis and Clark expedition be an ethnographic enterprise—something beyond sea otters and beaver pelts. Lewis and Clark were to gather material for another empire—the empire of the mind, the kingdom of knowledge. Like his friends at the American Philosophical Society, Jefferson wanted the expedition to make a lasting contribution toward the scientific understanding of North America. That was what he meant when he described the venture as a "literary expedition." The knowledge was not to be gathered by the explorers for its own sake, however, but in the service of government and commerce.

Finally, and not to be overlooked, there was Jefferson's vision of the future of the American republic. He believed that accurate information about Indians was essential in order to shape a peaceful environment for both peoples. The desire for fact to replace speculation about native Americans was nothing new in Jefferson's mind. From boyhood he had had a passionate interest in things Indian. "In the early part of my life," he wrote, "I was very familiar with the Indians, and acquired impressions of attachment and commiseration for them which have never been obliterated."[10] Jefferson's fascination with Indian life and lore was part boyish curiosity and part scientific enquiry, all bound up in the optimistic notion that if native Americans surrendered their traditional "savage" ways and adopted a white "civilized" life, both peoples could enjoy the continent in peace. "Acquire what knolege you can of [their] state of morality, religion & information" was the way Jefferson put it to Lewis.[11] It was a Jeffersonian fundamental that if the two peoples knew each other more fully, each would treat the other with respect and consideration. Ethnography could make federal policy better informed and hence more humane. With an optimism based more on Enlightenment faith than American reality, Jefferson assumed that a benevolent government would use such information to civilize and Christianize Indians. Whether or not native people would welcome the spiritual and cultural blessings of European civilization was, of course, the unasked question.

Ethnographical research was neither the prime nor the sole duty of the expedition. Jefferson wanted his explorers to take their scientific tasks seriously as they collected information and artifacts, but he had much more in mind. As representatives of the United States, Lewis and Clark were expected to pursue the Indian policy goals of the republic. By 1803 those goals for the tribes east of the Mississippi were quite clear. Reflecting long colonial experience, federal Indian policy sought to acquire native lands at low cost while urging tribal people to shuck off hunting and breechcloths for plows and trousers. Couched in the language of Christian

Jefferson Peace and Friendship Medal of 1801, obverse (left) and reverse (right).
Courtesy of Oregon Historical Society.

philanthropy, Jeffersonian Indian policy pursued national expansion with single-mindedzeal. But in the West of the Louisiana Purchase, Jefferson was less certain of both policy and strategy. Those new lands were for traders, not white settlers. They might even provide refuge for native people dispossessed by the farming frontier.

Jefferson's different approaches to tribes east and west of the Mississippi are plain in the language he used in addressing delegations from the various regions. In speaking to eastern delegations the president always coupled his program for civilization with land acquisition. To western delegations, including those organized by Lewis and Clark, trade was the prime focus. When Jefferson drafted instructions for Lewis in 1803, negotiations with France were underway but the outcome was yet unclear. For that reason the diplomatic objectives enumerated in the directions for Lewis focused on trade while tactfully ignoring questions of power and sovereignty. The expedition was ordered to acquaint Indians with "the position, extent, character, peaceable and commercial disposition of the United States, and of our dispositions to a commercial intercourse with them." The factory system, a chain of government trading posts, had been an integral part of American policy since the mid-1780s. Jefferson knew that attractive goods and suitable post locations were essential in the face of powerful British competition. For that reason Lewis was told to confer with Indians on "the points most convenient as mutual emporiums" as well as "the articles of most desirable interchange for them and us."[12]

Jefferson expected that Lewis and Clark would hold frequent conferences with Indians. But he also knew that the rigorous demands of travel made extensive talks

6

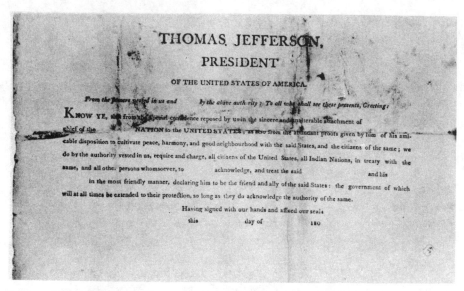

Lewis and Clark Indian Certificate. Courtesy of Western Americana Collection,
the Beinecke Rare Book and Manuscript Library, Yale University.

impossible. Therefore Lewis was instructed to organize delegations of chiefs and
elders to be sent to Washington. Just as colonial Indian agents once sent Mohawks
and Cherokees to London, Jefferson assumed that Omahas and Sioux in the Federal
City would be properly impressed with the wealth and power of the new nation.
And in an afterthought whose origins looked back to the earliest days of Indian-
European encounter, the president hoped the expedition might find some young
Indians willing to be "brought up with us, and taught such arts as may be useful to
them." It was a dream that had haunted missionary and bureaucrat alike—native
children gladly leaving their parents to embrace new fathers.

The creation of Indian delegations and a search for good trade sites were as close
as Jefferson got in June 1803 to giving his explorers explicitly imperial and political
directives. Although his commitment to an expanding nation was already plain,
Jefferson was not about to give Lewis and Clark instructions that violated territorial
bounds as they existed before the Louisiana Purchase. The spread of American commercial influence would be quite sufficient. But once the purchase was diplomatic
reality, announcing American sovereignty to native people became a vital part of
the expedition's Indian policy. Parts of Jefferson's January 22, 1804, letter to Lewis
can be seen as an appendix to the original instructions. Lewis and Clark were now
formally to extend American power up the Missouri and toward the mountains.
Jefferson's own words indicate how much the diplomatic role of the expedition had
expanded since the summer of 1803:

Being now become sovereigns of the country, without however any diminution of the Indian rights of occupancy we are authorized to propose to them in direct terms the institution of commerce with them. It will now be proper you should inform those through whose country you will pass, or whom you may meet, that their late fathers the Spaniards have agreed to withdraw all their troops from all the waters and country of the Mississippi and Missouri, that they have surrendered to us all their subjects Spanish and French settled there, and all their posts and lands: that henceforward we become their fathers and friends, and that we shall endeavor that they shall have no cause to lament the change.

In that same letter Jefferson gave Lewis the only order specifically naming a tribe and the policy to be pursued with it. The president drew on sources that included Jonathan Carver's *Travels through the Interior Parts of North America in the Years 1766, 1767, and 1768* (1778) and Alexander Mackenzie's *Voyages . . . to the Frozen and Pacific Oceans* (1801). More immediate information came from St. Louis contacts. Jefferson recognized the central role played by Sioux Indians in Missouri Valley trade and politics. He did not know the full complexity of the system that bound together British traders, Sioux hunters, and village farmers, nor did he realize just how far west Sioux power had expanded. But the president did know that a Sioux blockade on the Missouri could strangle an American fur trade empire based in St. Louis. "On that nation," he commanded Lewis, "we wish most particularly to make a favorable impression, because of their immense power." Jefferson's claim that the Sioux bands were "very desirous of being on the most friendly terms with us" was mostly wishful thinking. But that exercise in hope ultimately pointed the expedition toward what proved a nearly fatal confrontation with the Brulé Sioux.[13]

The expedition's success ultimately depended on friendly relations with the Indians. Jefferson was not about to unleash undisciplined adventurers to ride roughshod over them. Hostility between explorers and Indians could only endanger lives and weaken American influence. Jefferson knew firsthand what historian Charles Royster has written about American army officers in the late eighteenth century. Those men "saw threats and slights everywhere and reacted with fury."[14] Fear of overreaction, especially on the part of Meriwether Lewis, was also on Levi Lincoln's mind when he counseled Jefferson to avoid instructions that might lead the young officer to risk his life unnecessarily. "From my ideas of Capt. Lewis," wrote Lincoln, "he will be much more likely, in case of difficulty, to push too far, than to recede too soon." Jefferson saw the wisdom in Lincoln's comments and changed the sentence in the instructions that once contained the phrase "certain destruction" to read instead "we value too much the lives of our citizens to offer them to probable destruction."[15] Jefferson had shown considerable wisdom in making the exploration a military affair with proper organization and discipline. But he did not want the bumps and bruises of wilderness travel and encounters with strangers to provoke fatal overreaction. "In all your intercourse with the natives, treat them in the most friendly and conciliatory manner which their own conduct will permit." That advice was not intended to understate the potential dangers or deny the expedition the ability to defend itself. Jefferson understood the hazards. What he feared was that after months of hardship and frustration, some small incident might touch off a sudden burst of violence. Lewis and Clark were not to court self-destruction nor were they to wreak destruction on others. Survival would mean at least partial success; a glorious but futile death whether by accident or at the hands of an unknown foe would spell real failure.

Colonial experience taught that fruitful diplomacy and peaceful relations with native people required the exchange of gifts at each meeting. French and English forest diplomats learned that lesson early and did their best to offer goods of substance and quality. While some Europeans may have perceived those gifts as bribes to ensure compliance with treaty terms, heaps of blankets, pots, and guns meant something else to the Indians. In the act of reciprocal gift giving, different peoples symbolized their concern for each other. Neglecting to give gifts meant failure to "brighten the chain of friendship" that bound Europeans and Indians together. Giving and receiving soothed hurt feelings and reestablished broken relations. By the time Jefferson created the Corps of Discovery, gifts were a recognized part of the protocol of Indian diplomacy. To venture up the Missouri without a carefully selected store of goods was to challenge foolishly the river gods.

Lewis knew the gift-giving tradition and early in 1803 made note of funds to be set aside for presents for the Indians. In his initial tally of expedition costs, Lewis allocated $696 for trade goods.[16] Once in Philadelphia early in May 1803, he set about the task of locating and purchasing a wide variety of goods. In notes made on what might be obtained as trade items, Lewis demonstrated a sure grasp of frontier economics. Blue glass beads headed his list of most sought-after objects. It is probable that Lewis learned from sources in the Pacific Northwest fur trade that those beads were "far more valued than the white beads of the same manufacture and answer[ed] all the purposes of money." Second on his list were common brass buttons, which the same sources may have told him were "more valued than any thing except beads." The explorer was also determined to find red-handled knives of the sort used by North West Company traders. Axes, tomahawks, moccasin awls, and camp kettles rounded out Lewis's catalog of high priorities. In addition to those items, Lewis planned to purchase substantial quantities of wampum, tobacco, and textiles. Vermilion face paint, one hundred cheap rings with glass stones, and a number of pairs of scissors completed his stock of essentials.[17]

Using the services of Israel Whelan, purveyor of public supplies, and General William Irvine, superintendent of the Schuylkill Arsenel, Lewis was able to amass a substantial outfit of Indian goods. From merchants in and around Philadelphia came everything from 4,600 sewing needles and 500 brooches to 8 brass kettles and 2,800 fishhooks. There were stocks of hawks bells, thimbles, ruffled shirts, and eleven dozen of those red-handled knives. Lewis was to discover only later that there were not nearly enough blue beads or brass buttons, an oversight that cost the expedition dearly among the Nez Perce and Chinookan Indians. And at Jefferson's direct command there were two corn grinders. They were there, one might guess, for use in teaching native farmers how to make pone and grits.[18]

All of the gifts stowed in the expedition's luggage for transport to St. Louis had a purpose beyond diplomatic protocol. Those items, everything from ivory combs to calico shirts, represented what the United States offered to potential trading partners. As Jefferson repeated to every delegation of western Indians, Americans sought commerce, not land. Lewis and Clark were on the road to show American wares. The expedition was the mercantile and hardware display case for a trade empire on the move. Moccasin awls and brass kettles were as much symbols of American power as the medals and flags destined for headmen and warriors. Few of those manufactured products were new to Indians, but the promise of regular supplies and fair prices was bound to have some result. The Industrial Revolution had come to the Missouri Valley half a century before and it was equally well established on the Northwest coast. But Lewis and Clark, surrounded by bright mirrors and yards of red flannel, offered more than goods. They proposed membership in a system with well-established posts and dependable delivery schedules. And always in the background, visible but rarely mentioned, were guns and ammunition. Lewis and Clark did not carry a special supply of weapons to offer for trade or as gifts, but they were not reluctant to promise firearms to potential customers and allies. Although Jefferson and his explorers honestly pursued intertribal peace as a requisite to trade, arming friends seemed equally reasonable. What all those gifts represented was, in fact, the fundamental element in Jefferson's western Indian policy. Trade and diplomacy, commerce and sovereignty were all parts of the engine that drove American expansion and guided the Lewis and Clark expedition.

On a snowy day at the end of December 1803, William Clark moved into his hut at what has come to be known as Camp Dubois. Situated on Wood River across the Mississippi from St. Louis in present-day Illinois, the camp provided the Corps of Discovery with a convenient place to prepare for the first season of exploration.

The winter of 1803–1804 at Camp Dubois was more than a time to fit an odd lot of soldiers and frontiersmen to the discipline Lewis and Clark believed essential for the expedition's success. The Wood River interlude allowed explorers time to gather and evaluate a large amount of information about the Missouri River Indians. That material, coming from St. Louis sources and from Jefferson himself, constituted a crash course in Middle and Upper Missouri tribes: their numbers, locations, and possible reactions to the expedition.

No other city could have provided Jefferson's explorers with such a range and quality of information about the Indians. The currents of the Mississippi and Missouri brought to St. Louis not only pelts and skins but a vast store of knowledge and lore about the natives. Traders, merchants, government officers, and rough-handed engagés all had experience that could prepare Lewis and Clark for their Indian duties. The explorers needed to enter quickly that St. Louis world and tap its resources. That meant cultivating a friendly relationship with the brothers Chouteau, Jean Pierre and René Auguste, who had come to dominate the Indian trade around St. Louis and were anxious to expand their influence under the new American regime. The Chouteaus and their circle of friends and relatives quickly sought out the explorers. Social calls at Pierre's house combined good food, friendly company, and valuable information. Clark went so far as to boast that the Chouteau house became a virtual Corps of Discovery outpost during the winter.[19]

The Chouteau connection brought Lewis and Clark into contact with the city's best-informed merchants. There was so much information available that Lewis found it necessary to draft a form letter to give the data some structure. As he explained to Jefferson, "I have proposed many quiries under sundry heads to the best informed persons I have met with at St. Louis and within the vicinity of that place; these gentlemen have promised me answers in due time." A list of questions Lewis sent to René Auguste Chouteau early in January 1804 indicates the range of information the explorer was seeking. While most of the questions referred to white settlers and their current economic and political situation, there was room to comment on Indians and trade matters.[20]

Because the Chouteaus made themselves so available and accommodating to Lewis and Clark, there has been a tendency to overlook others who provided vital and perhaps more relevant Indian information. Chief among those were John Hay and James Mackay. Hay, United States postmaster at Cahokia, was an experienced Indian trader on the Mississippi. He also spoke French, and when Lewis visited St. Louis commandant Carlos Dehault Delassus, Hay and his fellow trader Nicholas Jarrot went along to interpret. Even more important, Hay provided the link to James Mackay. Mackay was perhaps the most widely traveled of the many traders Lewis and Clark met during the Camp Dubois winter. During the 1780s, Mackay explored the Assiniboine and Mouse rivers and visited the Mandan villages, along with North West Company employees from Fort Esperance on the Qu'Appelle River. By the mid-1790s the Scot had switched his political loyalties and was employed by the St. Louis–based and Spanish-controlled Missouri Company. When he met Clark early in 1804, Mackay had already ascended the Missouri River as far as the Omaha Indians in what is now Dakota County, Nebraska. Even more important, he had sent his Welsh lieutenant, John Evans, to the Mandans and had entertained notions of sending Evans across the mountains to the Pacific. Mackay's call at Camp Dubois on January 10, 1804, brought a lifetime of information on native people and Indian-white relations on the northern plains. Although Clark did not record what passed between the two explorers, there can be little doubt that their conversation was enlivened by Mackay's rich supply of experiences with the Indians.[21]

Lewis and Clark recognized that men like Hay, Mackay, and the Chouteaus could offer invaluable information. But there were other sources of information in St. Louis, men of the river perhaps less literate but with more immediate experience among Indians. Lewis and Clark needed that sort of firsthand knowledge. While the captains could question their own engagés, some of whom had logged considerable river time, there were others beyond easy reach. As Lewis explained it to Jefferson, "Some of the traders of this country from their continued intercourse with the Indians, possess with more accuracy many interesting particulars in relation to that people, than persons in a higher sphere of life." The problem was that those men lacked "both leasure and abilities to give this information in any satisfactory manner in detail." Determined to get that material, Lewis hit upon the idea of drawing "a form on paper containing 13 or 14 columns," each headed with a different topic relating to native people. Lewis had already circulated such forms by late December 1803 and felt certain that his plan would yield important data. The questionnaires may have proved successful, but unfortunately, neither blank forms nor completed ones have survived.[22]

Lewis and Clark got more than talk from their St. Louis contacts. Friendly meetings brought maps and journals produced by earlier expeditions up the Missouri. Of all the written material the explorers were able to study, none was more valuable for its Indian content than the journals and notes produced by James Mackay and John Evans. In a letter to Jefferson, Lewis reported that he had obtained Evans and Mackay's journal material dating from 1795 to 1797. Those entries, written in French, were being translated by the ever-useful John Hay.[23] No explorer destined for the northern plains could miss the import of those documents. Taken together, the Evans-Mackay file made several major points. There was the prospect of a rich trade to be exploited among both villagers and nomads. But success in that trade hinged on a reliable system with dependable Indian partners. Lewis and Clark could not have missed Evans and Mackay's singling out of the Mandans as the

Indians most helpful to traders. "The Mandaines," wrote James Mackay, "as well as all other nations that inhabit to their West, near the Rocky Mountains, are in general people as good as they are mild who lay a great value on the friendship of the Whites." The Evans-Mackay material also revealed the extent of international competition for trade on the Missouri. French, Spanish, and English interests were already on the river, and reading Evans and Mackay reminded the explorers that their diplomacy would be for high stakes. Mackay's observation that courting the Mandans could "put a Stop to the unjust progress of the English" was written for Spanish eyes, but its meaning was not lost on the Americans.[24] Finally, the Evans-Mackay journals brought home how much Indian opposition might be provoked by an American trade empire based in St. Louis. The Omahas, Arikaras, and some of the Sioux bands had already made life miserable for traders bound upriver. Lewis and Clark would have to deal with Indians who assumed it was their right to collect tolls on the Missouri highway.

The Evans and Mackay materials were of such great importance that Lewis and Clark probably took along Hay's translation of Mackay's journal. It is more certain that a second document from Mackay made the transcontinental passage. Sometime during the winter at Camp Dubois Mackay's "Notes on Indian Tribes" came into the possession of the expedition. That twelve-page report summarized the trader's early experiences with the Piegans and his 1787 visit to the Mandans. In the "Notes" Mackay offered a blend of current opinion on the origin and condition of the Indians and his own observations of their ways. He had something chatty to say on everything from religion to burials. Most important for the expedition's purposes, the trader made astute comments on the lives of the Missouri River villagers. Drawing on his own visit to the Mandans and Evans's experiences with the Arikaras and Mandans, Mackay briefly described the construction of earth lodges, the layout of towns, and the yearly patterns of farming and hunting. Mackay's "Notes" was yet another text in Lewis and Clark's education.[25]

The last piece of written material on Indian subjects had a St. Louis source but came to Lewis and Clark from Jefferson. In his November 16 letter to Lewis, the president sent along extracts from the Missouri River trade journal attributed to Jean Baptiste Truteau. Working for the Company of Explorers of the Upper Missouri, Truteau traded upriver as far as the Arikaras from 1794 to 1796. What Jefferson sent was a compilation of the tribes living along the Missouri and its tributaries. By studying the list, Lewis and Clark could gain further information about their numbers and locations. Many tribes that figured in the expedition's future were briefly noted in the journal. Those included the Otos, Omahas, the Sioux bands, Arikaras, and Mandans. Although the extracts did not plainly spell out the complex relations between those groups, Lewis and Clark were at least beginning to fix peoples and places in the mental geography of the expedition.[26]

Establishing hunting territories and village locations in their minds was made easier by several important maps Lewis and Clark examined during the winter at Camp Dubois. When Clark gathered and compared maps, he was primarily in search of information to guide the expedition over the best route to the Pacific. But Clark, who emerged as the expedition's cartographer, could not have missed the substantial body of Indian data contained in many of the maps he studied. Three maps in particular held valuable information on village sites and native populations. Those maps gave visual expression to the written material coming into Lewis and Clark's hands.

Among the maps that the explorers looked at was one Lewis described as "a general map of Uper Louisiana." It had been drawn by Antoine Soulard, surveyor general of Spanish Louisiana. Soulard prepared the Spanish version in 1794–95 at the direction of Governor Carondelet to guide the explorations of Jean Baptiste Truteau. Sometime after the journeys of Mackay and Evans, Soulard drafted versions of the map with English and French legends. It was the English version, entitled "A Topographical Sketch of the Missouri and Upper Mississippi Exhibiting the Various Nations and Tribes who inhabit the Country," that now came into Clark's possession. Soulard's map demonstrated with remarkable accuracy the locations of western Indians at the end of the eighteenth century. Along the Missouri and its tributaries Soulard placed the Oto, Pawnee, and Omaha peoples. Using simple circle and triangle symbols, the surveyor general noted Arikara and Mandan villages and the territories of nomadic Sioux, Cheyennes, and Assiniboins. Farther north Soulard sited the Blackfeet and Chipewyans. The Crows and Snakes (Shoshonis) marked the western limit of St. Louis knowledge. Looking at Soulard's map must have been a reassuring experience for the explorers: it showed the headwaters of the Missouri within easy travel to what Soulard labeled "Oregan or R. of the West." Indians that Lewis and Clark had heard about from St. Louis traders were on the map and in the expected places. This was not a map to chart a daily course on the river, but it did offer the sort of overview of the tribes that the explorers would need for much of their diplomacy. And because such diplomacy was closely linked to trade, Soulard's careful delineation of trade routes was a valuable bonus.[27]

Lewis and Clark certainly could have extracted a good deal of ethnographic information from the map. But at its best Soulard's creation did not reflect the kinds of immediate river and Indian contact the explorers sought. That sort of information could come only from maps drawn by James Mackay and John Evans. After Clark wrote to Indiana territorial governor William Henry Harrison seeking his help in locating accurate western maps, Harrison sent Mackay's chart of the Missouri from St. Charles to the Mandan villages. While having a far narrower range than the Soulard map, Mackay's work did offer a precise, firsthand view of tribes and villages along the river. Mackay's sequence of Indian sites on the Missouri was essentially correct, but his location of the Mandan villages at longitude 110° west put those earth lodges some four hundred miles farther west than they actually were. Whatever its geographical misconceptions, the Mackay map brought Lewis and Clark another step closer to knowing what Indians were around the next bend in the river.[28]

The Mackay map was an important addition to the expedition's understanding of the plains landscape and its people. But a map made by John Evans became what one recent scholar has called a major "road map" for the expedition for no less than seven hundred miles.[29] The Evans map of the Missouri River consisted of seven sheets depicting the course of the river and the location of the Omaha, Ponca, Arikara, Mandan, and Hidatsa villages. Those places along the river frequented by Sioux bands were also noted. By examining the Evans map along with the ones by Soulard and Mackay, Lewis and Clark could know with some certainty what Indians would be encountered next. The Evans map was taken on the voyage and became an invaluable tool for both navigation and diplomacy. All these maps completed what might be termed the expedition's academic education in the Indian geography of the Missouri Valley. The maps, journals, and river talk could not lessen the shock of encounter that lay ahead, but they might at least give the explorers a sense of the predictable in an uncertain land.

The first test of that education came even before leaving Camp Dubois. The Indian presents so carefully purchased in Philadelphia needed to be organized in some logical order. It made good sense to package trade goods, medals, flags, and fancy dress uniforms in the order in which they were to be distributed. Here again, John Hay proved indispensable. As an experienced trader he knew the finer points of packaging and merchandising. It was probably Hay who suggested putting a variety of gifts into bags protected by waterproof fabric. Those bags were first divided into two general groups, one for the Indians on the river up to the Mandans and a second set for "foreign nations." All told, there were to be twenty-one bags of Indian goods. As Hay worked on packing in late April 1804, the explorers showed that they had learned their lessons well. Bundles were made up for the Otos, Poncas, and Omahas. Knowing the great power of Omaha leaders like the late Chief Blackbird, they set aside a separate part of one bag for the leading Omaha chief. That bag had everything from a pair of scarlet leggings to a military officer's coat and American flag. There were similar bags for the Arikaras and Mandans. For those Indians beyond the Mandans there were five bales stuffed with peace medals, fancy handkerchiefs, hat bands, and mirrors.[30] The careful order in which those bales were packed and numbered testified to how much Lewis and Clark had learned during the months at Camp Dubois. On paper, at least, they knew the human contours of the land ahead. Those neatly tied packages should have been reassuring. But Clark was not confident. Just one day before leaving Camp Dubois he looked at the presents and thought they were "not as much as I think necessary for the multitude of Indians thro which we must pass on our road across the Continent."[31]

As the Lewis and Clark flotilla—keelboat and pirogues—rocked against the river current, it represented months of careful preparation. Armed with calico shirts, peace medals, and blank vocabulary sheets, the expedition seemed ready to carry out its many Indian missions. But there was still one unanswered question, one nagging doubt that no talk, map, or journal could resolve. How would the explorers cope with the inevitable tensions hidden in dozens of encounters with the Indians? Clark had long recognized the dangers. While working out travel schedules, he admitted that the accuracy of those time tables depended on "the probability of an oppision from roving parties of Bad Indians which it is probable may be on the R[iver]."[32] Unchecked emotions, moments of fury from either Indians or explorers, could cost lives and destroy the expedition. Perhaps the greatest uncharted space ahead was a human space.

Into that emptiness went men of diverse backgrounds and unknown temperaments. Young frontiersmen recruited by Clark might have been crack shots, but would memories of Indian warfare on the dark and bloody ground of Kentucky boil up whenever they saw Indians? The expedition matched young privates like George Shannon with old hands Hugh Hall and the Field brothers Joseph and Reuben. St. Louis engagés added river wisdom and colorful songs to the Corps. Among them François Labiche and Pierre Cruzatte stood out for their two winters spent at the mouth of the Nodaway River some 450 miles up the Missouri. Towering over them all as a frontiersman was George Drouillard. Born of French and Shawnee parents, he had spent years in the Illinois country. Woodsman, tracker, adept at sign language, Drouillard emerged as the expedition's chief hunter and scout. Young John Colter could not have had a better teacher. New Hampshire–born John Ordway quickly caught the captains' attention and became the Corps of Discovery's sergeant major. And there was York, Clark's slave, whose blackness would fascinate and frighten so many Indians.

Finally, there were the captains themselves. Despite Jefferson's assertion that Lewis was chosen for his "familiarity with the Indian character," the young officer had neither fought Indians nor lived with them.[33] He spoke no Indian languages. Jefferson's library might have been filled with books about Indians, but there is no direct evidence that Lewis read any of those volumes. His contacts with Benjamin Rush and other Philadelphia students of native cultures were all too brief. In fact, Lewis's frontier experience was limited to travel in the Ohio country on missions for army paymasters and recruiters. Those journeys gave Lewis firsthand knowledge of the officer corps—one of the reasons Jefferson selected him as private secretary—but they did not fit him to negotiate with confident chiefs and experienced warriors. Clark's life as soldier and surveyor did bring him into direct contact with Indians. Unlike many in his position, he had become an acute observer of native life and a confidant of chiefs and warriors—both ethnographer and diplomat. In ways that are beyond easy explanation, he enjoyed the company of Indians. Throughout his life Clark courted them, smoked with them, and shared food and stories with them. But this personal history was just a beginning. The expedition was to challenge each man in ways yet unimagined. Surveying their untested crew and themselves, Lewis and Clark could only hope that the patience, skill, and courage of some would sustain all until the Corps of Discovery found its own soul.

The "road across the Continent" began in mid-May 1804 as the expedition steadily left behind the familiar sights of Camp Dubois and St. Louis. In the days that followed there was time for a green crew to learn the dangers of falling banks, swirling currents, and hidden sawyers that could rip and overturn a craft. Those first weeks on the river brought reminders that the fur trade already reached far up the Missouri. The explorers saw rafts and canoes filled with furs from the Omaha and Pawnee villages. River traffic also brought the expedition some valuable information. Late in May, around the isolated village of La Charette, the explorers met Régis Loisel. A prominent member of the Missouri Fur Company, he was on his way back downriver after establishing a post to garner the Sioux and Arikara trade. The experienced Loisel gave Lewis and Clark "a good Deel of information" about Indian relations far up the Missouri. He may well have urged the explorers to obtain additional aid from his partners Pierre Antoine Tabeau and Joseph Garreau at their Cedar Island post.[34]

Early in June there was another fortunate meeting, this time with an Indian-language interpreter. The expedition was not well prepared to deal with translation problems, especially those involving important conferences with the Sioux. Pierre Cruzatte knew a few words and phrases and there were Drouillard's signs. Coming upon another St. Louis–bound party of traders, the captains met Pierre Dorion. The Frenchman had spent some twenty years with the Yankton Sioux and their neighbors. He was just the sort of agent Lewis and Clark needed to interpret at crucial conferences and to organize important delegations. Dorion was promptly hired with the understanding that he would remain with the Yanktons to promote the expedition's Indian policy.[35]

By the last days of July the expedition had passed the mouth of the Platte River, known to old river hands as the dividing line between the lower Missouri and the middle reach of the river. Mosquitoes, gnats, and a prairie landscape were all unmistakable signs of the expedition's progress. Information gathered at St. Louis and the words of engagés told Lewis and Clark to prepare for their first meetings with Indians. Along these parts of the river the explorers expected to see Oto, Missouri, Omaha, Ponca, and perhaps Pawnee Indians. On July 20, camped above present-day Nebraska City, Nebraska, Clark speculated that from his location a man could walk in two days to the Pawnees on the Platte and in one day to the Otos. Those Indians ought to be close at hand. Perhaps it was Labiche or Cruzatte who told Clark that at this time of year most river folk left their villages to hunt buffalo. Those hunts threatened to scuttle expedition diplomacy even before it was launched.[36]

Two days later, some ten miles above the Platte, Lewis and Clark settled into a place on the Iowa side of the Missouri with the delightful name of Camp White Catfish. From that spot the explorers planned to send out parties to invite Indians for formal talks. On July 23 George Drouillard and Pierre Cruzatte were given parcels of tobacco and ordered to find the Otos and Pawnees. Some signs, undisclosed in expeditionary records, suggested that at least a few river Indians had returned from hunting to obtain additional corn supplies. Taking this as a hopeful sign, Lewis and Clark confidently raised a flagstaff and waited anxiously for their native guests. Those preparations ended suddenly two days later when Drouillard and Cruzatte returned with unwelcome news. They had quickly found the major Oto town but it was quite empty. There were some traces of a small Indian party in the area, but neither scout could locate it. Disappointed and concerned, Lewis and Clark decided to press upriver in the hope that they might still come upon some Indians.[37]

The expedition's fortunes took a change for the better on July 28 when Drouillard happened on a Missouri Indian. Once back at the expedition's camp, the Indian revealed that his own band was quite small, no more than twenty lodges. Their numbers now seriously depleted by smallpox, the surviving Missouris lived with the Otos. The main body of Otos was still out hunting. Acting on that information, the captains sent the engagé La Liberté, who could speak the Oto language, back with the Indian to deliver a formal council invitation. The expedition planned to continue upriver and the Otos could find them farther along. At the end of July, in bottomland on the west bank of the river at what became Fort Atkinson, Nebraska, the expedition once again halted and waited for the Indians.[38]

After two days of patient waiting, Lewis and Clark were plainly worried. They knew it might take some time for "much scatred" hunters to be located and to make their way to the river. Nonetheless, Clark could not help admitting, "We fear Something amiss with our messenger or them." The captains sent out another man to hurry La Liberté and the Otos.[39] All that worry vanished at sunset on August 2 when a party of Otos and Missouris appeared at the Council Bluff camp. Along with them was a trader whose name Clark rendered as Fairfong, although he has never been properly identified. Fairfong knew the Otos and had their trust. The leading Oto and Missouri chiefs, Little Thief and Big Horse, were not with the delegation but Lewis and Clark were gratified to see six headmen. At dusk the explorers arranged a hasty greeting, sent gifts of roasted meat, and asked the Indians to attend a council the next day.[40]

As fog hung in the river bottoms on Friday morning, August 3, Lewis and Clark set about preparing for their first conference with the Indians. What the explorers did that morning linked them to generations of forest diplomats. The form and substance were dictated by common expectations resulting from years of woodland encounters. It was the sort of ritual Clark had seen at the council negotiating the Treaty of Greenville with General Anthony Wayne in 1795. If the subsequent history of the expedition is any guide, Lewis spent those early hours finishing his draft of a long speech proclaiming American sovereignty and the coming of new traders. Clark may well have spent the same time supervising the preparation of gifts. Opening bale number thirty, the men took out red leggings, fancy dress coats, and blue blankets. Setting aside flags and medals, they carefully packed the trade goods in individual bundles whose size and quality were determined by the rank of each chief. A special package was made up for the absent chief Little Thief. Although gifts and speeches had long been part of any Indian meeting, warriors and soldiers always made it a point to show military prowess as well. Lewis and Clark were determined to impress every Indian they met with the power of the young republic. Sergeants Ordway, Floyd, and Pryor must have been busy that morning readying their squads for a formal dress parade. At the same time, other men were detailed to convert the keelboat's main sail into a temporary awning to shield the diplomats from the August sun. A flag and flagstaff completed the setting. What would become routine in the months ahead was still new and fresh, and there must have been an electric excitement in camp as the Corps of Discovery waited for the Indians to arrive.

At midmorning the Oto and Missouri delegation, with trader Fairfong in tow, assembled under the sailcloth awning to watch something like a Lewis and Clark Medicine Show. At the command, the expedition's troops shouldered arms, dressed right, and passed in review. Lewis then stepped forward to deliver a long speech summarizing federal Indian policy. Because its language and themes were to be repeated many times in the coming months, the speech is worth careful attention.

Lewis began with the grand announcement of American sovereignty over the newly purchased lands. The Otos and Missouris were told bluntly that their Spanish and French fathers had retreated beyond the eastern sea and would never return. In their place was a new father, the "great chief of the Seventeen nations," and it was his will that all would "now form one common family with us." Explaining the nature of the expedition's mission always proved a difficult task; the first time Lewis tried it the best he could do was declare that the explorers were on the river "to clear the road, remove every obstruction, and make it a road of peace." Just who was to mark out that "road of peace" and where it might lead were matters Lewis addressed next. Urging the Indians to "shut [their] ears to the councils of Bad birds," the diplomat insisted that the new American father and his sons would bring peace and prosperity to "red children on the troubled waters." Those "red children" were required to make peace with their neighbors and trade with St. Louis merchants. If those words were heeded, advised Lewis, traders would come, a post would be built near the mouth of the Platte, and the Indians would "obtain goods on much better terms than . . . before." But Lewis's words had the edge of threat as well. If river Indians ignored American orders and followed the "bad birds," trade would be cut off and there would be much suffering.

Lewis concluded with what he saw as a crucial test of native willingness to accept the new order. He urged Oto and Missouri chiefs to form a delegation to visit the great Washington chief. Those delegates could see for themselves both the wealth of the American nation and the contentment of Indians already living under the federal father. And if they submitted to the great chief, those in the delegation would be showered with gifts and honors. Declaring that the traders of yesterday were gone, Lewis held out Jefferson and the American nation as "the only friend to whom you can now look for protection."[41]

Because chiefs like Little Thief and Big Horse were not in camp, the responses offered by those Indians who were present did not capture much of the expedition's attention. But what fragments are in the record remain important to gauge early native reaction to Lewis and Clark. Patrick Gass, soon to become a sergeant after the untimely death of Charles Floyd, said that the Indians were "well pleased" with the change in government. But that supposed pleasure at seeing new fathers was not widely felt by tribes along the lower river. Generated by news of the Louisiana Purchase, rumors had been flying for months that the Americans would radically change trading rules. In December 1804 a fearful Osage came to Camp Dubois filled with stories from an English trader who alleged that once the Americans had the country, trade would be disrupted.[42] The reaction of some Osages on the Arkansas River was even more forceful. When a Chouteau agent announced the purchase, his letter was seized and burned, "the Indians not believing that the Americans had possession of the Countrey."[43] Some Otos and their neighbors, who got goods from traders of various nationalities, may well have shared those concerns. The delegates at Council Bluff did nothing so dramatic, but they may have wondered about the economic consequences of new flags and medals hearing unfamiliar faces. In fact, what the chiefs did talk about was trade. The Otos and their neighbors wanted a dependable source of goods. After years of spotty contact with English and French traders, the Indians were intent on finding and joining a reliable system. Complaining that Spanish and French traders "never gave them as much as a knife for nothing," it was plain that the Otos and Missouris hoped the Americans would be more generous. Although Clark was unimpressed with the replies, calling the chiefs "no oreters," Ordway found the speeches "very sensable."

The day ended with more gifts—powder, whiskey, face paint, and fancy garters—and ceremony. Peace medals were distributed and Lewis gave the first of many airgun demonstrations. That silent weapon was impressive, but promises of trade meant more to the assembled Indians. And if the explorers could negotiate a peace between the feuding Otos and Omahas, that would surely add to American prestige. The Indians were both cautious and interested and Lewis and Clark finished the meeting with a sense of achievement. Although Little Thief and Big Horse had not spoken, the captains were confident that the wisdom of American policy, the lure of St. Louis trade, and the force of federal arms would prevail.[44]

Several days later Lewis and Clark followed up what they viewed as an initial diplomatic success by sending a copy of Lewis's speech and a parcel of gifts to Little Thief. That an equally suitable gift and a medal of proper grade were not sent to the Missouri chief Big Horse was an oversight due to the hurry to press upriver. The party transporting the goods was instructed to ask the Otos to send a delegation toward the Omaha village, there to cement good relations. By August 12 the expedition had passed the hilltop grave of the mighty Omaha chief Blackbird near present-day Macy, Nebraska, and expected to meet his successors at any moment. While the main body of the expedition stopped to prepare for an Omaha council, Ordway was sent to find the Indians. At Omaha Creek near present-day Homer, Nebraska, Ordway and his squad walked into the empty village of Tonwantonga. In the 1790s, during the years of Blackbird's leadership, the earth lodge village had held over one thousand Omahas. But the smallpox epidemic of 1800–1801 had dramatically reduced those numbers. Tonwantonga was vacant now as the Omahas were on the plains hunting buffalo. Although the Omahas were less powerful in the face of mounting Sioux influence, their absence from home was a major disappointment. Any hope of negotiating an Oto-Omaha peace and bringing the Omahas into the St. Louis trade system now seemed remote. Equally worrisome was the continued absence of the Oto and Missouri chiefs and the expedition party sent to find them.[45]

At least some of those problems were resolved on August 17. By this time the party had moved further up the Missouri, edging toward modern-day Sioux City, Iowa. Toward evening François Labiche came into camp; he had been with the group sent to find the Otos and track down a deserter, Moses Reed. He reported that the rest of the party, including Reed and the chiefs Little Thief and Big Horse, would arrive the next day. Labiche further explained that the Indians were intent on making peace with the Omahas. "As the Omahas are not at home," sourly wrote William Clark, "this great Object cannot be accomplished at this time." The explorers could only hope that this would not deter the Otos from accepting American proposals.[46]

On the following afternoon both the deserter and the chiefs came to camp. Making some shade near the keelboat, the captains briefly entertained the Indians before moving on to more immediate business—the trial of Moses Reed. As Little Thief and the rest watched intently, Reed was tried, found guilty, and sentenced to run the gauntlet four times. Shocked by this spectacle of public punishment and humiliation, the chiefs asked that Reed be pardoned. Had it not been for the need to establish firm discipline early in the voyage, Lewis and Clark might have sought to satisfy the visitors by granting their request. But it was not to be, and after they carefully explained the reasons for such punishment, the whole unhappy affair was done.

Even if the Omahas could not be part of the coming council, Lewis and Clark were anxious to know the reasons for trouble between those Indians and the Otos. Little Thief and Big Horse found no reason to conceal causes for the tensions. The chiefs promptly gave a quick lecture on the river realities of raid and truce. If the Americans expected Oto-Omaha conflict to turn on high policy disputes that could be settled by formal treaty, they were sorely mistaken. What unfolded was the tale of a horse-stealing raid by two Missouri warriors against the Omahas. The adventure had gone awry and in the fighting that followed, both men had been killed. Their deaths demanded retaliation. The Otos and Missouris also had stormy relations with the Pawnees. The chiefs admitted that theft of Pawnee corn while those people were off buffalo hunting was sufficient reason to fear revenge. What Little Thief recited were the common clashes that shaped prairie life. None of that denied the issues of trade and the struggles of the Otos, Omahas, and Sioux to secure that trade. But the Oto chief was offering a vision of the ordinary, the kind of affairs that Lewis and Clark had neither the time nor the talent to understand and control. The explorers listened but did not seem to comprehend. They were already prisoners of grand but ill-conceived designs to reshape Missouri Valley Indian politics and economics to the requirements of American policy and commerce. The realities of personal insult and family revenge must have seemed petty by comparison. Yet those were the human passions that outlived all official plans from any new father. Even so, that evening, as everyone enjoyed a dance and an extra gill of whiskey to celebrate Lewis's birthday, problems personal and national seemed far away.[47]

How different the Indian and expedition agendas were became plain the next day. Assembled under a shade awning, chiefs and warriors listened as Lewis again explained American plans for intertribal peace and trade from St. Louis. Only bits and pieces of the replies from Little Thief and Big Horse have survived, but what was recorded strongly suggests Indian expectations that did not match American designs. Little Thief agreed that peace would benefit all. He said that the Otos had always been friendly with white traders, whether they were English or French. What counted, so argued the chief, was not nationality but the price and quality of trade goods. Lewis and Clark could not have been pleased to learn that along the river the Stars and Stripes meant no more than the Union Jack or the Spanish ensign. Adding demand to insult, Little Thief wanted generous gifts from the hand of the new father. Big Horse added to the growing confusion by insisting that without "a spoonful of your milk"—a polite way to ask for alcohol—his younger warriors could not be restrained from attacking the Pawnees and Omahas. Whiskey for peace was not the price the expedition was prepared to pay, nor was it diplomacy on the level of virtue expected by Jefferson. And hard on this demand came a call from Little Thief for a delegation led by the trader Fairfong and François Labiche to make peace with the Pawnees. When this request was flatly rejected, all talk ended in sullen silence.

Uncertain of their next move and fearing that the whole conference might dissolve in confusion, the captains decided that gifts, medals, and certificates of good behavior might appease the Indians. Parcels of tobacco, beads, and face paint were quickly distributed. Medals and certificates went to warriors like Big Axe and Black Cat. But those well-intentioned items sparked fresh misunderstanding. When the explorers had prepared bundles of trade goods and medals for chiefs who had not attended the August 3 gathering, they had not realized the approximate equality of status between Little Thief and Big Horse. The Missouri chief had been sent a medal of lesser grade, and he now required one fitting his position. No sooner had that been accomplished than there was trouble in the ranks of the warriors. These men had expected substantial gifts and had received pieces of printed paper instead. No matter that the document proclaimed each Indian a "friend and ally" of the United States. One plainly disgusted warrior named Big Blue Eyes made it clear what he wanted and abruptly handed back the certificate. Some moments later the Oto had second thoughts and asked that it be returned. Angered at what seemed a lack of respect for official documents, Lewis and Clark refused and "rebuked them very roughly for having in object goods and not peace with their neighbors." Those pointed words may have been an accurate estimate of Oto and Missouri priorities, but they were hardly salve for bruised feelings. Little Thief finally put the matter to rest and asked that Big Blue Eyes be restored to the expedition's good graces. Not so quick to forgive, the explorers handed the paper to Little Thief, saying that he could present it to the offending warrior.

Lewis and Clark had expected the Indians' quick acceptance of American policies. All the gifts and military show were aimed at producing that result. On the other hand, the Otos and Missouris imagined wonderful giveaways of valuable goods from what seemed an endless supply on the keelboat. Little Thief and the other chiefs knew that their influence was in decline as Sioux and upriver villagers garnered a steadily larger share of the trade. Each expected too much from the other, and the day seemed to be ending in squabble and petty dispute. Trying to conclude the conference on a positive note, the explorers initiated a second round of gifts. Whiskey, keelboat curiosities like the ever impressive magnet and telescope, and an airgun show ended the council. Or at least Lewis and Clark thought that the gathering was finished. Discontented with skimpy presents, many Indians remained in camp asking for whiskey and trade items. What had been planned as an impressive day of solemn talk and American power tailed off in misunderstanding and confusion. Lewis and Clark were not about to alter either their goals or their tactics, but what happened in the Oto-Missouri talks should have been a warning of difficulties ahead.[48]

The meetings with the Oto and Missouri Indians were the first tests of the expedition's diplomatic skill. They were also a time to learn patience in the face of those who found the explorers' proposals either incomprehensible or confusing. Those August councils produced mixed results. Lewis and Clark might announce American sovereignty and assert that trade contacts were established, that sites were marked for future posts, and that intertribal peace was being promoted. The Corps of Discovery might be learning to live with the Indians. But a closer look makes those assertions appear less substantial. The Otos and their neighbors wanted trade. With what nation and under whose flag mattered not at all. Promises of peace with nearby Indians, no matter how honestly made, bound no one. As the expedition made its way up the Missouri and into Yankton Sioux territory, Lewis and Clark could realistically claim little success. They were now entering a plains world infinitely more complex than any they had encountered on the lower river.

On August 27, as the expedition passed the mouth of the James River, an Indian boy swam out to hail one of the pirogues. When the Americans pulled their boats on shore, two more Indian youths appeared. These Indians—two Yanktons and an Omaha—told Lewis and Clark that there was a large Yankton camp not far up the James. Eager to talk with these Indians, the captains sent Pierre Dorion and Sergeant Nathaniel Pryor to the Sioux village. Toward evening Pryor and Dorion reached the Yankton camp and received an enthusiastic welcome. Following tradition, the Yanktons wanted to carry Pryor into camp on a buffalo robe. It was to be more than a ride; it was a sign of honor and distinction. But the sergeant hastily declined, explaining that he was not the owner of the great boat now on the river. The Yanktons were not to be denied, however, and Pryor and Dorion were treated to a feast of fat dog, yet another sign of special attention.[49]

The warm greeting extended to Pryor mirrored the Yankton's eagerness to talk with Lewis and Clark. All of this was genuine hospitality and something more. What lay behind the offered buffalo robe procession and dog dinner were Yankton concerns about their own role in a rapidly changing plains world. The Yanktons did trade to the east with North West Company posts and had occasional visits from St. Louis merchants, but they needed a place in some dependable commercial system. They also needed protection from their more aggressive neighbors the Tetons. When Dorion, now joined by his son Pierre, and Pryor brought the Yankton delegation to the Missouri shore opposite Calumet Bluff, both the Indians and the explorers anticipated a successful meeting.

The morning of August 30 found the Corps of Discovery camped at Calumet Bluff on the west side of the river at the site of today's Gavins Point Dam. As the sun burned off an early fog, the explorers busied themselves with council preparations. What had been done for the Otos and Missouris was now readied for the Yanktons. Even before breakfast, some inquisitive Yanktons swam the river to watch the mysterious doings of the bearded strangers. At 9:00 A.M. Lewis and Clark were ready to begin their first conference with the Sioux. While the Oto and Missouri meetings were important as first forays in frontier diplomacy, the explorers knew that talks with any Sioux group would be of lasting significance. If the American fur trade empire was to move from the realm of Jefferson's imagination to commercial reality, Sioux cooperation and participation were essential. Knowing all that, Lewis and Clark dispatched a pirogue across the river to begin the proceedings.

If the stakes were high for American diplomacy in the new West, they were equally high for the Yanktons. Chiefs like Weuche and White Crane made that plain as they entered the precincts of Calumet Bluff in high ceremony. The whole Yankton delegation was preceded by four musicians, singing and playing as they paraded through the camp. That sense of drama was heightened when the captains ordered the bow swivel gun on the keelboat fired. Ritual payments of tobacco were made to the musicians; the conferees shook hands and then sat down to hear Lewis present the American proposals. His speech, translated by Pierre Dorion, Sr., lasted until late in the afternoon. The expedition's records do not contain a full text of the speech, but some clues in Ordway's journal suggest that it focused on peace with the Otos and Missouris and on arranging a major delegation of chiefs from several Sioux bands. Probably, Lewis proclaimed American sovereignty and promised reliable trade from St. Louis. When the speech ended, Lewis and Clark handed out medals to five of the Yankton chiefs. Weuche, sometimes known as La Liberator or the Handshake, was pronounced first chief and given a red-laced coat, military cocked hat, and American flag. The Indians retreated to the shade of some cottonwoods and divided the presents.

The Lewis and Clark expedition came to the northern plains as outsiders, but that night the explorers became part of a prairie community. In the late afternoon they provided beads as prizes when Yankton boys showed their skill with bow and arrow. At dark a crackling fire was built in the center of camp. Into the firelight came men in gaudy paint to dance and sing of their great feats in battle and the chase. Music came from a drum whose deerskin head was a gift from Lewis. While drummers beat out a powerful rhythm, other Indians kept time with deer hoof rattles. Later, Ordway recalled the vivid sights and sounds of that Calumet Bluff spectacle. "It always began with a houp and hollow and ended with the same, and in the intervales one of the warriors at a time would rise with his weapon and speak of what he had done in his day and what warlike actions he had done. This they call merit. They would confess how many horses they had Stole." Perhaps instructed by Dorion and his son, members of the expedition threw the dancers gifts of tobacco, knives, and hawks bells. For the Corps of Discovery, this would be a night to remember when times were harder and there was less to celebrate.[50]

Lewis and Clark were beginning to learn that the protocol of Indian diplomacy required time for chiefs and elders to hammer out replies to any proposal. But Weuche and his fellow Yanktons had no desire to keep the Americans waiting. Very early on the morning of August 31, the Indian delegation returned with their answers. That there were several responses and not one common reply from the Yanktons was another part of Lewis and Clark's education in native political realities. Weuche wasted no time revealing what was uppermost in his mind. Reliable trade connections were essential for the survival of the Yanktons. The chief reported that he and his warriors lacked both firearms and ammunition. Their women and children were destitute. Weuche wanted immediate relief, a request he thought not unreasonable in view of the riches of the keelboat. As an alternative, the chief suggested that his warriors be permitted to stop the next trade boat from St. Louis and help themselves to whatever was necessary.

But economics was not the only item on Weuche's agenda. As an astute plains politician, he quickly recognized that close ties to the new father would both protect and enhance the Yanktons' influence. Weuche cleverly offered his services to organize a large delegation from many bands the following spring. While not denying that men like Pierre Dorion and his son would be useful in that effort, the chief made it clear that ultimate success hinged on his good offices. And as for intertribal peace, Weuche again suggested that affairs be left in his hands. Explaining that other Indians "would hear him better," the chief assured Lewis and Clark that he could be trusted as a faithful intermediary. Finally, Weuche brought his comments full circle by returning to the trade issue. This time the chief took careful note of the international nature of the plains economy. Weuche reported that he had already held English and Spanish medals. But, he pointedly complained, the Yanktons needed more than bits of bronze and silver to fend off poverty. At this point, Lewis and Clark may well have become worried by constant references to trade goods. They had already chastised one Oto for paying undue attention to knives and beads. If the friendly Yanktons thought the expedition was really a trading venture, then less hospitable Indians farther upriver might stop and plunder the Americans. At the end of Weuche's talk and before the other chiefs began to speak, Lewis again attempted to explain the nature of their mission. He insisted that the explorers were not traders but had come only to open the road for others. He assured the Yanktons that honest traders with quality goods were not far behind. But the concept of exploration as a national undertaking had no precedent in tribal life. A keelboat filled with what seemed an endless store of goods only served to confuse the question.

Although the nature and purpose of the expedition was no clearer in Yankton minds, other chiefs like White Crane and Half Man needed to be heard. Their replies generally followed a common pattern. All agreed that trade and peace were worthy objectives. Of all the Yanktons who spoke during the day, none offered more important advice than Half Man. The chief made the expected promises, declaring his interest in peace with the Otos and a desire to see the great Washington chief. But at the end of his remarks, Half Man added a prophetic warning. "I fear," he said, "those nations above will not open their ears, and you cannot I fear open them."[51]

Half Man's dark words were hard to take seriously in an atmosphere of friendship and productive negotiation. The day ended with yet another show of airgun firepower and keelboat curiosities. Gifts of corn and tobacco to the Yanktons seemed to seal agreements while Dorion's plans to remain with them augured well for the organization of delegations. On the surface, at least, the council was a grand success. Here were Sioux headmen and warriors who welcomed the Americans and gladly joined the new trade system. The expedition's diplomacy appeared to have come of age. To that achievement was added the collection of important ethnographic information.[52] Just as significant, the expedition had enjoyed good relations with a powerful people. Worries about "the nations above" were easily discounted in the glow of proceedings at Calumet Bluff. Lewis and Clark were so confident of continued success in dealing with the Sioux that they did not think twice about leaving behind the only skilled interpreter. That the expedition's fortunes were about to slide into a morass of angry words and hostile gestures seemed remote. For now there were new plains sights to capture the explorers' attention. Again finding the Missouri channel, Lewis and Clark moved deeper into an Indian world that would both baffle and challenge the Corps of Discovery.

2

The Teton Confrontation

"These are the vilest miscreants of the savage race, and must ever remain the
pirates of the Missouri, until such measures are pursued, by our government, as
will make them feel a dependence on its will for their supply of merchandise."
—WILLIAM CLARK, 1804

On August 30, 1806, as the homeward-bound Lewis and Clark expedition swept
down the Missouri near present-day Yankton, South Dakota, the explorers caught
sight of more than one hundred well-armed Indians lining the northeast river bank.
Salutes of greeting were fired by both parties as the expedition pulled up its canoes
on the southwest bank. But the initial welcome vanished when Clark discovered
that the Indians were Brulé Sioux of Black Buffalo's band.[1] The captain had hoped
the Indians were Poncas, Omahas, or perhaps Yankton Sioux. But once their Brulé
identity was known, he turned on them with his own brand of invective.

Taking instructions from Clark, the interpreter René Jusseaume shouted across
the river that the Sioux were "bad people" and that "if any [came] near our camp
we should kill them certainly." In a second barrage, Clark had Jusseaume tell the
Brulés that future traders would be "sufficiently strong to whip any vilenous party
who dare[d] to oppose them." As a parting shot, Clark notified the Sioux that the
Americans had given guns, ammunition, and even a cannon to the Mandans and
Hidatsas—weapons that would surely be turned against Brulé raiders. While most
of the Indians retreated in the face of Clark's bombast, several warriors remained
on a hill, hooting, jeering, and proclaiming their readiness to kill the Americans.

Toward sunset, one man, probably Chief Black Buffalo, came to the water's
edge and invited the expedition to come across. Untongarabar, or Black Bull
Buffalo, is known in more recent literature as Black Bull. Lewis and Clark consistently called him Black Buffalo. He remained a powerful force in Brulé politics
and Missouri River trade until his death in July 1813. When Clark ignored his request,
the Indian returned to the top of the hill and angrily struck the ground three times
with his gun. "This I am informed," wrote Clark drily, "is a great oath among the
Indians."[2]

The expedition's members did not sleep well that night. Wet sand, gusty winds,
and an exposed campsite made them uncomfortable. Perhaps the unsettling jeers
and curses of the Sioux moved the captains and their men to recall another and even
more disagreeable clash just two years earlier with Black Buffalo and other Brulé
chiefs. A close look at that tense 1804 encounter can reveal much about Lewis and

Clark's relations with the Indians as well as the larger history of Upper Missouri Indian-white contact.

On the evening of September 23, 1804, as the men of the Lewis and Clark expedition rested at their camp just below the mouth of the Bad River, three Sioux boys swam across the Missouri to greet the explorers. The boys came from Teton Sioux villages along the Bad River, opposite present-day Pierre, South Dakota. From the very beginning of their enterprise, the captains had known they would have to face the feisty Tetons. Their reputation for harrassing traders, pilfering merchandise, and demanding large gifts was well known among St. Louis merchants. Jean Baptiste Truteau, whose party had been stopped by the Tetons in 1794, warned that "all voyageurs who undertake to gain access to the nations of the Upper Missouri ought to avoid meeting this tribe, as much for the safety of their goods as for their lives even." Lewis and Clark's conversations in St. Louis with Manuel Lisa, Antoine Soulard, the Chouteaus, and especially James Mackay, had made them aware of the risks in meeting the Tetons. The expedition's chance encounter with Regis Loisel, a trader just back from the Sioux country, had added to their information.[3] Now the Sioux boys told of two villages upriver. The captains, anxious to begin the talks, told the boys that their chiefs were invited to a conference the following day.[4]

After breaking camp on Monday morning, September 24, the expedition began serious preparations for the long-anticipated parley. Knowing that the Brulé chiefs would require substantial gifts for themselves and their people, the captains worked through their bales of trade goods to find suitable presents. Among the items selected for the chiefs were flags, medals, and a red military coat and cocked hat. Also prepared for general distribution were knives, small metal and fabric goods, and a large amount of tobacco. Because their St. Louis contacts had warned them about the often violent tactics used by the Tetons to control river traffic, the expedition was armed with more than gifts. Clark cryptically recorded that he and Lewis "prepared all things for action in case of necessity."

That "necessity" seemed to come closer in the afternoon when John Colter, who had been on shore hunting, reported that one of their horses had been stolen by some Teton warriors. No sooner had Colter made his report than five Indians appeared on shore. The expedition's flotilla, now near the mouth of the Bad River, anchored in the Missouri while the captains tried to talk with these Sioux. Lewis and Clark felt certain that they were the horse thieves and, employing an old ruse, told them the horse was intended for their chief. The American accusations and the fact that neither group understood the other made the meeting confusing and potentially dangerous. After the Indians left, the expedition made its way to an anchorage opposite the mouth of the Bad River. An island in the Bad was selected as the place for negotiations the following day.

Funeral Scaffold of a Sioux Chief near Fort Pierre, by Karl Bodmer. Courtesy of
The InterNorth Art Foundation, Joslyn Art Museum, Omaha, Nebraska.

Later Monday evening, after the event of the stolen horse seemed less confusing
and threatening, Lewis went to the island for a preliminary smoke with the Brulé
chiefs. They promised to return the missing horse and proclaimed their readiness
for serious talk the next day. Once back on the keelboat, Lewis seemed relieved to
report "all well" with the Sioux.[5]

Monday night was a time for Lewis and Clark to consider the intricate diplomacy
of the coming days. Jefferson's general instructions emphasized intertribal peace,
trade contacts, American sovereignty, and the collection of ethnological material.
But he had a special interest in the Sioux. Of all the Indians east of the mountains
known to whites, it was the Sioux that the president singled out for the explorers'
particular attention. Jefferson's concern with the Sioux was based on his appraisal of
both their military strength and their economic potential. The martial power of the
Sioux nation on both sides of the Missouri was well known. Jefferson was equally
sensitive to the economic possibilities and imperial rivalries present in any Sioux-
American negotiations. The journal by Truteau that Jefferson sent to Lewis in

November 1803 revealed those elements. Truteau described the Sioux as "the greatest beaver hunters," whose pelts were worth "double the Canadian for the fineness of [their] fur and parchment."⁶ Here was a grand opportunity for American enterprise. Profits from the Sioux fur trade would be an early vindication of the Louisiana Purchase. But, as Truteau had observed, the Sioux trade was firmly in the hands of the North West Company and its posts on the Des Moines and St. Peters rivers. If American sovereignty and commerce were to triumph, the Sioux would have to abandon John Bull for dealings with Uncle Sam.

Jefferson hoped Lewis and Clark might begin to lure the Sioux into the American orbit. But that would be no easy task. As he admitted to Secretary of the Navy Robert Smith, the United States was "miserably weak" in its newly gained western lands. In an important letter to Lewis, Jefferson urged the explorers to pay close attention to the Sioux. "On that nation," wrote the president, "we wish most particularly to make a friendly impression, because of their immense power, and because we learn they are very desirous of being on the most friendly terms with us."⁷ Jefferson engaged in wishful thinking when he wrote that the Sioux were looking for American friendship, but he was closer to the mark in noting "their immense power." Lewis and Clark would have to confront that power, convince the Indians that St. Louis merchants did not endanger the Sioux role in Upper Missouri trade, and persuade Teton trappers and hunters to bring their pelts and skins to American posts. The captains would have to deal with Indian leaders who clearly understood tribal needs and had both the diplomatic skill and the military force to command attention. With its tangle of economic, military, and imperial interests, the Teton Sioux negotiation was perhaps the most demanding piece of Indian diplomacy assigned to Lewis and Clark.

If the captains spent Monday night discussing the diplomacy for the next day, then surely men like Black Buffalo, the Partisan, and Buffalo Medicine did the same. For the Brulé bands and their leaders, the political and economic stakes were very high. In the intricate trade network of the Upper Missouri, the Teton Sioux played a dangerous and precarious game. Teton Sioux of the Brulé, Oglala, and Miniconjou bands traditionally traveled each year to a trade fair known as the Dakota Rendezvous, held on the James River in east-central South Dakota. There the Tetons met Sisseton and Yankton Sioux who had obtained manufactured goods from North West Company posts on the Des Moines and St. Peters rivers. The Teton bands used those goods and buffalo robes in their agricultural trade with the Arikara village farmers. With Teton population growing, a secure food supply was essential. So long as the Tetons could control the flow of European goods to the villagers, the Sioux position would be reasonably strong. But if the villagers gained easy direct access to St. Louis traders, the role of the Tetons as brokers and middlemen would be lost. These commercial considerations required the Tetons to, at most, blockade the Missouri River or, at least, exact considerable tribute from traders coming upriver. The well-armed Lewis and Clark expedition, representing St. Louis interests and determined to make direct contact with the Arikara, Mandan, and Hidatsa villages, was an intrusion that could not be ignored.[8]

But there was more than economic position at stake for the Brulé leaders. As Lewis and Clark would soon discover, they were about to enter the tangled web of band factional politics. In Brulé politics the leading players were Black Buffalo, Buffalo Medicine, and Tortohongar, known to the whites as the Partisan. Black Buffalo, chief of the largest Brulé band, was described by Tabeau as a man "of good character, although angry and fierce in his fits of passion." His authority and prestige had been challenged long before the advent of Lewis and Clark by the Partisan, chief of the second-ranked Brulé band. Tabeau, whose trade goods had been ransacked by the Partisan and some of his men, described this Teton as "a true Proteus, who is seen in the selfsame day faint-hearted and bold, audacious and fearful, proud and servile, conciliator and firebrand."[9] The role of Buffalo Medicine remains unclear; he was called by Lewis and Clark the "3rd chief" in the power struggle between Black Buffalo and the Partisan. That struggle for leadership often had unforeseen consequences. When Black Buffalo engineered a temporary peace with his Ponca and Omaha neighbors in 1803, the Partisan undercut the effort by organizing a horse-stealing raid on the Poncas. In retaliation, Ponca warriors stole nine Sioux horses and attacked a Brulé village. But the village they raided was Black Buffalo's and the peace was broken.[10] Now, as the negotiations with Lewis and Clark were about to begin, both Black Buffalo and the Partisan looked to use the talks to increase their own prestige. Playing to the Indian galleries, each chief would try to outdo the other in zealous defense of Sioux privilege.

Early on the morning of September 25, the expedition established a council place on a sandbar in the Bad River. A canvas awning was put in place and a flagstaff raised. By ten o'clock a large number of Indians began to gather along both river banks. About eleven o'clock Black Buffalo, the Partisan, and Buffalo Medicine appeared. Hoping to begin the conference on a generous note, the captains offered the chiefs and thirty Brulé warriors something to eat. Not to be outdone, the chiefs gave the expedition several hundred pounds of fat buffalo meat. Clark responded by offering the Sioux some pork. Both sides had now shown the required hospitality and it was time at last to talk. To their chagrin, the Americans discovered they lacked an interpreter skillful enough for this demanding task. The translator Pierre Dorion had remained with the Yankton Sioux to promote peace between that tribe and the Omahas. Clark unhappily noted, "We feel much at a loss for want of an interpreter." The diplomats would have to rely on "the old frenchman" Pierre Cruzatte, who Clark admitted, could "speak but little."[11]

At noon both sides seemed ready to settle in for the speechmaking. After the usual mandatory smoking, Lewis stood to make a short speech made shorter for want of an interpreter. No journalist recorded Lewis's words, but it is likely that at this early stage the captain spoke in no more than generalities. The speech probably followed the pattern established in earlier conferences with other tribes in which the explorer-diplomats touched on issues of intertribal peace, trade and American sovereignty.[12]

When Lewis's speech ended, the expedition put on its "traveling medicine show"—a demonstration of martial power and Western technology. This display, with its aim to impress the Indians with American might, had been successfully staged earlier for the Otos, Missouris, and Yankton Sioux.[13] The performance began with a military parade by uniformed troops marching under the colors of the republic. As the parade ended, Lewis and Clark sought to keep the military splendor and political significance of the moment alive by handing out gifts to the Brulé chiefs. Recognizing Black Buffalo as the leading chief present, the captains gave him a medal, a red military coat, and a cocked hat. In their rush to gain approval from Black Buffalo, the Americans evidently slighted the Partisan. Lewis and Clark may have been insensitive to the nuances of rank and precedence in Teton politics, but by trying to make Black Buffalo a client chief they were simply following long-established diplomatic practice. From the time of earliest contact, European and later American government officials had always sought out one Indian chief or headman, thinking he could both speak for and command the entire tribe. But neglecting the Partisan was a serious oversight, one that was sure to spark trouble in the coming days.

While the last presents were being distributed, the carefully orchestrated show was interrupted. The Brulé chiefs began to complain that the gifts were inadequate, as they had done to earlier traders. They demanded the expedition either stop its upriver progress and remain with them or at least leave a gift-laden pirogue behind as tribute.[14] While the captains must have known that such demands would eventually be made, they seemed unprepared that afternoon to deal with them directly. The niceties of diplomacy and the presence of many armed Teton warriors called for other measures. Lewis and Clark tried to divert Brulé attention by going on with the military hardware display. Lewis went through his now-familiar airgun demonstration, charging and firing it several times. Evidently unimpressed, Black Buffalo and the other chiefs continued to press their demands. Again hoping to divert the insistent chiefs, the captains offered to take them and some of their soldiers on the keelboat. Once on board, the Indians were shown "such curiossities as was strange to them." One Brulé warrior was given a government certificate proclaiming him "the friend and ally of the said states" and urging all citizens to treat him "in the most friendly manner."[15] Adding to the general milling about on the keelboat was the decision to break out some trade whiskey. Each chief was given one-fourth glass, "which [he] appeared to be very fond of." Clark observed that the Indians "sucked the bottle after it was out." Amid this confusion the Partisan made his move both to frighten the Americans and to impress bankside Indian spectators. Feigning drunkenness as a cover "for his rascally intentions," the Partisan became "troublesome." Fearing a bloody melee, Lewis and Clark struggled to get the chiefs back on shore. Those efforts were resisted, and it was only "with great relectiance" that the chiefs and their men boarded the pirogue for shore. Although the Partisan seemed intent on using the presence of the expedition as a means to advance his own power, Clark returned to land "with a view of reconsileing those men to us."

When the pirogue landed, an already difficult situation became potentially explosive. Three young Brulés, who may have belonged to the Partisan's retinue, seized the pirogue's bow cable. At the same moment, another warrior locked his arms around the pirogue's short mast. As the pirogue was being temporarily hijacked, the Partisan moved directly against Clark. The chief spoke roughly to Clark, staggered up against him, and told him that the expedition could not advance. The Partisan's actions were designed to test Clark, to make him weaken and back down as had previous white visitors. Given the presence of so many women and children, the Partisan had no intention of starting a shooting spree. Clark must have sensed the limits of the situation. His response to the jostling and "insolent jestures" was equally firm. Clark drew his sword and at the same time alerted Lewis and the keelboat crew for action. Lewis ordered the swivel guns readied while expeditionary soldiers around Clark prepared their weapons for firing. Then, as quickly as the Partisan had created the tension, Black Buffalo eased it. Obviously fearing heavy casualties if fighting erupted, Black Buffalo took the pirogue's cable and forcefully ordered the Brulé warriors away from the boat.

Surrounded by warriors with their bows strung and arrows out of quivers, the American captain and the Brulé chief now faced each other. The pointed and angry words they exchanged, passed through a very inadequate interpreter, reveal much about expedition-Indian relations and Teton Sioux policy. Clark told Black Buffalo that the expedition "must and would go on." To emphasize that determination, he told the Indians that his men "were not squaws, but warriors." Rising to this rhetorical challenge, Black Buffalo declared that "he had warriors too and if we were to go on they would follow us and kill and take the whole of us by degrees." Angered by the threats, Clark "felt My Self warm and Spoke in verry positive terms." Those terms included a reminder that the expedition was sent by the Chief of the Seventeen Fires, whose warriors could be summoned in a moment to punish the Sioux. And in a burst of temper, Clark boasted that he had "more medicine on board his boat than would kill twenty such nations in one day."[16]

The verbal sparring might have continued a bit longer except for the arrival of a canoe filled with twelve American soldiers "ready for any event." Most of the Indian warriors retreated and Clark was now left alone with the chiefs and a core of Brulé soldiers. Black Buffalo, still holding the pirogue's cable, asked if the women and children might see the keelboat and its curiosities. This was an easy request to grant, one that might allow both sides to emerge with honor and prestige intact. Clark agreed and Black Buffalo dropped the cable. Determined to have the last word, the chief declared that "he was sorry to have us go for his women and children were naked and poor and wished to get some goods, but he did not think we were merchants, nor that we were loaded with goods, but he was sorry to have us leave so soon." As Clark and his men stood by the pirogue, the chiefs walked down the bank for a private council. After waiting some time, Clark approached the chiefs and offered to shake hands. The captain was rebuffed and took that as a signal that discussions were over for the day.

As Clark and his party paddled back to the keelboat, Black Buffalo made one last demand. He and two of his warriors waded out ten feet from shore and asked to be taken on the keelboat. That night, as the Brulé chief and his men slept on board, Clark wrote simply of the day: "Their treatment to me was verry rough and I think justified roughness on my part." Clark neglected to add that their diplomacy was being drawn off course and onto the single point of continued upriver progress. The roughness of the day was hardly what Jefferson had in mind by "a friendly impression." The initiative was clearly in Brulé hands. All Lewis and Clark could do was react and hope to escape unscathed. And as an indication of the apprehensive mood felt throughout the expedition, the island named "Good humored" was changed to "Bad humored island as we were in a bad humor."[17]

The tensions of the previous day were not repeated on Wednesday, September 26. With Black Buffalo and his soldiers still on board, the keelboat sailed about five miles upriver. The shore was lined with Sioux spectators closely watching the progress of the chiefs and the explorers. Clark noted that "these people Shew great anxiety." With the failure of the bluff-and-bluster tactics the day before and the expedition now moving upriver, perhaps many Sioux feared they had lost the battle of wits and wills. Hoping to keep the expedition a bit longer, Black Buffalo asked the captains to land near his village so his women and children might visit the boat. Lewis and Clark agreed, perhaps feeling that more time with the Tetons might produce a change in the diplomatic climate.[18]

Anchoring the keelboat about one hundred yards from shore, the captains divided their forces. Lewis accompanied Black Buffalo to the Brulé village while Clark remained on board. The Brulé chief "appeared disposed to make up and be friendly." The Sioux village the expedition saw that day must have been an impressive sight. Ordway, one of the expedition's most careful observers, wrote:

"Their lodge [village] is very handsome in a circle and about 100 cabbins in nomber and all white, made of buffalo hides dressed white. One large one in the center, the lodge for the war dances."[19] Ordway and Gass estimated that with about ten persons in each tepee the total village population was eight or nine hundred persons. Gass thought that two-thirds of the Sioux in the village were women and children.[20]

As the morning slipped away and no word came from Lewis, those on the keelboat "became uneasy for fear of Deception." After about three hours, Clark sent Gass to find Lewis. Gass reported back that Lewis was well and that the Sioux were preparing a feast and dance to honor the Americans. That news was a clear indication of a shift in Brulé tactics. If the whites could not be easily bluffed, they might be flattered and impressed by a show of Sioux hospitality and military prowess. It was Black Buffalo's turn to demonstrate "medicine" as the Americans had done earlier. Throughout the afternoon many Brulé folk made "frequent selicitiations" for the expedition to remain one night longer so that they could "Show their good disposition towards us." Once the captains agreed, they were carried with much ceremony on white buffalo robes to the great council lodge.

The scene that night in the Brulé village made a lasting impression on many members of the expedition. Fires glowed through translucent tepees as women prepared vast quantities of food for the feast. Slabs of buffalo meat roasted over hot coals. In a circle inside the council lodge were seated some seventy elders and prominent warriors. The Americans were placed next to Black Buffalo. Directly in front of the chiefs a six-foot sacred circle had been cleared for holy pipes, pipe stands, and medicine bundles. American and Spanish flags were also displayed in the circle. Lewis and Clark noticed the Spanish ensign but decided to ignore it. There is no evidence to suggest that the Tetons recognized the sovereignty of either Spain or the United States. The flags may have been used simply for colorful decoration.

The diplomacy of the evening began when a Brulé elder stood "and Spoke aproveing what we had done." Because the captains still lacked a reliable Sioux interpreter, they were uncertain about much of what the old man said. The import of his speech seemed to be that the Brulé bands were poor and that the expedition should trade with them, not the upriver tribes. No journalist recorded the American reply, but the explorers probably repeated their usual formula about peace with other tribes and the need for the expedition to press on. The concern for intertribal peace was a cornerstone in Jefferson's Indian policy and also reflected the needs of the St. Louis merchants. Because Lewis and Clark had learned earlier in the day that there were many Omaha prisoners in the Brulé villages, the Americans saw this as an opportunity to promote Teton-Omaha peace. Clark called upon Black Buffalo to free the Omaha captives. Black Buffalo's attempt at peacemaking with the Omahas had been disrupted by the Partisan in 1803, and there was little reason to think the chief would release valuable prisoners just to gratify what must have seemed the whim of a distant chief.

The council reached its dramatic climax when Black Buffalo "rose with great state" to address the gathering. Again hindered by the lack of a skilled interpreter, Lewis and Clark understood little of what the chief said. Clark recorded in his journal that the chief spoke "to the same purpose" as did the Brulé elder. It seems clear that Black Buffalo was employing his oratorical talents to further the fundamental Teton Sioux aim—to keep the expedition from opening direct trade with the Arikaras and other Upper Missouri village people. His speech finished, Black Buffalo took up the most holy of the pipes and pointed it in each of the cardinal directions. Before lighting the pipe, he offered a prayer. Still holding the pipe, the chief took some tender dog meat and made a "Sacrefise to the flag." These solemnities over, the pipe was passed around the circle for all to smoke.

Food was next on the evening agenda. The captains and their men were presented with all the Sioux delicacies, including platters of roast dog, buffalo, pemmican, and prairie turnips.[21] The whole assembly ate and smoked with an air of conviviality until dusk. At nightfall a large fire was made in the center of the village to light the way for musicians and dancers. Ten male musicians entered first. Their instruments were of two kinds: a tambourine-like instrument made by stretching a skin over a willow hoop, and various rattles made by tying deer and antelope hooves on a long stick. Clark noted that the rattles made a "gingling noise." As the men began to sing and play, women "highly Deckerated in their way" came forward and began to dance in time to the rhythm. In this war dance the women displayed scalps and other war trophies belonging to their male relatives. That night such a display was surely aimed at impressing Lewis and Clark with Brulé military might. One young man moved away from the players and toward the spectators. In a high singing voice he recounted the daring exploits of band members in combat with their enemies. His words were picked up by the performers behind him and repeated to add power to the whole spectacle.[22] Throughout the evening members of the expedition rewarded the singers and dancers with tobacco. When one warrior thought he had not received his proper due, he broke one drum, threw two more in the fire, and angrily left the dance line. The two drums were hastily retrieved from the fire and the dancing continued.[23] The entertainment, "done with great Chearfullness," went on until midnight. Ordway found the music "delightful," but by midnight Lewis and Clark were plainly weary. Tactfully, they suggested to the chiefs that everyone must now be tired. Taking the hint, the chiefs ended the festivities and returned with the captains to spend the night on the keelboat.[24]

As Lewis and Clark left the Brulé village, they were offered young women as bed partners. For the Sioux, the proposal combined hospitality and diplomacy. Clark understood the meaning of the offer, writing later that "a curious custom with the Souix as well as the rickeres [Arikaras] is to give handsom squars to those whome they wish to Show some acknowledgements to." Repeating the offer the following night, the Indians made clear to Clark that the woman stood for the whole band. He was urged "to take her and not dispise them." Although fully aware of the symbolic significance of sexual intercourse with the proffered woman, Clark dismissed her. That rejection must have bewildered the Brulés and surely did not foster the friendship and trust Jefferson was seeking.[25]

The late night entertainment was unquestionably a great emotional release from the tensions of earlier days, but Clark reported that at least he did not sleep well. On Thursday morning, September 27, both the captains and the chiefs were up early. Black Buffalo and the Partisan were given, or rather they simply appropriated, the blankets they had slept on. After breakfast Lewis and the chiefs went on shore "as a verry large part of their nation was comeing in" to see the expedition. Clark remained on the keelboat, where he wrote a letter to Pierre Dorion and prepared a medal and some certificates for Lewis to use later in the day.

About midafternoon Lewis, accompanied by Black Buffalo, the Partisan, and the "considerable man" Warchapa, returned to the keelboat. After about half an hour, the captains evidently thought it best that all return to the Sioux village. When Clark began to suggest they go ashore, the chiefs showed "great reluctance" to leave. That reluctance finally overcome, Clark first visited the Partisan's lodge. A crowd gathered outside the tepee as the American and the Brulé spoke "on various subjects." Continuing his round of courtesy calls, Clark stopped at the lodge of a Brulé elder and then moved on to Black Buffalo's tepee. From there Clark was conducted to a gathering of Teton elders. Toward evening Lewis arrived in the village and both captains enjoyed a display of the same dancing and ceremony as the previous night. And once again, on the way back to the keelboat, they were offered Sioux women. As before, the offer was rejected.

Tired by a full day of talking and visiting, the American party, along with the Partisan and one of his soldiers, made their way on the white pirogue back to the keelboat. The evening stillness was shattered when some clumsy steering caused the pirogue to slam broadside against the keelboat's anchor cable. The cable broke and both vessels began to swing dangerously. Clark at once shouted at his men to get their oars in order to prevent further damage to either vessel. His shouting and the general bustle of men moving quickly in the darkness frightened the Sioux. An alarm ran through the village as Black Buffalo spread the word that an Omaha attack was at hand. Within ten minutes the chief and two hundred armed men prepared for combat were on the river bank. After about half an hour, most of the warriors made their way back to the village. However, some sixty remained on watch throughout the night.

Both Lewis and Clark believed that the sudden appearance of so many warriors was a "signal of their intentions (which was to Stop our proceeding on our journey and if Possible rob us.)"[26] This harsh view of Brulé motives was not shared by others in the expedition. Sergeants Ordway and Gass and Private Whitehouse emphasized both the fear of Omaha attack and the genuine desire of the Sioux to help the endangered vessels.[27] In light of Brulé activities before Lewis and Clark's coming, Black Buffalo's fear of Omaha attack was well grounded. In early September, some two weeks before the expedition arrived, a Brulé war party had raided an Omaha village, burning forty lodges and killing more than seventy-five of the tribe. There were now some forty-eight Omaha prisoners in the two Brulé villages along the Bad River.[28] In the cycle of raid and reprisal, Black Buffalo had every reason to think the confusion in the night was due to something more than a broken cable and a missing anchor.

But the Americans also had reason to worry that night. Although Clark stressed the sudden arrival of Sioux warriors as cause for alarm, it was probably intelligence brought to the captains by Pierre Cruzatte that put the expedition on its guard throughout the night. On Wednesday, September 26, Cruzatte had been given some trade goods as presents for the Omaha prisoners. Now, in return, the prisoners told the interpreter that Lewis and Clark "were to be stoped." The value of that information gathered from Indians who saw the Teton Sioux as enemies is now hard to judge. Certainly it fit the overall evaluation of Sioux behavior held by the expedition. Clark's tense lines "we Shew as little signs of a Knowledge of their intentions as possible, all prepared on board for any thing which might happen, we kept a Strong guard all night in the boat, no Sleep" betray both fear of Sioux military power and an exaggerated readiness to fight.[29]

Lewis and Clark and their men had now been with the Teton Sioux for three days. Those were days filled with isolated moments of trouble and misunderstanding and long periods of friendly visiting and good company. The expedition gathered some important ethnographic data, tried to make its point about American sovereignty, and even practiced, albeit with dubious success, some intertribal peacemaking. But on the crucial issue of trade—safe passage up the Missouri for fur traders and St. Louis merchants—there had been little or no progress. The expedition planned to spend the rest of the year at the Mandan villages; with winter coming, it was now time to move on. That determination to press upriver collided with the equal determination of the Brulé chiefs both to advance their own prestige and to defend Teton Sioux economic interests. In the eyes of men like Black Buffalo and the Partisan, the continued presence of the American expedition posed something of a dilemma and an embarrassment. Both men needed to act forcefully to vindicate personal claims to power. Teton bands had come to expect their headmen to obtain gifts from river traders. A chief who could not deliver was bound to have his authority openly questioned. At the same time, faced with a well-armed party under strong leadership, the chiefs feared pressing their demands too far. If there was a bloody incident and Indian casualties were high, the chiefs would surely lose influence. Pressure tactics that proved effective in intimidating poorly armed traders who needed Sioux cooperation would not work against a military expedition whose goals went far beyond the ledger book. It was against this background of cross purposes, face saving, and Lewis and Clark's determination to leave the Bad River that the last day of the Teton Sioux confrontation was played out.

Much of Friday morning was spent in a fruitless search for the keelboat anchor. By midmorning, when the work parties took breakfast, nearly all the Brulés lined the river bank. As the captains were about to order the sail hoisted, Black Buffalo and the other chiefs appeared. Once on board, the Brulé leaders began their now-familiar demand that the expedition remain with them. Ordway noted that the warriors on the bank were well armed with guns, spears, "a kind of cutlashes," and bows with metal-tipped arrows.[30] Anxious to leave, the crew made preparations to cast off the bowline. At that moment several of the Partisan's warriors took hold of the cable. Clark, who was inside the cabin with Black Buffalo, saw what happened and complained to the chief. Evidently fearing that the seizure of the cable spelled the beginning of very serious trouble, and perhaps resenting the role of the Partisan in the affair, the Brulé chief hurried forward to assure Lewis that the warriors simply wanted tobacco. Lewis, weary of the constant demands for gifts, refused to give them anything. He ordered all hands ready for departure, had the sail hoisted, and detailed one man to untie the bow cable.

At this critical moment several things happened at once. The bow cable, first untied by a crewman, was again fastened by several of the Partisan's warriors. At the same time, the Partisan himself demanded a flag and some tobacco. Lewis angrily ordered all Indians off the boat while Clark threw a carrot of tobacco on the bank. Clark then took the firing taper for the port swivel gun in his hand and "spoke so as to touch his [Black Buffalo's] pride." Clark did not record the sarcasm in his journal but years later told Nicholas Biddle, "I threw him tobacco saying to the chief you have told us you are a great man—have influence—take this tobacco and shew us your influence by taking the rope from your men and letting go without coming to hostilities."[31] Clark also had a "rangleing" exchange with the Partisan. Violence seemed seconds away. Warriors hurried women and children from the bank. But it was Black Buffalo who finally calmed the situation. He promised the expedition safe conduct if tobacco, always a ceremonial tribute, was given to the warriors holding the cable. Lewis and Clark balked at the demand, saying that they "did not mean to be trifled with." Seeing the captains hesitate, Black Buffalo sarcastically observed that "he was mad too, to see us stand so much for one carrot of tobacco." Lewis tossed the tobacco to the Indians and Black Buffalo jerked the cable from their hands. At that moment the Teton confrontation was over.[32]

In those moments when Clark was ready to fire, when the Brulé warriors had bows strung, and when the Partisan was shouting defiance, it was Black Buffalo who showed both firmness and the ability to compromise. Perhaps by September 28 the Brulé chief realized that nothing further could be gained by delaying Lewis and Clark. There would be other parties from St. Louis, less well armed, with more goods, and easier to intimidate. Allowing one boat to pass was hardly a defeat. Black Buffalo had obtained ceremonial tribute from the Americans and had lost nothing in the eyes of his own people. But at the beginning of the final day of the confrontation, the political ambitions of the Partisan were as yet unfulfilled. His contest for influence with Black Buffalo still gave him reason to harrass the Americans. The Partisan, described by Buffalo Medicine's son as a "Double Spoken man," seized the initiative that day as one more means to gain precedence over Black Buffalo.[33] The last minutes of the Teton encounter were less a conflict between Indians and American explorers and more a tussle between rival band headmen. In the end it was Black Buffalo who engineered a compromise allowing each party to escape with some dignity intact and without bloodshed.

If Black Buffalo is credited with working to avoid violence, then Lewis and Clark also deserve a share of the glory. They took seriously their instructions from Jefferson to deal with Indians "in a most friendly and conciliatory manner which their own conduct will admit."[34] The captains also understood the flexibility they had as explorers. They could, with enough determination and good fortune, move up the Missouri. Unlike the St. Louis traders, Lewis and Clark did not have to stay with the Sioux, trade with them, and depend on their cooperation. Subsequent St. Louis parties, from Nathaniel Pryor's Sheheke expedition to Wilson Price Hunt's Astorians, would find the Teton Sioux as intransigent as ever.

The memory of the Sioux September was still fresh when Clark, writing from Fort Mandan during the winter of 1804–1805, described the Tetons as "the vilest miscreants of the savage race, and must ever remain the pirates of the Missouri."[35] Clark's harsh words masked a harsher reality. The Sioux talks had failed. The Sioux were no closer to becoming part of the St. Louis trade network. No delegation of Brulé dignitaries was prepared to visit the president. Jefferson's call for Lewis and Clark to make a "friendly impression" on Black Buffalo's folk was lost in a welter of conflicting band and personal quarrels. Lewis admitted as much when he informed Jefferson that Corporal Richard Warfington's return party bound for St. Louis in the spring of 1805 was sure to encounter heavy Sioux fire. Sioux hostility might endanger not only Warfington's men but the keelboat loaded with the expedition's journals, maps, and botanical specimens. The hazard was real enough that Warfington's men "pledged themselves to us that they will not yeald while there is a man of them living."[36] This was hardly the sort of diplomatic conclusion Jefferson sought. At best Lewis and Clark could say their efforts were inconclusive; at worst they may have exacerbated Sioux-American relations.

Nearly 150 years later, Bernard DeVoto voiced what has become historical wisdom about the encounter. DeVoto declared that Lewis and Clark defeated the Tetons, forced them to back down, and made them "women" in the eyes of their neighbors. Heaping abuse on the Sioux, he described Brulé soldiers as "bully boys" engaged in "storm trooper tactics." DeVoto maintained that after being defeated by the no-nonsense firmness of the Americans, the Tetons "were just beggars again."[37] But it was not the Teton Sioux who were defeated. Rather, it was American diplomacy that had been handed a stinging rebuff. As Lewis and Clark recognized in their 1806 letter to the North West Company trader Hugh Heney, the Sioux would always be a barrier to trade on the Upper Missouri "until some effectual measures be taken to render them pacific."[38] They had surely not been rendered "pacific" by three days of playing cat and mouse with Lewis and Clark. In the next two decades, as English traders retreated from the prairies and plains and Sioux population grew, the Teton bands did indeed turn to American merchants. But until that happened, Jefferson's assessment that the United States was "miserably weak" proved a painfully accurate appraisal of northern plains realities. Lewis and Clark had done little to transform those political and economic realities.

3

The Arikara Interlude

"Durtey, Kind, pore, and extravigent"
—WILLIAM CLARK, 1804

The Teton encounter had no quick ending and escaping its tangles proved no easy task. When the expedition resumed its progress up the Missouri River on September 29, Black Buffalo was on board the keelboat while the Partisan was waiting in the wings. Standing on a sandbar, the Partisan and two of his warriors demanded transportation as far as the Arikara villages. When the captains refused, Black Buffalo suggested that a carrot or two of tobacco and a ferry ride from one bank to the other might placate the Partisan. Lewis and Clark wearily complied, hoping this would be the last Teton request.

The expedition's attention was now turned to the first signs of the Arikaras. At the mouth of No Timber Creek, known today as Chantier Creek, the Americans found an abandoned Arikara settlement. Described by Truteau in the mid-1790s, the village had been occupied until the end of the century. Clark wrote that nothing remained of the village "but the mound which surrounds the town." Ordway, who always had an eye for simple but revealing detail, noted remains of cornfields in rich bottomland around the empty village.[1] In subsequent days the expedition would see more abandoned towns, all mute testimony to the many years of Arikara migration along the Missouri.

On the following day, September 30, some of the last scenes in the Teton drama were played out. With Black Buffalo still on board, the explorers brought their flotilla to a sandbar opposite a Sioux encampment. As the men ate breakfast, the captains talked with several warriors. The Indians were told about the "bad treatment" the expedition had suffered at the hands of the Teton bands lower down the river and were warned not to try the same. Those brave words were carefully matched by a generous amount of tobacco, and the American party moved on without incident. In the afternoon the wind picked up and the Missouri suddenly became a choppy lake. Rocking dangerously, the keelboat seemed ready to founder. Black Buffalo, fearing for his life, pleaded to be put ashore. Perhaps relieved to be free of their Indian passenger, the captains gave the chief some gifts and "advised him to keep his men away."[2]

In early October, as the weather turned cold and windy, the expedition encoun-

42

tered even more traces of the Arikaras. On the first of the month, they found another abandoned townsite, a fortified island settlement of substantial size. Clark described the ruins as "only a mound circular walls 3 or 4 feet high."[3] But Lewis and Clark found more than Arikara remains around the Cheyenne River; they also found Jean Vallé, an independent trader. The Frenchman was engaged in the Sioux trade and had a small supply of goods for that purpose. Vallé gave the captains an important bit of information about Upper Missouri trade patterns when he reported that many of the Sioux were currently at the Grand River Arikara villages.[4] Lewis and Clark would soon learn much more about that Arikara-Sioux connection, and disrupting it became one of the captains' leading diplomatic objectives.

Knowing that they would soon be with the Arikaras did not allay the ever present dread of Teton ambush. October 2 proved to be a day filled with alarms and fear of the Sioux. Suspecting a surprise attack, "We prepared our selves for action which we expected every moment." Action seemed at hand early in the afternoon when a large Teton band appeared on a hill overlooking the north bank of the river. One of the warriors came down to the bank and fired his gun into the air. Certain that the attack was upon them, the expedition prepared to defend itself. Whitehouse later wrote, "we were determined to fight or dye." But that firm resolve was unnecessary as the Teton party, whose intentions were never clear, left as quickly as it had appeared.[5] Sioux warriors would not again menace the explorers until they wintered with the Mandans.

As the expedition continued up the Missouri, there were more signs of the Arikaras. On October 4, the captains saw the island village of Lahoocatt, a fortified town of some seventeen earth lodges. Lahoocatt had been occupied by an Arikara tribe that Tabeau called the Laocatas. About 1797 they had abandoned Lahoocatt and moved north to join the larger body of Arikaras at the Grand River villages.[6] At the end of the first week of October, Lewis and Clark saw even more abandoned villages around the mouth of the Moreau River. Clark noted a substantial settlement of "about 80 neet lodges covered with earth and picketed around." A brief examination of the site turned up bullboats, mats, and baskets. Three different kinds of squash were still growing in the untended village fields.[7] The following day, October 7, Clark walked up the Moreau River bank about a mile to yet another vacant Arikara town, this one consisting of some sixty lodges. Occupied as late as the previous winter, the village was strewn with mats, baskets, and bullboats.[8]

Earth lodges, fortifications, and extensive fields of corn, beans, and squash were all signs of the culture of the Missouri Valley villagers. The Arikaras, or Star-rah-he as they called themselves, were the first of the northern plains villagers encountered by the expedition.[9] Virtually all European visitors to the Arikaras noted the linguistic affinity between the Platte River Pawnees and the Arikaras. Tabeau observed,

"The Loups and all the different Panis now on the River Platte, made, undoubtedly, with the Ricaras but one nation which time and circumstance have, without doubt, insensibly divided." Lewis and Clark agreed. The Arikaras, they wrote, "are the remains of ten large tribes of Panias."[10] The Arikaras met by the expedition were descendants of people who came out of what later anthropologists called the Central Plains Tradition. These people built nearly square lodges with rounded corners in what is now western Iowa, Kansas north of the Arkansas River drainage, and east and south-central Nebraska. Since the tradition is associated with the Caddoan language family, they were probably the predecessors of the historic Pawnees and Arikaras.

Sometime after A.D. 1400 these proto-Arikaras began moving north out of the central plains into the Big Bend region of the Upper Missouri. This migration may have been occasioned by severe droughts on the central plains. As the proto-Arikaras entered the Upper Missouri, they settled in territory claimed by the Mandans. Early relations between the two peoples were generally peaceful. Indeed, housing styles of the Central Plains Tradition influenced Mandan earth lodge construction. But by the middle-1400s, as the northern Mandans began to reoccupy the Bad-Cheyenne region, conflict erupted. One sign of conflict was the rise of fortified Arikara villages.[11] Meeting stiff resistance, the Mandans gradually withdrew during the 1450–1650 period, leaving the Upper Missouri south of the North Dakota border open for Arikara occupation. After the mid-sixteenth century and until the historic era, Arikara sites in the Big Bend and Bad-Cheyenne regions were unfortified, a fact suggesting that fear of Mandan attack had considerably diminished. But that fairly peaceful interlude was shattered in the eighteenth century when the Sioux migration to the northern plains and increased tension with the Mandan and Hidatsa villagers once again caused Arikara villages to be protected with enclosing ditches and palisades. As Lewis and Clark were to learn, the Arikaras were entering a time of trouble—trouble not to be made any less by the presence of outsiders with unpredictable behavior and uncertain motives.[12]

Characteristic of the Missouri village life-style was the compact settlement with dome-shaped earth lodges, gardens, and nearby fields. Arikara, Mandan, and Hidatsa towns were all located around the mouths of major western tributaries of the Missouri River. The Bad, Cheyenne, Moreau, and Grand Rivers were the foci of Arikara occupation in the historic period. Several related ecological factors determined the location of Indian villages. The rivers provided fresh water while the valleys offered a source of firewood. In addition, the east-west position of the valleys acted as natural highways guiding western tribes such as the Sioux, Cheyennes, and Kiowas to the agricultural towns.[13]

By the time Lewis and Clark reached the Arikaras in 1804, the villages were again fortified with ditches and palisades. The first extensive description of Arikara defenses of the kind seen by the captains comes from Truteau's 1795 journal. He noted that Arikara villages were ringed by palisades five feet high and reinforced with earth. The palisades were made of stout willow or cottonwood poles "as thick as one's leg, resting on the crosspieces and very close together." Against the palisades was an earth embankment at least two feet thick. "In this way," he wrote, "the height of the poles would prevent the scaling of the fort by the enemy, while the well-packed earth protects those within from their balls and arrows."[14]

Before the outbreak of smallpox in the 1780s, there were numerous Arikara villages, each containing upwards of thirty-five earth lodges. By the advent of Lewis and Clark, Arikara settlements clustered around the Cheyenne, Moreau, and Grand rivers had grown to accommodate refugees from war and disease. The captains noticed recently abandoned towns of sixty lodges; each of three villages visited during their interlude with the Arikaras had at least that number. The lodges were scattered in no apparent pattern, a deviation from the arrangement of them in rough lanes that recent anthropologists have identified as part of the Middle Missouri Tradition. When Henry Brackenridge visited the Arikara towns in 1811, he found the lodges built so close to each other that it was easy for a newcomer to become lost quickly. There was no central plaza, as in Mandan towns, although the large medicine lodge did provide some spatial focus.[15]

Arikara earth lodges were the first of that distinctive housing described by the expedition. The circular design of the domestic earth lodge can be traced back to what is known as the Central Plains Tradition. The essential features of the historic earth lodge included a fire pit at the center of the floor, four primary posts to hold up the superstructure, a smoke hole in the roof, and a tunnel-like entrance. The average Arikara lodge was about fifteen feet high and thirty feet in diameter. Replacing dirt washed away from the frame was an important task for women after every rain.[16]

Although many European visitors to the Arikara towns attempted to describe the construction of earth lodges, few could bring the practiced eye of a carpenter to the subject as did Patrick Gass.[17] On October 10, 1804, Gass and several other members of the expedition went to the Arikara village at Ashley Island. While there, the sergeant took time to study earth lodges and their construction. Gass's description remains the best firsthand account of Arikara housing.

> In a circle of a size suited to the dimensions of the intended lodge, they set up 16 forked posts five or six feet high, and lay poles from one fork to another. Against these poles they lean other poles, slanting from the ground, and extending about four inches above the cross poles: these are to recieve the ends of the upper poles, that support the roof. They next set up four large forks, fifteen feet high, and about ten feet apart,

in the middle of the area; and poles or beams between these. The roof poles are then laid on extending from the lower poles across the beams which rest on the middle forks, of such a length as to leave a hole at the top for a chimney. The whole is then covered with willow branches, except the chimney and hole below to pass through. On the willow branches they lay grass and lastly clay. At the hole below they build a pen about four feet wide and projecting ten feet from the hut; and hang a buffalo skin at the entrance of the hut for a door.[18]

The earth lodge towns and their sedentary populations were possible because the villagers developed a complex strategy to wrest a living from the Upper Missouri valley. Outsiders who visited the region in the summer months did not experience the demands placed on Indians for survival in the northern plains environment. Those demands included a climate of extremes from winters of $-44°$F to summers of $+116°$F and an average yearly rainfall of no more than sixteen inches. This rigorous climate yielded a frost-free growing season of no more than one hundred days a year.[19] Temperature, rainfall, and seasonal flooding meant agricultural uncertainties for Upper Missouri farmers. Despite these problems, Arikara farming was productive enough to sustain village life and produce a substantial surplus for trade.

Arikara agriculture centered on the production of several food crops and at least one ceremonial plant. *Zea mays,* the wild cereal grass, was the foundation crop for all Upper Missouri farmers. Edwin Denig, an American Fur Company official at Fort Union in the mid-nineteenth century, reported the Arikara corn "seldom exceeds two and a half or three feet in height." Denig noted that each cornstalk contained only a few ears with kernels "small, hard, and covered with a thicker shell than that raised in warmer climates."[20] Although corn was the essential staple for diet and trade, other crops were cultivated by Arikara farmers. Beans were planted in the corn hills so that their vines could climb the stalks. Some of those bean seeds were collected by the captains and sent to Jefferson, who in April 1807 planted them. He reported them "very forward" in progress by April 18. On the first of May of the same year, Jefferson planted some Arikara corn at Monticello and observed later that the plants produced ears suitable for roasting about a week after those coming from more familiar maize varieties.[21] Corn and beans, the two sister crops, were joined by a third, squash. Clark recorded in his journal that the Arikaras raised three kinds of squash.[22] Like Mandan and Hidatsa farmers, Arikara women boiled some of the squash for immediate use while slicing and drying most of the crop for winter consumption.[23]

The Arikaras also grew pumpkins, watermelons, and tobacco. The tobacco attracted much of the expedition's attention. Both Lewis and Patrick Gass quickly recognized that the Indian tobacco (*Nicotiana quadrivalis*) was something quite different from the Chesapeake varieties. Lewis, always interested in precise botanical descriptions, observed that Arikara tobacco grew about three feet high, was planted in hills, and was harvested in late summer. The captain found smoking this tobacco "very pleasant." Gass agreed about the pipe qualities of the blend but added that it was less suited for chewing.[24]

The land used by Arikara farmers was held by family groups as corporate property. Lewis and Clark reported, "They claim no land except that on which their villages stand and the fields which they cultivate." The fields were generally plots of about one or one-and-a-half acres. Each family's land was carefully marked with brush and pole fences. Apparently, there were two kinds of Arikara farm lands seen by the expedition and by later visitors. Very close to the villages were fenced garden plots. As trade demands for increased production mounted, fields up to a mile away from the village center were cleared. Planting began in April or May, depending on weather and ground conditions, and harvest of the major corn crop was in early August.[25]

As in many other American Indian tribes, Arikara women did the farming. Europeans, accustomed to seeing men in the fields, consistently misunderstood the native division of labor and labeled Indian women "squaw drudges." Clark was not immune to that cultural blindness and insisted that Arikara women "do the drugery as Common amongst Savages." Tabeau went further and charged that village women were virtual slaves to tyrannical husbands.[26] What Clark, Tabeau, and other Europeans did not understand was the seasonal nature of woman's work, their companionship in the shared labor, the elevated ritual status of Arikara women because of their role as earth mothers, and the substantial demands made on men in trade, war, and hunting. Arikara women farmed, using two simple but effective tools. Hoes or digging sticks were made from the shoulder blades of buffalo or deer. These scapular hoes were used to break ground and keep weeds from overgrowing the plots. A second implement was a rake fashioned by binding reeds to a long handle. Despite the uncertainties of climate and flooding, Arikara agriculture was very productive. As late as 1853, Arikara farmers grew five thousand bushels of corn for sale outside the villages.[27]

Agriculture was the foundation of the Arikara economy, but hunting buffalo and other game animals was also important. When the corn crop failed, as it did in the summer of 1803 because of severe flooding, many Arikaras left the Moreau and Grand River villages to hunt on the plains. Hunting was far more than an expedient in hard times. The extended winter buffalo hunt was a necessary part of the Arikaras' food supply. In October or November, hunting parties would leave the river villages in search of the herds. The mounted hunters carried skin tepees with them as they traveled far from the villages. Because of the close relationship between the

Arikaras and the Sioux, village hunters sometimes spent the winter alongside the Sioux. The Arikara buffalo hunt was, at least until the mid-nineteenth century, strictly regulated by warriors especially selected for the occasion. Those warriors would arrange the placement of hunters and give signals for the rush to kill the animals. Their buffalo hunting was sometimes limited by interference from the Sioux. Anxious to remain the prime suppliers of hides and meat to the Arikaras, Teton bands blockaded the villages and kept hunters away from the herds. This happened in October 1803 and was further evidence of Tabeau's observation that the buffalo was "a very uncertain resource" for the Arikaras.[28]

As Lewis and Clark neared the Grand River villages, they slowly learned about two aspects of Arikara life that would shape their relations with the Indians. Arikara politics might be best characterized as chaotic factionalism—a maze of interlocking lineage, village, and band loyalties complicated by the consequences of devastating epidemics. Just as Lewis and Clark had to thread their way through Brulé Teton politics, so would they have to cope with men like Kakawissassa, Kakawita, Pocasse, and Piahito. But with the Sioux encounter still fresh in their minds, it was a second dimension of Arikara life that commanded more of the captains' attention. During the troubled days at the Bad River, Lewis and Clark had heard about the complex web of trade that bound Upper Missouri villagers and many western nomads together in an intricate system of cooperation, exchange, and intimidation. The importance of that system would be brought home to the explorers with considerable force during their interlude with the Arikaras.

Arikara farmers were part of the Missouri Trade System. Their towns were the locale's focal points for the system while the Mandan and Hidatsa villages on the Knife River served as the upper exchange centers. The villagers were engaged in supplying the agricultural needs of the nomads. Lewis and Clark aptly described the Arikara farmers as the "gardners for the Soues."[29] They grew corn, raised horses, and processed hides in return for a wide variety of merchandise and foodstuffs brought by their western and southwestern customers. Clark listed among those customers the Arapahos, Comanches, Kiowas, Osages, and Tawehashs. But the most important customers of the Arikaras were the Cheyennes and the Sioux.[30] The Arikaras' dealings with these two tribes were quite different, and those differences played a central role in expedition-Indian relations.

The often-troubled relationship between the Arikara villages and Teton Sioux bands was an uneasy symbiosis. From a Teton perspective, some sort of control had to be maintained over the Arikaras. As Teton population expanded west of the Missouri, reliable sources of food had to be found. Both Black Buffalo and the Partisan made plain to the captains the long-term Sioux interest in controlling the flow of manufactured goods upriver to the village farmers. The overriding Sioux need was for the Arikaras' food products and horses. Just how strong that need was can be seen in a preexpedition incident involving Black Buffalo and his family. Sometime around 1800, one of Black Buffalo's brothers paid a visit to the Arikara town at Ashley Island. Kakawita, Tabeau's host, evidently had a grudge against the Brulé man. When he killed Black Buffalo's brother, the Brulé chief took revenge on five or six Arikaras and a larger conflict seemed imminent. But as the August trading time approached and Arikara corn ripened, all thoughts of warfare disappeared.[31] For the Sioux, corn was more important than blood. That August, as in every other late summer and early fall, Sioux bands flocked to the Arikara towns, bringing meat, fat, and hides from the plains and European-manufactured goods from the Dakota Rendezvous.

Lewis and Clark, like other non-Indian observers, consistently misunderstood the Arikara-Sioux connection. Already disposed to cast the Tetons as "that lawless, savage, and rapacious race," the captains viewed the relationship as one of colonial exploitation. Clark believed that this economic link meant Sioux political domination of the Arikaras. As he explained, the Tetons maintained "great influence over the Rickeres, poison [ed] their minds and [kept] them in perpetial dread." To the captains, Arikara villagers seemed helpless victims of Sioux aggression. In both their written records and in their diplomacy, Lewis and Clark argued that a disruption of the Arikara-Sioux alliance would free the village farmers from tyranny and might force Teton bands to accept American trade terms. The explorers, who had only limited experience with the Arikaras, were not alone in believing that the villagers were an oppressed people. The trader Tabeau insisted that the Arikaras functioned as "a certain kind of serf" for the Sioux. He declared that the Arikaras were so fully dominated by the Sioux that they were even compelled to buy their bows and arrows from the Tetons.[32]

But this harsh view of Arikara-Sioux relations was not shared by the Arikaras themselves. They saw many advantages in the connection not quickly evident to outsiders. The economic advantages included a source of manufactured goods, especially guns, and a reliable market for corn and horses. Tabeau and the captains tended to overstate the violence and intimidation present in Arikara-Sioux dealings. There was, in fact, far more cooperation in times of war and friendship in times of peace. Much of the tension Lewis and Clark were to encounter between the Arikaras and Mandans was based on raids carried out by joint Arikara-Sioux war parties against the Knife River Mandan and Hidatsa villages. Among the objects sent back from Fort Mandan was a buffalo robe painting of one such raid in 1797.[33] The Arikaras knew well the military power of the Tetons, but they also knew how important their corn was to Sioux survival. Truteau was close to the mark when he wrote in 1795 that "the Ricaras and this Sioux nation live together peacefully. The former recieve them in order to obtain guns, clothes, hats, kettles, clothes, etc., which are given them in exchange for their horses. They humor them through fear and to inevitably overpower them."[34]

The captains themselves ran into the determination of the Arikaras to continue their Sioux connection. When the expedition stopped at the Grand River villages on the return journey, the explorer-diplomats tried in vain to convince the Arikara chiefs to sever Sioux ties. Several chiefs, who grasped the Upper Missouri balance of trade and power better than the neophyte Americans, replied that they "must trade with the Sieoux one more time to get guns and powder; that they had no guns or powder and more horses than they had use for, [and] after they got guns and powder . . . they would never again have any thing to do with them."[35] The captains had been put off in the best traditions of international diplomacy; once again their desire to rearrange traditional patterns of Indian behavior was thwarted.

If the captains and the Arikaras had very different perceptions of the Sioux, both parties agreed that the Cheyennes were far more acceptable and less troublesome customers. The Cheyennes, who had abandoned farming in the eastern prairie valleys to become a plains people, depended heavily on the Arikaras for foodstuffs and tobacco. Each summer many Cheyennes journeyed to the Arikara villages to trade and renew old friendships. Some advance groups came in mid-June while larger parties arrived in mid-July. Some remained with the Arikaras well into the fall months, as Lewis and Clark discovered. Cheyenne traders brought to the Arikaras a wide variety of perishable meat products as well as exquisite skin clothing made by their women. The Arikaras especially valued "shirts of antelope skin, ornamented and worked with different colored quills of the porcupine." In addition to meat and fancy clothing, the Cheyennes also brought flour made from pounded prairie apples. Much of what they offered might be classed as luxury goods, but there was one Cheyenne commodity that Arikara middlemen were very anxious to possess. Cheyenne horses were essential to fill out herds in preparation for trading with the Sioux. The Arikaras wanted Cheyenne horses so badly that they were willing to trade precious guns, powder, and shot for them. During the Lewis and Clark period, the Arikaras were prepared to trade one gun, one hundred rounds of ammunition, and a knife for one horse. The result of this trade, however, was that Sioux-Cheyenne relations were often tense because the Teton bands resented seeing Arikara corn in Cheyenne mouths and English trade guns in Cheyenne hands."[36]

Lewis and Clark, arriving at the Arikara villages in October, did not see the festive trading days of August and September. Some fifteen to sixteen hundred people had thronged the trade fair, described by Tabeau as "this great gathering of different nations." Although there was always the threat of violence, especially between the competitive Sioux and Cheyennes, the trading days were better occasions to make bargains and visit old friends. "Times are lively," noted Edwin Denig, "feasting and dancing goes on constantly, both in the village and camp—horse racing, gambling in many ways. Bucks and belles dressed in their best and tricked out in all the gaudy colors of cloth, paints, and porcupine quills may be seen mingled in the dance or exchanging their professions of love in more solitary places. The old men smoke and eat without intermission. The middle aged exchange horses and other property. The soldiers gamble. And the young warriors spend both day and night in attempts at seduction of the young women in both camps. Strange scenes are witnessed here, much that would be interesting, much more that would be indescribable."[37] Although the captains had not experienced those scenes, they surely had to face the consequences of those trading days. The alliances and friendships forged during the trade fairs would shape the responses of the Indians to Lewis and Clark's diplomacy in the days to come.

Lewis and Clark saw little of the Arikaras' ritual life during their brief October stay. Had they come earlier, they might have witnessed the impressive blessing-of-the-corn ceremony done to ensure an abundant harvest. Tabeau, who saw the three-day celebration, wrote that "everything breathes gaiety at this festival." An elaborate altar was set up in the lodge of the principal village chief. That altar was festooned with large gourds, arrows decorated to look like corn stalks, green branches, and dried meat. Empty baskets and scapular hoes were placed before the altar to symbolize the hope for a bountiful harvest. Crowns of plaited straw were to ward off insects and green branches were offerings to the moon and stars to gain good weather. To honor their role in agriculture, women arrayed in their best clothing sat near the center posts of the lodge. Having missed this ritual, Lewis and Clark could not comment on it, nor on the many beliefs and rites surrounding the buffalo. Although the captains and their men spent considerable time visiting the Arikaras, no journalist in the expedition took note of the private altars and painted buffalo skulls present in every earth lodge. Nor did the explorers set down Arikara ideas about the many spirits in their universe and the central force, "the Master of Life."[38]

Because the expedition's members usually seemed aware of Indian architecture and village design, it is even more surprising that no journal contains any reference to the Arikara medicine lodge. This ritual lodge was often the largest earth structure in the village. Located near the center of the village, it shared some construction features with domestic lodges: four primary interior posts, a central fire pit, and a walled entrance passage. The lodge measured some fifty or sixty feet in diameter and, unlike the circular domestic lodges, was octagonal in shape. Inside the medicine lodge and opposite the entrance was a low platform or altar for ritual offerings.[39]

If Lewis and Clark were oblivious to the ritual ties that bound Arikara life together, they were very aware of the powerful force that threatened to unravel it.

Beginning in the 1780s, smallpox epidemics swept through the Missouri trench, wreaking terrible havoc on all Indians. In the period before the epidemics, the Arikaras numbered perhaps twenty thousand to thirty thousand persons.[40] They belonged to many bands and lived in dozens of villages along the Missouri. The general western pandemic of 1780–81 killed perhaps seventy-five percent of the Arikara population, causing the abandonment of many villages and the amalgamation of numerous political groups. When Truteau visited the Arikaras in 1795, he was told that there had already been three epidemics, reducing thirty-two villages to a mere handful.[41] That wave of disease was followed in 1801–1802 by another one. Tabeau, writing about the 1803–1804 period, reported that "of the eighteen fairly large villages, situated upon the Missouri at some distance from each other, the Ricaras are reduced to three very mediocre ones." Although Tabeau recognized the role of war in this dramatic population decline, he was emphatic in arguing that smallpox "unexpectedly made this terrible ravage among them." Lewis and Clark were only recording the obvious when they blandly noted that the Arikara were "much reduced" from previous numbers.[42]

For the history of expedition-Indian relations, the impact of the epidemics was most clearly seen in Arikara politics. Although there is little evidence that the Arikaras developed political integration beyond the village level before the 1780–81 pandemic, the waves of disease so shattered the ranks of chiefs, elders, bundle holders, and important women as to make future intervillage leadership highly unlikely. As their numbers dropped and survivors from many different villages and lineages clustered into what amounted to refugee towns, intense factionalism flared between dozens of once powerful chiefs and warriors. Just as Lewis and Clark had to confront Teton Sioux internal politics, now they would have to deal with the domestic rivalries present in the three Grand River settlements.

Truteau was the first non-Indian to analyze Arikara factional politics. The French trader recognized that the villages he knew around the Cheyenne River in 1795 were filled with the survivors of earlier epidemics. The chiefs were constantly engaged in "differences of opinion and wrangles for authority." Truteau believed that this factionalism, or "jealousy" as he termed it, was "the sole cause of their discord and their divisions." He reported that these factional controversies were sufficiently intense to cause some Arikaras to move north to the Mandan region while others drifted south to live with the Pawnees.[43]

Tabeau, who spent much more time with the Arikaras than either Truteau or the captains, added much valuable detail to Truteau's concept of factionalism bred by disease. Tabeau had firsthand experience with the rivalries between Indian leaders. When he arrived among the Arikaras, he became the object of much bickering between the Ashley Island village's civil chief Kakawissassa and a war chief named Kakawita. Both men wanted the honor and prestige of having Tabeau as a house guest. But the argument went well beyond hospitality. Whoever played host to the trader would reap considerable influence in village life. For Kakawita, leader of a small village recently come to Ashley Island, snaring Tabeau meant economic advantage and increased power. The Frenchman had another lesson in Arikara factionalism when in August 1803 he attempted to convene a grand council to discuss trade arrangements. Knowing how many Arikara males were designated as chiefs, the trader carefully invited forty-two of the leading men. To his surprise, he was berated for neglecting so many others. As Tabeau aptly put it, the Arikara towns were filled with "captains without companies."[44] Dialect differences, old rivalries, important families weakened by disease, and leaders without followers all made Arikara politics treacherous ground for any outsider.

At the time Lewis and Clark visited them, the Arikaras were living in three large villages on the Missouri near the mouth of the Grand River. These villages were founded sometime in the late 1790s after the Arikaras abandoned their North Dakota settlements.[45] The first Arikara village encountered by the expedition was Sawa-haini, which consisted of about sixty earth lodges on Ashley Island in the Missouri River. The island was fully cultivated, with corn and tobacco especially evident. Both Tabeau and the captains reported that Kakawissassa, or the Crow at Rest, was the leading civil chief in Sawa-haini. However, during the Lewis and Clark period his authority was challenged by Kakawita, or Man Crow, war chief of the small village of Narhkarica recently come to Sawa-haini. When the captains returned in 1806, Kakawissassa told them he had given his chief's medal to yet another Sawa-haini chief, a man named Grey Eyes. People living on the island, along with those at the second village, were known to the captains as Arikaras-proper in order to distinguish them from the ethnically diverse Arikaras of the third town. That second village was upriver a short distance from Sawa-haini. Part of what archaeologists call the Leavenworth Site (39Co9), Rhtarahe was the lower of the two villages to share this location. Rhtarahe had about sixty to seventy lodges. Pocasse or Hay was the leading civil chief. Cottonwood Creek separated the earth lodges of Rhtarahe from those of Waho-erha. European visitors to the Arikaras recognized that Waho-erha was different from the other villages in both language and ethnic mix. Answering a query from Nicholas Biddle in 1810, Clark reported that Waho-erha was composed of nine different tribes who had not been involved in recent (1790s) troubles with the Mandans as had the Arikaras-proper. Clark noted, "A difference in pronunciation and some difference of language may be discovered between them and the Arikara proper."[46] Tabeau, who had more experience with the Arikaras, agreed with Clark's observation. The French trader characterized the differing Arikara accents and inflections as "the tower of Babel." The leading civil chief in Waho-erha was Piahito, or Hawk's Feather. Unlike the

Hidatsas, who developed an intervillage council in the 1780s, factionalism and old suspicions kept the Arikara bands divided. Each village would face the American visitors alone.[47]

On October 8, 1804, as the Corps of Discovery passed the mouth of the Grand River, two of the explorers came upon the Ashley Island village of Sawa-haini. Clark described the three-mile-long island as "covered with fields, where those people raise their corn, tobacco, beans etc." As the flotilla passed the island, many Arikaras lined the banks to gawk at the strangers. The men were dressed in buffalo robes, leggings, and moccasins while the women wore fringed antelope dresses. Clark noted that most of the warriors were well armed with northwest trade guns.[48] On a sandbar opposite the village were more Arikara sightseers and a French trader. While Clark led most of the party to a campsite beyond the island, Lewis and several crewmen in a pirogue went to talk with the trader. The captains had been told in St. Louis that they might meet one "Mr. Tebaux," who could give the explorers "much information in relation to that country."[49] The Frenchman on shore was Tabeau's fellow trader, Joseph Gravelines. Clark described him as "a man well versed in the language of this nation [who] gave us some information relitive to the Country, nation etc."[50] Both Gravelines and Tabeau spoke the Arikara and Sioux languages, skills much in demand for the Arikara talks. Later in the evening Lewis, Gravelines, and some of the party went to Sawa-haini carrying tobacco for a get-acquainted smoke. Heartened by that event and reassured by Gravelines and Tabeau that the Arikaras were "all friendly and glad to see us," the captains prepared for serious diplomacy the next day.[51]

At camp during that first evening among the Arikaras, Lewis and Clark may well have discussed American diplomatic goals as applied to the Grand River villagers. The captains surely did not accept Truteau's claim that the Arikaras were "the key to the passages which we must traverse to reach all the nations higher up the Missouri."[52] That distinction was reserved for the Teton Sioux. Nonetheless, the explorer-diplomats did not underestimate the importance of the Arikaras both as military allies of the Sioux and as potential American trading partners. They knew from their St. Louis contacts that the Arikaras had harrassed traders and often blocked their access upriver to the Mandans. Clark was honestly concerned about the reception the expedition would receive when he wrote that the Americans were prepared for war or peace with the villagers. Jefferson had not given the explorers the kind of precise instructions for the Arikara negotiations as he had for dealings with the Teton Sioux. However, the general observations in the president's instructions to Lewis and the recent experiences with the Tetons served to clarify what the expedition hoped to achieve while at the Arikara villages. On one level these objectives were the same as pursued since the beginning of the voyage. The captains were to assert United States sovereignty over Louisiana Purchase lands. Military parades and airgun displays were put on to make Indians stand in awe of American power. As they had done with other tribes, Lewis and Clark planned to distribute medals and uniforms to chiefs ready to support American authority. Old rivalries were to be forgotten and peace was to obtain among all the tribes. Such a peace was a prerequisite for another cornerstone of American policy: the promotion of trade with American merchants. Although the captains knew from St. Louis informants and from conversations with Tabeau and Gravelines that the Arikaras could not supply beaver pelts, the market for goods to replace those of English manufacture was great.[53]

Sovereignty, client chiefs, and trade were all important subjects for discussion with the Arikara chiefs. But if the events of the interlude with the Arikaras proved any test, Lewis and Clark had other things on their minds as well. Those other concerns focused on the complex relations between the Teton Sioux, the Arikaras, and the Mandans and Hidatsas. The explorers only gradually sensed how intricate those relations were. As they began talks with the Arikaras, the captains perceived the Tetons as ferocious enemies to undercut, the Arikaras as unwilling dupes of the rapacious Sioux, and the Mandans and Hidatsas as a force of unknown dimensions. With a naive optimism typical of so much Euro-American frontier diplomacy, Lewis and Clark believed they could easily reshape Upper Missouri realities to fit their expectations. The Arikaras were to be weaned away from dependence on the Tetons. An American-inspired alliance of all Upper Missouri villagers might further weaken the Sioux. On the night before the negotiations began, those goals seemed within reach. Lewis and Clark knew from Tabeau and Gravelines that Arikara moves had been underway in the past six months to lessen tensions with the Knife River peoples. But the captains also knew that the Laocata band of Arikaras had done all it could to sabotage an Arikara-Mandan peace. The Laocata action was a reminder that the violent events of the 1790s were not forgotten. Weakening the Arikara-Sioux connection and promoting peace among all the Upper Missouri villagers seemed a rational and beneficial policy to both the captains and their trader allies.[54] To the surprise of the explorer-diplomats, virtually all Indian parties proved resistant to change and suspicious of American motives.

During the Teton face-off it had been evident that Brulé politicians like Black Buffalo and the Partisan had a clear concept of Teton interests and the personal stature to make decisions promoting those interests. In the Arikara political world of "captains without companies," it proved more difficult to articulate a policy toward non-Indian outsiders. Civil chiefs, leading warriors, elders, and important families found their authority fragmented and open to challenge in the troubled times after the epidemics. Having the remnants of several bands living in one village made for political tensions unknown in Arikara life before disease forced such amalgamation. This state of affairs would remain unchanged for years. When the Astorians were among the Arikaras in 1811, some village chiefs attempted to block the progress of that expedition unless substantial gifts were offered. This decision was openly opposed by several elders who urged the Arikaras to "behave well towards the white people," arguing that "the advantages they derived by intercourse with them" far outweighed any danger.[55] In the fall of 1804, village chiefs like Kakawissassa and Piahito had considerable influence, but their power to determine and enforce policies was limited by cultural attitudes toward leadership as well as by the presence of refugee bands who did not accept decisions made by others. Chiefs, leading families, and ordinary Arikaras saw little reason to exchange valuable and reliable dealings with the Teton Sioux for the uncertainties of St. Louis trade and Mandan friendship. Village chiefs would be polite to the white strangers and might even make some promises, but the real Arikara interest was to have the Americans move on with the least disruption to the old ways of war and trade.

Lewis and Clark hoped to begin talks with the Arikaras on October 9. Invitations had been sent by way of Gravelines and Tabeau to Kakawissassa, Pocasse, and Piahito. A flag pole had been raised at the expedition's camp and some preparations were underway to begin the now-familiar display of military pomp and hardware. Sometime before noon the three chiefs appeared and the obligatory smoking began. The visual impact of Lewis and Clark's diplomacy required good weather for marching, shooting, and distributing gifts. When it became plain that this Tuesday would be windy, rainy, and cold, all agreed to postpone discussions until the following day. The Arikaras and Americans spent the rest of the day visiting each other. During those visits, York proved to be the greatest attraction, as he would be on subsequent days. Clark wrote that the villagers were "much astonished at my black Servent, who did not lose the opportunity of displaying his powers, strength, etc."[56]

Clear weather the next day seemed promising for a council session. After breakfast with Tabeau and Gravelines, the captains made all the necessary preparations for the Arikaras' arrival. After the flag was raised and many of the men donned dress uniforms, the camp was ready to greet its Indian visitors. By midmorning Kakawissassa and several leading men from Sawa-haini had arrived. But to the captains' dismay, delegations from the two other villages were conspicuously absent. That absence was a clear indication of the tension between the Arikara towns. Pocasse, Piahito, and their respective village councils were fearful that Lewis and Clark might make Kakawassassa the "grand chief." Such an action would upset the Arikara balance of power and possibly had no precedent in Arikara history. The captains, having learned something about internal Indian politics while among the Tetons, recognized the source of the Arikaras' concern. Clark observed, "We have every reason to believe that a gellousy exists between the Villages for fear of our making the first chief from the lower village." But recognizing the problem did not mean that Lewis and Clark were willing to alter their decision to make Kakawissassa the first or grand chief. At noon, increasingly concerned over the delay and worried that the talks might crumble, the captains asked Gravelines to go over to the villages and again invite Pocasse and Piahito to the council.[57]

Early in the afternoon the two reluctant chiefs and several principal men arrived at the expedition's camp. After smoking the required pipe, Lewis stood and "read a speech to them giving them good counsel." This prepared talk, interpreted to the Arikaras by Gravelines, was probably the same one delivered to other tribes from the beginning of the voyage. As the captains told the Otos, "the great chief of the Seventeen great nations of America, impelled by his parental regard for his newly adopted children on the troubled waters, has sent us out to clear the road, remove every obstruction, and make it the road of peace between himself and his red children residing there."[58] The speech stressed the now-familiar themes of federal Indian policy in the early Trans-Mississippi West. The acceptance of United States sovereignty, peace between the tribes, and trade with American merchants would be rewarded by the protection and favor of the great chief of the seventeen fires.

As Lewis was slowly reading his speech, Clark's attention was seized by something in the audience that put a new urgency to the negotiations: the presence of two Teton Sioux, one of whom Clark recognized from the troubled days at the Bad River. Clark was certain that the Sioux were there to thwart the progress of the expedition and retain some measure of control over Arikara affairs. If the Teton ambassadors succeeded in playing on the Arikaras' fears, especially those of Pocasse and Piahito, Lewis and Clark might have to face a second Upper Missouri Indian confrontation.[59]

With Lewis's talk finished, the display of military firepower and the all-important distribution of gifts began. As if to put an exclamation point to Lewis's presentation, three shots were fired from the bow swivel gun on the keelboat. The captains may have hoped the two Sioux would be reminded of how close those guns had come to firing on their warriors just a few days before. When the smoke cleared, out came gift bale number fifteen, marked and prepared for the Arikaras' use months before in St. Louis. The bale contained a bewildering array of goods, all representing what the Arikaras might obtain by trading directly with St. Louis merchants. There was a pound of vermilion paint for the warriors, three pewter looking glasses for young girls, and over four hundred needles for Arikara women. Lewis and Clark laid out their country store of merchandise, ranging from cloth, beads, combs, razors, and rolls of wire to nine pairs of scissors, knives, tomahawks, and even six Jew's harps. For the chiefs there were military coats, cocked hats, medals, and American flags. Notably absent from the gifts was any alcohol. The Arikaras made it plain to all European visitors that the drink was unwelcome. As they explained to Clark, those whites who gave Indians alcohol were not friends but were simply interested in seeing natives act the fool.[60]

Knowing that there was "gellousy" among the three Arikara villages over whose chief was to be afforded highest honors, the captains might have exercised some caution in handing out uniforms and medals and in naming chiefs to certain ranks. But Euro-American practice had always been to designate one Indian as the principal chief, whether that particular group sanctioned such a position or not. Lewis and Clark were not about to break with tradition, even if it caused more tension within Arikara politics and made Sioux efforts at sowing discord easier. Kakawissassa of Sawa-haini was named "grand chief" with the appropriate medal, while Pocasse and Piahito were offered medals of lesser grades. At the same time, perhaps to soothe bruised pride, other goods were given to each chief in equal measure. To signal the end of the conference, the airgun was brought out and fired. Ordway observed that the chiefs "appeared to be astonished at the sight of it and the execution it would do." As was their custom, the Arikara chiefs told Lewis and Clark that an answer, or rather three answers, to the American speech would come the next day. This was neither an attempt to deceive the explorers nor a ploy to draw out the negotiations. Rather, it was an acceptance of the fact that all decisions were the result of a consensus reached by elders in a village council. Since there was no Arikara tribal council, each village would present a separate reply. The presence of Teton representatives and the naming of Kakawissassa as leading chief only complicated the Arikaras' task of responding to the American views.[61]

With the talks over, Ordway and one other expedition member went to visit Rhtarahe while Gass took a party to sample food and hospitality at Sawa-haini. That afternoon of sightseeing and friendly talk produced some valuable information about Arikara life as well as scenes of comic proportion. Ordway's congenial stay in Rhtarahe gave the sergeant and his companion a chance to sample the Arikara diet. Welcomed into Pocasse's lodge, the Americans sat on woven mats and were served by the chief's wife. They were brought a bowl of beans and corn, the staple of Arikara fare. Following that dish, three different but unnamed Indian foods were offered to the Americans. "We ate some of each," wrote Ordway, "and found it very good." If he was fascinated with Indian menus, the Arikaras were equally intrigued by the looks and manners of the explorers. Ordway wrote later that those Indians "were very friendly to us and seemed to be desirous to talk with us and scarcely kept their eyes off us."[62] Usually a keen observer of the common things in native life, Ordway strangely neglected to record anything about the interior furnishings of the earth lodge. In fact, no journalist in the expedition took note of lodge interiors.

While Ordway was tasting Arikara cooking, Gass's party made its way to Ashley Island. If Ordway failed to examine lodge furnishings, Gass did not neglect details of exterior construction. His careful description, quoted earlier, is the best surviving account of Arikara housing. He offered an earth lodge portrait that squares with archaeological studies done at the two upper villages.[63] But it was York who proved the center of attraction that afternoon. The Arikaras were both attracted to and terrified by his blackness. Having never seen a black man, they were quite unsure if York was a man, a beast, or a strange and powerful spirit being. Clark later explained that Arikaras who had seen whites but not blacks thought York "something strange & from his very large size more vicious than whites." On the other hand, those Arikaras who had seen neither whites nor blacks were convinced that all members of the expedition, regardless of color, were possessed with extraordinary powers. York thoroughly enjoyed his newfound celebrity status and had already "made himself more turribal" than the captains wished.[64] That afternoon York and hordes of Arikara children had chased each other, the black man bellowing at them that he was a wild bear caught and tamed by Captain Clark. What may have worried the captains in this playful sport was York's boast that he ate human flesh. The Arikaras practiced ritual cannibalism of their fallen enemies, but that was a far cry from consuming village youth.[65] With Arikara chiefs embroiled in factional disputes and Teton agents ready to use those tensions against the expedition, Lewis and Clark did not need rumors drifting through the earth lodges that the Americans kept a great he-bear ready to eat Indian children.

Some of the captains' fears about Arikara reactions evaporated the next morning. Toward noon, Kakawissassa arrived at the expedition's camp. In accordance with the notion of reciprocity in gift giving, the Arikara leader brought baskets of corn, beans, and dried squash. While those provisions were surely appreciated, Kakawissassa's reply to Lewis's speech was even more welcome.

The chief's speech contained three important elements. First, there was the immediate question of Sioux influence on the Arikaras' behavior toward the expedition. The two Teton emissaries had certainly argued for some direct action against the explorers. Although the Arikaras were not known as great warriors, in the years after Lewis and Clark they would be very effective in blocking American access up the Missouri. But Kakawissassa made it plain at the beginning that the Arikaras' weapons would not be turned against the explorers. "Can you think," declared the chief, "any one dare put their hands on your rope of your boat. No! not one dare." Proclaiming the road open, Kakawissassa turned to his second point. In reply to the call for intertribal peace, the chief asked the captains to "speak good words" to the Mandans on behalf of the Arikaras. Seeing two of their diplomatic goals seemingly accepted without opposition or argument, Lewis and Clark must have been pleased when the Arikara chief expressed an interest in becoming part of the St. Louis trade system. Although Kakawissassa lamented the fact that beaver pelts were not available for Arikara women to process, he promised a good supply of buffalo robes.

More important, he promised to aid American traders in entering Cheyenne and Arapaho markets.[66]

Taken at face value, what Kakawissassa told Lewis and Clark promised a real victory for American policy and the expedition's negotiating skill. After the Teton troubles, the captains needed such a victory. But Kakawissassa's speech was actually much more and much less than it appeared to be. That the captains accepted it literally only suggests how innocent they were of Indian realities. On the issue of Sioux-inspired attempts to forcibly detain the expedition, Kakawissassa was forthright in saying that Teton advice had been rejected. Lewis and Clark took this to signal a weakening of the Arikara-Sioux alliance. But postexpedition events did not bear out the captains' optimistic evaluation. The Arikaras were not about to abandon their Sioux trade connection for an uncertain link with St. Louis. American merchants, interested in beaver, could not take the place of Sioux middlemen as both suppliers of manufactured goods and customers for Arikara corn and horses. Arikara life was based on the production of agricultural surpluses that would have little place in an American fur trade. That the Arikaras did not envision severing the Sioux alliance was to be made painfully clear in 1807, when both Manuel Lisa and Nathaniel Pryor encountered hostility from Arikara-Sioux forces.

The Mandan peace overture, an integral part of Lewis and Clark Indian diplomacy, also was not quite what the Arikara speaker made it out to be. Despite their best efforts during the talks with the Arikaras and later during the winter at Fort Mandan, the captains found the old Arikara-Mandan tensions not easily overcome. The peace policy, actually part of a larger anti-Sioux thrust, was doomed to failure by both Teton military power and persistent villager rivalries. In 1810, an Arikara-Mandan alliance would field several war parties against the Sioux, but those joint ventures would be short-lived. More important, the Teton bands engaged in massive economic retaliation against Arikara towns, ensuring the demise of any villager alliance.[67] It may be that the willingness of the Arikaras to allow Lewis and Clark to pass unimpeded was an abberation. In the years after the expedition, as Manuel Lisa brought the Sioux into the American trading orbit, the Arikaras assumed the Tetons' old hostile role. Fearing that Mandan power was increasing by the St. Louis connection while their fortunes declined, the Arikaras successfully blockaded the Missouri. Certainly American agents and merchants like the Chouteaus and William H. Ashley found the Arikaras to be implacable foes. Only gradually did American diplomats learn that flowery speeches and a few gifts could not easily transform Indian loyalties.

But the nuances of Kakawissassa's speech eluded Lewis and Clark, and early in the afternoon, believing they had achieved their goals, the captains ordered the expedition a short distance upriver to a camp closer to the twin villages of Rhtarahe and Waho-erha. With Kakawissassa and one of his nephews on board the keelboat, the explorers made their way toward the upper villages. Pocasse joined the boat party and late in the afternoon the whole group landed at a sandbar just below Rhtarahe. They were greeted by knots of curious villagers anxious to catch a glimpse of the strangers. The whole scene was made more colorful by several American flags snapping in the river breeze. The captains paused for a moment to take a sextant reading, something the Arikaras were certain was just one more piece of the explorers' spiritual magic, and then walked up to Rhtarahe with Pocasse. The chief made Lewis and Clark a gift of corn and beans while others in the party ate Arikara porridge and bread. After staying some time at Rhtarahe "talking on various subjects," the Americans paid a brief visit to Waho-erha and its chief, Piahito. There, too, the explorers enjoyed Indian food and hospitality. Promises were exchanged about talks the next day, and Clark judged the situation that evening as "all tranquillity."[68]

October 12 was the last full day the expedition spent among the Arikaras; nothing happened to shake the captains' confidence that they had convinced village chiefs to accept American policies. Yet, had the explorers listened more carefully to speeches made by Pocasse and Piahito, they might have been less certain of their victory. Lewis, Clark, and Gass, in the company of interpreters, spent the morning listening to the chiefs' speeches while Ordway's boat parties did some small-scale trading.[69]

Those final talks began with the captains reminding the Arikaras of "the magnitude and power of our country." Clark confidently recorded that those words "pleased and astonished them verry much."[70] The speech delivered by Pocasse contained much that the explorers wanted to hear. Pocasse reaffirmed the obvious: the Arikaras planned no hostile action against the expedition. He declared his interest in a Mandan peace and also expressed some desire to visit with Jefferson. At the end of the talk, almost as an afterthought, Pocasse suggested yet another doubt about severing the Sioux connection. With the exposed location of the villages and the temporary nature of American forces, what guarantees of safety did the Arikaras have against retaliation by the Tetons? Pocasse put it simply: "After you set out, many nations in the open plains may come to make war against us, we wish you to stop their guns and prevent it if possible."[71]

The doubts and fears expressed by Pocasse were amplified when Lewis and Clark met with Piahito. This Arikara chief gave the captains a quick lesson in Upper Missouri power politics. The people of Waho-erha were distinct in language and past history from the other villages. Waho-erha had not taken part in the recent and still smoldering Mandan-Hidatsa war. Piahito was very skeptical that wounds still fresh could be quickly healed by some of the expedition's diplomatic salve. Had they more fully understood what Piahito had to say, Lewis and Clark might have sensed how formidable a task it would be to rearrange traditional alliances and cure old hurts.

Piahito opened his remarks by bluntly saying he would believe a Mandan-Arikara peace only when he saw it with his own eyes. As much as he doubted Mandan intentions, he also questioned Sioux motives, declaring that the Teton "has not a good heart." If Piahito offered the captains some healthy skepticism about inter-tribal relations, he also presented an equally realistic appraisal of intra-Arikara affairs. Piahito said he always followed the lead of Kakawissassa and Pocasse and that they would watch over Waho-erha while he went up to the Mandans. Lewis and Clark wanted their message to be accepted by the Arikara leadership, and Piahito reassured the explorers that at least Kakawissassa and Pocasse "believe your words." But the Waho-erha chief also seemed to issue a veiled warning about a unity of Arikara views more apparent than real. "Maybe we will not tell the truth" was hardly the strong statement of approval the captains wanted from the chief. Piahito again stressed his concern about a trip to the Mandans. What would an alliance with the Mandans mean, how might the Sioux react, and what possible benefits would the Arikaras gain from such a move? As the formal talks ended and one of the Arikara chiefs agreed to go with the captains to the Mandans, all those doubts and questions were unresolved.[72]

If official relations with the Arikaras were troubled by some unsettling issues, unofficial and personal affairs with Arikara women went on quite satisfactorily. For the first time since leaving St. Louis, the young men of the expedition had ample time and opportunity for sexual contacts with Indian women. Those liaisons must be understood from both sides of the cultural divide. To ignore them here and later would be to deny the humanity of the expedition and to turn a blind eye on much of the historical record.

Sexual experiences, like all intimate encounters, may mean very different things to persons of dissimilar cultures. The Arikaras' perception of sexual intercourse and the role of women in the act differed markedly from that of the expedition's males. First, it must be said that the Arikaras, like their Mandan and Hidatsa neighbors, placed a very high value on women. They were the principal agriculturists, and that economic position meant ritual prominence as well. Women were neither the drudges nor the pawns of Arikara men so often portrayed in the records of white visitors.[73] Further, Arikara matrilineal society did not place as much importance on exclusive sexual relations with male spouses. As one Arikara told Truteau, "When a man dies he cannot carry women with him to the regions of the dead; and . . . they who quarrel, fight, and kill each other about the possession of a woman, are fools or mad-men."[74] That young Arikara women were anxious for sexual encounters with non-Indians was noted by virtually every visitor. As John Bradbury put it, "Travellers who have been acquainted with savages, have remarked that they are either very liberal of their women to strangers, or extremely jealous. In this species of liberality no nation can be exceeded by the Arikaras, who flocked down every evening with their wives, sisters, and daughters, each anxious to meet with a market for them."[75]

Interest in sex with strangers was based on three distinct cultural sanctions. The Arikara villagers were eager to obtain European goods, and having sexual relations with traders meant receiving those objects in payment for favors. Ironware, paint, blue beads, and cloth were all part of the exchange. Arikara women demanded and got high prices for their services. As Bradbury testified, "I observed several instances wherein the squaw was consulted by her husband as to the *quantum sufficit* of price, a mark of consideration which, from some knowledge of Indians, and the estimation in which their women are held, I had not expected."[76] But having sexual relations with a trader provided more than a supply of scarce luxury goods. Because they were central figures in the staple food trade with other tribes, Arikara women hoped to forge commercial links with white merchants. Sex, as Lewis and Clark were to discover at Fort Clatsop, was an important way to seal a business arrangement.

Sex with visitors was also an integral part of northern plains hospitality. When Bradbury visited an Arikara lodge, he found that the welcome included not only a bed but a "bedfellow."[77] As the captains learned during the Teton confrontation, to reject such offers was to court misunderstanding and suspicion. If intercourse with non-Indian males strengthened trade ties and expressed traditional hospitality, it also signified something far more complex in northern plains life. The Arikaras and their neighbors, both villagers and nomads alike, perceived sexual contact as a means of transferring spiritual power from one person to another. The Mandan buffalo-calling ceremony was only the most spectacular example of this belief. In that ritual, women had intercourse with elderly men, taking the seminal skill of old hunters and passing it on to their husbands. Sex became a kind of conduit for power. In the same way, Arikara women sought sex with Europeans as a way to pass the strength and skill of the outsiders on to their mates. As John Ewers has written, the "concept of the transmission of power through sexual intercourse seemed to have played a part in the eagerness of Mandan women to cohabit with white men in the early days of the fur trade."[78] Lewis understood the sense of awe when he wrote, "The Indians believed that these traders were the most powerful persons in the nation."[79] Sex was a means to appropriate that power and place it at their disposal.

There is little doubt that the men of the expedition found Arikara women attractive. They surely did not agree with Tabeau's charge that Arikara females were "the most ugly and have the advantages of surpassing all the others in slovenliness." One who disagreed was Gass. Writing that the Arikaras were "the most cleanly Indians I have ever seen on this voyage," the sergeant added that village women were "handsome" and "the best looking Indians I have ever seen." Ordway agreed, noting that "some of their women are very handsome and clean." Even Clark, who characterized the Arikaras as "pore and Durtey," recalled to Nicholas Biddle that the "Ricara women [were] better looking than the Scioux."[80]

In the notebook journals of the expedition, there are only the most oblique references to sexual contact with Arikara women. Clark claimed that Arikara overtures were rejected while the expedition was at the villages but implied that once the party departed on October 12 it was quite a different story. Clark recorded that on the evening of the 12th two young women were sent by an Arikara man "and persisted in their civilities." In his plainest statement about intimate relations with the Arikaras written while the expedition was in progress, Clark noted that the women were "very fond of carressing our men." Clark was less reticent when he answered questions for Nicholas Biddle in 1810. He frankly admitted that the men "by means of interpreters found no difficulty in getting women." He believed that Arikara women were "lecherous" and engaged in sexual adventures "without the husband's knowledge." However, in the same note to Biddle, Clark reported that "the husbands etc. [gave] wives and sisters to strangers."[81] Other travelers observed that Arikara women usually initiated sexual encounters, and there seems to be little doubt that the men in the expedition accepted the offers.

The only fully documented case of this involved York. In the Arikaras' eyes, York was the central attraction of the Lewis and Clark expedition. Airguns, gifts, and strange doings with a sextant all paled in significance before York. The black man fascinated Indian adults and terrified their children. York's blackness was viewed by the Arikaras as a sign of special spiritual power, and they appropriately named him "the big Medison." To have sexual contact with York was to get in touch with what seemed awesome spirit forces. On one occasion an Arikara man invited York to his lodge, offered him his wife, and guarded the entrance during the act. When a member of the expedition came looking for York, "the master of the house would not let him in before the affair was finished."[82]

Perhaps the most telling comment on the sexual desires of visitors among the Arikaras came in a conversation that Henry M. Brackenridge reported having with a village chief: " 'I was wondering,' said he, 'whether you white people have any women amongst you.' I assured him in the affirmative. 'Then,' said he, 'why is it that your people are so fond of our women, one might suppose they had never seen any before?' "[83]

Early in the afternoon of October 12, with the talks completed and one of the village chiefs on board, Lewis and Clark left the Grand River settlements. It was a festive departure, with "the fiddle playing and the horns sounding." The days that followed were filled with small incidents that added to the sum of Indian-expedition relations. One of those revealing events took place on October 14 when Private John Newman was sentenced to corporal punishment for "mutinous expression." Newman's whipping "allarmed the Indian chief very much." Virtually all native

American cultures rejected public physical punishment of either children or adults, believing that conformity to social norms might be better achieved by more subtle group pressure. As the expedition moved toward its Mandan wintering quarters, there was time to record additional bits of ethnographic data. Clark noted an Arikara stone monument surrounded by votive offerings. At another time Clark and the Arikara chief walked along the shore as the Indian recounted "a number of their traditions about turtles, snakes, etc. and the power of a particular rock or cove on the next river which informs of every thing." Sadly for the ethnographic record, Clark believed that "none of those I think worth mentioning."[84]

As Lewis and Clark headed toward the Mandan villages, they left behind with the Arikaras a strange set of impressions. Although the villagers had been acquainted with whites for some time, they had never seen such a large group of visitors. The intentions and behavior of the captains, their technology, and the presence of York all produced a vivid folklore. Tabeau, who dutifully recorded some of the tales, found himself in "a bad scrape by treating them as ridiculous." Kakawita, Tabeau's leading Arikara informant, reported what was widely believed among the Arikaras about the Lewis and Clark expedition. In their opinion, the explorers were on a special vision quest and had met "obstacles perhaps invincible" on their journey. One of those obstacles was reputed to be an awesome beast without a mouth who ate by "breathing the smoke of the meat through the nose." Even more terrible, related the Arikara storytellers, was "a troop of Amazons who kill all their male children, pulverize their genitals and conceive again by the injection of the powder obtained." Just how the expedition overcame those monsters is not part of the surviving record. What finally impressed the Arikaras were the objects carried by the expedition. The sextant, the magnet, and phosphorous were talked about as evidence of the captains' spirit powers. And, of course, there was York. As Tabeau wrote, "The most marvelous was, though, a large fine man, black as a bear who spoke and acted as one."[85]

Lewis and Clark's party carried away from their time with the Arikaras many personal memories of the sort not readily committed to the pages of diaries or official reports. There can be no doubt that after the tense days with the Tetons, the relaxed hospitality of the Arikaras was a welcome change. It remained for Clark to record his impressions of the Grand River villagers. Of the people, he wrote, "They appear to be peaceful, their men tall and perpotiend, women Small and industerous." Recalling their hospitality, he described the Arikaras as "Durtey, Kind, pore and extravigent." Clark's expressive word *extravigent* was his way of drawing attention to the Arikaras' generosity with food and favors. Pleased to give gifts, the Arikaras took "what was offered with great pleasure."[86]

There was much about Arikara culture that the captains either did not understand or did not see. Politics, sacred bundles, band organization, and the yearly round of ritual and ceremony all eluded the explorers. What the expedition's journalists did record was the exterior of Arikara life—an exterior of substantial earth lodges, well-tended fields, and friendly people. American frontiersmen, who valued a secure house and good crops, found much to admire during their time with the Star-rah-he.

4

The Mandan Winter

"During the time I was there a very grand plan was schemed, but its being realized
is more than I can tell, although the Captains say they are well assured it will."
—FRANÇOIS ANTOINE LAROCQUE, 1804

As the fall days of 1804 grew colder and shorter, the Lewis and Clark expedition
struggled toward what has been called "the keystone of the Upper Missouri region"—the Mandan and Hidatsa villages.[1] The American explorers were only the
latest in a long series of traders and travelers making the journey to the earth lodge
villages along the Missouri. The Mandan and Hidatsa towns were the center of
northern plains trade, attracting Indian and white merchants over vast distances. At
trading times, especially during the late summer and early fall, the villages were
crowded with the Crows, Assiniboins, Cheyennes, Kiowas, Arapahoes, and, after
midcentury, with whites representing the North West Company, the Hudson's Bay
Company, and St. Louis interests. In the arena of frontier culture, few places gave
more evidence of the varied objects and diverse peoples making up North America
than the Mandan and Hidatsa towns. The winter at Fort Mandan would expose
Lewis and Clark to much of that variety and diversity. The winter would try the
expedition's diplomatic skill and expand its ethnographic horizons. At the same
time, the Mandan and Hidatsa people would get their first long look at the coming
wave of American traders and bureaucrats. Those long Dakota months were an
apprenticeship during which each group probed the other and formed lasting
impressions.

A traveler coming up the Missouri from St. Louis in 1804 would have found five
Indian settlements—two Mandan and three Hidatsa—strung out along the river in
what is now central North Dakota. Past the Heart River, the first town was the
Mandan village known to Lewis and Clark as Matootonha. More correctly named
Mitutanka, this village was located on the west bank of the Missouri. Clark described
Mitutanka as "situated on an eminence of about 50 feet above the water in a hand-
some plain."[2] Like its sister village across the river, Mitutanka was built by the
Mandans sometime around 1787. In most of their notes, the explorers referred to
Mitutanka as the "lower" or "first" Mandan village. Ordway reported that the
village had about forty earth lodges. Because Mitutanka was the closest Mandan
village to the expedition's winter quarters, the explorers became very familiar with

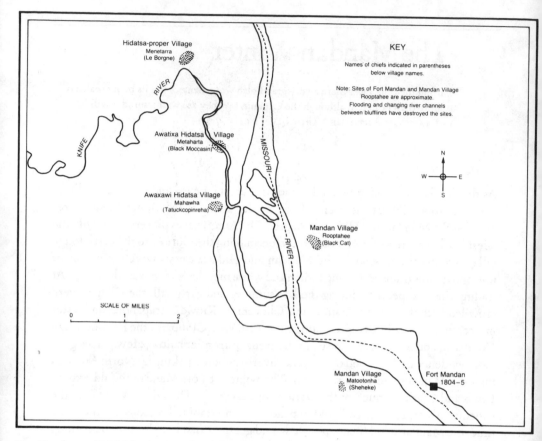

KEY

Names of chiefs indicated in parentheses
below village names.

Note: Sites of Fort Mandan and Mandan Village
Rooptahee are approximate.
Flooding and changing river channels
between blufflines have destroyed the sites.

Hidatsa-proper Village
Menetarra
(Le Borgne)

Awatixa Hidatsa Village
Metaharta
(Black Moccasin)

Awaxawi Hidatsa Village
Mahawha
(Tatuckcopinreha)

Mandan Village
Rooptahee
(Black Cat)

Mandan Village
Matootonha
(Sheheke)

Fort Mandan
1804–5

KNIFE RIVER

MISSOURI RIVER

SCALE OF MILES
0   1   2

Fort Mandan and Neighboring Mandan and Hidatsa Villages

Sheheke, by C. B. J. Fevret de Saint Mémin. Courtesy of American Philosophical Society.

both the town and its leading chiefs. Sheheke, known to Lewis and Clark as Big White, was the most prominent civil chief in Mitutanka. The captains named Kagohhami, or Little Raven, also a civil chief, as Second Chief.

Farther up the Missouri, directly north of Mitutanka and on the east bank of the river, was the second Mandan settlement. Throughout the expedition's records this town of about forty or fifty earth lodges was called Rooptahee. Rooptahee was a mispronunciation of Nuptadi, one of the four Mandan subtribes existing before the 1781 smallpox epidemic. Lewis and Clark often called Rooptahee the "upper" or "second" Mandan village. Because it was the home of Posecopsahe, or Black Cat, the civil chief designated Grand Mandan Chief by the explorers, Rooptahee took on special significance for the expedition's diplomacy. Cargarnomakshe, or Raven Man Chief, was made Second Chief of Rooptahee by the captains.

Directly across the Missouri from Rooptahee was a Hidatsa village so distinct from the two other Hidatsa towns that virtually every European visitor noted the differences. Known as Mahawha, the village was established about 1787 by the Awaxawi Hidatsas. Built on a terrace overlooking the confluence of the Knife and the Missouri rivers, Mahawha had about fifty warriors in 1804. The captains knew these people as the Amahami, Ahaharway, or Wattasoon Indians and always distinguished them in their records from the two other Hidatsa groups. Although the Awaxawis were linguistically distinct from their Hidatsa neighbors on the Knife River, they were not a separate tribe as Lewis and Clark believed. The Awaxawis called themselves Ahaharways or Ahnahaways; Wattasoon was their Mandan name. French traders nicknamed them the "soulier" Indians and Lewis and Clark occasionally termed the Awaxawis as the Shoe or Moccasin people. The captains had some contact with the Awaxawi Hidatsas of Mahawha through Tatuckcopinreha, or White Buffalo Robe Unfolded, the most prominent village chief.

Along the Knife River, Lewis and Clark found the two major Hidatsa settlements. On the right bank of the Knife, about a mile from the confluence of the Missouri, was the town Lewis and Clark called the "First Minnetaree Village," or "the little village of the Menitarras." Built about 1787 by Awatixa Hidatsas and home to a substantial number of Mandan families as well, the village was properly known as Metaharta. Village residents were sometimes named in expedition journals as Minnetarees Metaharta or the Minnetarees of the Willows. Metaharta has special significance for the history of the expedition since it was there that the Shoshoni woman Sacagawea and the North West Company trader Toussaint Charbonneau lived before joining the Corps of Discovery. Leadership in the village, as recognized by Lewis and Clark, came from First Chief Ompsehara, or Black Moccasin, and Second Chief Ohharh, or Little Fox. Metaharta would continue to be an important Hidatsa village of some forty lodges until its destruction, along with Mahawha's, by a Sioux raid in the spring of 1834.

The most remote of the Knife River Hidatsa villages, both in terms of distance and expeditionary diplomacy, was Menetarra, generally known in the journals as the "second Minnetaree Village." Established sometime before 1780 by the Hidatsas-proper, Menetarra was the largest of the Hidatsa towns, boasting some 450 warriors and 130 earth lodges during the Lewis and Clark era. Menetarra's assets were not only substantial population and considerable military force but exceptional leadership in the person of Le Borgne, or One Eye.[3]

Observing Mandan and Hidatsa villages during the summer of 1806, Alexander Henry the Younger described them as "a cluster of molehills or muskrat cabins." The trader explained that on closer examination "the nearly circular huts are placed very irregularly; some so close to each other as scarcely to leave a foot-passage, others again at a distance of 20 to 30 feet apart. But about the center of each village is an open space of about four acres, around which the huts are regularly built at equal

Black Moccasin, by George Catlin. Courtesy of National Museum of American
Art (formerly National Collection of Fine Arts), Smithsonian Institution; Gift of
Mrs. Joseph Harrison, Jr.

distances, fronting the open space."[4] For both Mandan and Hidatsa households
the village was the focus of important political, economic, and ceremonial
activities. In many ways the villages can be best understood as a collection of households all acting together to advance the welfare of the family, the clan, and the
village.

Just as the medicine lodge was the focal point for Arikara villages, the center of a
Mandan village was the sacred cedar post and the open plaza around it. The cedar
post represented Lone Man, the primary Mandan culture hero. On the north edge
of the plaza was the large medicine or Okipa lodge. Hanging on poles outside the
Okipa lodge were effigies representing various spirits. The Mandan villages seen
by Lewis and Clark consisted of about forty to fifty domestic lodges arranged
around the plaza. The social position of each household determined the location of

Back View of Mandan Village, Showing the Cemetery, by George Catlin.
Courtesy of National Museum of American Art (formerly National Collection of
Fine Arts), Smithsonian Institution; Gift of Mrs. Joseph Harrison, Jr.

lodges. Those families with important ceremonial responsibilities and those who owned powerful bundles lived near the plaza while less prominent households occupied lodges farther away. Mandan and Hidatsa earth lodges were usually occupied for anywhere between seven to twelve years. Each lodge housed from five to sixteen persons with the average number in a Mandan lodge being ten persons.[5] At the time of Lewis and Clark, Mandan and Hidatsa villages were defended by log palisades.

These villages, so familiar from the descriptions of explorers and traders like Lewis and Clark and Alexander Henry the Younger and nineteenth-century artists like George Catlin and Karl Bodmer, were in fact only part of the settled experience of the Upper Missouri villagers. They divided their time between large, permanent summer lodge towns and smaller winter camps. The winter lodges, built in wooded bottoms to escape the harsh winter storms, were neither large nor especially well constructed. Lewis and Clark did not comment on these winter camps, and it is possible that fear of Sioux attack kept many Mandans and Hidatsas within

Interior of a Hidatsa Lodge, by Karl Bodmer. Courtesy of The InterNorth Art
Foundation, Joslyn Art Museum, Omaha, Nebraska.

the protection of the more substantial summer villages. Looking down on the towns
from a high riverbank, David Thompson was reminded of "so many large hives
clustered together."[6] And so must they have seemed to Lewis and Clark seven years
later.

Lewis and Clark were not the first white men to see the Mandan and Hidatsa
villages and their surrounding fields of corn, beans, squash, and sunflowers. The
first recorded European visit to the villages had occurred on the afternoon of December 3, 1738, when Pierre Gaultier de Varennes de La Vérendrye, accompanied by
French traders and Assiniboin guides, entered a Mandan "fort" near the Heart
River. Attracted by tales of fair-skinned, red-haired natives who lived in large
towns and possessed precious metals, La Vérendrye had made the long journey
from Fort La Reine on the Assiniboine River to see those mysterious people. Although La Vérendrye did not find the fabled white Indians, he did record the first
European impressions of the Mandan lifeway. That record, taken along with evidence preserved from the 1742– 43 visit of La Vérendrye's sons to the region, offers
the picture of prosperous earth lodge people living along the Missouri River near
the Heart and already enjoying French and Spanish goods.[7]

With the disruptions caused by French and English conflicts that finally cost

Hidatsa Village at Knife River, by George Catlin. Courtesy of National Museum of American Art (formerly National Collection of Fine Arts), Smithsonian Institution; Gift of Mrs. Joseph Harrison, Jr.

France its Canadian empire, the tenuous foreign contacts with the Mandan villages were lost, at least to the written record. There is no doubt that European goods continued to enter the Upper Missouri carried by native middlemen. In the second half of the eighteenth century, some Canadians were beginning to reside in the villages as "tenant traders." These were men like the little-known Montreal trader Mackintosh, who visited the Mandans in late 1773, and the long-term resident Pierre Menard, who came in 1778. Mackintosh and Menard were among the last to see the Upper Missouri village Indians in the days of high prosperity before the devastating epidemic of 1781. In the years after 1781, weakened by disease and threatened by Sioux bands, the Mandans abandoned the Heart River villages. Their move north was toward the Knife River and an uneasy alliance with the Hidatsas. It was there that James Mackay found them when he came from the Qu'Appelle River to trade in 1787. Throughout the 1790s, contacts with both Canadian and St. Louis traders increased as men like Jacques D'Eglise, René Jusseaume, and John Evans waged economic war to gain control of the Mandan-Hidatsa trade. The presence of these men and their goods did not immediately threaten the well-being of the villagers. Quite the contrary, the trade items (especially guns and ammunition) strengthened the villagers against their Sioux and Arikara enemies. The traders were simply adopted as fictional relatives, a practice first noted by La Vérendrye and surely employed long before 1738 with Indian middlemen.[8]

The Mandan and Hidatsa villages have been aptly described as "the central market place of the Northern Plains."[9] It was this great Missouri River country store that attracted so many Europeans, as well as Indians. The transactions at this crossroads of cultures and goods touched the lives of people far from central North Dakota and in turn conditioned the Mandans' and the Hidatsas' relations with all outsiders. At that market one could find Spanish horses and mules brought by the Cheyennes, destined for Assiniboin herds; fancy Cheyenne leather clothing for Mandan dandies; English trade guns and ammunition eagerly sought by villagers and nomads alike; and the ever present baskets of corn, beans, squash, and tobacco upon which Mandan and Hidatsa economic strength was built. Forming the upper exchange center in the Missouri Trade System, the Mandan and Hidatsa villagers served as brokers in an international economic and cultural trade network that faced in three directions and stretched over thousands of miles.

Like their Arikara neighbors, the Mandan and Hidatsa villages shared an important western connection with the Cheyennes, Crows, and Arapahoes. These nomadic plains people brought a wide variety of meat products as well as luxury leather goods to the Mandan-Hidatsa market. But in the eyes of all villagers, the most valuable commodity brought from the West and Southwest were horses and mules. Just as the Arikaras sought those animals to supply the needs of the Sioux, so did Mandan and Hidatsa traders bargain for them to satisfy the requirements of their Assiniboin and Cree customers. Reaching east, the Knife River brokers also did some trading with Sioux bands who brought buffalo meat and some manufactured goods from the Dakota Rendezvous. However, the close trade ties between the Teton Sioux and the Arikaras and the frequent raids that alliance visited on the Mandan and Hidatsa towns made the Sioux connection somewhat risky.

If the Sioux could not be relied upon to bring European goods to the Knife River villages as they did to the Grand River towns, the Mandan and Hidatsa people had to find another and more reliable source of supply. So the third face of the Mandan-Hidatsa system looked north to the many bands of Crees and Assiniboins. Long before Lewis and Clark, the Crees and Assiniboins had been carrying English and French goods to the Mandan and Hidatsa towns to exchange for agricultural produce, tobacco, and horses. When La Vérendrye visited the Mandans in 1738, he saw the Mandan–Assiniboin trade in full swing. The French explorer, impressed with the Mandans' business skill, wrote that the villagers "knew well how to profit by it

Aerial View of the Big Hidatsa (Menetarra) Village. Courtesy of North Dakota
Highway Department and the National Park Service.

in selling their grains, tobacco, skins and colored plumes which they knew the
Assiniboin prize highly." As testimony to the penetration of European goods into
the northern plains well before the middle of the eighteenth century, La Vérendrye
observed that the most sought-after merchandise brought by the Assiniboins were
"guns, axes, kettles, powder, bullets, knives, [and] awls."[10]

Whenever Lewis and Clark analyzed an Indian trade system, they always thought in
terms of the distribution of political power in that network and possible future
competition with American merchants. Regarding the Missouri Trade System, they
believed that the Teton Sioux needed to be weaned away from North West Company traders and brought into the sphere of the St. Louis interests. Beyond that,
Lewis and Clark were always eager to cast the Sioux as colonial masters exercising
political and economic dominance over the innocent and vulnerable Arikaras. The
message was simple. The political and economic power of the Sioux needed to be
broken and the honest villagers freed so that they could participate in the new
American trade system.

Lewis and Clark's diplomacy attempted to impose the same simplistic model on the Mandan and Hidatsa trade with Assiniboins and Crees. Those tribes provided manufactured goods from English and Canadian sources that might be supplied by American merchants. Knowing there was often tension between the villagers and their northern trading partners, Lewis and Clark used such strife as a pretext to lecture Mandan chiefs on the reasons for abandoning the Assiniboins and Crees in favor of St. Louis traders. What the captains did not grasp was that the merchandise exchanged between the villagers and the northern peoples—food products and horses—did not in the least interest Americans increasingly obsessed with beaver pelts. Despite this, Clark still told Mandan chiefs, "You know yourselves that you are compelled to put up with little insults from the Christinoes [Cree] and Ossinaboins because if you go to war with those people, they will prevent the traders in the North from bringing you guns, powder, and ball and by that means distress you very much." Clark was determined to cast the Mandans and the Hidatsas in the same role as the Arikaras with the new oppressors as Assiniboins and Crees. If the Sioux were the masters lower down the river, Lewis and Clark seemed prepared to brand the Assiniboins as "great rogues" from the north.[11] Just as the captains had misunderstood Arikara-Sioux relations much to the detriment of the expedition's Indian diplomacy, so they failed to appreciate both the ability of the villagers to cope with the northern nomads and the essential equality of the trade arrangement. Because he saw actual trade bargains made between the two parties, La Vérendrye better understood the operation of the system. "The Mandan," he wrote, "are much more crafty than the Assiniboin in their commerce and in everything, and always dupe them." He called the Mandans "sharp traders, [who] clean the Assiniboin out of everything they have in the way of guns, powder, ball, kettles, axes, knives, and awls."[12] If the captains seriously entertained the notion that the villager-Assiniboin link could be broken, they did not account for the trading abilities and needs of either party.

Toward the end of October 1804, as the expedition passed the Cannonball River, the explorers began to notice abandoned Mandan villages. On October 19, the captains saw the ruins of a sturdy Mandan settlement on a hill some ninety feet above the river. In the days that followed, as the American party passed through the old Mandan homeland around the Heart River, there were even more signs of village life before the epidemic scourges of the 1780s and Sioux-Arikara attacks forced a northward flight toward the Knife. A Mandan sun dance post standing alone on the prairie was a silent witness to the past. Among the mounds and empty lodges of abandoned villages, the Americans found the scattered bones of both men and animals—grim reminders of the devastation of earlier days.[13]

Faced with these unsettling artifacts of a troubled past, there must have been a

certain measure of relief among the explorers when, on October 24, they encountered the first live Mandan Indians seen by the expedition. As the captains passed an
island in the Missouri, they came upon a Mandan chief on a fall hunt. Because one of
their central diplomatic objectives was to promote an alliance of all Missouri River
villagers against the Sioux, Lewis and Clark were anxious to foster peace between
the Mandans, Hidatsas, and the Arikaras. The captains were sure they had moved
one step closer to that goal when the Mandan chief and the Arikara chief traveling
with them met "with great Cordiallity and serimony." After smoking a pipe together, Lewis and Gravelines went with the Mandan chief to his lodge. When Lewis
and the group returned, "We admitted the Grand Chief and his brother for a few
minits on our boat." Ordway added his unofficial seal of approval to the day by
observing that the Mandans "had Some handsome women with them." As the
expedition camped that night below an old Mandan-Arikara town, all signs pointed
toward friendly relations on several levels.[14]

Expeditionary diplomacy, as well as personal expectations about those "handsome women," was slowed the next day as progress upriver became more difficult.
As the Missouri twisted its way north beyond present-day Bismarck, North Dakota,
its channel became choked with sandbars and hard to find. While the men struggled
throughout the day with the heavy keelboat, more and more Mandans came to the
riverbank to watch what must have seemed an outlandish spectacle. Clark described
the Mandans as sightseers intent on "satisfying their Curiossities as to our apper-
ance, etc." As the day wore on, knots of Indians called the Americans to come
ashore and talk. The demands of the river gave little time for such rest stops, but
Clark did take note of more vacant Mandan villages and "a large and extensive
bottom for several miles in which the squars raised their corn." Sometime during
the day the captains also heard a bit of news that further verified their bad opinion of
the Sioux and the Assiniboins. Sioux warriors had recently stolen some Hidatsa
horses and on the way home from the raid had fallen in with an Assiniboin band. The
Sioux had been killed by the Assiniboins, an incident reenforcing the image of
plains nomads as hostile and unpredictable. When several Mandans came to camp,
Clark had his first opportunity to study the villagers. His first impressions were
favorable and he wrote, "Those Indians appear to have similar customs with the
Ricaras, they dress the same, [and are] more mild in their language and justurs."[15]

As the Lewis and Clark flotilla neared the Mandan and Hidatsa villages, the pace
of the expedition's activity increased. There were all sorts of problems that called
for the captains' attention and most of those questions involved relations with the
Indians. The Americans needed to prepare for full-scale talks with Mandan and
Hidatsa chiefs, a prospect that required careful thought, reliable interpreters, and
plenty of gifts. The delicate truce proposed between the Arikaras, Mandans, and
Hidatsas had to be accepted by the Knife River chiefs and perhaps solidified with

some cooperative show of force against the Sioux. And there was the presence of Canadian and English traders on the Upper Missouri. These men, none of whom were American citizens, posed a unique challenge to Lewis and Clark's Indian diplomacy. Were they to be allowed to continue trading with the Indians, thereby undercutting St. Louis ventures, or were they to be expelled, perhaps with a show of force? In the confused days immediately after the Louisiana Purchase, the status of those foreign traders was unclear. Lewis and Clark would have to tread carefully, watching the words and actions of both Indians and traders, gathering valuable information but alienating no one. American sovereignty had to be proclaimed but not so stridently as to frighten Indian trading partners. Finally, and of no little concern, a suitable location for winter quarters had to be found.

Plans to resolve those questions began to take shape on the evening of October 26, when the Americans camped in a fallow cornfield just below Mitutanka. Earlier in the day, the captains had accepted two Mandan chiefs and their household goods as temporary keelboat passengers. Now as the whole party made camp, they were joined by scores of Mandan men, women and children who clustered around the expedition's gear. Poking and probing all the strange objects, the Indians seemed especially attracted to the corn mill. Because Clark was still suffering from a persistent rheumatic complaint and both men were unsure of their reception by the Mandans, Lewis alone joined the chiefs in making the short walk to Mitutanka. Fears of an unfriendly reception were quickly allayed when Lewis was given a warm welcome. Ordway's cryptic "found the nation very friendly" masks the real concern the expedition had about relations with the villagers. At this early stage perhaps neither the chiefs nor the captains were quite ready to pass final judgment on each other. But it was an encouraging sign of Mandan friendship when the chiefs came back to the expedition's camp later in the evening and smoked with Clark.[16]

That first evening of talking and smoking was important preparation for the days to come but it was, after all, only the beginning. Contact had been made with only one Mandan village. With much left to do, the expedition continued to make measured progress upriver on the following day. Saturday proved to be a day filled with informal visits to both Mandan villages, considerable socializing, and an important meeting with the trader René Jusseaume.

Leaving camp early on Saturday morning, the expedition made its first stop at Mitutanka. Clark hiked up the fifty-foot terrace to the stockaded town, noting as he went the earth lodges with many horses tethered outside. Once in the village, the explorer was greeted by several chiefs. Although Clark did not record which chiefs were present, it is most likely that he met Sheheke and perhaps Little Raven, the Second Chief. After smoking, Clark was invited to remain at the village for some food. Anxious to impress their powerful visitor and perhaps make a valuable trade connection, the Mitutanka chiefs were very displeased when Clark rejected their offer of corn and beans. That displeasure was eventually dispelled when the captain explained that he felt "indisposed" and was not prepared to take on the Mandan menu.

Perhaps the most important event during the two-hour visit at Mitutanka was the meeting with René Jusseaume. A free trader with ties to the North West Company, Jusseaume had been living among the Mandans for some fifteen years and spoke their language fluently. Few whites could match Jusseaume's knowledge and experience on the Upper Missouri. Many fellow traders did not like the Frenchman, including Alexander Henry the Younger, who described him as a man whose ways were "much worse than those of a Mandane." The dour Henry asserted that Jusseaume was "possessed of every superstition natural to those people, nor is he different in every mean, dirty trick they have acquired from intercourse with the set of scoundrels who visit these parts." Although Lewis and Clark were eager to hire Jusseaume as an interpreter and informant on Upper Missouri life, they had an equally low opinion of him. Later that evening, after Jusseaume told Clark that he had once served the elder Clark as a scout in the Illinois country during the Revolution, the explorer described him as "a cunin artful an insonce [insolent] ar—— [?]."17

His visit at Mitutanka over, Clark returned to the river. As the expedition passed the Nuptadi village called Rooptahee, the banks were lined with Mandan children intent on not missing a single move made by the white strangers. Opposite the Hidatsa village of Mahawha, the keelboat and pirogues were anchored and camp was established. Lewis then took an interpreter, perhaps Jusseaume, and paid a courtesy call at Rooptahee. Most of the men who were out hunting had now returned, and Lewis spent an hour talking with the village leaders Black Cat and Raven Man Chief.

With the Mandan villages all properly visited, Lewis and Clark now turned their attention to preparing for the important council planned for October 28. The three Hidatsa villages had not yet been invited, and it was imperative that they be part of any negotiations. The captains selected three runners, perhaps young Mandan warriors, to carry carrots of tobacco to the Hidatsa towns to symbolize the Americans' cordial wish to talk. Erecting a flag pole, checking the supply of gifts, and sending invitations were only part of the preparations made that night. There was the pressing matter of political intelligence. Lewis and Clark needed to know the names of the Mandan and Hidatsa chiefs and prominent men, as well as something of the way they might respond to the proposals offered by the captains. For all their dislike of Jusseaume, it was to him that Lewis and Clark turned for "some information of the chiefs of the different nations." Jusseaume's thorough knowledge of village politics is reflected in the complete list of Indian notables Clark composed on October 29. With all these matters in hand, the expedition welcomed overnight Mandan visitors and bedded down for another night along the Missouri.18

The grand council bringing together Mandan, Hidatsa, Arikara, and United States representatives was to take place on Sunday, October 28, 1804. Ordway described the level flood plain across the river from Mahawha as "the most convenient place to hold a council with the whole nation." By midmorning Hidatsas representing all three villages began to gather at the conference ground. Everything seemed in order before noon except the weather. Just as high winds had delayed talks with the Arikaras, so now a strong gale from the Southwest turned the captains' plans upside down. Blowing sand picked up by the fierce wind stung everyone's face, and the Missouri became so rough that Sheheke and the other Mitutanka chiefs could not cross to the meeting site.

Their plans gone awry, the captains spent the day entertaining the chiefs who were already there. Tours of the keelboat were conducted for the visiting dignitaries, who promptly pronounced it and York to be "great medicine." Lewis, Clark, the Mandan chief Black Cat, and an interpreter then walked about a mile and a half up the Missouri looking for a good location for the future Fort Mandan. Although many places seemed promising, all lacked sufficient supplies of timber. The captains also used their time with the Mandan chief to ask him about leadership in the five villages. Black Cat, whom Lewis and Clark came to rely on more and more during the winter, provided the names of twelve prominent chiefs to flesh out the information obtained from Jusseaume. There was also time for some friendly gift giving. Several women brought corn and boiled hominy; Clark responded by offering a large glazed earthenware jar to Black Cat's wife, "who receved it with much pleasure." Other members of the expedition indulged in some sightseeing. Ordway poked around Rooptahee, noting the design of the village and marveling at the way Mandan corpses were arranged on scaffolds outside the town. George Drouillard, who had caught two beavers the night before, probably did some more pelt hunting.[19] Hoping that the weather on Monday would be more favorable, the explorers again made their diplomatic arrangements. The Hidatsa chiefs were asked to smoke with Black Cat and remain in his village until the next day. Despite these delays, Lewis and Clark were confident that they could persuade the Indian delegates to accept what might be called "the American Plan."

As Lewis and Clark entered the crucial talks, they had several objectives in mind. Some were the same as those pursued in meetings with Indians lower down the river while others were unique to the Mandan-Hidatsa situation on the Upper Missouri. Of the goals that represented a continuity with earlier Indian conferences, two must have seemed especially important to the explorer-diplomats that Sunday evening. First, there was the vital matter of announcing American sovereignty over lands of the Louisiana Purchase. As they had done before, Lewis and Clark were anxious to impress on the minds of "dutiful Indian children" that they had a new and powerful father in a distant place. But sovereignty meant more than simply proclaiming

Thomas Jefferson as the new Indian father. If American influence was to be substance and not shadow, men like Black Cat and Sheheke had to be made willing
agents of United States policy. The second goal was closely tied to the first. American policy toward the Indians linked trade with sovereignty. Proclaiming ownership of new territories meant little unless some economic good would come from
them. Everything that Lewis and Clark had seen so far indicated the rich possibilities for St. Louis–based traders. That trade could serve many purposes. Strengthen-
ing American influence while reducing the power of British agents was not the least
of the captains' concerns. Lewis and Clark never thought that trade followed the
flag. They assumed that sovereignty and business enterprise marched as one.

Commerce and nationalism were certainly important objectives to be pursued in
the Mandan-Hidatsa talks. But what now captured most of the captains' attention
was a plan whose outlines had been forming from the earliest days of the expedition.
As Lewis and Clark saw it, the various Sioux bands, but especially the Teton, were
the most dangerous and disruptive force on the Missouri. After spending some time
on the Upper Missouri, the explorers were ready to add the Assiniboins to the list of
hostile tribes. For Lewis and Clark, the response to the Sioux and Assiniboin challenge was the creation of a villager alliance against the plains nomads. Such an
alliance would strengthen, so thought the captains, the power of the earth lodge
people so that they could more fully participate in the American trade system. At the
same time, such an alliance might force the Sioux and Assiniboins to abandon their
British suppliers and join the American traders. The vital first step in forging such a
villager alliance had been taken when Lewis and Clark convinced some Arikara
chiefs to make peace with the Mandan and Hidatsa towns. As the captains entered
the Mandan-Hidatsa conference, they still believed that a few words, a bit of military pomp, and some gifts could rearrange tribal politics to suit American interests.

The weather on the morning of October 29 did not bode well for the sort of
meeting the explorers had in mind. Lewis wrote, "The winds was so hard that it was
extreemely disagreeable, the Sands was blown on us in clouds."[20] Fearing that
further delays might permanently damage their prospects for success, Lewis and
Clark decided to proceed with the gathering. To shield the participants from the
nasty weather, the captains ordered an awning put up and pieces of sail cloth stretched
between stakes to block the wind and flying sand.

By midmorning all seemed in order, and at eleven o'clock the bow swivel gun on
the keelboat was fired to signal the start of the meeting. Expeditionary records do
not make it clear how many Mandan and Hidatsa chiefs were present. It is certain
that Le Borgne, the powerful Hidatsa-proper chief, was not present, nor was
Sheheke. Those who did attend included Black Cat and the important Hidatsa-
proper chief Caltarcota. Lewis began the session by giving a long speech interpreted through Jusseaume, "the Substance of which [was] Similer to what we had

Delivered to the nations below." That stock speech stressed the themes of United States sovereignty, American trade, and intertribal peace. Such proposals did not seem novel to the captains, but they did amount to substantial changes in the ways the five Mandan and Hidatsa villages did business with both native and white outsiders. Even before Lewis introduced the touchy matter of peace with the Arikaras and a villager alliance against the Sioux, there were signs of displeasure. The most visible one came from Caltarcota. Although he had given up much formal power to Le Borgne, Caltarcota retained considerable influence among the Hidatsas-proper. As Lewis spoke, the chief became increasingly restless and finally seemed ready to leave the council. When questioned, Caltarcota excused his unhappy reaction to the American proposals by claiming that his village stood in imminent danger of attack from unnamed but hostile Indians. One of the chiefs quickly saw through this deception and "rebuked [Caltarcota] for his uneasiness at Such a time as the present." Caltarcota's "uneasiness" was probably a reflection of the close ties Menetarra and the other Hidatsa villages had to English traders, as well as a dislike for outsiders who dared dictate policy to the Hidatsas. But at this point in the proceedings Caltarcota's actions did not seem worrisome and the captains had no reason to think that there would be serious Hidatsa opposition to any part of the American design.

At the end of the speech, the captains introduced the most controversial element on their diplomatic agenda. The assembled Indians must have known that the Arikara chief sitting in the council was more than window dressing. Now was the time to open the issue of an Arikara peace with the Mandans and the Hidatsas as a preliminary to a general villager coalition. The captains did not record the words they used to propose the peace treaty, but what does survive is evidence of a significant gesture. Clark, by now acquainted with the protocol of plains diplomacy, took a pipe, smoked it and passed it to the Arikara chief. That pipe was in turn handed around to the Mandan and Hidatsa representatives. Clark noted later, "They all smoked with eagerness out of the pipe held by the Ricara chief."[21] To demonstrate the importance of the Arikara chief and to enhance his status among the other chiefs, Clark gave him an American dollar coin as a medal, "with which he was much pleased," as well as a certificate verifying his "sincereity and good conduct."

Lewis and Clark did not know until much later that the Mandan chief Big Man had privately blasted the Arikaras as "liars and bad men." Speaking directly to the Arikara chief sometime after the council, Big Man accused the Grand River villagers of treachery in killing Mandan representatives who had earlier sought peace. Whenever there was conflict between the Mandans and the Arikaras, the Mandan chief insisted that the instigators were always the Arikaras. But Big Man boasted that in those violent encounters Mandan warriors killed the Arikaras "like the buffalo." With a candor not shown to Lewis and Clark, Big Man said to the Arikara chief, "We will make peace with you as our two fathers have directed, and they shall see that we will not be the Ogressors, but we fear the Ricares will not be at peace long."[22] Lewis and Clark did not hear about that acrimonious exchange until the end of November. Had they known about Mandan reservations earlier, the American diplomats might not have been so sanguine in their expectations.

Relieved that the peace overture had evidently been well received, Lewis and Clark moved on to the next item—designating chiefs and distributing gifts. As they had done before, the captains were determined to "mint" chiefs whether the American stamp meant anything or not. Indians accepted the uniforms, medals, certificates, and flags as symbols of respect but had no intention of relinquishing political autonomy or cultural identity. Appointing men like Black Cat or Sheheke was essentially a meaningless exercise, but it fulfilled bureaucratic imperative. "With much serimony," the expedition handed out medals, coats, hats, flags, and other goods to those selected to receive American honors. Knowing that Le Borgne was too important to be overlooked even though he was out hunting, the captains gave Caltarcota a suit of clothes for the chief. For the old Hidatsa-proper chief himself, there was a supply of gifts, a flag, and some wampum. Because Lewis and Clark knew so little about the politics of Metaharta and Menetarra, they named no chiefs for those villages but simply listed a number of prominent warriors for the expedition's record. Unlike other earlier Indian conferences that ended with a general distribution of gifts to natives of all sorts and ranks, Lewis and Clark limited their presents to the chiefs and elders. That action caused considerable resentment, since most Indians persisted in viewing the expedition as a trading venture.

With the conference nearly over, Lewis and Clark asked the Indians for their replies as soon as possible. The proceedings ended as they began with a display of American firepower. Lewis fired his airgun, "which appeared to astonish the natives very much." The council concluded, most of the Indian participants drifted away, perhaps still wondering just what all the high-flown words and gifts really meant.

But for Lewis and Clark, the day was not yet over. Later that evening the Arikara chief came to Clark with an unwelcome request. The chief was beginning to feel uncomfortable in the company of so many recent enemies and wanted to return immediately to the Grand River villages. With negotiations on the Arikara peace still in progress, his departure could cause delay and suspicion. With a string of wampum and a promise that the talks would be successful, Clark was able to forestall the Arikara's departure. Having done that, Lewis and Clark might have noted how busy the day had been. Indeed, it had been so filled with diplomatic comings and goings that Lewis forgot to wind the expedition's chronometer.[23]

If Lewis and Clark expected quick answers to the American proposals, they were to be disappointed. There was no Mandan tribal council; each village had to spend considerable time formulating a response. There was a Hidatsa tribal council, created about 1797 or 1798, but each of the three villages retained virtual autonomy in dealings with powerful outsiders.[24] Despite their experience in earlier negotiations with the Indians, Lewis and Clark still assumed that they were dealing with nation states possessing bureaucratic machinery able to formulate and enforce a single response to a diplomatic proposal. In the three weeks that followed the grand council, the captains got not one answer but many. And they encountered more questions and hostility than expected.

On the day after the conference, Sheheke and Ohheenar, an adopted Cheyenne living in Mitutanka, came to the expedition's camp. Out hunting the day of the meeting, they were now eager to hear the speeches and share in the honors and gifts. Lewis and Clark offered the Mandan chiefs a synopsis of the American plan and ceremoniously placed a medal around Sheheke's neck. Knowing that they would have to wait a bit longer for responses to their plans, the captains divided the rest of the day between continuing the search for winter quarters and trading with the dozens of Mandans who were now becoming a regular part of camp life. From the camp opposite Mahawha, Clark took eight men in a pirogue and sailed seven miles up toward the Knife River. On one of the islands in the Missouri, he found a good supply of wood but decided that the site was too distant from the water. Clark was beginning to think that a location lower down the river and closer to the Mandan villages might prove the best choice. Throughout the afternoon the expedition's camp was filled with Indians eager to exchange corn and cornmeal bread for a variety of trade goods. The expedition needed to lay in a substantial store of food for the long winter. These trading days fulfilled that need while furthering good relations between the explorers and their neighbors. As the cool October afternoon slipped into evening, everyone danced and drank, "which pleased the Savages much." And in the twilight there was something else that pleased the captains. Into camp came the Raven, Second Chief at Rooptahee, with an invitation from Black Cat. The Mandan chief wanted to talk, and he promised to give many bags of corn as a sign of good faith. The Raven also said that he was prepared to accompany the Arikara chief back to the Grand River to cement the villager alliance. Lewis and Clark may not have known where to build Fort Mandan, but at least it appeared winter diplomacy was well launched.[25]

The last day of October 1804 marked the first of the Mandan and Hidatsa's formal replies to the Lewis and Clark diplomatic offensive. Because the captains believed that Black Cat was the single most powerful Mandan chief, they were anxious to know his response. About noon, Clark and Jusseaume walked down to Rooptahee. At the village Clark was welcomed "and with great ceremoney was Seeted on a roabe by the Side of the Chief." Black Cat placed a fine buffalo robe over Clark's shoulders, "and after smoking the pipe with several old men around" Black Cat began to speak.

His speech was a carefully worded reply to the American proposals—a response designed to reassure Lewis and Clark of Mandan friendship without tying the villages too closely to an uncertain policy. The Mandan chief went directly to the heart of the explorers' plan. Declaring that he believed what the captains said about an end to violence, Black Cat felt certain that a general peace would "not only give him Satisfaction but all his people." The chief graphically illustrated the benefits of such a peace, saying it would mean "they now could hunt without fear, and their womin could work in the fields without looking every moment for the enemey." The idea of a general Indian peace was fundamental to American policy, but in the case of the Upper Missouri villagers that peace had to be achieved among themselves before it could be widened to include others. Black Cat seemed to indicate that was a real possibility. Pointing to the Raven and several warriors seated nearby, he indicated that these men would accompany the Arikara chief back to his village "to smoke with that people." Saying that the way was now open, Black Cat also showed some interest in going to see the Great Father in Washington.

If Black Cat had things to say that pleased Lewis and Clark, the Mandan also had complaints. Those complaints were based on the captains' inability to explain the nature of their mission. Previous Indian-white contact had always been within the context of trade. Indians of the region had yet to encounter white soldiers or bureaucrats. The very concept of exploration as an activity apart from war or trade simply made no sense to the Indians. As the expedition went upriver, Lewis and Clark did give away substantial stocks of goods. The rumors that preceded the party stressed that display of wealth and raised expectations that many Indians might share in it. If the captains left behind among the Arikaras a vivid folklore, what went ahead were tales of cloth, beads, and ironware for all. When Lewis and Clark did not immediately distribute gifts in the amounts expected after the first council, there was dissatisfaction. As Black Cat put it plainly, "When you came up the Indians in the neighboring Villages, as well as those out hunting when they heard of you had great expectations of receiving presents. Those hunting immediately on hearing returned to the Village and all was Disapointed, and Some Dissatisfied." Black Cat admitted that he was pleased with his gifts but reported that most in Rooptahee expected more.

The Mandan chief concluded his speech by restoring some stolen French beaver traps whose return had been requested earlier by Lewis and Clark. Two of the traps were laid at Clark's feet, along with twelve bushels of corn and several buffalo robes. After more smoking "in great cerimony," Clark replied to Black Cat's speech. The expedition's record does not contain any hint of what the captain said except that his words "Satisfied them verry much." If Black Cat and his elders seemed "satisfied" with the meeting, Clark also had every reason to be pleased. Black Cat's village appeared ready to smoke in peace with the Arikaras. Complaints about not enough presents seemed inconsequential, and the chief's careful avoidance of criticism of either the Sioux or the Assiniboins did not disturb the confident captains.

On his way back to the keelboat, Clark met Tatuckcopinreha, chief of Mahawha, and Little Crow, a prominent Mandan and second chief at Mitutanka. Clark invited the two to join him on the boat, where they spent about an hour talking and smoking. Since this was the first official contact the expedition had had with any Hidatsa chief since the grand council, Clark probably hoped that Tatuckcopinreha would respond to at least part of the American proposal. Either the village council had not decided on its answer or the decision was to wait and see what the other villages would do, since all Clark got out of the Mahawha chief were "a fiew words on various subjects not much to the purpose." After some more smoking and a quick airgun demonstration, the Indians left. Clark was plainly disappointed and peevishly wrote, "Those nations know nothing of regular councils and know not how to proceed in them, they are useless."[26]

Although the failure to get any clear statement from Tatuckcopinreha was unfortunate, this first day of gathering Indian reactions was successful from the captains' perspective. And the explorers' mood surely brightened later in the afternoon when Black Cat and two of his sons came parading into camp to show off the fancy clothing given to them the previous day. In high spirits, Black Cat wanted to see the Americans dance to the music of Pierre Cruzatte's fiddle, a request "which they very readily gratified him in." The festive air in camp that night seemed a fitting end to a day in which the expedition edged closer to its diplomatic objectives.[27]

The following day it was Sheheke's turn to speak with the captains. About ten o'clock the Mitutanka chief, accompanied by Big Man and Ohheenar, came into the expedition's camp. Sheheke had two things on his mind, the Arikara peace and the future location of the expedition's winter quarters. The explorers were more interested in the Mandan's response to their proposals; he appeared far more concerned about the site of Fort Mandan. As it turned out, Sheheke was the one who had his priorities in order, at least as far as Mandan needs were concerned. But because the white strangers were so insistent, the chief began with words about peace and the Indian alliance. Sheheke agreed to make peace with the Arikaras and promised to send a delegation down to the Grand River to smoke with his new brothers. But the chief was not about to let Lewis and Clark think that the Mandans were in the past anything other than innocent victims of Sioux and Arikara aggression. He maintained that conflict was always instigated by Arikara-Sioux forces. Some years before, a chief sent by the Mandan villages to smoke for peace had been murdered by the faithless Arikaras. Such acts fueled the continued violence and distrust, Sheheke declared. He boasted, "We have killed enough of them. We kill them like birds." But at the same time, Sheheke agreed that perhaps now was the time for a peace. Without making any long-range promises or binding the village to a potentially troublesome ally, Sheheke simply said, "We will make a good peace."

Those were the words Lewis and Clark wanted to hear. The captains were intent on accomplishing their diplomatic assignments, and obtaining assurances from both Mandan chiefs must have been satisfying. What continued to elude Lewis and Clark was the nature of Upper Missouri tribal and village relations. "A good peace" was not the same as a lasting one, nor was it intended to be. Black Cat and Sheheke were not talking about a fundamental rearrangement of relations between villages or tribes. They certainly had no power to commit Mandans to such changes. Sheheke asked simply, "Are you going to stay above or below during this cold season?" The chief's solicitude for American comfort during the winter was more apparent than real. His real concern was to keep the expedition nearby for a regular supply of trade goods and for protection against Sioux raids. And there was the always troubled state of Mandan-Hidatsa relations. Sheheke wanted a Fort Mandan, not a Fort Hidatsa. Having the Americans within the orbit of his village would enhance his prestige at the expense of his neighbors. All of this was couched in terms of available food for the winter, Sheheke claiming that it would be easier to supply the expedition's needs if the fort was closer to the Mandan villages. The chief made this plain when he admitted, "We were sorry when we heard of your going up but now you are going down, we are glad." He had made his point, although the captains did not yet know how far the Mandans would go to keep Hidatsas away from the fort. If the price for having the winter quarters nearby was seeming assent to Lewis and Clark diplomatic proposals, Sheheke thought the cost low enough for gain received.[28]

In the days that followed, the diplomatic pace slowed. Dropping temperatures, hard frosts, and the first signs of ice on the river were all warnings of the impending plains winter. Indian negotiations now seemed less important than building warm shelter and laying in a good supply of meat and corn. Joseph Whitehouse summed up the expedition's activity in early November by writing that "all the men at Camp Ocepied their time dilligenently in Building their huts and got them Made comfertable in that time to live in."[29] As Fort Mandan slowly took shape, other parts of the company's routine also fell into place. Jusseaume brought his family into the American compound, thereby allowing quicker access to his interpreting skills. The daily visits of Mandan men and women bringing corn, beans, squash, and buffalo meat for trade now became not only a ritual of friendship but an important source of provisions. With the Arikara chief and a Mandan-Hidatsa delegation having left for the Grand River villages on November 2, the captains had every reason to believe they had achieved both good relations with their native neighbors and the goals of Upper Missouri Indian policy. That there were no Hidatsa chiefs in the delegation and that the Hidatsa villages had not replied to the captains' proposals seemed relatively unimportant.

The predictable rhythm of those busy November days was broken by the arrival of Assiniboins to trade at the Mandan and Hidatsa villages. Jusseaume reported that about fifty lodges of the Little Girl Assiniboins were close at hand. Long before the La Vérendrye era, Assiniboin middlemen had made regular journeys to the Upper Missouri to trade with the villagers. Their arrival signaled not only trade but some tension as well, since the Assiniboins often tried to enhance their own standing by stealing Mandan and Hidatsa horses. The coming of the Assiniboins was of special interest to Lewis and Clark. Just as the tributaries of the Missouri might provide St. Louis merchants access to the fur-rich region of the Saskatchewan River, contact with the Assiniboin Indians might advance American trade prospects. The captains were always concerned with ways to undercut British traders, and although they distrusted the Assiniboins, they knew that northern Indians might play an important role in future American plans. If Jefferson's view that the Louisiana Purchase included lands north of the 49th parallel proved valid, ties with the Assiniboins would be essential.

By the middle of November, Jusseaume counted some seventy Assiniboin lodges with a scattering of Crees. All were camped close by, busily preparing to trade with the village folk. Toward evening on November 13, most of the Assiniboins and Crees joined the villagers at one of the Mandan towns for an adoption dance and ritual "giveaway." These ceremonies allowed customary enemies to become temporary fictional relatives and trade in peace.[30] Because the adoption idea might be used by Americans as a means to enter the intense competition for Upper Missouri trade, Lewis and Clark were interested in recording and analyzing this apsect of plains culture.

Although the captains were eager to make contact with the Assiniboins, they were unsure just how to proceed. That uncertainty was resolved when Black Cat obligingly brought the Assiniboin band chief Chechank, or the Old Crane, and seven "men of note" to Fort Mandan. Eager to make a good impression on the visitors, Clark offered Chechank a carrot of tobacco "to smoke with his people." Because the Assiniboin bands spent most of the year on British soil in what is now Saskatchewan and Manitoba, any official dealings with them would be both awkward and irregular. The captains certainly could not create chiefs, hand out medals and flags, or distribute substantial gifts to those Indians. Clark wisely made a gesture that steered clear of those dangers while still showing American interest and respect for the Assiniboins. Taking a piece of gold braid, perhaps from a dress uniform, Clark gave it to Chechank "with a view to know him again."[31]

The presence of the expedition and promises to bring American goods from St. Louis had changed the villagers' feelings about the Assiniboins. As some Mandans saw it, manufactured goods could be gotten from another source besides the troublesome Assiniboin middlemen. This potential shift in economic strategy became plain on November 18 when Black Cat made a surprise appearance at Fort Mandan.

The chief began his visit by tactfully making "great inquiries respecting our fashions." But it soon became clear that there was more on Black Cat's mind than curiosity about another culture. He revealed that on the previous night there had been a major Mandan council involving chiefs and elders from both villages. In view of the fact that there was no Mandan tribal council, nor even a clear concept of a Mandan tribe, such a meeting was an extraordinary event. The council session had centered on the problems posed by dealing with the Assiniboins. Some in the council, taking seriously the offer of direct access to metal and textile goods from St. Louis, urged others to no longer trade with the northern Indians. However, that proposal was not well received by most at the assembly. Those who favored an immediate severing of old trade ties and a quick reliance on the Americans were forcefully reminded of lingering ill feelings over John Evans's treatment of them in 1796–97. These Mandans claimed that Evans had deceived them and never fulfilled his promise to return and provide them with arms and ammunition. Lewis and Clark, they said, might well do the same. Feelings such as these rightly worried the captains. If so many Mandan chiefs and elders distrusted the Americans, the whole scheme of a villager alliance and a St. Louis trade system might be in jeopardy. But all Lewis and Clark could do was urge the Indians "to remain at peace" and assure them "they might depend upon Getting Supplies through the Channel of the Missourie, but it required time to put the trade in operation."[32] Such soothing words could not take the place of bales of trade goods, nor could they allay the fears expressed in the council. As the expedition settled in for the winter, Mandan doubts about American promises were a discordant note in a tune that had played well so far.

Two days later, on November 20, there was more unsettling news. No sooner had the captains been forced to confront Mandan discontent than they heard about serious trouble between the Brulé Sioux and the Arikaras. Because the expedition's Indian policy depended on isolating the Sioux and luring the Arikaras into the American-sponsored coalition, anything that took place between those two Indian groups was of intense concern. Three chiefs from Rooptahee reported that Brulé Sioux camped above the Cheyenne River were threatening to attack the Mandan villages during the winter. Even more ominous, the men said that the Sioux had roughed up two Arikara peace emissaries. Anxious to maintain their hold on the Grand River villages, the Sioux were plainly "much displeased with the Ricares for making peace with the Mandans etc. through us."[33]

Lewis and Clark were now confronted with a set of grave diplomatic problems. The Mandans' acceptance of American economic leadership, seemingly so certain in late October, now appeared uncertain. The Arikara peace mission had been disrupted by Sioux opposition and now there were open threats of Teton raids during the winter. The entire Lewis and Clark Indian strategy rested on peace between the tribes and a growing acceptance of the villager alliance. It now became plain that the coalition was more imaginary than real. Mandan discontent, possible Arikara defection, and the danger of Sioux assaults all pointed to yet another nagging and unresolved problem. Since the last days of October, the captains had had no official contact with the Hidatsa villages. Those villages had never replied to the American proposals, nor had they taken any substantial part in the delegation sent to negotiate with the Arikara towns. As these problems began to flood in on the captains, it was essential that talks be opened with leaders at Metaharta and Menetarra.

Those talks began on November 25, when Meriwether Lewis, René Jusseaume, and Toussaint Charbonneau rode from Fort Mandan to the Hidatsa villages. Six additional members of the expedition took one of the pirogues up to the Knife River. Their destination was Menetarra, largest and most powerful of the Hidatsa settlements. For reasons that are not clear, the American party went directly to the lodge of a Hidatsa chief named the Serpent. Lewis seemed especially interested in talking with another chief named the Horned Weasel. Oddly, there is no record of any attempt to talk with either Le Borgne or Caltarcota. Charles Mackenzie, a North West Company trader living in Metaharta, was told by Lewis that when the Americans attempted to talk with the Horned Weasel they were politely but forcefully rebuffed. The Hidatsa chief let it be known that he was "not at home." Lewis admitted to Mackenzie that "this conduct surprised me, it being common only among your English Lords, not to be 'at home' when they did not wish to see strangers."[34] Although Lewis and the rest of the American party did manage to find lodging that night, they were not given the chance to present American views to any Menetarra chiefs.

Lewis did not know that while he was being cold-shouldered in Menetarra, Clark was in the midst of entertaining at Fort Mandan some of the very men Lewis wanted to meet. Sometime during the day of the 25th, with Lewis and all the interpreters away from the fort, two Hidatsa chiefs, one of them Waukeressara, appeared at the expedition's quarters. Clark recognized the significance of the visit, noting that the chiefs were "the first of that Nation who has Visited us Since we have been here." Handicapped by the absence of the interpreters and anxious to pay "a perticular attention" to the visitors, Clark was reduced to handing out some paint, a piece of lace, a handkerchief, and "some other few articles" in hopes of making a favorable impression. The captain believed that the gifts "pleased them very much" but it would take more than an assortment of presents to change Hidatsa attitudes.[35]

Unaware of the events at Fort Mandan and feeling rejected by the Hidatsas-proper in Menetarra, Lewis rode over to the Awatixa Hidatsa village on the morning of November 26. Perhaps the American diplomat hoped that among Black Moccasin's people he might gain a more sympathetic hearing. Sometime during the day, after complaining to Mackenzie about his unpleasant experiences in Menetarra,

Lewis convened a council of the Awatixa chiefs. Just who attended this meeting in Metaharta is not clear since the only account is from a sketchy narrative written by Mackenzie. Certainly there were Awatixa Hidatsas present, and it is possible that some curious Hidatas-proper also showed up. Lewis began the proceedings by trying to explain the nature and purpose of the American presence. There had been confusion on this point, and the diplomat was eager to clarify the objective of the party as exploration, not trade. But this was a minor point, or so it seemed to Lewis. Mainly, he promoted the twin themes of American policy toward the Indians on the Upper Missouri: peace among the tribes and a villager alliance. To emphasize United States sovereignty and good will, Lewis distributed clothing, medals, and flags. Although some Hidatsas took the gifts, others made a show of rejecting them. At this point several of the Hidatsas gave voice to their feelings, declaring that no matter how many presents were offered, they "could not be reconciled to like these 'strangers' as they called them." The Hidatsa chiefs then complained that "had these Whites come amongst us with charitable views they would have loaded their 'Great Boat' with necessaries. It is true they have ammunition, but they prefer throwing it away idly than sparing a shot of it to a poor Mandan."

Lewis's response to these complaints was oddly inappropriate. Unlimbering his airgun, he gave a quick demonstration of its accuracy and fire power. The assembled Indians were certainly impressed with the weapon and "dreaded the magic of its owners," but Lewis had hardly quieted their fears. Nor had he gained any converts for the American gospel. The complaints continued, and at last one Hidatsa chief boasted that if his young warriors ever caught the Americans on the plains they would share the fate of hunted wolves. Unimpressed with either the expedition's weaponry or Lewis's diplomacy, the same chief insisted that there were only two sensible men in the entire American expedition, "the worker of iron and the mender of guns."

Despite these allegations and veiled threats, Lewis may well have thought his mission was at least partially successful. The explorer extracted a promise from some Hidatsa chiefs not to wage war on distant peoples such as the Shoshonis and Blackfeet. But such a promise was hardly binding, and no sooner had Lewis left Metaharta than the chief of the Wolves, a society of young warriors, took a party of fifty to raid the Blackfeet. Lewis also may have thought he had made some diplomatic progress because two Hidatsa chiefs, Marnohtoh and Mannessurree, agreed to return with him to Fort Mandan for further talks.[36]

Once back at Fort Mandan, there were more talks and now some of the sources for Hidatsa distrust of the expedition were revealed. The chiefs unleashed a torrent of pent-up anger and poorly concealed abuse on the captains. The first part of that torrent concerned rumors spread by the Mandans and designed to keep the Hidatsas from coming to trade at the fort. The Hidatsa chiefs claimed the Mandans had told them that the Americans were in league with the Sioux and were preparing a secret winter attack. This rumor was added to another Mandan-inspired tale which insisted that any Hidatsa who went to the expedition's quarters would be killed by the explorers. These rumors gained weight among the Hidatsa villagers as they witnessed a number of events for which there seemed no explanation except a sinister one. When René Jusseaume moved his family into Fort Mandan, many Hidatsas saw this as a sign of a coming attack. The Hidatsas were further worried by the sheer size of Fort Mandan and its well-armed occupants. A number of chiefs were offended also at what they called "the high-sounding language the American captains bestowed upon themselves and their nation, wishing to impress the Indians with an idea that they were great warriors, and a powerful people, who, if exasperated, could crush all the nations of the earth." As Alexander Henry the Younger later explained, such saber rattling did not set well with the proud Hidatsas.

Rumor, misunderstanding, and a dash of American swagger were not the only things that had alienated the Hidatsas. There was the matter of economic ties with British traders and what Lewis and Clark believed to be illegal political activity by North West Company agents. The captains knew long before they got to the Upper Missouri that they would encounter British citizens working for the two great trading companies. As Lewis and Clark understood it, American policy was to allow such business activity by foreign nationals to continue so long as it did not threaten federal sovereignty. The explorers had made it plain in their earliest meetings with Mackenzie and François Antoine Larocque that North West Company agents would not be forced out of the new lands of the Louisiana Purchase as long as they did not distribute any symbols of political authority such as flags and medals. After listening to the Hidatsas' charges, the captains were convinced that Jean Baptiste La France, a North West Company clerk working for Larocque and Mackenzie, was speaking "unfavorably" among the Hidatsas about American actions and intentions. There is no doubt that the Indian villagers felt close enough to the British traders to exclude American economic overtures. They did not need someone like La France to remind them of the important role played by both the Hudson's Bay Company and the North West Company. Le Borgne himself made his preferences known in a conversation with Charles Mackenzie. The chief "said a great deal in favor of the [North West] Company, but he did not praise the Americans."

And there was one final sentiment voiced by the Hidatsas at the end of November. Lewis and Clark believed that an Indian policy promoting peace between the tribes was both humane and rational. Many younger Hidatsa warriors did not share that view. They explained that forswearing raids on enemies would leave unavenged the deaths of relatives. More important, without the status gained by deeds of valor there would be no way to select village leaders. Lewis recorded one young warrior's concern that "if they were in a state of peace with all their neighbors what would the nation do for chiefs?" This man saw the unfortunate cultural consequences of peace, explaining that "the chiefs were now old and must shortly die and that the nation could not exist without chiefs."

Lewis and Clark may well have been overwhelmed by both the vehemence and the number of Hidatsa grievances. Just how Lewis answered them is not recorded in the expedition journals. Clark only noted with forced optimism that "all those reports was contredicted by Capt. Lewis with a conviction on the minds of the Indians of the falsity of those reports." But little had really changed. The Hidatsas were no more prepared to become part of the American grand design than before. All the concerns that had forced Lewis's Hidatsa mission were still unresolved. In fact, now that the captains knew just how much tension there was between the Mandans and Hidatsas as well as what many Hidatsas thought about the expedition, there may have been more reason to fear for the future.[37]

Determined to do whatever they could to preserve a policy toward the Indians that now seemed on the verge of complete collapse, Lewis and Clark decided to call in the Nor'Wester Larocque for a severe tongue-lashing. Unable to change Indian realities, the captains evidently fixed on the Nor'Westers as the source of the expedition's difficulties. Although La France had probably done all he could to keep the Hidatsas loyal to their North West Company partners and Larocque had sometimes made a nuisance of himself in pressing his request to accompany the Americans to the Pacific, Lewis and Clark had no real evidence to suggest that British traders were inciting opposition to American authority. Nonetheless, on November 28 the captains met with Black Cat and other Mandan chiefs for "a little talk on the Subject of the British Trader M. Le rock Giveing meadals and Flags." The chiefs were told that if they accepted such gifts they would "incur the displeasure of their Great American Father."[38]

With the Indians properly warned, Lewis and Clark turned directly to Larocque. On the following day the trader and one of his men came to Fort Mandan just as a soldier in the expedition was setting out to summon him. Larocque was treated well enough; in fact, relations between the traders and the explorers were to remain genial during most of the winter. There was a good deal of mutual visiting between the two groups and the captains found men like Larocque, Mackenzie, and Hugh Heney to be valuable sources of information on a wide variety of subjects. But now the tension of the past several weeks began to show as Lewis and Clark accused Larocque of intending to distribute medals and flags. He quickly replied that, in failing to carry such objects with him, he "ran no risk of disobeying" their orders. Apparently put off by that disclaimer, the captains then brought Charbonneau into the discussion. Charbonneau, with the expedition's permission, had been working part-time for Larocque in the trade with the Hidatsas. Charbonneau was "strictly enjoined not to utter a word to the Indians which might in any way be to the prejudice of the United States, or any of its citizens," even if Larocque ordered him to do so. Turning to Larocque, one of the captains added sarcastically, "Which we are very far from thinking you would." The air temporarily cleared, the explorers and traders spent a pleasant evening at the fort. Larocque was told about American trade policy on the Upper Missouri and the extension of the factory system into the region. "In short," recalled Larocque, "during the time I was there a very grand plan was schemed, but its being realized is more than I can tell, although the Captains say they are well assured it will."[39]

Nothing of substance had changed. Lewis and Clark may have felt confident about Larocque's "fair promises," but the fundamental problems undermining that "very grand plan" were no nearer resolution. All the fears and concerns that drove Lewis to make his ill-fated journey to the Hidatsa towns had not gone away. Like virtually all white diplomats on the North American frontier, Lewis and Clark found it difficult to believe that they could not easily rearrange Indian realities to serve non-Indian interests. The captains were not the masters of Upper Missouri Indian affairs. They were simply players in a complex game made more intricate by their very presence. Just how helpless the expedition was to shape native actions became painfully clear at the end of November.

Friday morning, November 30, seemed like the beginning of any other routine day at Fort Mandan. There had been a hard frost overnight and now hut fires were stoked up to beat back the cold. At eight o'clock the quiet was broken by a voice shouting from the other side of the Missouri. A Mandan called for a pirogue to ferry him across the river, explaining he had "something of consequence to communicate." Once in the fort, the Indian presented the captains with news that alarmed them and at the same time offered a unique opportunity for the expedition to flex its military muscle. He explained that five Mandan hunters had been surprised and attacked by a party of Teton and Arikara warriors. In the struggle that followed one villager was killed, two were wounded, and nine horses were stolen. There had also been trouble between the raiders and hunters from Mahawha. Four Hidatsas from that village were missing and rumors were flying of an imminent Sioux-Arikara attack.

Although news of a joint Sioux and Arikara raiding party had obvious implications for the future of a villager alliance, Lewis and Clark felt that the first order of business was a firm demonstration of American force to punish those who had attacked the Mandans. Where words had failed, the explorers were now ready to use military action. "We thought it well," explained Clark, "to Show a Disposition to ade and assist them against their enemies, perticularly those who Came in oppersition to our Councels." After a hurried discussion, the captains organized a large armed party of soldiers from the fort. Lewis and Clark expected to swell their own ranks by obtaining volunteers from Mitutanka, Rooptahee, and Mahawha.

By midmorning Clark had his men ready for action. The putative expedition consisted of Clark, Ordway, Jusseaume, and about twenty soldiers. Crossing the Missouri, the group headed for the Mandan village of Mitutanka. Once across the river, Clark arrayed his troops in battle formation with men out on each flank and a covering rear guard. Sergeant Ordway, who was on the left flank, recalled later that heavy brush matted down with snow made the march slow and difficult. Finally making their way out of the river bottom, the Americans broke onto the level plain behind Mitutanka. Clark had planned the show of force as a means to impress and reassure the Mandans. But his unannounced arrival had just the opposite effect. "The Indians not expecting to receive Such Strong aide in So Short a time was much surprised, and a little allarmed at the formadable appearence of my party." When Clark and his men were about two hundred yards from the village, a very worried Sheheke and several other chiefs came out and nervously invited the Americans into the town. While the soldiers went into several lodges to rest and warm up, Clark tried to explain the nature of his mission. Hoping to calm the Mandans' fears, the captain declared that he and his men were there to "chastise the enemies of our Dutifull Chieldren." Turning to Black Cat, who was evidently in Mitutanka on other business, Clark asked him to verify the assault on the Mandan hunters. This done, Clark then recommended that war parties from both Mandan villages join the American forces "to meet the Army of Souex and chastise them for taking the blood of our Dutiful Children."

If the Mandan chiefs were alarmed by the arrival of heavily armed soldiers, they were astounded at Clark's proposal. For a large Mandan-American force to venture out in the cold and snow in search of an elusive Arikara-Sioux party made no sense to the chiefs. They had taken the attack as just one more in a long series of episodes between the nomads and the villagers. The dead man could be avenged in the spring. Clearly the chiefs found the American suggestions both puzzling and disturbing. After a brief talk among themselves, Big Man explained that all the villagers were impressed with the readiness of the Americans to defend them. Trying to accept some of the blame for the attack and thereby defuse the situation, the chief said that his people "carelessly went out to hunt in small parties believing themselves to be safe from the other nations." Although Lewis and Clark tended to portray the Tetons as the instigators in this and other attacks, Big Man saved his harshest words for the Arikaras. Recalling the discussion of the Arikara truce at the meetings in late October, Big Man revealed for the first time his harsh words directed at the visiting Indian diplomat. "I knew," insisted the Mandan chief, "that the Panies [Arikaras] were liers, and told the old Chief who Came with you (to Confirm a peace with us) that his people were liers and bad men and that we killed them like the Buffalow, when we pleased." Big Man again expressed the common

Mandan view that any peace with the aggressive Arikaras was bound to be unstable. He added that two Arikara men who had been in Mitutanka at the time of the raid were sent packing by the chiefs for fear that revenge might be taken on them. According to Big Man, those visitors reported that two of the Arikara towns "were making their Mockersons," a sure sign of preparation for war, and that the Mandans "had best take care of [their] horses." Big Man admitted that there were some Teton warriors in the Arikara villages who were "not well disposed towards us," but the Mandan chief felt certain the real blame rested with the troublesome Arikaras. Even so, the prospect of rushing out to "chastise" the Arikaras in the dead of a Dakota winter had little appeal to any of the villagers. "My father," said Big Man, "the Snow is deep and it is cold, our horses Cannot travel through the plains, those people who have spilt our blood have gone back." Not wanting to seem ungrateful in the face of American support—support the Indians were not sure they really wanted—Big Man offered the alternative of a joint war party when spring came.

By now Clark must have realized that an attack on the Sioux and Arikara raiders with Mandan support was not to be. His enthusiasm for fighting dampened by Mandan reluctance and the simple passage of time in a warm lodge, Clark used the remaining hours for more diplomatic talk. Once again he emphasized the readiness of American forces to defend friendly Indians against any enemy and urged the Mandans to report the presence of hostile warriors directly to the captains. Substituting tough words for strong action, Clark boasted that he "wished to meet those Seeoux and all others who will not open their ears, but make war on our dutiful Children." The captain had made his point about the use of force. He now knew that rumors about Arikara faithlessness were being treated as truth by Mandan chiefs. Allowed to go unchallenged, such sentiments could destroy any hope for the villager alliance. Clark cautioned the chiefs against indicting all Arikaras for what he termed the actions of a few "bad men." "Do not get mad with the recarees," he counseled, "until we [know] if those bad men are countenanced by their nation, and we are convinced those people do not intend to follow our Councils." Returning to his understanding of the economic relationship between the Teton Sioux and the Arikara towns, Clark tried to make a case for the Tetons leading the Arikaras "astray." He also used the opportunity to remind the chiefs that just as the Arikaras were forced to accept Sioux domination, the Mandans had to swallow Assiniboin insults rather than risk war with the northern Indians and a possible interruption of trade goods from Canada.

Talks went on for some time until coming darkness made Clark decide to return to Fort Mandan. The journey back in failing light and deep snow proved to be "verry fatigueing." To boost their spirits once inside the fort, each man was given an extra liquor ration. But for the captains even extra spirits could not change the fact that their venture into gunboat diplomacy had proved a dismal failure and something of an embarrassment.[40]

The day must have been an unsettling climax to a troubled month. At the end of October, with the initial Mandan and Hidatsa councils finished, Lewis and Clark had believed they were well on the way to achieving their Indian policy goals. Then the Arikara peace seemed assured and unity among the village peoples appeared probable. But events throughout November challenged those assumptions. The captains' best efforts to salvage something of their plans failed. Their response to the attack on the Mandan hunters was symbolic of how little white outsiders could alter Indian realities. Held prisoner by their own political and cultural values, the captains were determined to use the incident as an excuse for the display of their military might and, with some luck, to strike a blow against the Teton Sioux. Differing perspectives on warfare and diplomacy meant that the Mandan chiefs found the American desire for winter revenge at best baffling and at worst stupid. Lewis's unhappy Hidatsa foray could now be matched by an equally fruitless Clark journey into the complicated Upper Missouri Indian world.

As the snow and cold of a Dakota December closed in, the captains found more of their time taken up with the demands of food, warm clothing, and reliable fires. They had no intention of ignoring the uneasy state of Indian affairs around them, but travel conditions and lack of sufficient information narrowed their options and limited what actions could be taken. Believing that the Mandan chiefs had been both impressed and reassured, they had only to discover the current state of Arikara-Sioux relations. In the first week of December the explorers sent a letter to the traders Tabeau and Gravelines, who were at the Grand River villages, pleading for news. But it was more than simple news gathering that the explorers wanted from the St. Louis men. They asked the traders "to interseed in preventing hostilities." Lewis and Clark wanted both the Arikaras and the Sioux to be warned of "what part we intend to take" if either group broke the peace. Lacking any real power to back up such threats, the captains probably hoped the personal influence of the traders would carry the day.[41]

The Mandan winter was neither all high diplomacy nor a nerve-racking round of alarms and confusions. Most of the five months spent at Fort Mandan were taken up with demands for food and shelter. Explorers and Indians got to know each other in ways that had little to do with federal policy or grand councils. Visiting, hunting, trading, and sexual adventures were all common ground where people from different cultures could talk, joke, haggle, and compete in the shared struggle for life on the northern plains.

Fort Mandan was no isolated frontier outpost, caught in the grip of a Dakota winter and cut off from the simple pleasures of human companionship. Long before Lewis and Clark came to the Upper Missouri, Mandan and Hidatsa villagers had brightened their winters with a steady round of visits to the lodges of friends and neighbors. Life in the winter camps could be harsh and hungry, but there also were times for storytelling and gossip. Once Fort Mandan was built, the Americans simply became part of that social web that bound the villagers together. Nothing seemed more natural than the desire of explorer and Indian alike to see each other at home and share some food and friendship.

From the moment the expedition reached its winter quarters, Indian visitors came in a steady stream. Fascinated by the "great boat," the endless variety of curious objects, and the Americans themselves, village men, women, and especially children, could not get enough close looks at the bearded strangers. Although some Indians came to trade, Clark remarked later in the winter that most were "lookers on" simply attracted by the presence of the expedition.[42] By the end of the councils in late October, any initial reserve each group had about the other was gone. When Clark returned on October 30 from a trip upriver looking for a suitable fort location, he found his men gaily dancing sets and reels, "which pleased the savages much."[43]

Once the expedition's workmen began to build Fort Mandan, there was even more reason for Indians to come down and watch the construction of a great lodge the size and shape of which they had never seen. Just how much good-natured banter was possible between Indian onlookers and American workers is not part of the expedition's record, but throughout November there was hardly a day in which numbers of Indians did not come to inspect the construction.[44] By the end of the month, as the fort took shape, it was possible for the explorers to invite selected Indian visitors—usually chiefs, elders, and their families—into their rooms. On November 20, for example, three chiefs from Rooptahee paid a visit, stayed all day, and were "verry Curious in examining our works."[45]

Indians were drawn not only to the fort itself but to the many "curiosities" they found inside. It had long been the expedition's practice to display all sorts of weapons and scientific instruments to Indians in an effort to impress them with American technology. When Le Borgne and other Hidatsas came to the fort in early March 1805, they were shown everything from Lewis's airgun to his spyglass. The Hidatsas promptly proclaimed these devices to be "Great Medicines." Whether impressed or not, many visitors found the objects both mysterious and compelling. Thermometers, quadrants, writing paper, and metal objects of all sorts were worth a special trip. It was as if Fort Mandan had become a living museum of white American life, familiar in some ways but novel in so many others.[46]

During most of the winter, Indians were welcomed at Fort Mandan with unfailing hospitality. Only once during the entire season were Indians asked not to visit the fort. On Christmas Day, 1804, the expedition wanted to do its own celebrating. Native neighbors were told that the festivities were part of a special "medicine day" for whites only. On every other day the gates were open. When a group of Cheyennes appeared in early December, the captains "gave them victuals & used them friendly." Lewis and Clark's hospitality was well known; Indians often came early in the day, slept overnight inside the fort if invited, and left the next morning. When meat became very scarce in mid-January, many Indians came to the fort hoping to be fed. Although the expedition was not any better supplied than the villagers, Ordway reported that "we use them as well as possible."[47]

Indian visitors brought to the expedition's huts a sense of friendship and "good company." Visits from Indian neighbors usually meant sharing food and enjoying a dance or some fiddle music by Pierre Cruzatte. There must have been time to appreciate a fine bow, a good gun, or a skillfully decorated pair of moccasins. Older men like Black Cat often told what Clark described as "Indian aneckdotes." Although none of those stories was set down in their journals, the Americans may have heard the sorts of stories and tales told in lodges among friends.[48]

The sheer numbers of that company sometimes tested patience on both sides of the cultural divide. Lewis called the Indians "good company" and in the same breath complained that "they usually pester us the ballance of the day after once being introduced to our apartment." Ordway peevishly recalled that on one day in mid-December he had fourteen Indians all eating in his squad room at the same time. On another occasion, when the weather suddenly turned warm at the end of December, "great numbers of indians of all discriptions Came to the fort." In fact, there were so many visitors during the day that Ordway complained, "We found them troublesome in our huts." Misunderstandings were inevitable. When an Indian did something to annoy Joseph Whitehouse, the soldier struck the man on his hand with a spoon.[49]

Despite the tensions that would naturally come when people meet each other at close quarters, the daily round of Indian visitors was a welcome part of the Fort Mandan routine. Later, at Fort Clatsop on the Pacific, the captains would feel compelled to issue strict regulations controlling the presence of Indians inside the palisade. The Fort Mandan rules were much looser. The only serious attempt at limiting native guests came in early February when the sergeant of the guard discovered that women belonging to the Charbonneau and Jusseaume households "were in the habit of unbaring the fort gate at any time of night and admitting their Indian visitors." Concerned about this breach of security at a time when Sioux attacks were still a real fear, Lewis ordered a lock placed on the gate and restricted Indians sleeping at the fort to those either attached to the Corps of Discovery or those with invitations from the captains.[50]

Social calling was a two-way affair during the winter with the Mandans. Members of the expedition managed to make frequent trips to the Mandan villages. Those trips were usually for trade and occasionally for personal affairs, but some were simply for good company. When Gass and a friend went up to the Mandan towns during a break in the January weather, they were given a warm welcome and plenty to eat. These visits were a regular part of the explorers' lives during an otherwise difficult winter.

Perhaps the grandest, and certainly the loudest, visit paid by the expedition to the Indian towns was in celebration of New Year's Day, 1805. Both English and French traditions called for a boisterous, joyful romp to usher in the new year. On January 1, after firing two swivel guns to mark the occasion, the captains allowed sixteen men "with their Musick" to visit Mitutanka "for the purpose of Dancing." The merry men of the expedition had told Clark that their visit was made at "the perticular request of the Chiefs of that Village." Led by John Ordway, the party left the fort carrying a fiddle, a tambourine, and a sounding horn. At the entrance to Mitutanka the Americans fired their weapons and played a brisk tune. Welcomed into the village, they marched to the central plaza, fired another round, and began to dance. The Mandan onlookers were especially charmed by the ability of François Rivet to dance upside down on his hands. All joined in a circle around Rivet, dancing and singing. After some time all the revelers were invited into the lodges for food and gifts of buffalo robes.

Toward noon Clark appeared with York, Jusseaume, and a third man. Clark's walk up to Mitutanka combined pleasure and diplomacy. "My views," he explained, "were to alay Some little Miss understanding which had taken place Thro jelloucy and mortification as to our treatment of them." When Clark arrived at the Mandan town, he found the festivities in full swing. To add to the merriment, he called on York to dance, "which amused the crowd very much, and somewhat astonished them, that so large a man should be active." As the good times continued throughout the afternoon, Clark visited the lodges of all except two of Mitutanka's leading men. Those who did not merit a holiday greeting were guilty, so Clark charged, of "some expressions not favorable towards us, in comparing us with the traders from the north." Clearly some Mandans believed that agents of the North West Company and the Hudson's Bay Company continued to offer better trade agreements and gifts than the Americans. But all this was put right when other Mandans reassured the captains that the remarks were made "in jest and laftur." Late in the afternoon the eating and dancing finally played out and most of the men in the expedition went back to Fort Mandan. Some stayed in Mitutanka overnight to enjoy other kinds of Mandan hospitality.[51]

One day of New Year's celebrating simply led to another, and with a second Mandan village nearby, no one needed any more reason to make a second round of holiday cheer. This time it was Lewis's turn. Along with Gass, the captain and most of the garrison went out on January 2 toward Rooptahee. At the village there was more of what Ordway described as "frolicking." Eating, dancing, and a general good time were enjoyed by soldiers and villagers alike.[52]

The expedition and its Indian neighbors were drawn to each other not only by the shared desire for friendship but by the needs of business and trade. The explorers had an insatiable appetite for Mandan corn and other produce. The kills made by expeditionary hunters had to be supplemented by buffalo and antelope brought by Indians. Filling the larders of Fort Mandan brought Indian suppliers and white consumers together to haggle over what a basket of corn was worth and just how many hoes could be mended for a side of buffalo.

Although Indians occasionally brought food to the fort as a gift, the expedition learned early in its stay that the Mandans were skilled traders who expected good measure for their crops. At the end of October, just as the Americans were establishing winter quarters, Mandan women began to bring corn and cornbread into camp. As Ordway observed, "They expect us to give them some small article in return for their produce."[53] As winter drew on and word spread that the fort was a good market for food products, a steady stream of Indian men and women came to trade. In one typical exchange, Little Raven and his wife brought a quantity of corn meal and were given some dried buffalo meat, a pot, and an axe. On another occasion Sheheke had his wife pack down one hundred pounds of buffalo, which was exchanged for "some small presents to the squar and [the] child [received] a small axe [with] which she was very much pleased." There is no evidence that Lewis and Clark ever worked out a uniform price and exchange schedule in which certain amounts of corn or meat would automatically receive a set quantity of trade goods or blacksmith services. Rather, it appears that each purchase was bargained on the spot. The captains were willing to barter almost anything in their store of goods in order to maintain a steady supply of food. However, they refused to trade in firearms. When an old man came looking for a pistol in return for some corn and four buffalo robes, his offer was firmly rejected.[54]

Because the expedition so desperately needed Indian corn and the captains knew that there was a tremendous demand among the natives for metal goods, an interesting exchange system gradually developed between Fort Mandan and the nearby villages. That system involved Indians bringing corn as payment for blacksmith work done at the Fort Mandan forge. Under the direction of John Shields, a skilled smith, the expedition's forge and bellows were put in place at the end of December. Iron hoes were mended, firearms were repaired, and later a brisk business was done fabricating battle axes. Indian visitors to the fort were "much surprized" by the workings of the machinery and once the captains let them know of the new arrangement for trade, corn supplies quickly increased.[55]

Until late January 1805, this system seemed to work well. Indians got hoes mended and axes sharpened while the expedition maintained a dependable store of provisions. But this exchange economy had a curious flaw. There were only so many hoes in need of repair and only a limited number of dull axes. By the end of January, the blacksmith-corn trade stood in danger of shutting down for want of Indian interest. Lewis and Clark then shrewdly analyzed the requirements of their Indian customers. Despite the fact that intertribal peace was a mainstay of the expedition's diplomacy, the captains decided to enter the weapons business. Their plan was both to manufacture and to repair war axes, a weapon much in demand by Upper Missouri warriors. This new aspect of expedition-Indian trade demanded an expansion of Fort Mandan's industrial capacity. More charcoal was needed for the forge, and on January 24 work parties were detailed to begin cutting timber. Several days later prairie grass was cut to cover a makeshift charcoal kiln. By January 29 Clark reported, "We are burning a large Coal pit to mend Indians hatchets, and to make war axes." The captain readily admitted that the weapons trade was vital for the expedition's survival, noting it was "the only means by which we procure corn from them."[56]

For the rest of the winter the smiths were busy filling Indian orders for war axes. When the forge ran far behind on orders, an old burned-out stove was salvaged and cut up to make arrow points and buffalohide scrapers. Because unworked metal was so scarce at this point, Lewis established a short-term exchange schedule. The smiths were to charge seven or eight gallons of corn for each four-inch piece of sheet iron. Just how important this trade had become was plain when Lewis wrote that "the blacksmiths have proved a happy resource to us in our present situation as I believe it would have been difficult to have devised any other method to have procured corn from the natives." As the winter began to break in March and warriors started to talk about the spring raids, the pace of war axe production increased. By March 13, Clark observed, "Many Indians here today all anxiety for war axes the smiths have not an hour of idle time to spare." Because the captains had so often emphasized the American desire to end intertribal wars, arming warriors with weapons made at Fort Mandan put the explorer-diplomats in an odd position. The captains never intended to fuel the fires of raid and ambush, but neither were they so naive as to think that the "impliments of War" from the Mandan forge were for defensive purposes only. Typical of this dilemma was the request from a Menetarra war chief who came to purchase an axe and obtain permission to attack Sioux and Arikara warriors. For the proper price in corn the axe was handed over, but the request to use it was denied. The Hidatsa chief must have wondered just what sort of man would arm a warrior and then tell him not to engage the enemy. The war axes were prized possessions and some ended up being traded with other Indians for equally desirable goods. How far those products of the Mandan forge traveled was discovered some fourteen months later when the expedition, on its way home, stopped at the Pahmap Nez Perce village. Ordway discovered that the Fort Mandan axes were being used as pieces in an Indian gambling game. The Nez Perce players explained that they had gotten the axes from some Hidatsa traders.[57]

If trading brought explorers and Indians closer together as business partners, those same transactions provide modern students of Indian-European relations with some valuable evidence about how each culture saw the other. The men of the expedition were often bewildered by watching the Indians bring in valuable food supplies in exchange for what seemed worthless bits of metal and fabric. Gass insisted that Mandan men and women were eager to have "old shirts, buttons, awls, knives, and the like articles." Other journalists in the party, as well as many early traders, agreed with that evaluation.[58] It was equally true that Indians wondered why whites were so ready to part with precious metal goods for corn that could be grown every year. Neither group fully realized that cultures value objects and goods differently, depending on the needs and circumstances of that particular culture. A classic case of the differing perspectives on material culture was the use made by the Mandans of a corn mill given to them by the expedition during the winter. Although the Indians were fascinated by the device, they had no use for it in its present state. On the other hand, the metal in the grinder was a scarce and valuable commodity to be made into arrow points and hide scrapers. The Mandans promptly dismantled the mill to serve their own cultural needs. The largest piece was attached to a wooden handle and what emerged was a fine pounder for making grease from buffalo marrow bones. When Alexander Henry the Younger saw the skillful transformation of the corn mill, he quickly labeled the Mandan mechanics "foolish fellows."[59]

But the Indian interest in European goods of all kinds was more than a matter of obtaining the fruits of western iron technology. Native peoples throughout North America often saw European goods as something more than just material objects. This was especially the case with guns, peace medals, Christian missionary relics, and coins. Those things were venerated as both symbols and transmitters of the strong medicine and spiritual energy the whites seemed to possess. Lewis had some inkling of this when he wrote in 1807 that the Indians believed the first white traders "were the most powerful persons in the nation."[60] The power of the whites could be shared with others by wearing or using things associated with them. Some Hidatsa-proper villagers gave voice to that belief when they claimed that the gifts, flags, and silver medals distributed by Lewis and Clark contained powerful evil forces that reflected the dangerous intent of the expedition. Fearing the "bad medicine" in the objects, the Hidatsas thought the best thing to be done with such hazardous goods was to pawn them off on unsuspecting enemies.[61] Just as white Americans a century and a half later would prize bits of pottery and arrow points as reminders of a distant and mysterious native past, so Mandan and Hidatsa men and women valued buttons and tobacco boxes as links, for good or ill, to powerful strangers.

Although visiting and trading were important parts of life shared by Indians and explorers during the long winter months, few activities bound the men of the fort to the villagers as did hunting. Both cultures valued the hunter for his skill in a dangerous pursuit. Throughout the winter there were many joint hunting parties. Those trips, often in bitter cold and through deep snow, served to increase the sense of sharing a common life on the plains.

One such hunting venture took place in early December. When buffalo were discovered nearby, Sheheke sent word to the fort and invited the expedition to join the chase. Always ready to replenish their food stores, Lewis, Gass, and fourteen other men gathered with the Mandans for the hunt. The explorers watched with admiration as the mounted Indian hunters guided the buffalo herd away from broken ground and on to a level plain where each man cut out an animal for the kill. Lewis and his men were able to kill ten buffalo, five of which were packed back to the fort. The remaining dead animals were, according to plains custom, available for any hunter to butcher and take along. On the second day of the hunt, as the temperature fell to $-12°$F, Clark joined the chase. The expedition's guns brought down several more buffalo, but the harsh cold and broken ground extracted a high price for the meat. Several of the hunters had frostbitten feet, two men had badly bruised hips from falling on hard ground, and York had a frostbitten penis. This rigorous two-day adventure added food to Fort Mandan larders and surely impressed the explorers with the Indians' hunting skills. Clark certainly understood the physical requirements of the winter buffalo hunt when he admitted he "felt a little fatigued haveing run after the Buffalow all day in Snow many Places 18 inches Deep, generally 6 or 8." It was that kind of understanding that made hunters from both cultures value and appreciate each other.[62]

The need for medical attention was yet another force that brought Indians and explorers together during that winter. Native doctoring focused on the healing of cuts, bruises, and abrasions. Because the captains had the reputation as powerful spirit beings, some Indians believed that white medical techniques might be especially effective in serious cases. At the end of December, for example, a woman brought her child who was suffering from a severe abscess on the lower back. Anxious to obtain "some medisin," the worried mother promised "as much corn as she could carry" as payment. Clark laconically wrote that "Capt. Lewis administered," but his method of treatment and the outcome were not recorded. Perhaps the most serious Indian case the captains dealt with involved the young adopted son of a Mitutanka family. At temperatures around $-40°$F, the young boy had wandered away from the village and had spent the night on the prairie protected only by a buffalo robe. When the boy was found, his feet were severely frostbitten. The lad's feet were put in cool water and Clark had hopes that the circulation would return. But the captain's expectations were too optimistic. By January 27, some seventeen days after the initial treatment, the toes on one foot were clearly infected. Lewis decided that in order to prevent gangrene, the toes would have to be removed. The amputation was evidently successful and it may be presumed that the boy recovered.[63]

The sorts of sexual encounters between expedition men and Indian women that began at the Arikara villages continued during the winter among the Mandans. The young Americans were looking for something to soften the rigors of a Dakota winter, and the Mandan women were willing for the same reasons as their Arikara sisters. There is little doubt that the explorers found village women attractive. Ordway noted after the first Mandan meeting that the Indians "had Some handsome women with them."[64] He became involved in Fort Mandan's first troublesome sexual affair. One morning, toward the end of November, the sentry on duty reported that an Indian was about to kill his wife. Hoping to stop such a violent act, Clark went outside the fort for a talk with the angry husband. From that conversation came a complex tale of sexual jealousy. About eight days before, the Indian couple had had a bitter argument and the woman had left the village and spent several days with the Charbonneau and Jusseaume women. After a cooling-off period, the Indian woman had returned to her husband only to have the quarrel flare up again. Beaten and stabbed three times, the terrified woman fled once again to the safety of Sacagawea and her sisters. When Clark tried to quiet the angry husband, the captain was told that Ordway was somehow involved in the nasty business. The Indian claimed that Ordway had slept with his wife, and "if he wanted her he would give her to him." Clark then ordered Ordway to give the irate man some trade goods to soothe his ruffled feathers. But at the same time, the captain chided the Indian, saying that "not one man of this party had touched his wife except the one he had given the use of her for a nite, in his own bed." Tacitly admitting that there was a good deal of intercourse between his men and the village women, Clark claimed that they would not "touch a woman if they knew her to be the wife of another man." Exactly how Clark knew the means used to select only unmarried bed partners is unknown, but perhaps believing that Fort Mandan soldiers only slept with single women eased his conscience. In this particular case, the captain ordered that "no man of this party have any intercourse with this woman under penalty of Punishment." As for the unhappy Indian couple, Clark played marriage counselor and advised the pair to go home and "live hapily together in the future."[65]

Although not usually so violent as the Ordway affair, sexual liaisons were an accepted part of Fort Mandan life. Regular visits to nearby villages and the large number of women who frequented the fort offered the opportunities sought by both sexes. Lewis and Clark knew well in advance of their departure from St. Louis that sexual relations would be part of the expedition's experience. Understandably, they included the sorts of medical instruments and remedies believed effective against venereal diseases. Symptoms of venereal complaints were first recorded in mid-January 1805. By the end of the month at least one in the party was "very bad with the pox." As the explorers were preparing to leave Fort Mandan at the end of the winter, Clark made yet another revealing statement about the widespread incidence of sex with Indian women and its medical consequences. The captain reported that his crew was "generally healthy except Venerials complaints which is very common amongst the natives and the men catch it from them."[66]

Most sexual affairs during the winter were private matters that satisfied the personal needs of the different partners. But there was one Mandan ceremony that involved sexual relations far beyond the personal and the private. The buffalo-calling or walking ritual involved younger men offering their wives to elderly warriors and hunters for sexual intercourse. Essential to the rite was the belief that power, in this case the hunting abilities of old men, could be transferred from one person to another by sexual relations. Buffalo calling was not simply to lure a herd close to the village but also a means of giving young men special skill in the chase. White males were also sought after as sources for great power. As Clark himself noted, "The Indians say all white flesh is medisan." The Hidatsa chief Le Borgne agreed, saying that "the white men are powerful, they are like magic." Just how many men in the expedition obligingly took part in the ritual is unknown, but the trader Tabeau reported that many Mandans believed their prompt success in the January hunts was due to white participation in the ceremony. As Tabeau wryly put it, the explorers were "untiringly zealous in attracting the cow."[67]

Lewis and Clark would have been the first to agree that the months of November and December 1804 were troubled ones for their Indian diplomacy. What seemed a set of reliable agreements negotiated at the end of October were undermined by rumor, distrust, and the power of the Sioux-Arikara alliance. The expedition's efforts to repair the damage appeared futile. Although Lewis and Clark could only wait as Tabeau and Gravelines tried to woo the Arikaras back into the American fold, they could take action to settle Hidatsa concerns and squelch Mandan rumor-mongering. On the afternoon of January 15, four "considerable men of the Mene-tarre" paid a call at Fort Mandan. Knowing how infrequent were Hidatsa visits, the captains were determined to pay special attention to men "who had been impressed with an unfavorable oppinion of us." Because the Hidatsas were flattered by Lewis and Clark's hospitality, the captains evidently believed some sort of diplomatic thaw was in the air.[68]

On the next day, the four Hidatsas still at the fort were joined by some thirty Mandans. What followed did nothing either to allay the expedition's worries about Mandan-Hidatsa tensions or to build confidence in a stable villager alliance. Seeing the Mandans, the Hidatsas immediately accused them of being liars. The Hidatsas charged they had been told by the Mandans that expeditionary soldiers would kill any Hidatsa who came to the fort. Clearly nothing had changed since Lewis and Clark first heard the same sort of Mandan rumors at the end of November. The Hidatsa guests were plainly pleased and relieved with their reception at Fort Mandan, but they were not about to accept the Mandans as either allies or friends. The Mandans were "bad and ought to hide themselves," declared the Hidatsas. Lewis and Clark now found themselves in a difficult position. As the most powerful military force among the villagers, the Hidatsas were essential for American policy. At the same time, Hidatsa raids against the Shoshonis and other western tribes endangered not only federal Indian policy but the immediate security of the expedition once it left Fort Mandan. All these considerations called for closer ties with the Hidatsa villages. But it appeared that those ties would have to be forged at the expense of Mandan good will. This was a knot that no expedition blade could cut. Simply urging a young Hidatsa war chief to abandon a horse-stealing raid on the Shoshonis and calling for peace among the village folk would only produce an illusion of diplomatic progress.[69]

That so much was still unsettled was brought home with great force in the middle of February. On February 14, George Drouillard, Robert Frazer, Silas Goodrich, and John Newman were sent downriver with three horses and sleds to retrieve meat cached from an earlier hunt. Some twenty-five miles from Fort Mandan, the Americans stumbled into the middle of a large Teton Sioux raiding party. "Hooping and yelling," the warriors cut the horses from the sleds and "jurked the halters from one to the other through several hands." Two horses, a fine gelding belonging to Charles Mackenzie and a mount in the expedition, were taken by the warriors. The third horse, a grey mare, was returned to the explorers "by the intersetion of an Indian who assumed some authority on the occasion, probably more through fear of himself or some of the Indians being killed by our men who were not disposed to be robed of all they had tamely." It was well after dark when the men finally straggled in to make their unhappy report.

News that part of the expedition had been attacked by Sioux warriors who might still be close by galvanized the Americans at Fort Mandan into action. The captains quickly sent two men to the Mandan villages asking for Indian support to chase down the Sioux. About midnight Sheheke, several other chiefs, and a number of older Mandan men arrived at the fort. Explaining that most of the young men in Mitutanka were out hunting and had taken the best guns with them, Sheheke could not offer much in the way of armed support. A few warriors and only two guns proved to be the final Mandan contribution.[70]

At dawn on February 15, Lewis, Ordway, and twenty-some soldiers and Indians left Fort Mandan to pursue the Sioux raiders. From the beginning it was a mission destined to fail. The weather was bad, the snow deep, and the men soon had their feet cut and bleeding on the sharp ice. As the day wore on, most of the Mandans abandoned the search. They knew the trail was cold and the cause hopeless. Near the end of the day, after some thirty miles of grueling march, Lewis and his men found two abandoned tepees. Exhausted by their journey, the men slept in the tepees overnight. The next day Lewis realized that a continued pursuit of the Sioux was senseless. Until returning to Fort Mandan on February 21, the party conducted a successful hunt, eventually bringing to the fort some 2400 pounds of much-needed meat.[71] The meat was a valuable consolation prize, but it only served to remind the captains that their words and weapons had not yet changed Upper Missouri realities. The Teton Sioux were still their own masters, the Arikaras appeared unreliable and unwilling to abandon their Sioux trading partners, and the Mandan and Hidatsa villagers seemed bent on squabbling with each other.

In the wake of the Sioux attack, it was more important than ever for the captains to know just where the Arikaras stood. The raiding party had attempted to implicate Arikaras in the assault on Drouillard and his men by leaving behind some telltale kernels of Arikara corn. Although the captains saw through this ruse, the need for accurate information about Arikara sentiments was even more urgent than it had been in November when Tabeau and Gravelines were asked to investigate the question. It was not until the end of February that the results of their inquiry became known. On February 28, Gravelines, two French engagés, and some Indians came up from the Grand River with a letter from Tabeau. Although the text of the letter has not survived, Clark's summary of it indicates that at least some of the news was reassuring. Tabeau reported that the Arikaras had nothing but "peaceable dispositions" toward the Mandans and Hidatsas. He closed by noting the supposed intention of the Arikaras to abandon their Grand River villages and live in the Knife River region. This move, Tabeau explained, would make an alliance against the Teton Sioux much easier to sustain. When the explorers told several Mandan chiefs of the Arikara plans, the Indians declared that "they had always wished to be at peace and good neighbors with the Recaras, and it is also the sentiments of all the Big Bellies and Shoe nations." The reply must have further pleased the captains, although the Mandans' sincerity in welcoming the Arikaras as neighbors again was questionable.

If Lewis and Clark were relieved to hear Tabeau's news, they were anything but pleased to hear the more ominous and realistic evaluation of the tribal situation from Gravelines. He had heard that the Sisseton Sioux and three of the Teton bands intended "to come to war in a short time against the nations in this quarter and will kill every white man they see." Ordway, who heard Gravelines' report, understood that the Sioux saw the Americans as "bad medicine." While the Frenchman explained that neither Black Buffalo's band of Brulé Sioux nor the Arikaras were part of the threat, enough Indians were supposedly involved to give the captains more than a moment of real concern. Gass described the expedition's fears with characteristic bluntness. The Sioux, wrote Gass, were preparing "to massacre the whole of us in the Spring."[72]

The accuracy of Gravelines' prediction of a Sioux attack on Fort Mandan and the surrounding villages cannot be known. There was no doubt that many Tetons saw Lewis and Clark as a dangerous force. The Americans had challenged Teton economic power, threatened the important Arikara connection, and were attempting to forge a military and commercial alliance against the nomads. There was surely sufficient reason for any number of war parties to move against the expedition. But there is no evidence that such a move was planned by any of the Teton bands. For all the talk of a spring massacre, the captains did not appear to take Gravelines' warning seriously. It may have been that by the end of the winter the diplomatic education of Lewis and Clark was sufficiently advanced so that they knew something about the difference between rumor and reality. More likely, their knowledge that they would leave the region in early spring made the threat less menacing.

March was the last full month the expedition spent at Fort Mandan. To the daily routine of trading, hunting, and tending the hut fires were now added the time-consuming preparations for the second year of western travel. Canoe builders were busy making four craft while others were checking ropes, clothing, and vital hardware. Ice breaking up in the river and the return of biting gnats were sure signs of spring and the time of departure.

Preparations were interrupted early in March by the arrival of a Hidatsa delegation. On a cold, windy March morning, as Clark walked up to inspect the canoe builders, he met the Hidatsa-proper chief Le Borgne. The chief was surely the most influential of the Hidatsa village leaders, and his apparent refusal to parley with Lewis and Clark throughout the winter was a real defeat for their diplomacy. Le Borgne had made no attempt to hide his disdain for the captains. Charbonneau had reported earlier in the year Le Borgne's barbed sarcasm aimed at the explorers. Taunting the Americans, the chief declared that he would visit Fort Mandan only if the captains would give him their largest flag.[73]

That remark seemed to justify the impression most white travelers on the Upper Missouri had about the Hidatsa chief. Henry M. Brackenridge, calling Le Borgne "one of the most extraordinary men I ever knew," described the chief as "sometimes a cruel and abominable tyrant" who ruled with "unlimited control." Brackenridge's fellow traveler John Bradbury agreed. The English naturalist used words like "monster," "savage" and "ferocious" to portray Le Borgne. Tales relating Le Borgne's violence and strength gained wide currency in the region; Clark told Nicholas Biddle one such story about the chief's murder of a faithless wife. While Le Borgne was unquestionably a man of personal strength and ability, he was neither the tyrant nor the brute presented in the records of those who actually saw little or nothing of him. Alexander Henry the Younger did have much experience with Le Borgne and this trader's observations suggest a very different sort of man. Now in his mid-forties, the Hidatsa chief had become a skilled warrior and astute diplomat. Under his leadership the Hidatsas had made important trade alliances with the Cheyennes while gaining considerable advantage over the Mandan villages. During July 1806, Henry watched with admiration as Le Borgne pursued complex negotiations with Sioux and Cheyenne bands. "He does everything," wrote the trader, "in a composed, deliberate, and cool manner."[74]

Although it is now unclear what sort of calculation brought Le Borgne to Fort Mandan on March 9, 1805, it was a move the chief would not have taken without careful thought. Because Clark spent much of the day with the canoe builders and later at Rooptahee, just what passed between Le Borgne and Lewis is unknown. It is certainly plain that the chief was shown all the respect due his position and was showered with gifts. Hearing that Le Borgne had not received the presents sent to him after the October 1804 meetings, Lewis made a special point to offer a wide variety of goods, including a shirt, some scarlet cloth, a flag, and a metal gorget. To impress the chief with western technology, Lewis brought out the airgun, the quadrant, and a spyglass, all of which Le Borgne pronounced "Great Medicines." Perhaps the most charming moment of the day came when Le Borgne spotted York standing nearby. The chief had heard about York's blackness from young warriors. Doubting what they had seen, the chief called for York to be brought to him. Thinking that perhaps York's color was paint, Le Borgne spit on his own hand and vigorously rubbed York's skin. When York removed the handkerchief from his head and showed Le Borgne his hair, the chief was astonished and promptly declared that the black man "was of a different species from the whites."

The meeting with Le Borgne must have seemed strangely anticlimatic. So much had happened over the winter that made the captains need the support or at least the understanding of the Hidatsa chief. But on the vital questions of Upper Missouri diplomacy the expedition's record for March 9 is strangely silent. If Lewis and Clark broached the subject of a villager alliance and trade with St. Louis, perhaps Le Borgne showed no interest in pursuing such matters. Whatever his feelings, Le Borgne made no promises. The two swivel guns fired in his honor at the end of the meeting signaled nothing except the failure of Lewis and Clark's diplomacy to change Hidatsa minds.[75]

When the Mandan winter was nearly over, two incidents occurred that symbolized the experience of that season for both the expedition and its Indian neighbors. Toward the end of March, Lewis and Clark heard that two Hidatsa war parties had left the Knife River villages and a third was soon to depart. It was not the kind of news that would give much comfort or sense of accomplishment to diplomats seeking intertribal peace. Intent on counting coup against the Shoshonis or other western peoples, the Hidatsa warriors had paid no more than passing attention to proposals so earnestly promoted by the captains. Had the expedition's diplomats carefully checked Hidatsa weapons, they might have been even more dismayed. Many of their war axes probably bore the marks of having been made at the Fort Mandan forge. Hidatsa war parties venturing out this spring, as they had for many springs, were a simple reminder of how little had changed. The much talked-about villager coalition against the Teton Sioux was still more real in the captains' minds than in the actions of men like Black Cat or Le Borgne. Tensions between Mandan and Hidatsa villages were certain to flare up once American traders came from St. Louis. Each village would want to corner the market on manufactured goods, just as the Mandans had tried to monopolize the expedition and frighten away potential Hidatsa customers. The future of trade between St. Louis and the Upper Missouri was equally uncertain. How Arikara villages and Teton Sioux bands would react to a flood of goods passing them on the way upriver was unknown. There was no evidence that North West Company men like Larocque were about to concede the northern plains to St. Louis interests. Nor was there any hint that Mandan and Hidatsa Indians were ready to abandon traditional trading partners like the Assiniboins for the untried Americans. All the lively and complex issues Lewis and Clark had been talking about with Missouri River Indians since the days of August at the Council Bluff camp were still unresolved.

But if Lewis and Clark's diplomacy produced few if any of the changes sought by the explorers, it would be misleading to declare the Mandan winter either a failure or a disappointment. In many ways the months at Fort Mandan were both productive and peaceful. During the 1805–1806 winter at Fort Clatsop, surrounded by dampness and subjected to an unending fare of foul elk meat and dried salmon, many in the party would recall the bracing plains climate and tasty diet with considerable nostalgia. Personal relations between explorers and villagers during the Mandan winter were marked by genuine good feeling with only few misunderstandings. Those friendships made it possible for the expedition to spend a winter on the plains with a sense of security unrivaled in the history of North American exploration. That sense of harmony, security, and good spirits can be felt in the last visit Lewis and Clark paid to Black Cat on an unseasonably warm day in early April. Lewis smoked with the Mandan chief "as is their custom," and when Clark arrived the Mandan presented him with a pair of beautifully decorated moccasins. If the Hidatsa war parties were an unpleasant reminder of unachieved goals, those moccasins symbolized what good neighbors both peoples had been. The simple rituals of hunting, eating, trading, and sleeping together had bound the explorers and villagers together during a Dakota winter.

5

Lewis and Clark as
Plains Ethnographers

"Our information is altogether from Indians collected at different times and
entitled to some credit."
—WILLIAM CLARK, 1804

The winter at Fort Mandan gave Lewis and Clark their first extended opportunity
to fulfill one of the expedition's most important objectives. Jefferson had instructed
Lewis in June 1803 to gather, record, and analyze a vast amount of information about
the Indians in the West and Pacific Northwest. Although Jefferson's final document
did not quite match the complex set of questions about the Indians proposed by his
scientific consultants, Lewis and Clark had little doubt that their ethnographic
assignment had a high priority. The captains understood that they were to do more
than count native noses and list languages. From the beginning of the expedition,
virtually every diarist in it diligently recorded all sorts of information about Indian
life. But the demands of time and travel made thorough study difficult. It was not
until the winter with the Mandans that Lewis and Clark could seriously undertake
studies in Indian ethnography.

Disguised as travelers, traders, missionaries, and explorers, ethnographers were
part of the American frontier from its earliest times. They recorded their impressions of the strange and exotic cultures they encountered, often without fully realizing they were engaged in ethnographic study. These pioneer ethnographers described
Indian life on a part-time basis, considering such activity incidental to their primary
tasks. They included Jesuit missionaries in Canada, who studied Indian ways in order
to save lost souls, and fur merchants, who noted native exchange systems to facili-
tate future trade operations. As part-time observers of native cultures, Lewis and
Clark belonged to a long tradition in North America that included Father Paul Le
Jeune, James Adair, Nicolas Perrot, and the captains' contemporaries Alexander
Henry the Younger and Zebulon Pike. Everything these men noted about the
Indians—clothing, houses, village locations, languages, customs, and economy—
they recorded in the service of business enterprise, government policy, or religious
zeal. They made no pretense at being scientific observers: As valuable as they are,
their ethnographic records are imperfect, incomplete pieces of evidence. It would
be unreasonable to expect that Lewis and Clark painted a unified, coherent portrait
of any Indian culture. They simply did not think in those terms. But they did leave
behind journals and maps that comprise pieces of an intricate puzzle.

Lewis, Clark, Ordway, and the other journalists in their party were ethnographers, not ethnologists. The distinction is important since it bears directly on how the explorers viewed their work and the results of it. Ethnologists study diverse cultures with an eye toward creating widely applicable concepts of social development and behavior. In this century they have become full-time specialists committed to accurate, objective observation.[1] Lewis and Clark would have understood the modern desire for accuracy but not the passion for impartiality. Only rarely did they assume an air of cool detachment and scientific objectivity in their dealings with the Indians. Disinterested observation was the farthest thing from their minds. Because the captains were confident of their own cultural superiority, they never doubted the wisdom of judging Indians by white standards. For Lewis and Clark, every observation was also a judgment. Those judgments are plain in the explorers' comments about the feisty Teton Sioux and the sharp Chinook traders. For instance, Patrick Gass could not describe the Mandan practice of feeding buffalo skulls without pausing to damn native superstition.[2] But the captains' confidence did not often become swaggering arrogance—something that cannot be said for those who came later. Fortunately, their cultural biases did not prevent them from asking the right ethnographic questions. Equally fortunate, they had the good sense to write down most Indian answers, including many that seemed bewildering at the time.

Lewis and Clark began their ethnographic work at Fort Mandan by simplifying and streamlining Jefferson's detailed questions covering seventeen areas of Indian life and culture. Those questions touched on everything from language and law to trade and technology. The expedition was to record what the Indians wore, what they ate, how they made a living, and what they believed in. But long before coming to their winter quarters, Lewis and Clark realized that they would have neither the time nor the linguistic ability to ask all of Jefferson's questions. Their "Estimate of the Eastern Indians" contained nineteen questions that now seemed important to the expedition. Special attention was given to each Indian group's tribal name, location, population, language, and potential for American trade. Questions about religious traditions, medical practices, or cultural values were quietly dropped from the official list. This did not mean the expedition was unwilling to record that sort of data. During the winter with the Mandans, journal entries noted creation myths, migration legends, burial practices, and sacred rituals. It does suggest that the captains very sensibly recognized their limitations during the winter and decided to use their time and resources to gather material on the externals of Indian life. They concentrated on how Indians looked but did not give systematic attention to native souls and psyches. Their commitment to externals can be seen in their treatment of Indian architecture. Although the expedition's record contains fine exterior descriptions of tepees, earth lodges, and plank houses, it has little to say about their interiors. Later, artists like Karl Bodmer, George Catlin, and Paul Kane would take us inside those houses.

Time, circumstances, and talent limited the expedition's study of Indian subjects. The explorers were inquisitive about the world around them, and they had Jefferson's methodical approach to guide them. But the Corps of Discovery was not quite prepared for the vast ethnographic enterprise proposed in the "Estimate." Relying on their good sense, Lewis and Clark used four techniques that had long been the mainstays of North American ethnography. First, the captains directly questioned both Indians and whites, often at great length. Second, they collected objects—everything from Arikara corn and tobacco seeds to a Mandan buffalo skin painting. Third, they reported what could be concluded from firsthand observation. Occasionally, they obtained information a fourth way, by participating with the Indians in hunts, games, or ceremonies.

Of the four methods used by Lewis and Clark, interviews yielded the most valuable information. Since the fort was within easy walking distance of the two Mandan villages, there were more Mandan informants than Hidatsa ones. Scores of Mandan men and women visited the expedition's quarters for all sorts of reasons, but when it came to ethnographic research the most welcome guests were Black Cat, Sheheke, Little Raven, and two leading men from Mitutanka, Big Man (Ohheenar), an adopted Cheyenne, and Coal (Shotaharrora), an adopted Arikara. It was very important that these chiefs and "considerable men" be courted and closely questioned. For generations, chiefs and elders had served as tribal historians, committing to memory a whole body of past experience and tradition.[3] Without the help of these men, the Lewis and Clark ethnographic record would have been meager and unreliable. Of the two principal Mandan chiefs, Black Cat was the most valued by the expedition's ethnographers. Lewis characterized Black Cat as a man of "integrety, firmness, inteligence and perspicuety of mind."[4] The chief made at least seventeen visits to Fort Mandan, some lasting many days. During those visits he often related "little Indian aneckd[ts] [anecdotes]."[5] But like the Arikara traditions Clark dismissed as not worth mentioning, many pieces of Mandan history and belief shared by Black Cat were not recorded in the journals. Later in the voyage, when the captains had sharpened their ethnographic skills, they would now and then take time to preserve that sort of priceless detail.

If there were plenty of Mandan informants, there were far fewer from the Hidatsa villages. As noted earlier, several factors limited the expedition's access to Hidatsa information. Some Hidatsa chiefs, including Le Borgne, were away on winter hunts. More important, there was lasting suspicion and hostility among the Hidatsas, especially in Menetarra, about the intentions and behavior of the American party. Many of them were alarmed by the expedition's weapons and the size of Fort

Mandan. Some elders resented what they called the captains' "High sounding language" and several warriors were angered by the explorers' boasts about American military might. Such tensions, often fueled by the Mandans' malicious rumors, kept many Hidatsas away from the fort and made them reluctant to entertain the captains at the Knife River villages.

The simple fact was that Lewis and Clark desperately needed the Hidatsas' information. The explorers knew that Hidatsa (but not Mandan) raiding parties ranged far west to the slopes of the Rockies. These parties could provide knowledge not only valuable for the second year of the expedition's travel but essential for its ethnographic assignment. Since Hidatsa visitors to Fort Mandan were few, those who did come were given special attention.[6] They included Tatuckcopinreha, chief of the little Awaxawi village, and his neighbor the Awatixa chief Black Moccasin. On one occasion Tatuckcopinreha related "many strange accounts of his nation," but Clark recorded only the bare outlines of recent Awaxawi migrations.[7] Notably absent for most of the winter were any Hidatsa-proper folk from Le Borgne's village. Not until the end of the season did the chief and one of his brothers pay court at Fort Mandan—Le Borgne to hear about American diplomacy and his brother to repeat Hidatsa words for an expedition vocabulary. Although the Hidatsa contacts were few, they did yield significant information. From them, Lewis and Clark learned about the size and locations of the Crow, Flathead, Shoshoni, and Blue Mud (Nez Perce) Indians.[8] Without Hidatsa cooperation, however grudgingly given, there would have been substantial gaps in the expedition's ethnography.

Throughout the winter there were other important interviews with Indians who were neither Mandans nor Hidatsas. Black Cat brought in the Assiniboin band chief Chechank, or Old Crane, to talk with Lewis and Clark, thereby expanding their knowledge of northern peoples and trade routes. There were also a number of Cheyennes in the Mandan villages who perhaps told the captains about tribes to the West and Southwest. And of course there was the Shoshoni woman Sacagawea, whose contribution is simply impossible to verify. It seems more likely that whatever Lewis and Clark knew about the Shoshonis came from Hidatsa sources.[9]

In all these talks the central problem remained language translation. Charles Mackenzie, a North West Company trader who lived in Black Moccasin's village during the winter of 1804–1805, left some vivid impressions of those difficulties in communicating. Mackenzie recalled watching Lewis and Clark struggle to record a Hidatsa vocabulary in which each word had to pass along a cumbersome translation chain stretching from a native speaker through Sacagawea, Charbonneau, Jusseaume, and on to members of the expedition. Heated arguments among the various translators were frequent, slowing the whole process and worrying many Indians. The way Mackenzie remembered it, "The Indians could not well comprehend the intention of recording their words, [so] they concluded that the Americans had a wicked design on their country."[10]

Fortunately, Lewis and Clark encountered no such language barriers in their conversations with white traders living in the villages around Fort Mandan. Traders and explorers spent a good deal of time with each other that winter, enjoying friendship and sharing information. Although there was some passing tension when North West Company employees were suspected of spreading anti-American rumors among the Hidatsas, Mackenzie insisted that "we lived contentedly and became intimate with the gentlemen of the American expedition, who on all occasions seemed happy to see us, and always treated us with civility and kindness."[11] Their specific ethnographic contributions cannot always be traced in the expedition's record, but it is plain that men like Mackenzie, Jusseaume, Charbonneau, Larocque, and Heney provided much material for the "Estimate of the Eastern Indians" and Clark's 1805 map of western North America. The explorers were especially impressed with Heney's experience and knowledge. This trader had spent many years among Upper Missouri and Upper Mississippi peoples and seemed quite ready to share his experience with the captains. They questioned him closely about Upper Mississippi tribes and the many Sioux bands.[12] Heney's imprint is clearly on the Sioux and Chippewa sections of their "Estimate of the Eastern Indians." Other North West Company men like Larocque and Mackenzie offered their personal observations on the Assiniboin and Cree Indians. And despite his unsavory reputation, Jusseaume did have the kind of firsthand information the expedition needed. Some of the most valuable comments in the journals about Mandan beliefs and intertribal relations came from him.[13]

Because formal interviews demanded both time and translation, much ethnographic information came from personal observation. While always seeing and evaluating through non-Indian eyes, the Americans usually managed to record what they witnessed with considerable accuracy. The expedition's ethnographers were especially interested in observing and setting down details of Indian material culture. What fascinated them were the ordinary things of Indian life—clothing, weapons, food, and houses. During the Mandan winter, Lewis, Clark, and Ordway made important observations on Upper Missouri native life. A look at their distinctive contributions can help chart the growing sophistication of their ethnography.

Clark's observation was sharpened by his growing skills as a frontier diplomat and negotiator. Although the future St. Louis superintendent of Indian affairs sometimes found time to record the presence of a Mandan sun dance post or a Hidatsa migration story, his real interest was what might be called political ethnography. He wanted to know who had formal political and military power, the ways that power was exercised, and how it was passed from generation to generation. Whenever possible, Clark questioned both Indians and whites about native leadership. But when that was not possible, he relied on his own eyes. He carefully watched Indians such as Black Cat and Sheheke for clues in their behavior that might reveal the patterns of Indian polity.

Interested in the etiquette of Indian politics and diplomacy, Clark quickly recognized the role of tobacco and smoking in all decision-making. Tobacco was, he wrote, "an article indispenceable in those cases."[14] When the explorer took part in discussions with chiefs and elders, he was careful to record the ritual procedures that dominated all native councils. Clark had been a perceptive political observer from the beginning of the voyage, although in many cases his perceptions were not translated into diplomatic action. By the first winter, he had grasped the fundamentals of Indian diplomacy as well as any veteran of northern plains life. After visiting Black Cat at the end of October 1804, he painstakingly described the protocol of the meeting with its rituals of smoking, proper seating, and the placing of a buffalo robe over his shoulders.[15] Behind Clark's recording of such observations was an intensely practical motive. Future American diplomats in the West would need to know Indian ways just as the French and English had had to bend their diplomatic manners to suit the requirements of the Hurons and Iroquois.[16]

Although there are many traces of Clark's political observations scattered throughout his winter journal entries, his ability to understand native politics was best expressed in notes taken by Nicholas Biddle. In answer to Biddle's general question about Mandan and Hidatsa chiefs, Clark offered a long summary of his political observations. "The throne of the Mandans," he explained, "generally descends from the chief to his son if he is able, or promises to be able to direct the military movements of warriors." Unlike so many other non-Indian observers, Clark did not suggest that the "throne of the Mandans" assumed some sort of coercive power over ordinary villagers. Grasping the essential reality of Indian leadership on the northern plains, he realized that "the power of the chief is rather the influence of character than the force of authority." Clark found that chiefs could not become petty tyrants without incurring the disapproval of others equally powerful. "Power," he wrote, "is merely the acquiescence of the warriors in the superior merit of a chief." Extensive observation had taught him that Indian decisions on everything from war to individual transgressions were reached after careful, often time-consuming deliberation in council. Clark told Biddle, "The chief does nothing without consulting the old men." He noted that the council was "formed not by appointment, but the most respectable old men are asked for their advice."[17]

Clark's observations and questions did not reveal that ownership of important tribal bundles as well as military prowess was essential for chiefs. And he did assume incorrectly that there was one Mandan nation with a single Grand Chief. But those shortcomings aside, Clark proved to be an astute observer of the chiefs, the councils, and the polity they represented. Unlike most Europeans who insisted on imposing their notions of coercive leadership on native cultures, he got the fundamentals right.[18]

If Clark's observations were directed toward studying public politics, the sharp eyes of Sergeant John Ordway were consistently drawn to the commonplace in Indian life. Ordway's journal is filled with notes on those ordinary objects and actions that characterized Upper Missouri Indian cultures. The sergeant was never systematic in his observations. He simply looked at and wrote about what seemed unusual or interesting to him. Blessed with an inquisitive mind, a good vocabulary, and a clear writing style, young Ordway set down those telling details ignored by others. One of his habits throughout the journey was to do some informal exploring on his own, poking and probing around Indian villages to satisfy his curiosity. On one such jaunt early in the winter, Ordway examined and described Mandan burial practices. With an accuracy that rivals George Catlin's later painting of the same subject, the explorer explained that "the form of these savages burying their dead is after they have deceased they fix a Scaffel on raised 4 forks about 8 or 10 feet from the ground." Ordway noted that corpses were wrapped in buffalo robes and placed on top of the burial scaffolds. Without mentioning the skull circles observed later by Catlin and Prince Maximilian, Ordway correctly noted the location of burial grounds outside village palisades. He also made a telling observation about Indian mourning practices: "When any of them loose a particklor friend or relation they morn and cry for some time after."[19]

On subsequent visits to Mandan villages, Ordway took note of Indian cooking and food preservation. The Mandan diet of beans, corn, squash, and meat appealed to him, and in his simple style he reported that the Indians "live very well." Methods of storing food also attracted his attention. Villagers had long constructed elaborate underground bell-shaped food caches to preserve corn, beans, sunflower seeds, and dried squash over the winter. When Ordway accompanied Sergeant Nathaniel Pryor's detail assigned to obtain corn at Black Cat's village, he observed that large amounts of corn were taken out of the underground pits.[20]

Perhaps Ordway's most arresting ethnographic observation during the winter with the Mandans was a description of one of the most popular games played throughout Indian North America. Known as the game of hoop and pole, the sport was found among almost every Indian group north of Mexico. Although there was considerable diversity in equipment and scoring, the game basically involved hurling a spear or shooting an arrow at a hoop or ring. Scoring depended on the accuracy of the strike toward the ring. Among the Upper Missouri villages the game called for a large cleared, level playing space, long sticks with thongs to catch in the target rings, and flat clay targets. Because the long throwing sticks looked like billiard cues, later white observers insisted that the Mandans and Hidatsas played billiards.

Hidatsa Winter Village, by Karl Bodmer. Courtesy of The InterNorth Art Foundation, Joslyn Art Museum, Omaha, Nebraska.

On a cold, stormy day in mid-December 1804, Ordway and two friends made their way to the Mandan villages for some corn trading. Despite the inclement weather, the Americans found a number of chiefs and warriors outside playing the hoop and pole game. Ordway wrote the following account of the game:

> They had feattish [flattish] rings made out of clay Stone & two men had Sticks about 4 feet long with 2 Short peaces across the fore end of it, and neathing on the other end, in Such a manner that they would Slide Some distance. They had a place fixed across about 50 yards to the 2 chiefs lodge, which was Smothe as a house flour. They had a Battery fixed for the rings to Stop against. Two men would run at a time with Each a Stick & one carried a ring. They run about half way and then Slide their Sticks after the ring.

Ordway was interested enough to want to play the game, but his efforts were thwarted when he could not understand the scoring system.[21]

Even the most casual reader of the Lewis and Clark record soon learns that Lewis was the expedition's most skillful observer of Indian material culture. He probably kept a full journal during the winter, but only a few sheets of it have survived.[22] Those few scraps reveal an astute observer of Indian life. Three of his observations show his growing skill as an ethnographer.

One entry concerns the brisk trade in war hatchets that developed between the villagers and the Fort Mandan forge, which gave Lewis an opportunity to study battle-axe styles used by the warriors. He described the weapon as a thin, iron blade "from 7 to nine iches in length and from 4¾ to 6 inches on its edge, from whence the sides proceed nearly in a straight line to the eye where its width is generally not more than an inch." Mounted on a handle some fourteen inches long, the whole weapon weighed about a pound. Lewis found the weapon's blow "uncertain and easily avoided." The American soldier was even less impressed with earlier versions of the instrument. This precise description of the axe was accompanied by a quick but accurate sketch of the weapon.[23]

In March 1805, Lewis had the chance to observe French trader Joseph Gravelines demonstrate an important Indian industrial process: the intricate means Arikara craftsmen used to make glass beads. The Frenchman indicated that the Arikaras learned the skill from Shoshoni prisoners, but Tabeau heard from his Arikara friends that the process came to them from a "Spanish prisoner," perhaps an Indian held captive somewhere in the Southwest and traded up to the Grand River villages. As Gravelines went slowly through the steps, Lewis watched intently and probably took ample notes. From those notes and his own memory he was able to write a remarkably graphic and precise description of glass bead-making. That description included not only the steps in the process but the materials and equipment necessary for a successful result. Not satisfied with simply recounting the molding, firing, and tempering techniques, Lewis also noted how the beads were used. "The Indians," he explained, "are extreemly fond of the large beads formed by this process. They use them as pendants to their years [ears], or hair and sometimes wear them about their necks."[24]

Lewis's third ethnographic observation came at the end of the Fort Mandan season as the expedition was preparing for its second year of travel. To provide shelter for themselves, the interpreters, Sacagawea, and her child Jean Baptiste, the captains purchased a buffalo skin tepee. The expedition had seen tepees early in the journey among the Sioux bands; Lewis now wrote one of the best descriptions yet drafted of that distinctive plains dwelling.

> This tent is in the Indian stile, formed of a number of dressed Buffaloe skins in such manner that when foalded double it forms the quarter of a circle, and is left open at one side. Here it may be attatched or loosened at pleasure by strings which are sewed to its sides for the purpose. To erect this tent, a parsel of ten or twelve poles are pro-

Leather Tents of the Dakota Tribe on the Upper Missouri, by Karl Bodmer.
Courtesy of The InterNorth Art Foundation, Joslyn Art Museum, Omaha,
Nebraska.

vided, fore or five of which are attatched together at one end, they are
then elivated and their lower extremities are spread in a circular
manner to a width proportionate to the demention of the lodge; in the
same position orther poles are leant against those, and the leather is
then thrown over them forming a conic figure.[25]

Sometimes burdened with an overblown vocabulary and an ornate style, Lewis was
nonetheless well on his way to becoming the expedition's premier ethnographer.
He had neither Clark's talent for political analysis nor Ordway's penchant for the
homey detail. He did have the naturalist's ability to describe objects with almost
photographic fidelity. Lewis brought to ethnography the practiced eye of one who
delighted in describing and cataloging the creatures of the natural world.

From their earliest travels in the Americas, Europeans collected and sometimes
stole what seemed to them attractive Indian souvenirs. At first those artifacts were
seen as mere curiosities, conversation pieces for princes and merchants. But by the
eighteenth century such "cabinets of curiosities" had become the core of serious
scientific collections of ethnological specimens. Jefferson shared that impulse to

assemble and analyze objects from cultures throughout the world. Just as the Royal Society instructed Capt. James Cook to gather representative samples of South Pacific material culture, so did Jefferson urge his captains to collect articles typical of Indian life along the route.

Most of the expedition's collecting reflected Lewis's interest in natural history as well as Jefferson's desire to catalog the plants, animals, and mineral resources of the newly acquired territories. Despite a focus on the land and its products, there was time to gather some Indian objects. On April 3, 1805, as the expedition was making final preparations for leaving Fort Mandan, Clark drafted a list of all those specimens and samples sent back to St. Louis with Warfington's keelboat crew. Among the boxes, trunks, and cages were a number of objects illustrating Indian life. Knowing Jefferson's interest in scientific agriculture, the explorers included a generous sample of the produce of Upper Missouri villagers. Arikara tobacco seeds, a carrot of their distinctive tobacco, and an ear of Mandan corn were the captains' harvest for the gardener of Monticello. Clothing was also included in the Indian collection sent downriver. Four buffalo robes and "some articles of Indian dress" wrapped in a Hidatsa robe were placed in the second numbered box to show the curious back home something of native fashion.

That second box also contained the most arresting object collected during the winter. On a large buffalo skin a Mandan artist had portrayed in vivid detail a 1797 battle between Arikara-Sioux raiders and Mandan-Hidatsa warriors. Warfare was further represented by a Mandan bow and quiver of arrows. The bow is the only object in the assembly whose provenance can be traced in the expedition's journals. Early in February 1805, Lewis paid a social call on Black Cat. During the visit he was presented with a bow by the Mandan chief, most likely the same bow sent along with some arrows in the St. Louis–bound boxes. Rounding out the Indian collection was a Mandan clay pot "used for culinary purposes."[26]

A review of the Indian objects collected by the expedition reenforces the impression that the explorers were bent on studying the externals of native life. Weapons, clothing, pottery, seeds, and a skin depicting a battle all suggest what Lewis and Clark thought was important for understanding villager ways. Nothing was sent back to reveal the rich ceremonial life in Mandan and Hidatsa towns. For the pragmatic Americans more interested in natural resources than in supernatural practices, collecting seeds made more sense than trying to get Indians to part with pieces of ritual paraphernalia. What emerged from the Mandan winter collection was a perception of the village Indians as warriors and farmers. It would take nineteenth-century artists like George Catlin and Karl Bodmer and explorers like Prince Maximilian to broaden that narrow image.

Much of the winter of 1804–1805 was a shared experience with Indian neighbors. With so many friendly villages close at hand, it was natural that both explorers and natives should participate in all sorts of activities. From formal rituals and large-scale hunts to more intimate encounters, the expedition's members learned about Indians by living parts of villager culture. Because the Mandans and Hidatsas did not schedule major rituals like the creation drama called the Okipa during the winter, the explorers did not witness those powerful ceremonies. However, the Americans did participate in the buffalo-calling rites during January 1805 and saw a Mandan war medicine dance the same month.

Excluded by the calendar from the important public rituals, the explorers did gain much information about Indian life by taking part in less spectacular but perhaps more typical events. On a hunting trip with Sheheke, Lewis observed the plains custom of marking ownership of downed animals. As he related it to Clark, buffalo carcasses without identifying arrows in them could be claimed by anyone needing meat.[27] From eating in earth lodges the explorers learned about village menus and food preparation. Participation in some aspects of Indian daily life did not mean that the Americans changed their own cultural identity. But sharing some of the joys, troubles, and labor of a Dakota winter did give the expedition's ethnographers a sense of authority when they wrote about Indian life.

Lewis and Clark did not gather information out of idle curiosity. Although never attempting any complete picture of village life, they gave purpose and method to their ethnographic enterprise. That methodology can be best seen in their "Estimate of the Eastern Indians." More than random entries in their journals, the "Estimate" was the showpiece of their ethnography. Drafted by Lewis and Clark during the winter, the document was a massive effort to organize and compare data on nearly fifty tribes and bands. In concept and design it was as scientific as expedition ethnography ever got. Organized in tabular form and structured around nineteen questions, the "Estimate" recorded such things as tribal names, location, population, languages, and potential for American trade. Although Lewis and Clark composed an "Estimate of the Western Indians" during the winter at Fort Clatsop, that later document was not nearly as intricate or comprehensive.

Questions from the
"Estimate of the Eastern Indians"

a   The Names of the Indian nations, as usially spelt and pronounc'd by the English.

b   Primitive Indian names of Nations and Tribes, English Orthography, the syllabels producing the sounds by which the Ind^s themselves express the names of their respective nations.

c   Nick-names, or those which have generally obtained among the Canadian Traders.

d   The Language they speak if primitive marked with a * otherwise derived from, & approximating to.

e   N^{os} of Villages.

f   N^{os} of Tents or Lodges of the roveing bands.

g   Number of Warriours.

h   The probable Number of Souls, of this Numb^r deduct about ⅓ generally.

i   The Names of the Christian Nations or Companies with whome they Maintain their Commerce and Traffick.

j   The places at which the Traffick is usually carried on.

k   The estimated amount of Merchindize in Dollars at the St. Louis prices for their annual consumption.

l   The estimated amount of their returns in dollars, at the St. Louis prices.

m   The kind of pelteries, & Robes which they Annually supply or furnish.

n   The defferant kinds of Pelteres, Furs, Robes, Meat, Greece & Horses which each could furnish for trade.

o   The place at which it would be mutually advantageous to form the principal establishment, in order to supply the Several nations with Merchindize.

p   The names of the nations with whome they are at war.

q   The names of the nations with whome they maintain a friendly alliance, or with whome they may be united by intercourse or marriage.

r   The particular water courses on which they reside or rove.

s   The Countrey in which they usually reside, and the principal water courses on or near which the Villages are Situated, or the Defferant Nations & tribes usually rove & *Remarks*. [28]

The "Estimate" and its questions sprang in part from the explorers' own efforts to pare down the lists of complex questions proposed by Jefferson and Rush. But the document was more than an expedient response to dwindling time and short abilities. The eighteenth-century Enlightenment stressed the careful gathering and thoughtful comparison of all knowledge. Learning needed to be practical, as the American Philosophical Society recognized when it dedicated itself to "Promoting Useful Knowledge." And in that age of encyclopedias, information required organization in order to be useful. The chapter organization and comparative charts in Jefferson's *Notes on the State of Virginia* may have been the progenitor of Lewis and Clark's "Estimate."

Typical of the informants Lewis and Clark sought out for the "Estimate" were two Indians, Greasy Head and an unnamed Arikara, who came to Fort Mandan early in March 1805 and "gave some account of the Indians near the rockey Mountains." Hugh Heney provided "the names and charecktors of the Seeaux" and the Chippewas. From Mandan and Hidatsa contacts came information on the Crow, Shoshoni, Blackfeet, and Nez Perce Indians. Reaching back to their days near St. Louis, the explorers used traders' information on the three Pawnee divisions as well as the Iowa and Osage peoples. Clark's careful list of Indians who traded with the Arikara villages proved invaluable when filling out the sections dealing with the Arapaho, Sutaio, Kiowa Apache, Comanche, and other central plains and southwest Indians.[29]

All that questioning, analyzing, and comparing produced accurate data about the names, numbers, and locations of Indians from the western Great Lakes to the Continental Divide, and from the Canadian plains to north Texas. What Lewis and Clark wanted, at least during the winter with the Mandans, was a kind of statistical geography of those tribes they had already met, those yet to be encountered, and those who might influence United States Indian policy. And that is really what the "Estimate of the Eastern Indians" proved to be—a limited but practical document for government agents and fur traders.

Although the "Estimate" was the key document produced by the expedition's ethnographers during the Mandan season, other records from that period contained information about the Indians. Thomas Jefferson, who had long been interested in Indian languages, provided the captains with blank vocabulary sheets as a means to collect and preserve native words and phrases. Clark told Nicholas Biddle that great care was exercised in getting each sound properly recorded. Writing years after the expedition, Jefferson declared that Lewis "never miss [ed] an opportunity of taking a vocabulary." The trader Charles Mackenzie verified the explorers' commitment to language study, noting their struggles to capture words translated through several speakers. Knowing just how tense relations were between the American party and the Hidatsas-proper makes the expedition's successful effort to obtain a vocabulary from one of Le Borgne's brothers a genuine accomplishment. All told, the captains gathered some fourteen word lists to be sent downriver at the end of the winter. One of the lasting tragedies was that all that work was lost or misplaced after the expedition returned.[30]

Although those lost lists cannot be studied for their linguistic content, it is important to recognize the sorts of words and phrases sought out by the expedition. Reflecting Jefferson's commitment to useful knowledge, the blank vocabularies reveal a set of some 315 words needed for simple conversations between Indians and traders or government officials. The explorers were to gather classes of words ranging from Indian equivalents for simple numbers to the names of common animals. Names of the seasons, kinds of trees and plants, labels for family relationships, and words for basic human emotions were all to be included in the collecting process. Neither so utilitarian as the simple trading phrase vocabularies written by Hudson's Bay Company employees nor so complex as the dictionaries compiled later in the century by linguists working for the Bureau of American Ethnology, the Lewis and Clark vocabularies represent an attempt to gather information useful to men of science, government, and business.[31]

Most of the ethnographic data collected by the expedition was recorded in journal entries, the "Estimate of the Eastern Indians," and the now-lost vocabularies. But there were two additional sources of Indian information, which bring to light important aspects of native life as well as the fundamental contribution made by Indians to the expedition. Throughout the winter with the Mandans, Clark carefully gathered material in order to draw a large map of western America he called a "Connection of the Countrey." Writing in his journal on January 7, 1805, Clark reported that he was busy drafting "a connected plott from the information of Traders, Indians & my own observation & ideas." One historical geographer has called Clark's map "the foremost" result of the period of information gathering and analysis, while a specialist in historical cartography has described it as "one of the most significant maps produced by the expedition."[32]

Usually noted as an example of the way Lewis and Clark pictured the West before leaving Fort Mandan, the map also contained important tribal locations and population estimates. How Clark obtained such Indian ethnographic and geographic information and how he fitted that data into his own mental framework amount to a unique cultural confrontation. His cartography also suggests the Indians' views of their own physical environment as well as their ways of conveying those views to strangers. Just how much information about the proposed route from Fort Mandan to the mountains came from Indian sources can be judged by another document—Lewis's "Summary View of the Rivers and Creeks which discharge themselves into the Missouri." Composed during the winter of 1804–1805, this detailed study of rivers and streams between St. Louis and the Continental Divide is often cited as further evidence of the expedition's skill at gathering and analyzing a mass of geographic data. At the same time, a careful reading of the document reveals both the amount and quality of geographic knowledge available from the Indians around Fort Mandan.

Histories of North American exploration have often slighted the role of the Indians as suppliers of essential information to white explorers. Undue attention to the supposed efforts of Sacagawea to "guide" Lewis and Clark has tended to obscure the vital contributions of Mandan and Hidatsa mapmakers to the American enterprise. During the months of December and January, as Clark was hard at work on his western map, three important Indian-mapping sources became available to him. On December 17, he got from Heney "some sketches which he had obtained from the Indians to the West of this place." Just who those western Indians were or what information was contained in those sketches is not clear from the surviving evidence. However, Heney was highly regarded by the captains and any data he had from Indian sources was bound to get serious consideration. Early in January, as Clark continued work on his map, the Mandan chief Sheheke visited the fort and provided more valuable information. Sheheke gave Clark "a Scetch of the Countrey as far as the high Mountains, & on the south Side of the River Rejone [Yellow-stone]." The chief explained that six small rivers emptied into the Yellowstone on the south, that the land was hilly and heavily timbered, and that there were "Great numbers of beaver." Guided by Sheheke's words or perhaps his drawing, Clark drafted a map of the Yellowstone from its confluence with the Missouri to its assumed headwaters somewhere in the Rockies.[33]

The "sketches" provided by Heney and Sheheke may not have been visual representations but rather verbal descriptions of lands and rivers toward the mountains. On January 16 the expedition did receive an unmistakably Indian map from a visiting Hidatsa chief. "This war chief," wrote Clark, "gave us a Chart in his way of the Missourie." Because Hidatsa raiders had personal knowledge of lands and peoples up to and sometimes beyond the Continental Divide, Lewis and Clark always placed high value on their reports. But Clark's phrase "a Chart in his way" hints at both the means the Hidatsa cartographer chose to construct his map and the problems the American explorer had in interpreting it.

As Clark explained later to Biddle, Indian maps came in several shapes and forms. Some were flat drawings made on skins or mats while others were three-dimensional relief maps made in sand, "hills designated by raising sand, rivers by hollow etc." Although it is not certain which method had been employed in making this Hidatsa map, there was no doubt that working with it posed serious problems. Accustomed to dealing with flat maps having North at the top, locations plotted by latitude and longitude, and distances measured in miles, Clark must have found the Hidatsa map bewildering. Both Indians and whites made maps, but the interests of those peoples and their cartographic conventions were quite different. Indian map-makers often oriented their maps along sunrise and sunset lines or toward the direction of travel. Distances were measured in terms of travel time while directions were expressed in words such as *above* and *below*. Because Indians mapped what was important to them, the concerns of the expedition must have sometimes appeared strange or illogical. Used to travel overland by horse, plains people found it difficult to answer questions about the heads of navigation on the Missouri and other rivers. Lines drawn in the sand might mean creeks, game trails, or often-used war routes. Language itself compounded the problem. Simple prepositions such as *to* and *from* could be crucial in explaining the direction of a river's flow. The shape of the Hidatsa map, its unfamiliar conventions, and the cultural assumptions behind it must have challenged Clark's abilities. That the explorer and the Indian were will-ing to attempt such communication across an especially treacherous cultural divide testifies to the skill and persistence of both men.[34]

It was easier for Clark to fix tribes and villages on his own western map than to interpret native charts. In many ways Clark's 1805 map was a visual statement of the "Estimate of the Eastern Indians." The peoples classified and tabulated in the

"Estimate" were located spatially on Clark's map. From his vantage point at the Mandan villages, the explorer looked north and properly located the several Assiniboin and Cree bands in what is now Manitoba and Saskatchewan. Farther to the North and West, in northern Montana and Saskatchewan, he correctly placed two of the Blackfeet divisions, the Bloods and the Siksikas. On the North Saskatchewan River, Clark precisely spotted the Sarsi Indians. Turning west, he accurately recorded the locations and populations of the Crow, Comanche, Cheyenne, Kiowa, Shoshoni, and Flathead Indians. Drawing on information from Hidatsa sources, he noted the important links between the Hidatsas and the River Crows. Recognizing the distant travels of Hidatsa warriors, Clark took pains to trace "the war path of the Big Bellies" from the Knife River villages, along the Missouri, across the mountains, and on to the Flathead Indians in the present-day Bitterroot Valley in Montana.[35]

While Clark was occupied in recording Indian information on his map, Lewis was gathering equally significant native data to incorporate in his compilation of Missouri River waterways and prominent geographical features. For his description of the creeks and rivers flowing into the Missouri between St. Louis and Fort Mandan, Lewis could rely on the expedition's firsthand experience. But for details beyond the mouth of the Knife River, the explorer admitted that "the subsequent description of this river [the Missouri], and its subsidiary streams are taken altogether from Indian information." Convinced that such information was "entitled to some confidence," Lewis nonetheless was careful to explain that he and Clark had closely questioned natives during the entire winter, compared their answers, and accepted only those that could be cross-checked. What came from mostly Hidatsa sources was a remarkably accurate picture of the Missouri River from the Great Bend to its headwaters. But just as the Indians' different cultural perceptions made mapping from their data difficult, so did those same problems distort Lewis's analysis. Nowhere was that distortion more evident than in the ways explorers and Indians understood the nature of the Great Falls of the Missouri. The Indians' description was especially vivid, telling of the power and thunderous sound of the falls. But because Hidatsa warriors had no experience carrying heavy boats and cumbersome luggage around the falls, they reported that the portage was "not greater than half a mile." As it turned out, the expedition struggled over a bruising eighteen-mile route around the falls. Despite misunderstandings about the identity of the Marias River, the nature of the Great Falls portage, a purported easy passage over the Continental Divide, and the imagined south fork of the Columbia River just over the divide, the Indians' information proved not only accurate but invaluable.[36]

To evaluate Lewis and Clark's ethnographic contributions, three related questions ought to be posed. First, what did the explorers see, understand, and accurately record? Determined to study the externals of Indian culture, Lewis and Clark excelled at describing village locations, weapons, food, clothing and other material aspects. Journal accounts of village meals illustrate the point. With obvious relish, Clark described Little Crow's wife stirring "a kettle of boiled Cimnins, beans, corn and choke cherries with the stones." Ordway went further, describing with cookbook accuracy the ingredients and shaping of Indian corn ball bread. The sergeant found that this part of the Indian diet "eats verry well."[37] With a common-sense curiosity that characterized so much of the expedition's ethnography, the explorers observed and tasted the stuff of Indian life.

On occasion, Lewis and Clark were able to understand and record other aspects of Indian life, including trade, a subject of intense interest to them. Although sometimes confused by Indian notions of what was valuable in an economic exchange, the explorers did comprehend one of the central rituals in intertribal trade. Because Indians who traded at the Mandan and Hidatsa villages were for most of the year potential enemies, or relatives of those killed in combat, means had to be found to forestall possible violence and allow peaceful relations. Reflecting the fundamental Indian social reality that defined relatives as friends and outsiders as enemies, villagers and nomads created a ceremony in which strangers were made temporary, fictional relatives. Men who might later fight each other could for a brief time exchange goods, trade stories, and even share religious practices as fathers and sons.[38]

Sieur de la Vérendrye was the first European to record this practice of adoption, reporting that the Assiniboin Indians who accompanied him asked to be adopted as his "children," thus repeating the formula they had long employed with the Mandans. In mid-November 1804, with a large number of Assiniboin and Cree Indians camped nearby, Clark took note of "a serimony of adoption, and interchange of property." Relating the process to Nicholas Biddle, Clark explained that "every man of the North makes a *comrade* of the Mandan or Ricara with whom he had to deal." An exchange of gifts sealed the adoption, established certain bargaining limits, and signaled the opening of peaceful trade.[39]

But there is a second question equally worth asking. What did the expedition see, record, but not understand? During that long Dakota winter the explorers encountered many things well beyond their own cultural experience. Ritual behavior or social customs often eluded their grasp, especially if they had no counterparts in white American life. Berdaches, those plains Indian men who dressed and acted as women, caught the captains' attention but evaded their understanding. First mentioned by Clark in late December 1804, the berdaches were described as "men dressed in squars clothes." In conversation with Biddle, Clark amplified that original description, adding that young Hidatsa boys showing "any symptoms of effeminacy or girlish inclinations" were raised as women, married men, and fulfilled all the functions assigned to Hidatsa women. But Clark had missed the spiritual nature of the berdache while imposing an interpretation of sexual deviation where none belonged. What he perceived as gender confusion or homosexuality was actually something quite outside his own experience. Men became berdaches not early in life but usually as teenagers or later. The berdache role could be assumed only after a series of dreams from the Holy Woman Above. Only brothers or sons of men owning ceremonial rights to the Woman Above and Holy Woman bundles could become berdaches. After having the required dreams and assuming women's clothing, berdaches were viewed as persons of great and sometimes mysterious spirit power.[40]

The explorers were equally confused by the few native religious rituals they witnessed. One of those was the practice of feeding to buffalo heads or skulls a ceremonial meal. When Gass saw a Mandan offer food to a buffalo head, he ridiculed the devotion, saying, "Their superstitious credulity is so great, that they will believe by using the head well the living buffalo will come and that they will get a supply of meat." After the expedition's hunters killed a buffalo and put its head on the bow of the keelboat, an Indian passing by stopped and spent some time smoking to the buffalo. Asked what he was doing, the man replied that the buffalo was his medicine and required this ritual.[41]

Although the ceremony was accurately described by Gass and Clark, its meaning escaped them. The Americans did not sense the connection Indians made between living things and those apparently dead. Feeding buffalo heads could appease the spirits of dead animals while reassuring those that were to be hunted and killed. Hunters always made a small offering to a skull before beginning the hunt. Buffalo skulls were often included in the most powerful of the medicine bundles. Unaware of the sanction given to buffalo feeding by the buffalo culture hero in the Sacred Arrows myth, the explorers could interpret the practice as only savage superstition or childish fantasy.[42]

One of the rituals of village life most carefully recorded and least understood was the Mandan buffalo-calling ceremony. The open sexuality of the rite certainly attracted some of the American party, but the purpose of that ritual intercourse simply baffled Clark. Several men in the expedition obligingly took part in it, and their experiences enabled Clark to write a remarkably detailed description of buffalo calling. He realized that the ceremony was undertaken to attract the herd and guarantee a successful hunt. But he simply could not fathom how sexual relations between old men or white men and the wives of younger Indians could bring the animals closer and ensure good kills. Admiring much about the Mandan way, Clark found it difficult to reconcile what seemed random promiscuity with his own positive evaluation of village life. He did not understand that northern plains cultures assumed that sexual intercourse was like a pipeline that could transfer spiritual power from one person to another. Old men had that special power and, as Clark himself noted, "the Indians say all white flesh is medisan." Giving their wives to old men or white strangers was a way aspiring young men could appropriate powerful spirit forces for themselves. Nothing in his cultural heritage prepared Clark to comprehend all this, but he had the good sense to make an accurate record of the event. It is important to recall that Clark was not prudish about buffalo calling. He wrote his account in plain English. It was only later that the proper Philadelphian Nicholas Biddle put Clark's forthright words into genteel Latin.[43]

Finally, Lewis and Clark's ethnography needs to be assessed by what the explorers did not see. Since it was the wrong season of the year, they did not witness the awesome Okipa. Because many essential social aspects of native life were culturally invisible to most white outsiders, the captains did not take note of the clans and age-grade societies that gave shape to Upper Missouri Indian life. Some objects were hidden from all strangers: Lewis and Clark neither saw nor wrote about the sacred bundles, the turtle drums, and the ceremonies that surrounded those objects. Just how much Indian religious practice the explorers understood is not clear from the evidence. Clark did write about "medicine" and tried to explain the idea to Biddle by recounting part of a Mandan creation story.[44] But it is doubtful if any member of the expedition understood the plains belief in power or medicine as a tangible force that pervaded all life. Lewis and Clark never saw the interior of the Mandan and Hidatsa universe. That universe—the amalgam of behavior and values that made villagers who they were—was simply beyond the explorers' cultural horizon.

During the winter at Fort Mandan, Lewis and Clark served their apprenticeships in ethnography. They saw much and recorded most of it in simple, common-sense language. Migration stories, selective prairie burning, and warriors' weapons—all were described in the expedition's record. By the time Lewis and Clark got to the Shoshonis, they were journeymen ethnographers on the way to becoming masters.

6

Across the Divide

"Men with faces pale as ashes"
—SHOSHONI ORAL TRADITION

On a windy day in early April 1805, Meriwether Lewis surveyed the Corps of Discovery and its "little fleet" of canoes and pirogues, and declared that the expedition was ready "to penetrate a country at least two thousand miles in width, on which the foot of civilized man had never trodden." The long months at Fort Mandan now over, Lewis enthusiastically wrote that he "could but esteem this moment of my departure as among the most happy of my life."[1] But even before that long-anticipated move upriver, the explorers had formulated plans and goals that directly involved Indian peoples in the West and Pacific Northwest. Foremost was the need to locate the Shoshoni Indians and obtain horses from them. Lewis explained how important those horses were to the expedition's success when he wrote that "the circumstances of the Snake Indians possessing large quantities of horses is much in our favour as by means of horses, the transport of our baggage will be rendered easy and expeditious over land, from the Missouri, to the Columbia river."[2] Led to believe that the Shoshonis would be encountered somewhere between the Great Falls of the Missouri and the Three Forks, Lewis and Clark made finding them a central goal in the second season of exploration.

The journey up the Missouri and on to Three Forks necessitated travel through territories frequented by Indians that Lewis and Clark believed were hostile to an American presence. As the expedition left Fort Mandan, its second goal was to avoid the various Assiniboin bands known to hunt along the banks of the Missouri beyond the Great Bend. Branded by the explorers as people with a "turbulent and faithless disposition," the Assiniboins were viewed as a potential threat to the expedition's progress. As Lewis explained later in the spring, "We do not wish to see those gentlemen just now."[3]

Searching for Shoshoni horses and avoiding Assiniboin warriors were tactical goals—ones that needed to be achieved in order to guarantee a successful voyage. But Lewis and Clark always understood that they were more than mere travelers making a grand western tour at government expense. They went west as diplomats and agents of an American empire. Proclaiming United States sovereignty, establishing intertribal peace, and promoting trade with American merchants were unchanging objectives of the expedition. Symbolizing those goals was an unnamed Mandan man who went along with the expedition when it left on April 7. He was on board, explained Lewis, "with a view to restore peace between the Snake Indians and those in this neighbourhood."[4] Although the Mandan peace emissary decided two days later not to hazard the journey, Lewis and Clark were still committed to the policies toward the Indians they had promoted from the outset.

In the weeks that followed the departure from Fort Mandan, the expedition made good progress against the spring current of the Missouri. Busy navigating the twists and turns of the river channel, they had little time to notice how few Indians were to be seen. An occasional Hidatsa hunting party or abandoned camp was the only reminder of a native presence. Yet the concern over potential trouble with the Assiniboins haunted the expedition. In mid-April the Americans began to see traces of recent Assiniboin activity; horse tracks and empty hunting camps were worrisome signs, but they did not put the explorers on any special alert.[5] They were far more intent on reaching the Yellowstone confluence. But on April 17, as the expedition was on the Big Bend of the Missouri, its fears about the Assiniboins seemed justified. At sunset, fresh Assiniboin tracks and four timber rafts were spotted along the river bank. Both Lewis and Clark believed that an Assiniboin war party on its way to raid the Crows was nearby. If the expedition overtook the warriors, there could be serious trouble.[6]

Despite fears of an untimely collision with the Assiniboins, the rest of April proved peaceful. As the explorers passed the Yellowstone confluence and entered present-day Montana, signs of the Assiniboins and other Indian tribes continued to appear. Stick lodges, hunting camps, Assiniboin prayer cloth offerings, and sweat lodges all told that the expedition was not alone on the Upper Missouri.[7] Early in May, when the Americans were in northeastern Montana, increased evidence of Assiniboin movement once again put Lewis and Clark on guard. On May 8, at the Milk River, the explorers came upon a place "where an Indian had recently grained, or taken the hair off of a goatskin." Lewis's belief that the Indians were Assiniboins and Clark's report of possible smoke and tepees some distance up Milk River convinced the captains that real danger was near.[8] Two days later there was another alarm. During the morning, as the explorers made a brief stop just past Stick Lodge Creek upriver from present-day Fort Peck dam, a dog wandered into the expedition's camp. Taking this to be a sure sign that Indians were close at hand and certain they were Assiniboins, Lewis and Clark sent out hunters "to scower the country." Fearing an attack by Indians Lewis characterized as "a vicious illy disposed nation," the captains set the whole party to checking weapons and ammunition. When the scouts returned and reported no warriors about, the alert ended as quickly as it had come.[9]

For the rest of May and well into June, the expedition's energies were taken up in navigating the river through the Missouri Breaks. Although the Breaks and the White Rocks region offered what Lewis poetically described as "seens of visionary inchantment," there was little time to appreciate such natural wonders. Sandbars, rapids, and falling banks made the task of pulling boats against the current ever more demanding. Struggling toward the Judith River, the explorers continued to note "strong evedences of Indians being on the river above us, and probably at no great distance."[10] More deserted stick lodges, a tepee pole that bore signs of use as part of a travois, and other native goods were steady reminders of the crowded wilderness. On May 29, at the Judith River, there were two vivid marks of Indian life. Walking along the Missouri at a point just above the mouth of the Judith, Lewis counted the fires of 126 recently occupied tepees. Close by, Clark observed the rings of an older tepee encampment numbering some 100 lodges. Once again anxiety about the Assiniboins surfaced as the captains brought Sacagawea some worn-out moccasins from the sites for her identification. After careful examination, she declared that they were not of Shoshoni origin but were probably made by Atsinas. Relieved that they were not the Assiniboins', the explorers may have been equally disappointed that the camps were not Shoshoni. If the moccasins were visual signs of Indian life along the Missouri, the powerful stench of rotting buffalo carcasses was an equally potent reminder of the native presence. Although recent archeological studies by W. Raymond Wood have indicated that the route of travel for May 29 did not pass a buffalo jump, the mass of buffalo remains did prompt Lewis to write a detailed description of a *pishkun* or jump and the dangerous techniques used by Indians to lure animals over the edge.[11]

By the time Lewis and his advance party reached the Great Falls of the Missouri on June 13, 1805, the expedition had been traveling for over two months, and once past the Yellowstone there had been no encounters with Indians. The goal of avoiding Assiniboins or other potentially hostile natives was achieved more by good fortune than skill. But as the explorers labored over the grueling Great Falls portage, the captains thought increasingly about finding Shoshoni horses. Their growing concern can be measured by an important decision made during the portage. Earlier in the journey, Lewis and Clark had given some thought to sending one canoe and a few men back to St. Louis from the falls carrying news of the party. That plan was now quietly abandoned, partly because it might have discouraged the whole group and, perhaps more important, because "not haveing seen the Snake Indians or knowing in fact whither to calculate on their friendship or hostillity, we have conceived our party sufficiently small." Although it is not clear from the expedition's record whether Sacagawea led the explorers to expect to find the Shoshonis near the falls, there certainly were indications that those Indians had been in the area recently.[12] On July 16, one day after the explorers finished the portage, Lewis was taking one of his usual walks along the Missouri when he came upon a large and recent Shoshoni camp. Spotting what would later be familiar to him as the cone-shaped Shoshoni brush wickiup and also noting much horse sign, Lewis concluded that he had "much hope of meeting with these people shortly."[13]

Convinced that the Shoshonis were just days away and could provide both horses and "information relative to the geography of the country," Lewis and Clark made an important decision. On July 18, Clark took an advance party consisting of York, Joseph Field, and John Potts on ahead. Moving quickly, Clark hoped to find the Shoshonis before they were frightened by hunters' guns from the larger group.[14] In the days that followed, both Clark's forward team and Lewis's main contingent strained for any hint that their Shoshoni search was over. Saturday, July 20, brought more Shoshoni signs but no Indians. Early in the morning Lewis saw smoke up Potts' Creek. Unsure of the smoke's significance, the explorer thought it was either accidental or a deliberate Indian signal. According to his journal entry for the day, he learned later that some Shoshonis had seen either his or Clark's men, feared they were Blackfeet warriors, and fled from the river. Later the same day Clark's force, painfully working its way up a path filled with sharp rocks and prickly pear along Pryor's Valley Creek, saw a second smoke signal. Eager to let Indians know they were friends, not enemy raiders, Clark and his men took to scattering pieces of clothing, paper, and linen tape along their route.[15] Despite these efforts, the Shoshonis seemed as tantalizingly out of reach as their smoke signals.

Frustrated by their failure to contact the Shoshonis and increasingly tired by the rigors of a difficult river passage, the expedition pressed on toward Three Forks. Although the explorers never expected Sacagawea to guide them in the usual sense of the word, they did hope she would recognize some of the country once the expedition entered Shoshoni hunting grounds. But it was not until July 22 that the Indian woman began to see country remembered from those days before her kidnaping by Hidatsas. As the main body of the expedition neared Pryor's Valley Creek, Sacagawea pointed out familiar landmarks and assured Lewis that this was "the river on which her relations live [d], and that the three forks [were] at no great distance." Tacitly admitting just how worried the whole Corps of Discovery was at not yet finding the Indians, Lewis wrote that Sacagawea's news "cheered the sperits of the party who now begin to console themselves with the anticipation of shortly seeing the head of the missouri yet unknown to the civilized world." Later that evening, with both the advance party and the main body reunited, Lewis and Clark planned strategy for what they felt was an imminent meeting with the Shoshonis. Believing that the Indians would be found at Three Forks, the captains decided to send Clark again with a small group to reconnoiter the route and make initial contact.[16]

Excited by the prospect that their Shoshoni quest might soon be ended and that

Indian horses would carry them over an easy portage to Pacific waters, the two groups set out the next morning. Clark took with him Robert Frazer, Joseph and Reuben Field, and Toussaint Charbonneau. To reassure Indians that they were friends, Lewis ordered that small American flags fly from every canoe. While Clark followed Indian paths toward Three Forks, Lewis and the boats pressed upriver. Each group found the going difficult and exhausting. Hiking over broken terrain filled with sharp rocks and prickly pear, Clark's men suffered twisted ankles and lacerated feet. The boat crews had it no less easy. The Missouri was now a narrow channel choked with willow islands, rocky shallows, and unexpected rapids. Towing their craft from the shore exposed the men's moccasined feet to the needle spines of the prickly pear. Working boats in the water became a back-breaking, bone-chilling enterprise. Ordway understated the obvious when he wrote, "The party in general are much fatigued." But swollen feet and aching bones would have been gladly accepted had the effort produced a Shoshoni encounter. When Clark reached Three Forks on July 25, he found a fire-blackened prairie and horse tracks but no Indians. Two days later Lewis and the main body came to Three Forks, found Clark's note detailing what he had discovered thus far, and saw for themselves that the valley held only silence.[17]

The Three Forks of the Missouri was what Lewis described it to be, "an essential point in the geography of this western part of the Continent." But one of the essentials was missing. Without Indian horses the expedition would be stranded on the wrong side of the Great Divide. Facing a second winter east of the mountains, on short rations and unsure of the route ahead, the expedition was at a desperate point. Lewis put it bluntly: "We begin to feel considerable anxiety with rispect to the Snake Indians. If we do not find them or some other nation who have horses I fear the successful issue of our voyage will be very doubtful or at all events much more difficult in it's accomplishment."[18] The explorers did not understand that Shoshoni and Flathead bands did not come across the mountains and into the Three Forks region until September. At the very moment when the worried captains were holding talks plotting what to do next, the Shoshonis and Flatheads were still busy fishing along the Lemhi and Salmon rivers.

The expedition camped at Three Forks, where Sacagawea had been kidnaped from a Shoshoni band some five years earlier. It was a time to treat blistered and infected feet, repair clothing and moccasins, and dry dampened papers and trade goods. But the most important task at Three Forks was formulation of a plan to locate the elusive Shoshonis. Perhaps guided by information supplied by Sacagawea, the explorers now believed the Indians were either further up the Jefferson River or across the mountains still fishing.[19] Wherever they were, they had to be found. Using a tactic employed before, Lewis and Clark decided to send a scouting party ahead while the main group continued up the Jefferson. Since Clark was still recovering from an infection caused by prickly pear punctures, Lewis led the scouts.[20]

The first week of August 1805 must have seemed an eternity to the frustrated and exhausted men of the expedition. Everything that could go awry did. Laboring up the Jefferson in a channel that was barely navigable, Clark's boat crews slipped in the mud, tripped over hidden rocks, and spent hours waist-deep in cold water. Men who usually did not complain in the face of hardship were now "so much fortiegued that they wished much that navigation was at an end that they might go by land."[21] Canoes overturned, tow ropes broke, and the air was blue with tough talk. As a last straw, a beaver had gnawed through the green willow branch holding a message from Lewis, causing the boats to make a needless and painful detour up the Big Hole (Wisdom) River. And George Shannon got lost on a hunting trek up the Big Hole. The efforts of Lewis's scouting party to locate the Shoshonis were no more successful than previous ones. There were signs of Indian activity, but as before they yielded neither people nor horses. When the two captains again joined forces on August 6 and proceeded up the Jefferson, they had to face some harsh realities. Several men, including Clark and Whitehouse, were injured and in pain, while many others were near exhaustion. Valuable trade goods, medicine, and powder were wet and damaged. Food supplies were uncertain. And above all, there was the inescapable fact that unless the expedition found horses very soon it would have to pack only a fraction of its supplies across the divide and look for a place to winter in mountains known for their scarcity of game. The men's spirits and prospects would not be as low again until the bitter days in the snows of the Lolo Trail.

These bleak prospects began to change on August 8. With the explorers just below the mouth of the Ruby (Philanthropy) River, Sacagawea recognized "the point of a high plain to our right which she informed us was not very distant from the summer retreat of her nation on a river beyond the mountains which runs to the west." Known to Indians as the Beaver's Head because it reminded them of a swimming beaver, the rock brought both hope and a sense of urgency to the expedition. "As it is now all important with us to meet those people as soon as possible," the captains decided to once again send Lewis on ahead with George Drouillard, Hugh McNeal, and John Shields. Lewis vowed to find horses if it took a month of hard travel.[22] On the next morning, August 9, Lewis and his men swung on their packs and began to follow the Jefferson River toward the mountains. The whole future of the expedition depended on Lewis's success in finding the Shoshonis and trading for horses in something less than a month.

All day on August 9, Lewis and his men tracked along the Jefferson. Seeing the river "very crooked much divided by islands, shallow, rocky in many places and very rapid," Lewis worried that Clark's boats might not be able to make the passage. On the following day the explorers "fel in with a plain Indian road" which took them past Rattlesnake Cliffs to a fork in the Beaverhead River. Because the path also forked and Lewis did not want to waste time on the wrong trail, he dispatched Drouillard up one way while Shields took the other. Sensing that this fork also marked the end of navigable waters, Lewis left a note for Clark telling him to go no further until the advance party returned. Lewis and his men now set out along Horse Prairie Creek, a small stream that flowed from the West. Horse Prairie Creek led the explorers into Shoshoni Cove, described by Lewis as one of the "handsomest" coves he had ever seen. Camping that night in the cove, Lewis and his men ate venison roasted over a willow brush fire and wondered what lay beyond the dividing ridge.[23]

Sunday, August 11, proved to be one of the most important days for the expedition. It was a day equally important for the Shoshonis of Cameahwait's band camped over the divide along the Lemhi River. Soon after Lewis and his men set out from their camp in Shoshoni Cove the Indian trail vanished in dense sagebrush. Anxious not to miss what proved to be Lemhi Pass over the Beaverhead Mountains, Lewis ordered Drouillard to walk on the captain's right flank while Shields would cover the left. McNeal was to remain with Lewis as the whole formation moved slowly through the cove and toward the pass. Five miles of this maneuver got Lewis closer to Lemhi Pass, but it still seemed no nearer to the Shoshonis. Then suddenly, some two miles off, Lewis spotted an Indian horse and rider cantering toward him. With the aid of his small telescope, Lewis identified the Indian as a Shoshoni. The armed warrior was riding an "eligant" horse and had not yet seen the Americans. Overjoyed at the prospect of finally meeting the Shoshonis, Lewis walked slowly toward the Indian. The explorer was certain that once the Shoshoni saw his white skin any fears would disappear. With about a mile now separating the two, the Indian stopped and Lewis likewise halted. Determined to make some friendly gesture, Lewis took his blanket and waved it three times in the air. Perhaps Drouillard had told him that this was the accepted sign for peaceful conversation between strangers. But the Shoshoni apparently discounted Lewis's signal and watched with mounting suspicion as Drouillard and Shields drew closer. Unable to catch the attention of either man, Lewis feared that their continued march would frighten the Indian and dash any hopes of a friendly meeting. Lewis took a few strands of beads, a mirror, and some other trade items and began to walk alone toward the still-mounted Indian. When the men were no more than two hundred paces apart, the Indian slowly turned his horse and began to ride away. In desperation Lewis shouted out the word "tab-ba-bone," which he believed was Shoshoni for whiteman. The explorer knew that Drouillard and Shields had to be stopped or all would be lost. Risking a shout and some vigorous waving, Lewis commanded both men to halt. Drouillard obeyed but Shields evidently did not see the signal. The Indian moved off a bit more and then stopped a second time. With steady determination Lewis resumed walking toward the man, again saying "tab-ba-bone," holding up the trade goods, and even stripping up his shirt sleeves to show white skin. But none of this worked and when the two were no more than one hundred paces apart, the Indian whipped up his horse and vanished into the willow brush.

"With him," wrote Lewis, "vanished all my hopes of obtaining horses for the present." Depressed and angry, Lewis rounded up his men and "could not forbare abraiding them a little for their want of attention and imprudence on this occasion." Although Lewis blamed Drouillard and Shields for the failure at Shoshoni Cove, other factors were also at work. The Lemhi Shoshonis had just suffered a punishing raid at the hands of Atsina warriors and were bound to view any stranger with considerable suspicion. More important, there was the matter of the word "tab-ba-bone." Lewis had probably asked either Charbonneau or Sacagawea for a word meaning "whiteman." Since that word did not exist in the Shoshoni vocabulary, the explorer was given the term for stranger or foreigner. The Indian kinship world was divided between relatives who were friends and strangers who were potential enemies. Shouting "tab-ba-bone" to an already fearful Shoshoni was hardly the way to begin a successful talk.

Knowing that the day's opportunity was lost, Lewis decided to pause in the cove for breakfast. While the rest of the men cooked, Lewis prepared a small parcel of beads, moccasin awls, paint, and a mirror. Tying the goods to a pole stuck in the ground near the campfire, Lewis hoped the gifts would attract Shoshoni attention and convince them that the strangers were interested in trading, not raiding. A sudden rain shower made following the Shoshoni's tracks impossible. Wet grass hampered walking and a maze of horse prints made deciding which track to follow difficult and frustrating. Camping that night at the head of Shoshoni Cove, Lewis may well have wondered whether the Shoshonis would forever remain just beyond his grasp.[24]

For the Lemhi Shoshonis of Cameahwait's band, August 11, 1805, had seemed like any other day in late summer. Groups of women and children were out on the prairies digging roots. Others were busy at fish weirs or gigging for salmon with sharp, barbed sticks. Most men were occupied with hunting or tending to the needs of horses and weapons. One man who had been out riding near a creek on the other side of the mountains saw strangers whose faces he had described as "pale as ashes." But the report seemed preposterous and after some talk it was dismissed as an idle boast. What counted that day was that the band would soon join Flathead friends in journeying toward the Three Forks for the buffalo season. They would no longer be *ágaideka'a*, or salmon eaters, but *kutsendeka'a*, those who ate the buffalo. There would be danger from enemies like the Atsinas and Blackfeet, but there would also be fresh meat to end days of near starvation. That anything might alter the familiar seasonal rhythm was almost unthinkable.[25]

Lewis expected the next day to bring the long-hoped-for Shoshoni encounter. Early that morning Lewis sent George Drouillard out to track. Continuing on the trail as it led toward Lemhi Pass, Lewis saw places where Indian women had been digging roots. Brush lodges were also signs that the Shoshonis were near. Although Lewis's party did not find the Shoshonis on August 12, it was a memorable day. Near the crest of the pass the explorers found "the most distant fountain of the waters of the Mighty Missouri." Later recalling McNeal standing astride the headwaters creek, Lewis exalted that "thus far I had accomplished one of those great objects on which my mind has been unalterably fixed for many years." After drinking from the stream and resting for a moment, Lewis and his men crossed the Continental Divide—the first Americans to make the passage—and stood looking at the Bitterroot Mountains. Not even those "immence ranges of high mountains still to the West of us with their tops partially covered with snow" could dampen Lewis's enthusiasm as he drank at the Lemhi River and for the first time tasted western waters.[26] For all the glory and excitement of the day, Lewis must have known that the expedition's essential problem remained unsolved. Seeing one Shoshoni, observing many Indian signs, and crossing the divide did not bring horses into the explorers' corral.

Breaking camp on August 13 somewhere down a mountain slope toward the Lemhi River, Lewis and his men followed the Indian trail as it led into the Lemhi Valley. After covering about four miles, the explorers' attention was drawn to a ridge directly in front of them. Up on the ridge, watching them intently, were two Shoshoni women, a man, and several dogs. Frightened by the sudden appearance of strangers, two of the Indians sat on the ground as if preparing for the arrival of enemy raiders. When the Americans were no more than half a mile from the Indians, Lewis ordered his men to halt. Leaving his rifle and pack, Lewis picked up a large American flag, unfurled it, and walked slowly toward the Shoshonis. Despite Lewis's cautious approach, the Indians fled. Perhaps once again the word "tab-ba-bone" was more damaging than he understood. The Shoshonis were gone but their dogs were more inquisitive, sniffing and barking at the strangers. Seizing on any tactic that might convince the Indians of his peaceful intentions, Lewis tried to tie trade goods to the dogs' necks. But the animals were too skittish and the plan failed.

Intent on finding the Shoshonis, Lewis and his men began to backtrack along a dusty trail that "appeared to have been much traveled lately both by men and horses." After about a mile of moving through the steep ravines of the Lemhi Valley, the explorers suddenly stumbled on three Shoshoni women. One immediately fled in terror, but an elderly woman and a young girl calmly sat on the ground with their heads down, waiting for what they must have thought was certain death at the hands of hostile strangers. Lewis walked up to the two frightened Indians, took the older woman by the hand, and repeated the now-familiar "tab-ba-bone." At the same time, he pushed up one shirt sleeve to reveal white skin. Seeing that the women were somewhat more calm, he handed out some gifts. Worried that the one woman who ran away might alarm nearby Shoshoni warriors, Lewis made signs for the older woman to call back her companion. The explorer knew from Sacagawea that vermilion symbolized peace for the Shoshonis, and he promptly daubed the women's faces with paint as one more way to communicate his intentions. Once again using signs, he asked them to guide the Americans to the main Indian encampment.

Led by the Indian women along a trail beside the Lemhi River, Lewis and his men were suddenly confronted by a band of some sixty mounted warriors riding at full speed. Warned by one of the Indians who had seen Lewis earlier in the day, Cameah-wait had marshaled his warriors and was now prepared to do battle. Acting quickly, Lewis dropped his gun, held up a flag, and walked toward the advancing Indians. Out ahead of the main warrior party rode the band chief Cameahwait and two lesser chiefs. Seeing Lewis and the women, the chief reined up his horse, had a hurried talk with the women who excitedly showed them their gifts, and then rode on toward Lewis. In that moment when Cameahwait and his fellow chiefs were coming toward him, Lewis must have wondered just what sort of reception to expect. Any fears he had quickly evaporated as the Shoshoni chiefs warmly embraced him and repeated the word "ah-hi-e," "I am much pleased." What followed was a great festival of embracing and shouting as the Americans were "all carressed and besmeared with their grease and paint" until Lewis admitted he was "heartily tired of the national hug." Following proper plains diplomatic protocol, Lewis sat on the ground with the Shoshonis and smoked a pipe. To show their good faith and genuine welcome, the Indians removed their moccasins during the ritual smoke. Once the smoking was finished, Lewis moved to cement good relations with his new-found friends. While he distributed trade goods—including a generous amount of blue beads and vermilion—Lewis used signs to explain briefly that he and his friends were in Shoshoni country for peace and trade. Hot and thirsty from what had already seemed a very long day, Lewis was anxious to get on toward the Lemhi River Shoshoni camp. But Cameahwait was in no particular hurry and preferred to savor the moment by giving two long speeches to his warriors. It was not until late in the afternoon that the explorers and their native escort came to the Indian camp along the Lemhi.

If Lewis thought that he and his men could rest for the remainder of the day, he had not taken the measure of just how much the Americans were a curiosity and a social happening. Ushered into a skin tepee, the only one still owned by the band after the recent Atsina raid, the explorers were ceremoniously seated on green boughs and antelope skins. Once again there was ritual smoking, as explorers and

Indians sat facing each other across what Lewis characterized as a "little magic circle." The ceremony complete, Lewis spoke through Drouillard's signs to explain who they were, what their mission was, and what they hoped to obtain from the Shoshonis. As Lewis talked, the crowd around the tepee swelled with women and children intent on seeing the outlandish pale beings. Now late in the evening, Lewis recalled that he had eaten nothing since the previous night. His request for food brought some serviceberry and chokecherry cakes, plain food but for Lewis and his men a welcome meal. The berry cakes satisfied Lewis's stomach, but a small bit of salmon did more to gratify his mind. That salmon convinced him that "we were on the waters of the Pacific Ocean."

But any hope Lewis had of an easy passage to the Columbia was shattered when Cameahwait told him about the treacherous course of the Salmon River. For now, Lewis consoled himself with the belief that "this account had been exagerated with a view to detain us among them." Exhausted by one of the most momentous days in the life of the expedition, Lewis left Drouillard, Shields, and McNeal to dance with the Shoshonis while he sought "a tolerable sound night's repose."[27]

The day had been every bit as momentous for Cameahwait's people. Their familiar patterns of hunting, fishing, gathering, and preparing for the annual buffalo hunt had been interrupted by the arrival of strangers whose appearance was disturbing and whose intentions were unknown. Although northern Shoshonis had long been exposed to European goods from Spanish sources, there is little evidence to suggest that anyone in the Lemhi bands had ever seen a white man. It is difficult to know just what the Shoshonis thought of Lewis and the others. Certainly they were fascinated and delighted with the gifts, including mirrors that were described in one oral tradition as "things like solid water, which were sometimes brilliant as the sun, and which sometimes showed us our faces." Dazzled by those mirrors and the sudden arrival of pale strangers, many Shoshonis imagined Lewis and his men were "the children of the Great Spirit."

But not every Shoshoni in camp that night was filled with wonder and delight. There was a great deal of suspicion. A number of warriors believed that Lewis's party were really agents for the Blackfeet or some other hostile people. That fear was increased by the weapons carried by the explorers as well as by Lewis's request that the band go to Shoshoni Cove to aid Clark's party. Despite all the dancing and good cheer in camp that night, the Indians' fears were growing. Those fears would have to be confronted and resolved if the expedition was to gain the Shoshonis' cooperation.[28]

Knowing he had to give Clark's weary boat crews time to navigate the Beaverhead River as far as the forks, Lewis decided to spend a day at the Shoshoni camp. That extra day would serve Clark's needs as well as give Lewis an opportunity to gain additional geographical information from Cameahwait. The explorer spent most of the morning working on his journal and talking through Drouillard's signs with the chief. At midday Lewis decided to organize a Shoshoni move toward the rendezvous with Clark. Lewis wanted Cameahwait to provide porters and at least thirty horses to carry the expedition's baggage over Lemhi Pass and on to the Indian village. The chief seemingly agreed and, after a long speech to his warriors, told Lewis that everyone would be ready to move the next morning. That news, and a report from Drouillard that the Shoshonis had some four hundred fine horses and mules, gave Lewis reason to believe that his effort to gain Indian support was succeeding.[29]

Lewis had hoped that on the following morning, August 15, Cameahwait's band and their horses would be ready to make the journey back across the divide. But despite his efforts at gentle persuasion, it became increasingly clear throughout the morning that the Indians were reluctant to leave camp. Cameahwait repeatedly encouraged his people to leave their river village and follow Lewis, but the chief's efforts failed and an exasperated Lewis finally demanded to know what was wrong. As Cameahwait explained it, "Some foolish persons among them had suggested the idea that we were in league with the Pahkees [Siksika Blackfeet] and had come on in order to decoy them into an ambuscade where their enimies were waiting to receive them." While Cameahwait claimed that he did not share his warriors' apprehensions, the chief's behavior both that day and the next suggests that he was quite worried. For these Shoshonis there was ground for fear even if it infuriated Lewis. The band had suffered severe economic and personal losses at the hands of everyone from the Knife River Hidatsas to the Blackfeet. Outgunned and perhaps outmanned by an unknown force, the Indians had every reason to be wary.

At the same time, Lewis realized the necessity of Shoshoni cooperation in ferrying men and equipment over the pass and their overall support in providing horses if no water route to the Columbia could be found. Seeking both to reassure and prod the Shoshonis, Lewis told them he was disappointed in their lack of confidence in his good character. Aware of how much the Indians wanted manufactured goods, he threatened to block any future trade in guns and ammunition. As a final shot, the explorer raised doubts about the valor of Shoshoni men, saying that those who refused to help him were cowards. Lewis believed he had "touched the right string" when he questioned native courage. Whatever caused the turnabout, several warriors now joined Cameahwait and declared their readiness to make the trip. Theirs was not a popular decision, and as the joint Shoshoni-American party left camp "several of the old women were crying and imploring the great spirit to protect their warriors as if they were going to inevitable destruction."[30] As explorers and Indians camped that night at the upper end of Shoshoni Cove, Lewis might well have pondered his fate and that of the expedition if Clark's party did not appear the next day.

What should have been a pleasant reunion between Lewis and Clark on August

16 proved instead to be a day filled with tension, fear, and deception. Early in the morning, Lewis sent out Drouillard and Shields to do some hunting. Without meaning to, the explorer promptly increased the Shoshonis' suspicions when he asked the Indians to be quiet lest they frighten the game. Thinking that they were now the hunted quarry, two groups of Indians rode off down the cove to shadow Drouillard and Shields. It was not a good way to begin the day, and things soon became even more tense. As Lewis and Cameahwait made their way down through the cove, one of the Indian scouts came riding up the plain at full whip. Lewis's first thought was that by "some unfortunate accident" a hostile war party was in the neighborhood and had been confused with the main expedition group. All fears were quickly allayed when the Shoshoni announced his news, explaining that Drouillard had killed a deer and all were invited to feast on it. As hungry Indians ate the uncooked meat, Lewis took note that the fear of possible ambush had reduced the caravan to no more than twenty-eight men and three women. Since the women were expected to play the porter role, his count was not reassuring.

With the bloody meal over, Lewis carefully explained to Cameahwait just where the main body of the expedition would be encountered. The chief replied by placing skin tippets or mantles around the necks of the Americans. Although impressed with the tippets, Lewis believed that they were an attempt to disguise the explorers as one more move to prepare for a possible ambush. Not wanting to arouse any suspicions, he accepted the tippet and gave Cameahwait his army cocked hat. Wearing a buckskin shirt and sporting a dark summer tan, Lewis looked "a complete Indian." By now his central concern was that Clark would not be at the appointed place and that the Shoshonis would turn either violent or uncooperative. When the explorers and their Indian escort came to within two miles of the forks of the Beaverhead, Lewis could see that Clark's boats were not there. Genuinely worried, he watched as the Shoshonis cautiously slowed their pace. Writing later in his journal, the explorer admitted that he simply did not know what to do. With a determination bred of desperation, Lewis handed Cameahwait his gun, telling him that "if his enemies were in those bushes before him that he could defend himself with that gun." Lewis claimed that for his part he did not fear death and challenged Cameahwait to shoot him if the Americans were guilty of deception. Following Lewis's bold move, the other explorers gave their guns to the warriors. Lewis's quick thinking temporarily quieted the Shoshonis' fears. It also gave the captain time to seize on a second stratagem to retain the Indians' confidence. Recalling the notes he had tied to a stake as a means of communication with Clark, Lewis now claimed that the letters were actually written by Clark. Lewis boldly told Cameahwait that the expedition was having difficulty navigating the Jefferson and "was coming up slowly." Lewis later admitted that lying to the chief, although justified by the occasion, "set a little awkward."

Neither Lewis nor the Shoshonis slept well that night. Most of the Indians camped away from the fire light, hiding in the brush to avoid being caught in an enemy raid. Many of them continued to doubt the wisdom of trusting the strangers. Bitterness mounted against Cameahwait as several warriors charged the chief with exposing them to unnecessary danger. Perhaps seeing through some of Lewis's tales, some Shoshonis insisted that the Americans were telling different and contradictory stories. Still smarting from the recent Atsina raid, these wary warriors found only a fitful sleep. Lewis's night was no less troubled. Filled with gloomy thoughts, he turned over in his mind all the possible causes for Clark's delay. His greatest fear was that Clark had found the river so difficult that the main body had halted well below the forks. If Clark's group did not appear the next day, the Indians would abandon Lewis and his men. "I knew," wrote Lewis later, "that if these people left me that they would immediately disperse and secrete themselves in the mountains where it would be impossible to find them or at least in vain to pursue them and that they would spread the allarm to all other bands within our reach & of course we should be disappointed in obtaining horses, which would vastly retard and increase the labour of our voyage and I feared might so discourage the men as to defeat the expedition altogether." Feigning unconcern but in reality as worried as "the most affrighted Indian," Lewis tried to maintain the Indians' confidence with stories, told around a willow brush fire, of York, Sacagawea, and the great store of goods the Shoshonis would get in trade for their horses.[31] Among the many remarkable days and nights of the expedition, this day and its tension-filled night must have long remained in Lewis's memory. For the Lemhi Shoshonis, it was their last night before entering the world of white men.

Lewis's guess that Clark and the boat crews were having great difficulty navigating the Beaverhead River proved correct. Its swift current and shallow channel had tested the expedition's strength almost to the limit of endurance. Early on the morning of August 17, 1805, the boat crews set out for another day's battle with the Beaverhead. At the same time, Lewis nervously sent out Drouillard and an Indian companion with a note urging Clark to come on with all possible speed. By mid-morning Clark was at the forks of the Beaverhead. Anxious not to miss any trace of Lewis or the Indians, Clark, Charbonneau, and Sacagawea walked out ahead. About a mile from the forks, Clark saw several mounted Indians riding toward him. Sacagawea and Charbonneau, who had evidently gotten ahead of Clark, "began to dance and show every sign of joy" as they recognized the Shoshonis. Sacagawea sucked her fingers as a sign that these men belonged to her own people. As the explorer and the Shoshoni party neared each other, Clark recognized George Drouillard. The meeting took place with "great signs of joy." Some time later, as Clark moved up toward what would soon become Camp Fortunate, one of the Indians reported to Lewis that whites had been seen and were coming upriver. The stage was now set for a grand reunion and serious Shoshoni negotiations.

The arrival at Camp Fortunate had all the elements of pageantry and fictional romance. In his understated way, Lewis was "much gratifyed" by Clark's appearance. But there was nothing understated about the Indians' reception. Clark's hair was festooned with shells and he was subjected to the usual round of "national hugs." While Cameahwait was busy welcoming Clark as something akin to a visiting god, other Shoshonis watched in astonishment at the parade of men, boats, and equipment. Not only fascinated with clothing, guns, and canoes, the Indians gaped at York's blackness and "the segassity of Capt. Lewis's dog." In the midst of all this excitement there was another reunion yet more dramatic and improbable. As the baggage was being taken from the canoes, one of the three Shoshoni women in Lewis's group recognized Sacagawea. The two women had been captured in the same Hidatsa raid. No sooner had these two sat down than Sacagawea began to stare at Cameahwait. Suddenly recognizing him as her brother, "she jumped up, ran & embraced him, & threw her blanket over him and cried profusely." In a week that had seen tension, fear, deception, and determination, Sacagawea's homecoming was not out of place. Once again the stars had danced for Lewis and Clark.

Toward late afternoon, with baggage and people sorted out, the captains prepared for some serious talk with Cameahwait and the other Shoshoni chiefs. Sitting under an enclosure of willow brush and sail cloth, Lewis and Clark began their usual diplomatic litany. Not trusting to Drouillard's signs, the captains employed a cumbersome translation chain consisting of Sacagawea, Charbonneau, and François Labiche. By this means, Cameahwait was told "the objects which had brought us into this distant part of the country." But even more important than explaining the expedition's goals or fitting the Shoshonis into the American trade system was the need for Indian horses. Hoping to interest the Shoshonis in horse trading, the captains declared that their principal purpose for making so hazardous a journey was to discover a practical trade route for American merchandise. Because the trade could not begin until the explorers had fulfilled their mission, Lewis and Clark pointedly reminded Cameahwait it would be "mutually advantageous to them as well as to ourselves that they should render us such aids as they had it in their power to furnish to hasten our voyage and of course our return home."

Cameahwait certainly got the message. Faced with well-armed enemies and an uncertain supply of manufactured goods from Spanish sources, he could hardly reject the opportunity to have a place in the new American trade system. Guns and ammunition, especially, were on the chief's mind. Ordway counted only two or three guns and no ammunition among the warriors at Camp Fortunate. Cameahwait's personal war name, Too-et-te-con'l or Black Gun, was just one more indication of the special emphasis northern Shoshonis placed on firearms. Without thinking much about the consequences of arming the Shoshonis—consequences that would be felt by Hidatsa, Blackfeet, and Nez Perce warriors—Lewis and Clark made any promise in order to obtain the necessary horses. Cameahwait's apparent agreement to provide whatever was required was followed by the usual program of handing out medals to chiefs, distributing gifts to onlookers, and showing off the always impressive airgun.

Lewis and Clark finished the eventful day plotting strategy for crossing the Continental Divide and finding western waters. Their plan called for Clark, Charbonneau, Sacagawea, and eleven men to cross the divide and follow the Lemhi River. Charbonneau and Sacagawea were to remain at the Shoshoni village, organizing the Indians' efforts to carry expedition baggage over the pass. Clark and his men were to reconnoiter possible water routes to the Columbia. While these efforts were taking place west of the divide, Lewis proposed to remain at Camp Fortunate to supervise the transportation over Lemhi Pass. Both expedition parties would eventually join forces at the Lemhi River Shoshoni camp.[32]

The six days Lewis spent at Camp Fortunate were his first extended opportunity to study and record major features of northern Shoshoni culture. Lewis's descriptions of the objects that made up the daily life of the Indians revealed just how much he had learned during the Fort Mandan apprenticeship. With Sacagawea gone, Lewis lacked both a knowledgeable Shoshoni informant and a reliable translator. Nor could he depend on well-informed white traders like those at Fort Mandan. Rather, he had to rely on careful observation; an occasional detail would be added later by Sacagawea or Cameahwait. Despite such problems, Lewis discovered and recorded a vast store of information about Shoshoni life.[33]

Although Lewis had begun to note important aspects of Shoshoni life as early as August 13, it was not until August 19 that the explorer undertook a systematic description of Shoshoni material culture. Using the now-familiar categories first employed to analyze Upper Missouri villager ways, Lewis wrote about Shoshoni physical appearance, population, disease, clothing, and weapons. Hunting techniques, fishing methods, cooking pots, spoons, and tobacco pipes all were noted in the explorer's record. So long as there were objects for him to look at, Lewis was able to provide masterful descriptions. But when dealing with social values and personal relations, he tended to rely on traditional European stereotypes of Indians.

Because Lewis could handle clothing and observe it with his keen naturalist's eye, he filled his journal with words about moccasins, leggings, shirts, robes, and ornaments. Every piece of clothing, and often its method of construction, was described with his typical attention to detail. But no article in the Shoshoni wardrobe so captivated the explorer as the ermine tippet given to him by Cameahwait. Lewis described it as "the most eligant peice of Indian dress I ever saw."[34]

Always interested in weapons, Lewis took special note of the various kinds of Shoshoni bows and arrows. Recognizing that sacred forces were often attached to

certain weapons, Lewis took time to record the construction of and special ceremonies surrounding Shoshoni hide shields. As he explained it, the preparation of a
buffalo-hide shield required several days of feasting and ritual during which band
elders and shamans carefully worked the skin. If both the sacred and secular pro-
cesses were properly done, the Shoshonis believed that the shield would repel
arrows and bullets.[35]

Skilled at describing the shapes and uses of native objects, Lewis found it more
difficult to discuss the Indian band's social behavior without falling back on the
clichés used by Europeans for centuries. He depicted Shoshoni men as lazy husbands who mistreated their wives while lavishing attention on a favorite horse. He
saw Indian women as squaw drudges who did all the heavy work and hardly paused
during a supposedly painless childbirth. Indian parents spoiled their sons and sold
their daughters to the highest bidder. The explorer insisted that Shoshoni men and
women engaged in easy sex, and although he noted that virtue among women was
more valued than in the Missouri River villages, he asserted that it was not above
price. The expedition's commitment to ethnographic externals suited Lewis's skills
and some of his cultural biases. He could bring to life a weapon or a skin shirt, but
the people who created those objects always seemed just beyond his reach.

No place was that more plain than in Lewis's attempt to describe the Shoshoni
character. By the time Lewis and Clark reached the Shoshonis, the explorers had a
well-developed set of ideas about plains natives. The Missouri River villagers were
potential customers and allies to be courted and protected. They were, in Clark's
memorable phrase, "durtey, kind, pore, and extravigent." But buffalo and horse
plains people like the Sioux and Assiniboins held a very different place in the
explorers' minds. Those tribes were viewed as hostile, unreliable, and innately
violent. When Lewis attempted to evaluate the Shoshoni temperament, he was
caught between those negative judgments and the fact that he and others in the
expedition found much to admire about Cameahwait's people. Lewis's Shoshonis
were honest, well-behaved, and considerate. They would share food with strangers
without question even if there was little to go around. Lewis admired their personal
bravery and recognized the rough equality that made "every man a chief." But at
heart he saw Shoshoni men and women not as adults but as mercurial and ignorant
children. Angry at the necessity for Indian support to cross Lemhi Pass, Lewis
lamented the fate of the expedition "which appeared at this moment to depend in a
great measure upon the caprice of a few savages who are ever as fickle as the wind."
When he watched some starving Shoshonis eagerly eat raw venison, Lewis loftily
wrote, "I really did not untill now think that human nature ever presented itelf in a
shape so nearly allyed to the brute creation."[36] Some of the American party might
have reminded the captain how tasty white pudding or *boudin blanc,* made from
buffalo intestines, was when prepared by the skillful hands of Toussaint Charbon-

neau. Lewis's whole evaluation of the Shoshoni personality can be seen in one vivid journal entry. Writing on August 19, he declared that "from what has been said of the Shoshones it will be readily perceived that they live in a wretched stait of poverty. Yet notwithstanding their extreem poverty they are not only cheerful but even gay, fond of gaudy dress and amusements; like most other Indians they are great egotists and frequently boast of heroic acts which they never performed. They are also fond of games of wrisk. They are frank, communicative, fair in dealing, generous with the little they possess, extreemly honest, and by no means beggarly."[37] Lewis's Shoshonis were guileless children, fond of dressing up, telling tall tales, and too poor to know they ought to be unhappy without the blessings of civilization.

As Lewis made his catalog of Shoshoni culture, there was much he missed or misunderstood. During the long Fort Mandan winter, Lewis and Clark had heard a good deal about the Shoshonis, especially from Hidatsa informants. Although the captains understood that Shoshoni bands ranged over a wide territory, they did not know the considerable variety and diversity among Shoshonean peoples. Using Sacagawea and other northern Shoshoni captives as models, Lewis and Clark first imagined the Shoshonis to be a plains people something like the Teton Sioux bands but with a less warlike disposition. In fact, there were two very distinct traditions, two ways that joined to make Lemhi Shoshoni life.

Throughout the long days of searching for the Shoshonis beyond Three Forks, Lewis and Clark thought only of horses. But the mounted warrior and hunter was a quite recent development among Shoshoneans. By far the older tradition in northern Shoshoni life came out of the southern Great Basin, especially Nevada and Utah. Indians of the southern Shoshoni lifeway lived in small family groups, were hunter-gatherers, and built wickiup dwellings in a conical shape from brush and grass. Southern Shoshonis did not have horses, nor did they focus their lives on a warrior ideal. When Shoshoneans moved into Montana and Idaho some time in the six-teenth century, they carried that Great Basin culture with them. When Lewis and Clark saw Cameahwait's people eating fish and living in brush wickiups, the ex-plorers were witnessing the persistence of old ways.

But the northern Shoshonis were more than *ágaideka'a*, salmon eaters. In the years after 1700, with the introduction of the horse and contact with plains cultures, there was a revolution in northern Shoshoni life. That social and cultural upheaval turned pedestrian small-game hunters and fishermen into equestrian hunters of the buffalo and antelope. Changes in social values and organization paralleled the economic ones. After 1700 the northern Shoshonis developed a culture more like their plains neighbors than their Great Basin relatives. By regional standards, most northern Shoshonis were not the poverty-stricken people portrayed by the captains but rather well-to-do, possessing material goods and horses beyond the imagination of most Great Basin peoples. But the acceptance of the horse and some plains nomad traits did not mean that the old ways disappeared. The two traditions were not mutually exclusive. Lewis and Clark saw a people who scheduled their lives and habits to suit salmon runs west of the divide and buffalo herds east of it. Lewis provided in his journal entries a survey of the material culture of people whose lives were poised between a Great Basin past and a plains present. Skin tepees and brush lodges, salmon weirs and buffalo hunts all pointed to Indians who had achieved a balance in a difficult land.

Sandwiched between Lewis's ethnographic work at Camp Fortunate and Clark's difficult reconnaissance of the Salmon River country were two important conferences with Cameahwait. Described by Clark as "a man of Influence Sence & easey & reserved manners, [who] appears to possess a great deal of Cincerity," Cameahwait had proved to be a cooperative and friendly host.[38] The chief was willing to continue in that role, but he wanted specific things from the expedition in return for his help. And he had no intention of allowing the expedition's desires to thwart the needs of his people. All of this became plain as Clark entered Cameahwait's Lemhi River village on August 20. Ushered into the only skin tepee the band still had, Clark was fed berry cakes and salmon before beginning his talk with the chief. First, the explorer needed geographical information. The future of the expedition now depended on finding a practical route to western waters, whether that path required horses or canoes. Cameahwait listened intently to Clark's request for directions and then constructed a detailed relief map depicting the Lemhi, Salmon, and Bitterroot rivers as well as the Bitterroot Mountains. Cameahwait's report was both accurate and discouraging. Pressed further by Clark, the chief mentioned for the first time "persed nose Indians" who lived on a river "below the rocky mountains [which] ran a great way toward the setting sun and finally lost itself in a great lake of water which was illy tasted, and where the white men lived."

That was just the sort of news Clark was looking for, but he was not yet prepared to decide that this northwestern route was the most acceptable. Turning his attention to an old man said by Cameahwait to know much about the lands to the southwest, Clark asked him about possible trails to the sea in that direction. What Clark got was an image of barren terrain filled with hostile Bannock Indians and a route that eventually led to the Spanish domain. Promptly rejecting such a path, Clark returned to the suggestions offered by Cameahwait. The chief indicated that Nez Perce hunters made annual treks over the mountains to the Missouri. Although Cameahwait insisted that "the road was a very bad one" and lacked game, Clark quickly decided that if Indian hunters could make the crossing on short rations his men could do the same.

Cameahwait was certainly willing to provide Clark with vital geographical information and a guide named Old Toby, but in the chief's mind the meeting had a very different purpose. Faced with a food supply that was precarious and enemies who were well armed, Cameahwait wanted a serious talk about Shoshoni power, American trade, and plentiful supplies of manufactured goods. Although the Atsinas, Blackfeet, and Hidatsas had a ready access to firearms from Canadian traders, the Shoshonis were forced to rely on capturing an occasional gun. Shoshoni trade, which centered on Spanish goods obtained either through direct contact or Ute middlemen, did not provide the needed weapons. Spanish borderlands policy sought to keep weapons out of native hands. What Spanish policymakers saw as an effort to protect their borders and restrain Indians from killing each other was perceived by Cameahwait as "leaving them defenceless and an easy prey to their bloodthirsty neighbors to the east." Hunched over the council fire, "his ferce eyes and lank jaws grown meager for want of food," Cameahwait imagined how different Shoshoni destinies would be if he and his warriors had American guns. "We could then live in the country of the buffalo and eat as our enemies do and not be compelled to hide ourselves in these mountains and live on roots and berries as the bear do." Perhaps caught up in the intensity of that vision, Clark made promises impossible to keep and destined to anger other plains people. The explorer told Cameahwait that the Missouri River villagers had promised to stop raiding the Shoshonis. Clark knew that Hidatsa war parties had left their villages that very spring, but it was news he was not about to share. Restraining the Hidatsas was not possible, nor was it realistic for Clark to promise that Atsina and Blackfeet warriors might accept peace on the plains. Falling back on what was now firm expedition policy, Clark promised that "whitemen would come to them with an abundance of guns and every other article necessary to their defence and comfort." All the Shoshonis needed to do was provide American traders with fur, and the bounty of Western technology would be theirs. Clark did not realize that by arming the Shoshonis and making them fur-trade allies, he ensured bitter responses from the Blackfeet and the Atsinas.[39]

Two days later, as Clark's reconnaissance of the Salmon River country continued, Cameahwait, Charbonneau, Sacagawea, and some fifty Shoshoni men, along with unnumbered women and children, appeared at Camp Fortunate. Now it was Lewis's turn to trade words with the chief. Although the expedition's record for this meeting is not as full as for Clark's, it is plain that Cameahwait once again emphasized his insecure position and its consequences for the band's food supply. Lewis's reply was once again to stress the value of American trade and the possibilities it offered Shoshonis for a better life. Like Clark, Lewis made Cameahwait a promise of guns. To satisfy more immediate needs, the explorer provided corn, beans, and fish for the hungry band.[40] Had he been more observant, the captain might have realized that the demands for food were running counter to the needs of the expedition. At some point Cameahwait would be forced to decide between feeding his people or continuing to provide support for the explorers.

On August 24, after some delays, Lewis finally moved out of Camp Fortunate. What seemed to him an essential move must have worried Cameahwait. Just how long, he may have wondered, would his band have to wait before leaving for the Three Forks buffalo hunt? That worry grew into a full-scale confrontation with Lewis the following day. Early in the morning of the 25th, Cameahwait quietly sent some of his young warriors across the pass to the Lemhi River camp. These men were to round up the rest of the band, and all would then travel to their eastern hunting grounds. Cameahwait was not abandoning the expedition. He was simply responding to a food crisis among his own people. But Lewis knew none of this until late in the afternoon when Toussaint Charbonneau casually mentioned that he soon expected to see all the Shoshonis on their way east. Lewis was furious with Charbonneau for withholding vital information, but his real concern was to stop the Shoshoni move until the expedition was across the mountains and had the horses it needed. Lewis knew he needed to act quickly. Calling Cameahwait and two lesser chiefs to meet with him, the explorer bluntly asked whether they were honorable men whose word could be trusted. He forcefully reminded the chiefs of all their promises to aid the expedition across the divide and on to western waters. Not content to challenge their honor, Lewis resorted to a direct threat. "If they wished the whitemen to be their friends," he declared, "and to assist them against their enemies by furnishing them with arms and keeping their enemies from attacking them . . . they must never promise us anything which they did not mean to perform." After an awkward silence, the two lesser chiefs claimed that the decision was made by Cameahwait. Waiting a long time before replying, Cameahwait admitted that his decision had been wrong. The chief explained that he "had been induced to that measure from seeing all his people hungry." Lewis had seen the hunger too and had commented on it repeatedly. Cameahwait's choice had not deserved Lewis's harsh blast. That the chief finally chose honor over starvation deserved more credit than Lewis was willing to grant.[41]

The last act in the Shoshoni encounter was played out at the end of August when the captains were reunited at the Shoshoni village on the Lemhi River. Once the explorers decided to follow the advice of Old Toby and take their chances on the Nez Perce path over the mountains, there was a flurry of horse trading. Those days of bargaining reveal how quickly the Shoshonis learned to deal with the expedition as a captive market. In the earliest days of the encounter, the Indians were so fascinated with the explorers and their manufactured goods that they were willing to exchange a horse for an old checked shirt, a pair of worn leggings, and a knife. "The Indians," wrote Lewis, "seemed quite as well pleased with their bargain as I was."[42] But Shoshoni traders soon learned that they could get much more if they bargained more sharply. On the day Lewis moved out of Camp Fortunate he noticed some spare horses. Offering to trade for them, the explorer was bluntly told to display his wares before business could begin. Ragged clothing and mirrors were plainly not sufficient to attract the attention of the Indians. Digging deep into his store of trade goods, Lewis came up with objects that had been the staple of exchange at Fort Mandan. Those iron war axes that had so pleased village warriors had a similar effect on the Shoshonis. With the rate of exchange for horses now changing, Lewis was compelled to offer a battle-axe, a knife, a handkerchief, and some paint for one horse. For a Spanish mule, valued for its surefootedness, the American had to add another knife and some clothing.[43]

Once over Lemhi Pass and at the Indian village, Lewis began serious trading. On August 23, the first day of bargaining, it was plain that the free and easy days of cheap horses were long gone. Lewis was forced to pay increasingly larger amounts of merchandise for each horse. He had no choice but to accept the Indians' demands. On the second trading day, Lewis bought five or six more mounts and paid a considerable price for each one. When Clark joined Lewis on August 29, he had to offer his pistol, a knife, and one hundred rounds of ammunition for one horse. Offering guns for horses was a sure indication of both the expedition's need and the Shoshonis' trading skill. Despite their best efforts, the captains did not prove to be especially astute traders. When Clark carefully examined the twenty-nine horses in the expedition's corral, he found them to be "nearly all sore backs, and several pore, and young."[44] Lewis and Clark had paid dearly for castoffs of the Shoshoni herd. The Shoshonis had proven to be better Yankee traders than the Americans.

Led now by Old Toby, the expedition struggled along the north fork of the Salmon River through country made difficult by heavy timber, steep hills, and dense thickets. Progress was slowed as horses slipped and fell. A snow and sleet storm made the going even more treacherous. The explorers had heard about the Flathead Indians during the winter with the Mandans. The Shoshonis had indicated that the Flatheads might be met as the expedition moved north, but since the Flatheads regularly joined Shoshoni bands for hunting across the mountains at this season, a meeting this late in the year seemed unlikely. Nevertheless, on September 4, as the expedition crossed Lost Trail Pass and entered the Bitterroot Valley, the Americans encountered a large Flathead Indian camp in a place known later as Ross's Hole.

Lewis and Clark's progress toward the Flathead camp had not gone unnoticed. Early that morning an old chief named Three Eagles had grown concerned about possible raiding parties who might steal the band's horses. Out scouting during the day, Three Eagles was the first to see the expedition. Hiding in the brush, he was both bewildered and concerned by the sight. Here were men and horses moving along without any effort to conceal their presence. Seeing that they had no blankets, the Flathead assumed they were a group of travelers who had been robbed by hostile Indians. Uncertain of the strangers' intentions, he hurried back to camp to warn his people.

Still apprehensive about the strangers, Three Eagles returned to a stand of timber where he could watch without being seen. As the Americans drew closer, Three Eagles caught sight of York, whose face, he supposed, was painted black in preparation for war. The Indian assumed that the expedition must have recently emerged from a battle in which they had lost only their blankets. Now convinced that the strangers would soon come upon the Indian camp, Three Eagles once again returned to spread the warning. Because the expedition did not act like a war party, the Flathead chiefs decided to remain quiet and wait for the strangers to arrive in the valley.[45]

Throughout the day the expedition had seen fresh signs indicating that Indians were nearby. Toward evening the party entered Ross's Hole and saw thirty-three lodges dotting the valley floor. Already convinced that the Americans were not a war party, the Indians greeted Lewis and Clark with a Flathead version of the "national hug" employed by the Shoshonis. While the captains were ceremoniously conducted to Flathead tepees, the rest of the expedition was offered what little food could be found. Because it was late, serious talk had to be postponed until the following day.

Those Indians whom Lewis and Clark and their men insisted on calling the Flatheads were, in fact, Salish-speaking people. They later told the captains that they were Ootlashoots of the Tushepaw nation. "Ootlashoot" was probably from the Salish word for red willow, the native name for the Bitterroot River. The name Flathead proved to be a source of endless confusion from its first appearance in the expedition's records. The Salish seen by Lewis and Clark did not practice head flattening, a fact quickly pointed out by Clark in conversation with Nicholas Biddle. The captains first heard about the Flatheads while at Fort Mandan, and Clark's 1805 map places them approximately where they were found in September 1805. The name Flathead appears to have been the result of interpreting the visual sign language gesture for the Salish. They were signed by pressing both sides of the head with the hands in a flattening motion.

Much of Flathead life was like the cycle of the Shoshoni year. The Ootlashoots maintained close ties with the Lemhi Shoshonis and joined them each year for the Three Forks buffalo hunt. Flathead culture was an adoptive way of life. By the time the captains came to Ross's Hole, these Salish speakers had created a lifeway that blended their plateau past with many plains traits. After 1700, Flathead life became increasingly dominated by horse and buffalo patterns. Perhaps the most significant difference between the Flatheads and their Shoshoni neighbors was language. Both Clark and Ordway noted the difference on the first night in the valley. For Ordway,

Salish speakers sounded as if they were lisping or had "a bur on their tongue." The sergeant speculated that this odd way of speaking meant the Flatheads were really the long lost Welsh Indians! Without knowing it, the expedition had passed from the Uto-Aztecan language family, to which Shoshoni belonged, to the Salish family. What Clark graphically described as "a gugling kind of language spoken much thro the throat" was in fact Salish.[46]

Lewis and Clark did not intend to spend much time among the Flatheads. The Indians were in a hurry to join their Shoshoni hunting partners and the expedition was anxious to make their mountain passage. Thursday, September 5, was a busy day filled with talk and trade, both of which were made difficult by translation problems. Neither Old Toby nor Sacagawea spoke Salish. As luck would have it, among the Flatheads was a Shoshoni boy who had been taken captive by some northern raiding party, was later freed by the Flatheads, and now lived with them. Using the boy's language skills, the captains constructed a translation chain that required each word to pass through the captains' English, Labiche's French, Charbonneau's Hidatsa, Sacagawea's Shoshoni, and on to the boy's Salish. By this cumbersome means, the explorers briefly explained their mission, awarded several medals and flags, and generally made friends. But the real business of the day was horse swapping. The Flatheads generously took a number of worn-out horses in exchange for some of their healthy and "ellegant" ones. Twelve good mounts were added to the expedition's herd. During the day Clark took time to note Flathead hair and clothing styles, observing that they were quite similar to Shoshoni fashions. Whitehouse probably spoke for many when he found the Flatheads to be "the likelyest and honestst Savages we have ever yet Seen."[47]

The following day the expedition did some more horse dealing, adding two fine animals to the herd. Meanwhile, Lewis struggled to draft a Salish vocabulary. According to Whitehouse, many believed such a vocabulary would prove once and for all time whether these Indians were descendants of Prince Madoc and the Welsh Indians. Here so many miles from the Missouri were echoes still of that persistent myth which had the power to capture the imaginations of men as different as John Evans and Thomas Jefferson. Working in a steady drizzle, the expedition's horse handlers hurried to lighten loads and tighten packsaddle cinches. At mid-afternoon, as the rain let up, a memorable cavalcade marched out of Ross's Hole. The expedition pressed on north while the Flatheads galloped out for Three Forks and the buffalo hunt.[48]

The next three weeks held some of the most demanding and dangerous days in the history of the Corps of Discovery. After spending a brief time at Travelers' Rest, the explorers turned west to hazard the Lolo Trail across the Bitterroot Mountains. Talks with Old Toby and Cameahwait had prepared Lewis and Clark for a difficult crossing. But information from two Flatheads met near Travelers' Rest had taken the sting out of the Shoshonis' warnings. The Flatheads insisted that the trail took only five days and would bring the expedition directly to Indians who were Flathead relatives. Heartened by those words, the explorers marched out to cross what Gass called "the most terrible mountains I ever beheld."[49]

From the beginning, the Lolo Trail proved a cruel and unforgiving passage. A clearly marked, well-traveled trail at the outset, it soon became a faint trace often lost in a tangle of fallen timber and dense thickets. Serious trouble struck on September 14 when Old Toby's memory failed and he led the party off the main track, down a fishing path, and to the Lochsa River. On short rations already, the expedition killed one of their horses and remembered how lost and hungry they were by naming a nearby stream Killed Colt Creek. In order to rejoin the trail, the explorers had to make a painful climb up the side of Wendover Ridge. Horses slipped and fell, rolling down in tangles of brush and broken equipment. For hungry and bone-tired explorers, the Lolo was already coming to symbolize the kind of physical challenge they had not experienced since the days at the Great Falls portage and on the Beaverhead River.

Monday, September 16, was perhaps the grimmest day in the expedition's memory. Sleeping on any level places they could find, the explorers awoke to find themselves covered with a heavy blanket of snow. Whitehouse caught the general mood that morning as he watched men without stockings fumble in the cold to wrap rags around already numb feet. Gasping for breath in the thin air, the expedition marched thirteen painful miles "with great dificulty." Clark, never one to complain in the face of adversity, admitted, "I have [never] been [as] wet and as cold in every part . . . in my life." With no end in sight, there would be another night sleeping in the snow and struggling to survive on meager rations.

By the night of September 17, it was plain that drastic measures had to be taken. The expedition was nearing the limits of its physical endurance. Believing that Nez Perce territories were just ahead, the captains decided that Clark would press ahead with a small band of hunters while Lewis worked to bring along the main group. On the morning of September 18, Clark and his men set out toward a broad valley they could see in the distance. Ahead lay two more days of difficult going. Rescue from the bitter snows was now at hand, but few would forget what Gass called "this horrible mountainous desert."[50]

Sometime on September 20, Clark and his hunters at last escaped the Lolo Trail and broke out on a small upland plain known afterward as Weippe Prairie. Long a gathering place for Nez Perce families to dig and cook camas roots and fish in the nearby Clearwater River, the prairie was filled with signs of Indian activity. Riding some three miles through the plain, Clark and his men could see many Nez Perce lodges in the distance. When the Americans were within a mile of the first cluster of lodges, they suddenly came upon three young Indians. Seeing the strangers and fearing a raid, the boys scattered and hid in the high prairie grass. Clark worried lest they alarm the village and make the first expedition–Nez Perce meeting a troubled one. He quickly dismounted, handed his gun to one of the hunters, and began to search the tall grass. That hasty search turned up two very frightened boys. To quiet their fears, Clark gave each one several small pieces of ribbon and then urged them with gestures to announce the arrival of friendly visitors in their village.

Clark's party waited nervously as the boys hurried away. A short time later, one man emerged from the village and walked cautiously toward the explorers. The Nez Perce used signs to invite the Americans into a large tepee. He explained that the lodge belonged to the band's chief Broken Arm, now absent on a raid. Most of the men in the band were with the chief and would not return for two weeks. By now Clark and his men were surrounded by a few elderly men and many women, all eager to see the bearded strangers. Although the Nez Perces had heard about white men, only a handful had ever seen them. Clark sensed that curious Nez Perce eyes betrayed both fear and genuine pleasure. Why they might have been pleased to greet the Corps of Discovery did not become clear until later. But now food was the order of the day and pieces of buffalo, dried salmon, and camas bread were passed around. Not knowing the consequences of that diet, Clark and the others ate the camas with unthinking abandon. After handing out a few small gifts, the captain moved on to the second Nez Perce camp.

At the second camp, a cluster of fifteen lodges, Clark finally had time to take note of the Indians around him. Although Nez Perce dress and ways seemed similar to what he had seen at Ross's Hole, Clark's ears told him that Nez Perce language was quite different from the Salish spoken by Flatheads. Without knowing it, the explorers had crossed an important linguistic boundary and were now in the territory of Sahaptian speakers. Clark recorded that these Indians called themselves "Chopunnish or Pierced noses." Chopunnish may have been Clark's fractured effort to spell "Sahaptian," the Salish word used by Flatheads and their neighbors to describe the Nez Perces as "those who lived to the south."[51] Looking at Nez Perce men, Clark found them large and "portly" while the women appeared small and "handsome featured." With an eye toward future trade, Clark noted Nez Perce bead-color preferences (blue and white) and the ornamental uses for brass and copper. Perhaps remembering how good camas bread tasted, Clark took time to record the method Indian women used to steam the roots and prepare the bread. Later in the evening the explorer began to regret his healthy appetite. As it would for days, the root bread produced diarrhea and painful intestinal gas. Clark may have made a mental note to warn Lewis not to eat the bread![52]

On the following day, Clark dispatched hunters to find something to vary the camas and fish diet while he stayed with his Nez Perce host. The captain hoped to settle any Indian fears about the expedition's intentions and obtain much needed information about the route ahead. Anxious to help, a Nez Perce chief drew a hasty chart of the Clearwater and Snake rivers. Clark was told about the Great Falls of the Columbia and also led to believe that whites lived at the falls, where the Nez Perces obtained beads and metal goods. Although the Indians did trade for beads, copper, and brass at The Dalles and the Celilo Falls, there were, in fact, no white traders in the territory so jealously guarded by Wishram and Wasco Indian middlemen. Probably a misinterpretation of sign language was to blame here. When Clark asked for additional information, he was told that a more important chief named Twisted Hair was at a fishing camp farther up the Clearwater. After purchasing some extra provisions and sending Reuben Field back toward the Lolo Trail to locate Lewis, he made his way to Twisted Hair's camp.

Traveling over unfamiliar ground without an Indian guide, Clark became lost in the darkness. Fortunately, he stumbled on a Nez Perce man who was willing for the price of one handkerchief to direct the explorer toward Twisted Hair's camp. It was close to midnight when Clark finally reached the fishing camp. Twisted Hair, properly known as Walammottinin, meaning "hair or forelock bunched and tied," was about sixty-five years old, "a Cheerful man with apparant siencerity." Clark's first meeting with Twisted Hair was cordial, and both men smoked together well into the night.

Among the women and children at Twisted Hair's camp was an elderly woman named Watkuweis. In the first draft of his journal for that day, Clark took note of her presence, explaining that she "had formerly been taken by the Minitarries of the North & seen white men." Her name did not appear in his revised journal entry. Clark did not know how important the old woman had been in insuring a friendly reception for the expedition. Watkuweis, whose name meant "returned from a far country," had been captured by Blackfeet or Atsina raiders sometime late in the eighteenth century. Taken into Canada, she had been purchased by a trader and had lived for several years among whites before finding her way home. Watkuweis had been treated well and had never lost her favorable impression of whites. When Clark came to Twisted Hair's camp, Watkuweis urged her people to treat the expedition with all hospitality. Nez Perce oral tradition records that when Watkuweis heard of Clark's arrival, she said, "These are the people who helped me. Do them no hurt."[53]

But the Nez Perce welcome was based on more than the word of a former captive. Like their Flathead and Shoshoni neighbors, the Nez Perce bands were desperate to obtain guns and ammunition. As weapons from Canadian traders fell into Blackfeet and Atsina hands, Indians without firearms found their situation increasingly precarious. Nez Perce buffalo hunters were threatened, and undefended villages were at risk. Faced with an urgent need to find guns, three warriors from Broken Arm's band had joined Crow traders in a journey to the Knife River Hidatsa towns. That trip, made in the spring of 1805, brought the Nez Perces their first six guns as well as news of Lewis and Clark. More than anything else, it was the need for guns that conditioned the Nez Perces' behavior toward the expedition. The desire for trade and the words of Watkuweis made the expedition's first encounter with the Nez Perces a friendly one.[54]

September 22 was the day of grand reunion for the Lewis and Clark parties. While Clark spent most of the morning with Twisted Hair and his son, Lewis and his contingent traveled the last few painful miles along the Lolo Trail. Early in the afternoon, the main party came off the trail and was met by Reuben Field. At about five o'clock, Lewis's group reached the first Weippe Prairie village. When all the Indian women hurried to gather their children and flee on horseback into the woods, Lewis was plainly worried since Clark was supposed to have prepared the Indians for his arrival. Lewis feared that moving the women and children out of range now was the first step in a hostile action. But his fears were stemmed when several unarmed men emerged from the village carrying gifts of camas bread for the expedition.

Just at sunset, Clark walked up to the first Nez Perce village to find the main party "much fatigued and hungry." Recalling his own unpleasant experience with the camas bread and fish diet, Clark "cautioned them of the consequences of eating too much." In the twilight, Weippe Prairie was covered with inquisitive Nez Perces, all anxious to catch a glimpse of the strangers and their fascinating equipment. That fascination was evidently too much for some Nez Perces because later Reuben Field discovered his knife, compass, fire steel, and gun wiping rod were missing. Ready to overlook minor pilfering, Lewis and Clark were intent on obtaining accurate geographical information from the Nez Perces. But communication was difficult since neither Old Toby nor Sacagawea could speak Nez Perce. Although forced to rely on sign language, the captains managed to obtain valuable data about the way ahead. Twisted Hair took a whitened elk skin and drew an accurate map of the rivers that would take the expedition to the Columbia. The chief claimed a bit optimistically that five days of travel would take the Americans to the Falls of the Columbia and places where white traders lived. Always the cautious cartographer, Clark finished the evening gathering "maps of the Country & river with the Situation of Indians, Towns from Several men of note Seperately which varied verry little."[55]

Lewis and Clark did not intend to remain long among the Nez Perces, no matter how friendly they were. With the Columbia and Pacific waters so close, the explorers were anxious to find winter quarters somewhere along the coast. The expedition's most immediate needs were to replenish food supplies and exchange horses for canoes. There might be time for some ritual diplomacy, but linguistic and ethnographic studies would have to wait until the return trip. On September 23, Lewis and Clark called a council at the first Nez Perce village. Although Broken Arm was still absent on a raid, other chiefs joined Twisted Hair in listening to the captains recite the usual formulas of United States Indian policy. But efforts to inform the Nez Perce chiefs of American intentions were hampered by translation problems and once again all relied on Drouillard's signs. With serious diplomacy cut to a minimum, gifts of tobacco, clothing, flags, and medals had to convey the expedition's message. Just what Twisted Hair and his fellow chiefs gathered from the conference remains unclear, but Clark claimed that the gifts and American policies "appeared to satisfy them much." Determined to cultivate friendship with the Americans, the Nez Perce diplomats might have been more satisfied with direct talk about guns.

While the diplomats were occupied in exchanging gestures and gifts, most of the expedition was busy trading for food and getting to know their Nez Perce neighbors. John Ordway's usual eye for telling details did not fail him as he caught sight of copper kettles and other metal goods obtained from middle Columbia traders. The sergeant also noticed something that indicated the adoptive nature of so many plateau peoples: among the plains-style skin tepees were reed or "flag" lodges reminiscent of those seen in Shoshoni country. But ethnography was not the order of the day. Trade for camas, dried fish, and berries was far more important, and the Nez Perces were eager to barter for precious cloth and metal. Blue beads were the most sought-after commodity, but Whitehouse saw real Indian interest in "a small piece of red cloth, as wide as a mans hand." Although Clark later complained that the Nez Perces were "very selfish and stingey," both peoples appeared pleased with their trade bargains.[56]

Lewis and Clark planned to brand their horses, leave them with the Indians, and begin canoe building as quickly as possible. The Nez Perces were no hindrance to that plan, but their food was. In the evening after the conference, Lewis and two men began to suffer from severe gastrointestinal distress. Whether it was the change in diet or bacteria in the food is not clear, but the consequences were serious. Constant debilitating diarrhea and gas pains sometimes so pressing as to make breathing difficult afflicted others in the expedition. On September 24, when the captains wanted to get closer to the Clearwater River, many men were sick and Lewis himself was "scarcely able to ride on a jentle horse." Explorers who had weathered the Great Falls portage and the Lolo Trail were now lying along the path doubled over with pain and too weak to walk.[57] Despite the fact that he was still unwell, Clark joined Twisted Hair and two of his sons in searching for good canoe timber and a boat-building site close to the river. The place they found was a narrow pine bottom on the south side of the river, opposite the junction of the north fork of the Clearwater and the main stem.

Despite widespread illness, the expedition made their canoe-building camp on September 26 and began to work. It quickly became apparent that the small axes Clark distributed were simply inadequate for the task. Not enough able workers and the wrong tools made progress slow. Looking to the Nez Perces for help, the expedition followed Indian practice in making dugout canoes by burning the centers of the logs. Even with that labor-saving technique, it took the Americans ten days to construct five canoes. If Nez Perce technology made the construction possible, Nez Perce skill of another sort was to be available for the journey on to the Columbia. Twisted Hair and a younger chief named Tetoharsky had promised to accompany the expedition and serve as intermediaries between the explorers and the Sahaptian-speaking peoples.[58]

Toward midafternoon on October 7, the Lewis and Clark expedition was at last prepared to begin the final leg of its journey to the western sea. With canoes loaded, balanced, and in the water, all seemed ready to seek the Columbia and a saltwater tide. Disappointed that the two Nez Perce chiefs had not yet appeared, the captains decided that they could wait no longer. It was not until the next day that Twisted Hair and Tetoharsky joined the expedition. No sooner had the Nez Perce guides appeared than Old Toby and his son left. Deciding that their term of enlistment was complete, the Shoshonis were last seen running along the riverbank, having neither announced their departure nor waited to be paid. Just why Old Toby fled is not clear, although Gass believed that a canoe accident in dangerous rapids earlier in the day frightened the Indian. Old Toby may have been equally concerned about traveling farther among unknown and potentially hostile tribes.[59]

On the night that Old Toby slipped away, the expedition and its Indian contingent stopped to make camp along the Clearwater River. Feeling stronger now and filled with the expectation that their canoes would soon ride in saltwater, the explorers were ready to celebrate. Gathered around blazing fires, they joined hands with the Nez Perces and "were very merry." The whine of Pierre Cruzatte's fiddle and the shouts of dancing men cut the chilly air. Frenchmen like Labiche and Drouillard enjoyed roasted dog while others picked at salmon and camas staples. But the night suddenly became stranger when a Nez Perce woman was seized by an apparent fit. Shouting and singing, she attempted to give gifts of camas roots and brass bracelets to one of the startled Americans. When the gifts were refused, the woman angrily cut her arms with sharp flint. What Clark and Ordway recorded as a seizure was perhaps the woman's *Wyakin* or guardian spirit at work. Whatever the cause, the entire night was both festive and disconcerting.[60] In the firelight and shadows it was time to remember how far they had all come since the winter with the Mandans. While Cruzatte's fiddle music accompanied Nez Perce shrieks, there may have been a moment to recall Cameahwait's lean face as he talked about guns or to recall the strange gurgling sound of Salish speakers at Ross's Hole, who many thought were the long-lost Welsh Indians. But retrospective romance was never the stock-in-trade of the expedition. Tomorrow promised to be another demanding day on the river.

7

Down the Columbia

"Our Situation well calculated to defend our selves from any designs of the natives,
Should they be enclined to attack us."
—WILLIAM CLARK, 1805

When Lewis and Clark pulled out of the Nez Perce Clearwater villages in boats in early October, they were moving toward worlds wholly unlike any they had yet experienced. In the next two months the expedition left the mountains and ponderosa pines of the plateau and sailed through the awesome and seemingly desolate Columbia Plain. Navigating hazardous rivers, the Corps of Discovery paddled the Clearwater to the Snake and on at last to the Columbia. Driven to reach the western sea before winter and challenged by treacherous white water, Lewis and Clark had little time to describe the dark-walled canyons and treeless plains around them. But in one memorable passage, Clark tried to capture something of the strange landscape. "The face of the Countery on both Side of the river above and about the falls," wrote the captain, "is Steep ruged and rockey open and contain but a Small preportion of herbage, no timber a fiew bushes excepted."[1] But below the Cascades of the Columbia the terrain and climate once again changed dramatically. Rain, fog, and dense ground cover all signaled that Lewis and Clark had at last reached a marine environment. They were in territory that received more than sixty inches of rain annually, more than six times the amount that fell on the land they had seen around The Dalles. Days marked by high winds, terrifying storms, monotonous meals of pounded salmon, and a damp that rotted clothing and tents pointed to what lay ahead during the winter at Fort Clatsop.[2]

Moving through climates and landforms striking for their abrupt changes tested the expedition's endurance, as did the Columbia itself. But even more striking were the physical and cultural differences among the Indians down the river and toward the coast. At the confluence of the Snake and the Columbia, Lewis and Clark entered an Indian world increasingly distant from the plains traditions that had been so much a part of expedition-Indian relations since those early days along the Missouri. On the Columbia, salmon was king and fishing the enterprise that gave shape to native life. Large houses with wooden frames, clothing a strange admixture of native and European fashions, graceful canoes with "curious images" at their bows, and practices like head-flattening—all pointed to a native environment dominated by Pacific ways.

To these sights were added the strange clucking sounds of the Chinookan speakers and the smells of tons of stacked salmon drying in warm winds blowing up the Columbia gorge. In flea-infested plank houses or at hastily made camps along the river, Lewis and Clark contended with Indians long accustomed to dealing with English, American, and native traders. The Columbia River Sahaptians and Chinookans could outbargain the sharpest Yankee in dealing for dog meat or precious firewood. In those transactions it was the Indian middleman—whether Wishram or Chinook—who expected to set the price, while outsiders of whatever cultural stripe were to pay or go without. An unfamiliar material culture coupled with hard bargaining methods a bit too close to home hinted that relations with the Indians in the Pacific Northwest were going to be distant at best and troubled at worst.

But much if not all of this was unimagined during the first days of travel beyond Canoe Camp. For nearly a week the expedition struggled with the twists, turns, and rapids of the Clearwater and Snake. As Lewis and Clark neared the Columbia-Snake confluence, they constantly had to deal with dangerous rocks, capsized canoes, and wet gear. Fully occupied in navigating through the many Snake River rapids, the explorers perhaps missed the subtle signs that they were approaching the eastern edge of the great Columbia Plain. One indication they did record was the growing scarcity of firewood. The Indians who lived along the Clearwater and upper Snake very carefully gathered and stacked whatever wood was available. On October 14, at Pinetree Rapids on the Snake some thirty miles below the Palouse River, the Americans were so short of wood that they asked their two Nez Perce guides for permission to take and burn some of the Indians' wood.[3]

If hints of coming changes in land and climate were overlooked, it was harder to miss the human clues pointing to a life where salmon replaced buffalo. During the six days before coming to the Columbia, the party passed dozens of fishing villages. Those villages, typically containing four brush lodges, were located about eight to ten miles apart at good fishing runs. In the summer, lodges were built with willows and rushes in a style that may have reminded the explorers of Shoshoni wickiups. Winter lodges made with split pine rails wore a more permanent face. Attracting more of the expedition's attention were the graveyards prominently located in many villages. Unlike scaffold burial places seen on the plains, these cemeteries were marked by picket fences surrounding bodies interred in the earth.[4]

From their Nez Perce guides Lewis and Clark knew that they were quite close to the Snake-Columbia confluence and the territories of Indians having little contact with whites. Thus informed, the captains prepared for what proved to be the first of many meetings with Indians down the Columbia. Twisted Hair and Tetoharsky were sent ahead on October 14 to announce the expedition's advance. Those Sahaptians scouted by the chiefs were known to Lewis and Clark as Sokulks and Chimnapams. The Sokulks proved to be Wanapams who lived on the Columbia above the Snake-Columbia confluence, while the Chimnapams were Yakimas whose villages dotted the great river around present-day Pasco, Washington.[5]

Twisted Hair and Tetoharsky did their advance work skillfully; on October 16 near the Snake-Columbia junction, Clark saw five Indians coming upriver "in great haste." Anxious to make a good first impression, the captains brought out tobacco and smoked with the new arrivals. Each was given additional tobacco to distribute among other Indians. The native party, either Yakimas from nearby villages or visiting Wanapams, eagerly took the tobacco and hurried back to spread the news of an impending great event.

By midday the expedition was at the Snake-Columbia confluence and, as had so often happened on the Upper Missouri, the Americans quickly became objects of intense curiosity. Scores of Yakimas and Wanapams lined the riverbanks to stare in astonishment at the bearded strangers and all their fascinating baggage. Those Indian sightseers bold enough to approach Lewis and Clark were rewarded with small twists of tobacco. As the Indians watched closely, the explorers made camp and waited for official delegations from the river peoples.

Later in the evening, the expedition was treated to a spectacle the likes of which they had not seen since their grand welcome by Cameahwait's Shoshonis. Led by their chief Cutssahnem, two hundred Wanapam men came striding into the American camp singing and beating on small drums. In the firelight the Wanapams formed a half circle and continued to chant a festive greeting. After the obligatory smoke, the captains got down to serious talk with Cutssahnem. But as was so often the case in the Northwest, Lewis and Clark were handicapped by translation difficulties. American intentions were explained in signs to Twisted Hair and Tetoharsky, who then had to be relied upon to present a faithful summary to their fellow Sahaptian speakers. Lewis and Clark wanted the Wanapams and Yakimas to know "our friendly disposition to all nations, and our joy in Seeing those of our friendly Children around us." If the Nez Perce translators failed to get the message across, the explorers knew from long experience that gifts were a powerful declaration of "friendly disposition." For Cutssahnem there was a large medal, a shirt, and a handkerchief. An unnamed "second chief" and a headman from one of the Wanapam villages were given smaller medals. With all parties properly welcomed and in good spirits, the Americans ended the day by purchasing eight fat dogs, some dried salmon, and twenty pounds of dried horsemeat.[6]

The junction of the Snake and the Columbia rivers had long been a favorite place for Yakimas and Wanapams to gather for fishing, trading, and visiting. Lewis and Clark decided to camp for an additional day or two at the junction to repair broken equipment, dry dampened papers, and purchase additional provisions. On the morning of October 17, while Cutssahnem and several of his principal men traded dogs and vocabulary phrases with Lewis, Clark took two men in a small canoe for a short reconnaisance up the Columbia. The mat-lodge fishing villages and drying scaffolds he saw along the banks were of the sort that would be described in the expedition's records for many days to come. At one cluster of lodges, Clark stopped for a closer look. In one house he found a busy crowd of men, women, and children. Seemingly unafraid of their uninvited guest, the Wanapams politely offered Clark a sitting mat and some boiled salmon "on a platter of rushes neetly made." As Clark enjoyed his meal and the good company, he took careful note of his hosts' clothing, manners, and physical characteristics.

Once back at camp, Clark found time to write an extended commentary on the river folk. Following the categories that were now an integral part of expedition ethnography, he described their bodies, dress, and houses. His observations on Wanapam and Yakima clothing and ornament were written with his characteristic eye for detail. What especially captured Clark's attention that day were three barely related but arresting facets of native life. Following directions from Jefferson and Rush that economic relations between males and females be carefully noted, the explorers generally repeated the white wisdom proclaiming Indian women "squaw drudges" to tyrannical husbands. Along the Columbia, the explorers found societies in which the sharing of labor between men and women was much more in evidence. Those societies placed considerable emphasis on age and wisdom. At one mat lodge Clark met a centenarian who sat at the best place in the house, and "when She spoke great attention was paid to what she said." Mat lodges, so unlike Mandan earth lodges or plains tepees, also called for written description. Later in their Columbia voyage, the explorers would see large plank houses and pit dwellings, but from the Snake-Columbia confluence to The Dalles mat lodges were the most common native architecture. Clark noted that the houses measured from fifteen to sixty feet long and were "generally of an oblong sqare form." The whole dwelling was supported by interior poles and forks. Openings along the roof allowed smoke from cooking fires to escape. Quick to see the relationship between house design and climate, Clark noted that flat roofs "proves to me that rains are not common in this open country." Perhaps thinking of the kinds of medical information so eagerly sought by Benjamin Rush, Clark recorded the eye ailments and dental peculiarities present among river people. Looking over his new-found native friends, the explorer pronounced them "of a mild disposition and friendly disposed."[7]

The time taken with Indians at the Snake-Columbia junction was well spent because it allowed for repairing equipment and gathering vital geographic information. From Cutssahnem the explorers obtained a charcoal-on-skin map "of the rivers and Tribes above on the great river and its waters on which he put great numbers of villages of his nation and friends." An unnamed Yakima chief who joined the council on October 18 offered a second map of the same territory and its people. These maps and the numbers of people seen around the confluence made it plain to Lewis and Clark that daily encounters with Indians were to be expected. As the expedition left the junction and began to navigate the Columbia, Twisted Hair and Tetoharsky were sent on ahead again to prepare the way. When the two Nez Perce scouts returned later in the day and found the expedition past the Walla Walla River and ready to camp in present-day Washington, they carried news of chief Yelleppit and the Walla Walla Indians.[8]

Relayed by the Nez Perce guides, the greeting Lewis and Clark got that evening from the Walulas or Walla Wallas and their chief Yelleppit was as enthusiastic as that offered earlier by Cutssahnem and his kin. Yelleppit's message of welcome included an offer of scarce firewood as an additional sign of friendship. Later that night the chief and some twenty of his men came upriver and made camp a short distance from the explorers.

Early the next morning Yelleppit, two other Walula chiefs, and a chief from either a Cayuse or a Umatilla band appeared in camp for a grand council. Yelleppit was an imposing figure, described by Clark as "a bold handsom Indian, with a dignified countenance about 35 years of age, about 5 feet 8 inches high and well perpotioned." Struggling as always with translations, the explorer-diplomats did the best they could with signs to convey their "friendly intentions towards our red children perticelar those who opened their ears to our Councils." Lewis and Clark's words were not recorded, but the Walula chief probably heard the usual diplomatic speech directed to Indians. Presentations of a medal, a handkerchief, some wampum for Yelleppit, and additional strings of wampum for the other chiefs were all part of the expedition's good-will ritual.

Fascinated by the explorers and impressed with their store of goods, Yelleppit asked them to remain a day longer so that all his people could see them. His request betrayed something more than just native curiosity about whites. The chief had his eye on the weapons and goods carried by the explorers. If European objects were already in Walula hands (and no expedition diarist mentioned seeing any such until further downriver) they surely came from other Indian traders. Like the Teton Sioux or Arikaras who hoped to keep the explorers and their goods from moving on, so too did Yelleppit seek to persuade Lewis and Clark to remain a while longer. The chief's search for European goods would continue for years after the captains politely rejected his request. When David Thompson visited Yelleppit in July 1811, the chief made the same kind of request. In addition, Yelleppit wanted Thompson to build a trading house at the Snake-Columbia confluence.[9]

As the expedition continued down the Columbia and neared the mouth of the Umatilla River, Indian reactions began to change dramatically. The welcomes offered by Cutssahnem and Yelleppit vanished and were replaced first by fear and then by ill-concealed hostility. That fear became evident during the afternoon of October 19 as the explorers left Walula territory and entered that occupied by Umatillas.

Throughout the afternoon, the men saw hastily abandoned villages and frightened Indians. "At our approach," said Clark, "they hid themselves in their Lodges and not one was to be seen until we passed." Although the expedition's records offer no straightforward explanation for this sudden shift in native attitudes, an event later in that afternoon does suggest how Indians with little or no contact with whites responded to the expedition.

As Clark was walking on shore with a small party that included Charbonneau, Sacagawea, and the Nez Perce guides, he idly shot a crane. Clark thought no more about the incident. A cluster of mat lodges in the distance seemed more worthy of attention. Indians from those lodges were spotted running in terror back to their village. Anxious to quiet the Umatillas' fears, Clark decided to take Drouillard and the Field brothers on a visit. Once at the settlement, they found five mat houses with their doors firmly shut. Pipe in hand, Clark pushed his way into the first lodge and found thirty-two men, women, and children "in the greatest agutation." As the Indians cried, wrung their hands, and lowered their heads in preparation for death, Clark struggled to allay their fears. Handshaking, a proffered pipe, and gifts eventually soothed them. He repeated the performance at the other lodges and, with the help of the Nez Perce chiefs and the presence of Sacagawea, terror passed into what he claimed was "greatest friendship." Then the Umatillas spilled out the reason for their fear. As Clark explained it later to Nicholas Biddle, "The alarm was occasioned by their thinking that we were supernatural and came down from the clouds." The Umatilla perception of Lewis and Clark as sky gods had been sparked by Clark's random killing of the crane. "These shots (having never heard a gun), a few light clouds passing, the fall of the birds and our immediately landing and coming towards them convinced them we were from above."[10]

As the expedition moved closer to Celilo Falls and The Dalles, the Indians continued to show signs of fear and distrust. Perhaps the outsiders were identified with Paiute warriors who frequently raided in the region. For whatever reason, the river people traded warily with Lewis and Clark. Ordway recalled that these Indians acted "as if they were in fear of us."[11]

Noting that edginess, members of the party stayed close to their weapons, but something else increasingly captured their attention. On October 20, Clark saw the first piece of European clothing, a "salors jacket," on a river Indian. Even more trade goods were in evidence when the explorers visited the Upper Memaloose Islands. Known as the "place of the departed," the islands contained many large burial vaults filled not only with human and equestrian remains but with all sorts of trade goods of European manufacture. That those grave offerings were part of native daily life was verified when the explorers stopped at an Indian camp to purchase fish and found "some articles which showed that white people had been here or not far distant during the summer." By the time Lewis and Clark were

Drying Salmon at The Dalles, by Paul Kane. Courtesy of Stark Museum of Art,
Orange, Texas.

around the John Day River, non-Indian clothing and implements were everywhere.[12]

Sailors' overalls, brass bracelets, tea kettles, and scarlet blankets all pointed to the presence of a vast trade network centered at The Dalles of the Columbia. Although Lewis and Clark did not yet know it, they were about to encounter that center and cross a fundamental cultural and linguistic boundary. Just as the Middle Missouri trade network and the people involved in it had a profound impact on the expedition, so did the Pacific-Plateau system dominate Indian-explorer relations around The Dalles and down the Columbia. Understanding the Pacific-Plateau economic and cultural network is essential for comprehending the often tangled and tense encounters between river Indians and the American party.

On the broadest level, the Pacific-Plateau system involved exchanging huge quantities of dried salmon for other food and trade goods. What corn and buffalo were to the Missouri villagers, dried fish was to the Wishram and Wasco merchants at The Dalles. Stretching from the Pacific coast to Nez Perce territories and linked to the Middle Missouri system by way of the Shoshoni Rendezvous, the network joined Chinookan and Sahaptian-speaking peoples in an intricate set of personal and economic relationships. Through the trade system flowed not only fish, wappato bread, buffalo robes, and European goods but also games, songs, and stories. Preserving the system met the needs not only of The Dalles middlemen but also their more distant Chinookan and Sahaptian trading partners.

Geography, in the form of a dramatic narrowing of the Columbia at The Dalles and the resulting creation of ideal fishing stations, conspired with weather—warm dry winds blowing up the gorge—to make the Indian villages around the Long and Short Narrows, in Clark's words, "great mart [s] of trade."[13] The Wishram Indians lived on the north bank at The Dalles; the Wascos occupied sites on the south side of the river. Although trading and fishing took place from Celilo Falls down to The Dalles, the most intense bargaining was done at the main Wishram village of Nixluidix. That village, whose name meant "trading place," was located at the head of the Long Narrows. When Lewis and Clark visited it on October 24, they found some twenty large wooden plank houses. Each plank dwelling held three Wishram families. Asked by the explorers who they were, the Wishrams replied, "i'tcxluit," meaning "I am Ita'xluit." That phrase sounded like Echeloot to American ears; hence the expedition's maps and journals always referred to the Wishrams as Echeloots.

The towering stacks of dried salmon at Nixluidix, estimated by Clark at about ten thousand pounds, pointed up the vast quantities of goods exchanged in the Pacific-Plateau network. Trading took place from spring through fall during the three major salmon runs, with most activity reserved for the fall season. During September and October dried fish and roots were freshly prepared and in abundant supply. To The Dalles trade fair came the nearby Yakimas and Teninos as well as the more distant Umatillas, Walulas, and Nez Perces. Local Sahaptians brought to The Dalles food products, including meat, roots, and berries. At the trading places, the Wishram middlemen exchanged those goods for dried salmon and European cloth and ironware. Distant Sahaptians, especially the Nez Perces who had access to the plains, brought skin clothing, horses, and buffalo meat. Less interested in fish than their Columbia cousins, the Sahaptians of the plateau were drawn to The Dalles in search of European goods, especially metal and beads.

Centered at The Dalles and with one arm stretching east, the Pacific-Plateau system also extended west down the Columbia to the coastal Chinookans. Those Pacific peoples brought to the trade system a variety of European goods obtained from fur traders, as well as indigenous crops. Among the manufactured objects carried by them and eagerly sought by The Dalles merchants were guns, blankets, clothing, and the prized blue beads. Coming upriver in their graceful canoes, the lower Chinookans carried wappato roots to be pounded and made into a bread that even the explorers found tasty. Once at The Dalles, Chinookans obtained dried salmon, buffalo meat, and valuable bear grass used in making cooking baskets and the distinctive Northwest Coast hats.

Lewis and Clark observed and recorded much about the Pacific-Plateau network and the kinds of goods that passed through it, but they arrived too late in the season to witness the full flavor of a rendezvous at The Dalles. Although the smell of dead fish still hung in the air and clouds of fleas hovered everywhere, the real trading days were over by mid-October. The explorers grasped something of the economic significance of The Dalles because they could see physical signs of the trade. The Astorian Alexander Ross, who had extensive Columbia River experience soon after Lewis and Clark, caught the personal side of that trading before it was swept away by the great fur companies. Ross estimated that at peak trading times three thousand Indians gathered at the Wishram villages for bargaining. But Ross also understood that trading was more than a simple act of economic exchange. Here Indians met old friends, made new ones, and heard the latest news. Gambling, socializing, and sporting for the opposite sex were all essential features of the trading days. "The Long Narrows," said Ross, "is the great emporium or mart of the Columbia and the general theatre of gambling and roguery."[14]

Escaping the analysis of Lewis and Clark and later whites was the political significance of upper Chinookan control at The Dalles. In the Middle Missouri system, it was essential for Teton Sioux bands to dominate both the flow of goods up the river and access to crops produced by village farmers. Although Lewis and Clark consistently misconstrued the nature of the relationship between nomads and villagers, they at least sensed that trade and politics were closely joined along the Missouri. The captains were much less aware of the balance of power down the Columbia. Upper Chinookans such as the Skilloots did not have the military power possessed by the Teton bands, but they were willing to resort to force in order to protect their place as middlemen in the trade system. Just how far Indians from The Dalles to the Cascades would go to defend their place in the network would be revealed in 1812 and 1814 when the fur traders Robert Stuart, Alexander Stuart, and James Keith fought pitched battles with the river Indians for passage on the Columbia. Lewis and Clark never drew such a violent response from the river peoples; it is worth recalling that the only real trouble the expedition had while on the river was with the Skilloots, a people very protective of their role as traders.[15]

On October 22 the expedition came to Celilo Falls, the first physical barrier on the Columbia. Long a major salmon-fishing place, the falls area was filled with lodges and fish-drying scaffolds. It was plain from the flood of water over the falls that a portage of the expedition's baggage had to be organized. That portage required native help and soon the explorers enlisted a number of Teninos for that duty. All the hurry to prepare for the portage, as well as the outlandish appearance of the Americans, drew a large crowd of Indian onlookers. Ordway pointedly wrote, "The natives are very troublesome about our camp." The trouble Ordway had in mind was petty theft. Any object laid aside for a moment was bound to vanish. Clark recognized the problem and claimed that when the expedition established secure camps in the Celilo Falls–Dalles area the greatest concern was not Indian arrows but "the protection of our stores from theft."[16]

The issue of theft, which reached peak proportions during the trip along the Columbia between Celilo Falls and the Cascades, troubled the explorers as it would later students of the expedition. Lewis and Clark found it a growing annoyance and eventually a drain on their diminishing supply of trade goods. On the return journey up the Columbia they openly threatened to fire on the thieves. In an unusual outburst of anger and frustration, Lewis struck a Skilloot Indian caught stealing during the return portage through The Dalles. At one point the captains had to restrain some members of the expedition who seemed "well disposed to kill a few of them." [17]

What Lewis and Clark saw as troublesome and potentially dangerous behavior was perceived by the river Indians rather differently. Taking axes, clothing, or rifling through the expedition's luggage probably involved two patterns of behavior not understood by the captains or their men. On one level, river people saw the things they took from the expedition as proper payment for services rendered. As the Indians viewed it, the explorers had more knives and blankets than they could possibly use. What harm could there be in taking a blanket, especially when the whites had so many and the Indians had provided valuable support in portaging around dangerous places in the river? But the issue was more complex. The river peoples had a strong sense of private property. They left stacks of valuable dried fish standing unguarded without thought of loss. In pilfering small objects from the Americans, they sought Lewis and Clarks' acknowledgment of their importance. Taking an axe was done to remind the white men of the need to offer respect and attention to the trading lords of the Columbia. As a recent student of Wishram and Wasco life put it, "Thefts from whites would arise not from fundamental lawlessness or from defining whites as enemies but rather from a temporary dislocation of relations which might be remedied if pressure were applied, for example, through thefts or incidents. These [pressures] would serve to reestablish, not break, relationships." [18] Theft as a means of creating mutually rewarding reciprocal relations was a notion utterly foreign to the explorers. It made far more sense in their world to see river people as crafty traders and cunning thieves.

Throughout the day on October 23, members of the expedition struggled and sweated as they manhandled goods and canoes over the Celilo Falls portage. That difficult task was made even more unpleasant by swarms of fleas infesting the dried grass and by fish skins littering the ground. Tortured by the fleas, many in the party stripped off their skin shirts and breeches in an effort to rid themselves of the biting pests. The portage lasted all day and eventually provided work for a few Indians and entertainment for more who watched the whole undertaking with a mixture of amusement and wonder.

Near the end of the day, the strain of the portage effort was broken by an alarming piece of news. One of the Nez Perce chiefs appeared at the expedition's camp and with signs claimed he had heard from Indians around the falls that "the nation below intended to kill us." When the Sahaptians who had crowded around the Americans all during the day left earlier than usual, Lewis and Clark thought the rumor was confirmed. To prepare for the expected attack, they carefully checked weapons and issued each man a sufficient number of rounds. With a bravado born of unfamiliar surroundings and some real fear, Whitehouse boasted, "We were not afraid of them for we think we can drive three times our number." The arms and ammunition may have reassured men like Whitehouse, but the Nez Perce chiefs remained visibly worried throughout the night.[19]

Although the Teton Sioux and Hidatsa threats against the expedition had some real intention behind them, talk relayed thirdhand about the supposed plans of "the nation below" appears in retrospect to be less reliable. The Indians referred to as "the nation below" were certainly upper Chinookans, perhaps Wishrams or Cascades. Those Indians and their neighbors did show considerable hostility toward fur traders whose activities challenged The Dalles trade fair system. The rumor reveals not so much the planned actions of the Chinookans around The Dalles as the relations between the Nez Perces and the Chinookans. Twisted Hair and Tetoharsky admitted to the captains on October 24 that they feared for their lives if they remained with the expedition once it passed The Dalles. During trading times the Nez Perces and Chinookans maintained the same sort of partnership as did the Mandans and Assiniboins. But for most of the year there was considerably more tension and occasional raiding between the two peoples. The alleged preparations for an attack on Lewis and Clark may have been rumormongering or an effort to justify the desire of the Nez Perce guides to leave the party.[20]

Whatever the cause of the alarm, the expedition's plans for combat did not go unnoticed; as the Americans ventured through the dangerous Short and Long Narrows, Indians approached them with much caution. Some Eneeshur Sahaptians who lived around the Short Narrows watched in amazement as Lewis and Clark sent their canoes and best watermen to shoot the Narrows. As this daring venture in whitewater navigation was unfolding, Twisted Hair and Tetoharsky announced that they were ready to leave the expedition. The Nez Perce interpreters correctly reported that The Dalles was the boundary between Sahaptian and Chinookan speakers. Lewis and Clark recognized that the chiefs could do no interpreting past The Dalles, but because they hoped to effect a peace treaty between the Sahaptians and the Chinookans, they persuaded the chiefs to remain for two more days.

Once safely past the Short Narrows and into Chinookan territory, the expedition made camp near Nixluidix, the principal Wishram village. Attracted by the large plank houses in the town, Clark paid the Wishrams a visit. He was welcomed warmly and invited into one of the houses. Clark's journal entry for the day contains a careful description of the house and details of its construction. But it remained for the practical carpenter Patrick Gass to pronounce Nixluidix as a town filled with "tolerably comfortable houses."

Still bothered by flea bites and short of fuel for their fires, the explorers settled in at their Dalles camp. Later that evening an Indian whom Lewis and Clark vaguely described as "the principal chief from the nation below" presented himself and several of his men at the American camp. It remains unclear who this chief was and what group he represented. Whoever he was, the explorer-diplomats seized on his arrival as an opportunity to promote one more of their intertribal peace schemes. The expedition's records do not reveal the course of the negotiations, but Lewis and Clark claimed they had engineered lasting peace and friendship between the Nez Perces and the Chinookans. That claim had as much validity as did earlier optimistic reports of a Missouri villager alliance against the Teton Sioux. In both cases, Lewis and Clark simply did not understand the nature of tribal and band politics. But none of those unpleasant facts intruded on pleasant illusions. Medals and gifts heightened the illusion of lasting peace, and the evening slipped away to the sounds of dancing and of Pierre Cruzatte's fiddle.[21]

With the hazards of The Dalles behind them, Lewis and Clark continued their sweep down the Columbia. Reassured by the friendly Nixluidix reception and by an apparently successful piece of diplomacy, the explorers did not expect much Indian trouble beyond the now-familiar incidents of theft. But just as the physical and cultural landscape was persistently unsettling, so too did rumors of danger persist. No sooner had the boats gotten through the Long Narrows than the Nez Perce guides again began to talk about threats posed to the Americans by unnamed "nations below." But when Lewis and Clark landed at a Wishram village past the Long Narrows, they found no hostility but only a war chief and a number of warriors on their way to attack Paiute bands. When the Nez Perce chiefs finally left the expedition, each was given a medal. There was no sense of impending trouble as Twisted Hair and Tetoharsky went back upriver.[22]

Without Nez Perce guides and among people whose language was unknown to them, the Americans' safety now depended on the attitudes of the river people. At the same time, much rested on the ability of the captains to restrain a growing belligerence in the ranks directed against the Chinookans. From October 25 to the first days of November, the explorers had almost daily contact with a large number of Chinookans. Those encounters usually involved stopping at villages to purchase dogs and dried fish to replenish the expedition's larder. Because these stops never lasted long and communication was very difficult, pursuit of the usual diplomatic and ethnographic goals proved nearly impossible. Nevertheless, the explorers did manage to distribute medals and gifts to a number of village leaders. Years later, during the complex Anglo-American negotiations surrounding the Oregon Question, those actions of the expedition were used to bolster United States claims to the

Interior of a Ceremonial Lodge, Columbia River, by Paul Kane. Courtesy of Stark Museum of Art, Orange, Texas.

Northwest. Despite language and time limitations, Clark's journal entries contain an amazing amount of information about the river peoples and their ways. Vivid descriptions of clothing, canoes, house construction, trade, and burial practices can be found in expeditionary records for this period. Lewis even found time to piece together laboriously several Chinookan vocabularies, although how this was accomplished without interpreters remains unclear. Throughout the last days of October and into November, relations between the explorers and the Indians remained peaceful. Accustomed to the presence of European goods and the indirect influence of white traders, most Chinookans were not startled by the Americans. Many enjoyed the fiddle music and dancing. York remained the attraction he had always been. The days contained the usual trials of wilderness travel, but there was little expectation that the Indians on the Columbia would add to the trials.

Once the expedition passed The Dalles, travel was rapid and relations with the river Chinookans were reasonably good. Although theft was an ever present irritation, the expedition's need for food and information made the captains unwilling to make good on the sorts of threats that would surface on the return journey. For their part, the river Indians viewed Lewis and Clark as curiosities and potential trading partners, certainly not as a possible challenge to native domination in the region.

But much of that apparent good will evaporated on November 4 when the expedition encountered a large Skilloot village near the mouth of the Willamette River. The Chinookan-speaking Skilloots occupied both sides of the Columbia between the Washougal and Cowlitz rivers. Lewis and Clark met Skilloot traders all along the river and on the return journey found a Skilloot settlement as far east as The Dalles. During the early days of November, as the explorers entered Skilloot territories—near present-day Portland, Oregon, and Vancouver, Washington—they noted an ever increasing stock of European goods. That supply of guns, swords, clothing, and assorted copper and brassware suggested the economic role of the Skilloots. Ranging from the coast to The Dalles, they acted as secondary middlemen along the western arm of the Pacific-Plateau system.[23]

Landing at a large Skilloot village of twenty-five houses, Lewis and Clark were impressed by the many well-armed warriors as well as by the number of canoes drawn up in front of the settlement. Invited into one of the lodges by a Skilloot who had been hired earlier to pilot the expedition over this stretch of river, the captains enjoyed roasted wappato roots and apparent good company. After purchasing four bushels of wappato, Lewis and Clark's party moved several more miles downriver, hoping to locate a suitable place for the noon meal. As the explorers prepared their usual river diet of dried fish, dog meat, and roots, several canoes of Skilloots appeared. Dressed in garb that was a colorful mixture of native dress and European clothing, the Indians seemed bent on a festival or council. Anxious to accommodate them, the captains promptly invited the Skilloots to join them. It would be the last time Lewis and Clark ever allowed such a large number of heavily armed Indians into camp. What the explorers expected would be a friendly meeting soon turned unpleasant. For reasons that may have had something to do with a fear of losing their economic position to unknown newcomers, the Skilloot warriors became "assumeing and disagreeable." Adding injury to insult, one of the Skilloots managed to steal Clark's prized ceremonial pipe tomahawk. As the captains searched the Indians and their canoes, another Skilloot made off with a capote belonging to either Charbonneau or Drouillard. All this confusion and trouble added up to a thoroughly nasty afternoon. The expedition kept to the river for an hour after dark "with a view to get clear of the natives who [were] constantly about us, and troublesom." Now more than ever, the expedition looked upon the people of the Columbia with a wary eye. As the explorers prepared to spend their last weeks on the river, they were in no mood to accept Indians as anything other than necessary trading partners.[24]

For several days after the unhappy Skilloot encounter, the explorers kept up their guard as they floated past Multnomah, Kathlamet, and Wahkiakum villages. As with other river Chinookans, contacts with these villagers were brief and usually for trade in food stores. Now and again there was time for some ethnographic observations, as when Clark wrote an especially detailed description of Wahkiakum houses. But what continued to occupy Lewis and Clark's attention was the sizable number of European objects held by river people. In fact, European influence now went beyond material goods and could be heard in the language. It is not clear when Lewis and Clark first heard the Chinook trade jargon. English words and curse phrases were noted among the Skilloots and their neighbors early in November. The explorers also heard about the English trader, Mr. Haley. And it was on November 7 that William Clark wrote his memorable phrase "Ocian in view O! the joy." Although the ocean proper was not quite yet in view, all attention was now focused on reaching the coast and finding winter quarters as quickly as possible.[25]

Information from the river Indians led Lewis and Clark to believe that there were permanent trade establishments along the coast. Hoping to find traders and locate a suitable place for wintering over, the captains attempted to quicken the pace of travel. Thwarted by the rolling currents of the Columbia and the steadily deteriorating weather, they found themselves stalled at Gray's Point in Gray's Bay. From November 10 to November 15, the expedition camped on the east side of Point Ellice. Those were miserable, wet days that dampened spirits and rotted clothing already in tatters. Clark summed up the misery everyone felt when he wrote, "We are all wet as usual—and our Situation is Truly a disagreeable one; and our selves and party Scattered on floating logs and Such dry Spots as can be found on the hill sides and crivicies of the rocks."[26] Borrowing from native practice, the explorers made hasty shelters from poles and mats. Later those temporary lean-tos gave way to huts made from boards scavenged from an abandoned Chinook village. Getting their first taste of a coastal winter, the whole expedition may well have started to feel nostalgic for the cold but bracing days on the northern plains.

On November 15, after reconnoitering by John Colter and other members of the expedition, the Americans moved down the coast four miles to a sandy beach just below Chinook Point. Here, at an abandoned Chinook village, they spent the next nine days until November 24. With the weather now clearing, they could see Point Adams and Cape Disappointment. There in front of the weary explorers were the rollers of the Pacific—the goal Clark had once described as "this great Pacific Octean which we been so long anxious to see."[27] The days spent at the Chinook Point camp were filled with visits from many neighboring Chinooks and Clatsops. Although the explorers allowed only small numbers of Indians into camp and treated all natives "with great distance," there was a chance to meet Chinook chiefs like Comcomly and Chillarlawil. Besides trade in fish, there were the more personal exchanges between the men in the expedition and the young women offered by Delashelwilt's wife.

The camp at Chinook Point provided a temporary respite from the demands of constant travel. But the need to find a reliable food supply and a sheltered place for winter quarters required the expedition to move once again. The Indians told Lewis and Clark that lands along the south side of the river offered the best game and roots. After taking a vote on November 24, the expedition moved back upriver and crossed over to the south side of the Columbia. Early in December, following a search by a small party under Lewis's command, the site for Fort Clatsop was selected. Surrounded by marshes and towering fir trees, and invaded by a pervasive dampness, the Lewis and Clark expedition prepared to spend a second winter in the land of Jefferson's imagination.

Indian visitors to the rain-soaked camps at Point Ellice and Chinook Point could not have missed the tough talk and threats. The Chinooks, Kathlamets, and Clatsops were repeatedly warned that any false moves would be met with maximum force by the expedition. Sentries were ordered to fire on Indians suspected of theft if it appeared that firearms were being taken. Clark claimed that all these threats and verbal onslaughts produced the desired result. "We find the Indians easy ruled and kept in order by stricter indifference towards them." Symbolic of all that suspicion was the password "no Chinook" already in use by men of the expedition even before the construction of Fort Clatsop.[28]

The ill-concealed tensions between the expedition and coastal Indians was the legacy of experiences and misunderstandings on the journey down the Columbia. After the nasty encounter with the Skilloots, the explorers began to build a negative image of river and coastal peoples that colored relations throughout the winter. That powerful image was a composite of several related attitudes about Pacific Northwest people and their lifeways. A principal element was the perception of Chinookan peoples as incorrigible thieves. The theft of expedition goods and the fear of losing weapons was behind much of the provocative language directed at the Indians. Clark would have found substantial agreement in his ranks when he branded the Chinookans as "thievishly inclined."[29]

But it was more than a belief in their criminality that led the explorers to view their Indian neighbors with suspicion and sometimes open hostility. During the days at Point Ellice and Chinook Point, the expedition often depended on nearby Indians for food. The Chinooks and Clatsops, accustomed to hard bargaining with whites in the sea otter trade, expected to drive equally hard bargains with the hungry explorers. Lewis and Clark clearly resented paying "immoderate prices" for essential foodstuffs. When some Kathlamets came offering roots, skins, and woven mats, "they asked such high prices that we were unable to purchase anything of them."[30] What Indians saw as simply good business and the Yankee law of supply and demand looked quite different to hungry and wet Americans. The Chinookans, so it appeared to Lewis and Clark, were not only thieves but sharp traders bent on gouging the needy. There was no trace of admiration in Lewis's voice when he declared that the Clatsops were "great higlers in trade and if they conceive you anxious to purchase [they] will be a whole day bargaining for a handfull of roots." It did not take many days of fruitless trading for green fish and roots in a pouring rain to convince the explorers that coastal Indians were possessed of an "avaricous all grasping disposition."[31]

To the image of thievish and grasping Indians Lewis and Clark added a third element. They found many Chinookan customs and practices both incomprehensible and reprehensible. Although the expedition always viewed Indian life through the filter of its own Euro-American values, there were native ways, especially on the northern plains, that the explorers found praiseworthy. No such praise was offered to coastal peoples. Lewis and Clark repeatedly described the Chinookans as dirty, poorly clad people who engaged in such barbarous customs as head flattening and ankle binding. Coastal sexual practices also came in for much pointed comment. During the Fort Mandan winter, sexual relations between village women and men in the expedition had been commonplace. Although concerned about the spread of venereal complaints in the ranks, the captains had been muted in their criticism of those Indian women. There was no such reluctance to vilify the coastal women. From the time of the first sexual encounters with Chinook women in November, Lewis and Clark blasted them as promiscuous sellers of their own bodies for trinkets and bits of ribbon.[32]

Finally, and perhaps most important, there was the matter of the physical appearance of coastal Indians. Every culture promotes its own image of an attractive body. The Indians of the northern plains came quite close to the somatic norm held by the explorers. But the Indians Lewis and Clark found on the lower Columbia and on the coast did not fit the Euro-American image. Shorter in stature and possessing facial features quite unlike those of the plains natives, the Chinookans appeared to the explorers as "low and ill-shaped." The fact that these Indians were superb canoe navigators, masterful traders, and skillful fishermen was often overlooked as the expedition stressed what it saw as the negative aspects of a "badly clad and illy made" people.[33]

In many ways, reaching the Great Western Sea was an anticlimax. Certainly all members of the expedition were exhilarated by the sight of the ocean. There was a sense of achievement in knowing that they had passed the tests of a hazardous land. Clark's own enthusiasm emerged when, taking a cue from Alexander Mackenzie, he carved on a big pine tree: "William Clark December 3rd 1805. By land from the

U. States in 1804 & 1805." As Clark recalled, his men appeared "much Satisfied with their trip beholding with estonishment the high waves dashing against the rocks & this emence Ocian."[34] But those feelings of excitement and accomplishment were tempered by relations with new neighbors that were already less than cordial. Throughout November, as the explorers suffered in the rain and cold, they were increasingly willing to use threats against the Chinookans. Given their experiences with other river bands and the constant problem of theft, Lewis and Clark surely felt justified in telling the Indians that they would be summarily shot if caught stealing guns or other weapons. Short on provisions and confronted by native traders who demanded high prices for their goods, the explorers felt trapped. Resorting to threats satisfied their desire to be in control of a difficult situation, but it spread fear and suspicion among the very people the Americans needed as winter allies and friends. Hemmed in by an inhospitable climate, an uncertain and monotonous food supply, and a language foreign to all expedition ears, Lewis and Clark faced a winter whose hazards were no less real than they had been at Fort Mandan. Whether their Indian neighbors would exacerbate those dangers was still unknown.

8

The Clatsop Winter

"They are generally cheerfull but never gay. With us their conversation generally
turns upon the subjects of trade, smoking, eating or their women; about the latter
they speak without reserve in their presents, of their every part, and of the most
formiliar connection."
—MERIWETHER LEWIS, 1806

As the Corps of Discovery settled into winter quarters along the Netul (Lewis and
Clark) River, William Clark described the site of Fort Clatsop as "the most eligable
Situation for our purposes of any in its neighbourhood."[1] But neither Clark nor his
fellow explorers seemed quite able to fix those purposes clearly in mind. It was as if
once reaching the Pacific the expedition lost a sense of direction and purpose. The
reasons for raising Fort Clatsop seemed less compelling than those that had brought
Fort Mandan to life. On the coast the expedition needed time to prepare itself for a
demanding return across the continent. The store of notes and maps from the
outbound journey had to be consolidated. In the spruce and fir forests and marsh-
lands around the fort, plants and animals new to eastern eyes required observation,
description, and cataloging. To continue their ethnography, the explorers would
have to question Indians and court their chiefs. And, as always, they looked at the
land and its peoples with the needs of an expanding American trade empire in mind.
From natural history and economic geography to salt boiling and moccasin making—these seemed to qualify as "our purposes." But none of these could spark the
excitement and anticipation that had run through life a winter before at Fort Mandan. In the predictable procession of wind, storm, and fog, the months ahead loomed
as an endless round of rain-soaked days. A season at Fort Clatsop seemed to promise
mildew, spoiled meat, and numbing boredom.

Clark's "eligable Situation" would have pleased any Chinookan band seeking a
winter village site. They might have quickly appreciated the advantages provided
by the river and surrounding forests and wetlands. But what any native of the lower
Columbia knew to be a bountiful country was soon perceived by Lewis and Clark as
a damp prison stocked with meager fare. That there could be two such divergent
ways of evaluating the Pacific Northwest is fundamental in understanding expedition-Indian relations during the winter at Fort Clatsop. Americans and Chinookans
saw themselves, each other, and the physical environment in profoundly different
ways.

Symbolic of those differences was the expedition's obvious disgust with coastal
weather. A powerful entry in Clark's journal for December 16, 1805, captured a

Fort Clatsop, a modern reconstruction. Courtesy of the National Park Service.

sense of awe and fear. "The rain continues, with Tremendious gusts of wind, which is Tremendious. The winds violent   Trees falling in every direction, whorl winds, with gusts of rain   Hail & Thunder, This kind of weather lasted all day, Certainly one of the worst days that ever was!" Less memorable but perhaps more typical were the string of phrases "we are all wet and disagreeable," "cold and a dreadful day," and most common of all, "the rain continued as usual."[2] While explorers huddled in their dank quarters and cursed the foul weather, the Indians went about their daily routine knowing that wind, rain, and thunder were but spirit forces making their powers known for all to see. Paddling canoes that defied the worst waves and wearing hats and capes admirably suited to wet days, the Chinookans may have paused to wonder why the bearded men in the log lodge feared the weather and hid from it.

Those Indians perplexed by the strange behavior of their neighbors on the Netul had not lacked contact with other whites or their fascinating metals and textiles. A decade before Lewis and Clark wintered at Fort Clatsop, Europeans had come to the Columbia with stocks of tea kettles, copper sheets, and blue beads. By 1805 the annual spring visits of British and American ships to a rendezvous on the waters of Bakers Bay had become an eagerly anticipated event in the lower Chinookans' year. European-manufactured objects quickly pervaded native life. Guns, brass bracelets, and iron pots took an honored place among the goods in burial vaults up the Columbia and along the coast. As if to emphasize that outside contact, the Chinook trade jargon was amply filled with salty English words and phrases.

The contacts lower Chinookans had with whites before Lewis and Clark determined a substantial part of their reaction to the expedition. Those experiences had their recorded beginnings in 1792 when three distinct parties crossed the treacherous bar of the Columbia and entered the world of the Chinooks and their neighbors. In May of that year, Captain Robert Gray and his ship *Columbia Rediviva* sailed upriver on a merchant excursion that lasted until the end of the month. Gray, who had already made a journey to the coast, was intent on capturing some of the sea otter trade that had drawn so many ships farther north. The American captain found the Chinooks anxious to exchange skins for a wide variety of hardware and cloth. In the fall of the same year, the river had its second caller. The Royal Navy ship *Chatham,* under the command of Lt. W. R. Broughton and part of the Vancouver expedition, explored far up the Columbia. Broughton's purpose was not overtly commercial, but he did note the interest of river people in manufactured goods, an observation not lost on English maritime investors. The last visitor in that busy year was the British trader Captain James Baker in the ship *Jenny.* Baker pursued a brisk trade with the Chinooks at the bay named for him. The ships on the Columbia in 1792 were just the beginning of a whole fleet yet to come.[3]

By the mid-1790s, traders were making the lower reaches of the Columbia a regular stop on the sea otter network that now stretched from Boston and Bristol to Nootka Sound and on to China. Captains like those the Indians later listed for Lewis and Clark were attracted not only by sea otters and beavers but by arrowproof moosehide armor called clamons. These "leather war dresses" were then exchanged for pelts with the warriors of what is now British Columbia. Typical of those trading ventures and the relations between merchants and Indians was the voyage of the Bristol ship *Ruby* and her captain Charles Bishop. Late in May 1795, the *Ruby* braved the vicious currents of the Columbia bar to anchor at Bakers Bay. Already familiar with the trading routine, scores of Chinooks paddled out to the ship and asked Bishop to fire a gun announcing the start of business. If Bishop believed that his fine store of merchandise would tempt Chinooks to hand over quickly valuable skins and clamons, he was quite mistaken. The Indians had already learned about supply and demand. They had become, in Lewis's colorful phrase, "great higlers in trade."[4] Even if Bishop's array of kettles, brass rods, and brightly colored cloth tempted them, the Chinooks knew the value of tantalizing delay. "In the Evening," recalled the British skipper, "the whole of them took to their cannoes and paddled to shore, leaving us not more disappointed than surprized." Thinking they had made their point, the Chinooks returned the next day and began to set prices. But Bishop was equally willing to play the waiting game, and it was not until the following day that he "broke trade with the Natives." By June 5 the *Ruby* had on board more than one hundred sea otter pelts of fine quality. If the captain was pleased, so were the Indians. The rituals of trade had been properly observed and both peoples had increased personal wealth, a cherished goal that united traders on both sides of the cultural divide.[5]

Out of the sorts of encounters with ships like the *Ruby*, the Chinookans developed a set of expectations about Europeans. The whites were a trading people who came from the sea in large canoes to exchange valuable metal and cloth for skins. Traders could be violent, but their touchy tempers might be softened by having women do much of the bargaining for both goods and services. The Chinookans were convinced, at least by 1805, that whites would eventually pay any price for sea otter pelts. Trading became a ritual game enjoyed as much for sport as for material reward. But material rewards were never far from the center of all native coastal cultures, and when Lewis and Clark refused to play the trading game there was some confusion and considerable misunderstanding. The whites were traders from the sea, hungry for skins and occasional sex. That a party of them might come overland bringing neither large supplies of goods nor a passion for pelts gave Indians pause to wonder what manner of *pâh-shish'-e-ooks* or "cloth men" these were.

Maritime traders like Robert Gray and Charles Bishop saw only a small segment of the Indian village world. At Fort Mandan, Lewis and Clark had been quite close to their Indian hosts. Such was not the case during the 1805–1806 winter. The decision to establish Fort Clatsop two miles up the Netul River meant that the expedition was at some distance from any substantial Indian settlements. Situated northwest from the fort across the Columbia around Bakers Bay were several villages occupied by the Chinooks-proper. At the time of Lewis and Clark, the most important Chinook village was Qwatsa'mts, at the mouth of the Chinook River on Bakers Bay. This plank-house settlement was home to the powerful chief Comcomly. Although the explorers gave no village-by-village population figures for the Chinooks-proper, they did estimate the total number of houses at twenty-eight and the population at some four hundred.

Still on the north shore and northeast from Fort Clatsop were the two villages of people Lewis and Clark called "Wackiakums." As was so often the case, the explorers had a difficult time separating the names of villages, bands, tribes, and linguistic divisions. The Wahkiakums lived in two villages at the mouth of Elochoman River. The larger one, containing seven houses, was called Wa'qaiya·qam; the smaller, only four houses, was called Lo'xumin. The Wahkiakums were part of the Chinookan

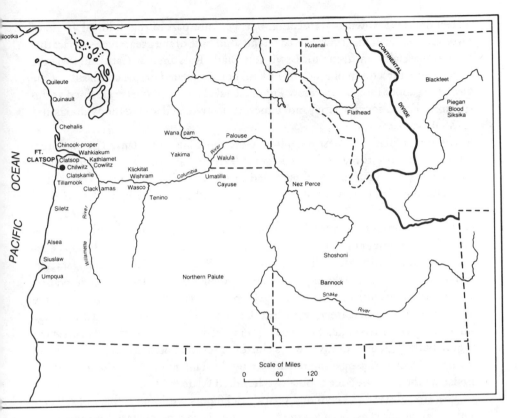

Nootka

Quileute

Quinault

Chehalis

Chinook-proper

FT.
CLATSOP
Wahkiakum
Clatsop
Chilwitz
Kathlamet
Cowlitz

Clatskanie

Tillamook

Clack amas

Wasco

Klickitat
Wishram

Wana pam
Palouse

Yakima

Walula

Columbia

Umatilla
Cayuse

Tenino

Siletz

PACIFIC OCEAN

River

Willamette

River

Alsea

Siuslaw

Umpqua

Northern Paiute

Kutenai

CONTINENTAL DIVIDE

Blackfeet

Piegan
Blood
Siksika

Flathead

Nez Perce

Shoshoni

Bannock

Snake

River

Scale of Miles

0   60   120

rt Clatsop and Its Indian Neighbors

dialect division known as Kathlamet, but were not part of the political world of those Cathlamet villagers who lived on the south side of the great river—a fact that proved especially confusing for Lewis and Clark. Kala amat or Cathlamet was the native name for a town of nine large plank houses located on the south side of the Columbia about four miles below Puget Island. The Cathlamets remained at this site until about 1810, when they moved across the river and joined the Wahkiakums at Wa'qaiya·qam.

Lewis and Clark's closest neighbors were the Clatsop Indians. The explorers knew and mapped three of their villages. Nearest to the fort was Lä't'cap, a name that meant "dried salmon" and provided Europeans with the name Clatsop. The "dried salmon" village was about seven miles southwest from Fort Clatsop. Situated on a branch of the Skipanon River near the ocean, the village had three houses with twelve families. To this village William Clark traveled in December and met Cuscalar, a prominent headman. It may also have been home to the Clatsop headman Coboway. North from "Dried Salmon" on Point Adams was the largest Clatsop settlement known to the expedition. Neahkeluk had eight large wooden houses; later in the nineteenth century, it would be palisaded for protection against hostile attack. For reasons that are now unclear, Lewis and Clark never visited this village nor had any recorded contact with its leaders. Farther down the coastal plain at the mouth of the Necanicum River was a cluster of seven houses. Three of those were occupied by the Clatsops; the remainder by the Tillamooks. So at least fourteen houses in the area contained some two hundred Clatsops.

The most distant of Lewis and Clark's neighbors were the Tillamooks. Their villages along the coast began at the Necanicum, with most centered around Tillamook Bay. Because the Tillamooks spoke the Chinook jargon to strangers, the explorers did not realize that these Indians were not Chinookan speakers but belonged to the Salish language family. Early in the winter, Lewis and Clark believed that villages like Necost, Natti, and those around Tillamook Bay represented distinct nations. Only gradually did this confusion clear. It was to the village of Necost, at the mouth of Elk Creek, that Clark traveled on his way to see a beached whale. In their "Estimate of Western Indians," the explorers recorded that there were fifty Tillamook houses with a population totaling one thousand.[6]

In a disconcerting way, the winter at Fort Clatsop has no narrative history. The winter at Fort Mandan had been a dramatic series of alarms and confusions punctuated by buffalo hunts, holiday celebrations, and occasional personal escapades. At Fort Clatsop the major events were Clark's trip to see a beached whale, Hugh McNeal's brush with death at the hands of a dangerous Tillamook, and the ill-advised decision to steal a Clatsop canoe. None of these can compare with the dangers of threatened Sioux attacks or the tensions of a diplomatic mission to a hostile Hidatsa town. At Fort Clatsop, there were only the elemental tasks of hunting, cooking, and mending. Even these had a timeless quality about them as they were repeated day after day. It was more than dampness and slow rot that pervaded life on the coast. Boredom was rife, to be fought off by every means available. Journal entries took on an almost copybook quality, while busy fingers turned out more moccasins than would ever be needed for the return journey. Lewis captured that sense of time in suspension when he wrote, "Every thing moves on in the old way."[7] Because Indian relations at Fort Clatsop do not follow a chronological pattern, this chapter uses topical categories such as visiting, trading, diplomacy, and ethnography to suggest the ways explorers and Indians dealt with each other.

The Lewis and Clark expedition was one of the greatest tourist attractions the native West had ever seen. Generally, crowds of Indians were attracted by the strangers and their fascinating array of weapons, clothing, and camp gear. Almost everywhere, visiting the explorers became a source of endless diversion and interesting conversation. Each visit had an element of personal discovery as both Indians and explorers eyed each other and then perhaps shared food or trade. At Fort Mandan there had been scarcely a day without a visit by Indians bent on seeing just what went on behind those log walls. Lewis and Clark encouraged visiting, knowing that it brought rewards in food, information, and security. During the winter with the Mandans, visiting was a two-way affair. Members of the expedition regularly paid calls at the earth-lodge villages. On New Year's Day, 1805, the explorers made especially festive trips to their Indian neighbors. Music, dancing, and hearty food marked that holiday fling. Although it would be too much to claim that the Missouri River villagers and the explorers made lasting friendships, the rituals of visiting in lodge and fort softened the rigors of a plains winter.

That kind of visiting, so characteristic of an earlier season, did not occur at Fort Clatsop. For all sorts of reasons, the Chinookans and the Americans did not share much of each other's company. When Indians came to the fort it was for business, not for companionship or curiosity. When Fort Mandan had been under construction, dozens of Indians had watched at every stage of the building. At Fort Clatsop there were far fewer riverbank superintendents. Early in December, four Indians appeared at the fort site and spent the better part of the day staring at the explorers. Later in the month, as work moved slowly on the huts, two other Indians came to observe the project. Social visits were so unusual that when one did happen it was sure to be noted in the expedition's journals. One of those rare calls took place on January 20, when three Clatsops came to the fort and spent the day. As if to underscore how remarkable this was, Clark wrote, "The object of their visit is mearly to smoke the pipe."[8]

If only a handful of Chinookans bothered to pay friendly visits at Fort Clatsop, there were even fewer white guests in plank houses. Clark's journey to the "Dried Salmon" village on December 9 and 10 and his later trip to the Tillamooks were not so much social calls as reconnaissance probes for a good salt-boiling site or a supply of whale blubber. Members of the expedition did not visit their neighbors. Perhaps blocked by the strong currents in the Columbia estuary, no explorer ventured to the Chinook villages at Bakers Bay. Even more surprising, there is no record of anyone in the expedition visiting the largest Clatsop village, Neahkeluk, located on Point Adams. Not even the usual holiday spirit moved men like Pierre Cruzatte to take his fiddle outside Fort Clatsop's gates. New Year's Day, always a time in the French and English traditions to visit neighbors, did not see any noisy greetings shared with Clatsop villagers. The only members of the expedition who may have visited in Indian homes were those who, like Joseph Field, William Bratton, and George Gibson, spent many days at the salt-boiling camp. At that site there were seven Indian houses, and it is possible that the men found them better shelter than their tents.

It was not from a lack of conviviality that Indians paid so few social calls at Fort Clatsop. When Clark first entered a Clatsop village he was treated with "extrodeanary friendship." His host, a man named Cuscalar, had new mats placed on the floor and presented the captain with platters of food. Lewis and Clark readily admitted that their neighbors could be "very loquacious and inquisitive."[9] But the social distance between them could not be overcome. Part of the explanation rests with the increasing commercialization of coastal life. Trade and the acquisition of material wealth had always been an important part of Chinookan life. With the coming of white merchants and the influx of manufactured goods, that facet became even more prominent. Contacts with whites were commercial, not social. The Indians found nothing at Fort Clatsop that was especially strange or interesting. Lewis's airgun might have drawn an extra look and Drouillard's marksmanship was impressive, but coastal people were already familiar with firearms, even if they did not own many. York was no attraction. Since American ships out of New England often brought black sailors, a man like York was not going to draw the kind of attention paid on the Upper Missouri. Few trade goods, language problems, and an isolated location served to make Fort Clatsop a place remote from the centers of Indian activity.

Perhaps the central reason for the lack of sociability during the second winter rested with the expedition's Indian policy. As noted above, Lewis and Clark distrusted and disliked the peoples of the region. The explorers viewed them as habitual thieves tainted with avarice and treachery. A long series of incidents and misunderstandings beginning with the expedition's descent of the Columbia seemed to justify such suspicion and ill-concealed hostility. The explorers might well have asked how one could find friends among badly clad, ill-shaped people who squatted like frogs and tied the ankles of their young women. They did not want such Indians as part of the expedition's daily life.

The captains' desire to keep the Indians at bay was made plain in special orders written at Fort Clatsop. Issued on January 1, 1806, they established strict procedures for dealing with Indians who came to the fort. Sentries were instructed to watch carefully for "the designs or approach of the savages." Once an Indian was seen coming toward the fort, sentries were required to inform the sergeant of the guard, who in turn was to notify either captain. The specific orders for the treatment of those Indians permitted inside the fort are important enough to be quoted in full.

> The Commanding Officers require and charge the Garrison to treat the natives in a friendly manner; nor will they be permitted at any time, to abuse, assault or strike them; unless such abuse assault or stroke be first given by the natives. Nevertheless it shall be right for any individual, in a peaceable manner, to refuse admittance to, or put out of his room, any native who may become troublesome to him; and should such native refuse to go when requested, or attempt to enter their rooms after being forbidden to do so; it shall be the duty of the sergeant of the guard on information of the same, to put such native out of the fort and see that he is not again admitted during the day unless specially permitted; and the Sergeant of the guard may for this purpose imploy such coercive measures (not extending to the taking of life) as shall at his discretion be deemed necessary to effect the same.

One further section of the regulation calls for some attention. At Fort Mandan, staying overnight had been an honor freely extended to many Indians. At Fort Clatsop, the sergeant of the guard, accompanied by Charbonneau and two armed sentries, was required to "collect and put out of the fort, all Indians except such as may be permitted to remain by the Commanding Officers." [10] Only rarely was that permission granted and even visiting chiefs found themselves unceremoniously ejected from the compound at sunset. Such restrictions on hospitality were not lost on the Indians. Accustomed to considerable freedom in dealing with white traders, they could only resent the suspicion directed toward them from the fort on the Netul.

Although the restrictions on hospitality at Fort Clatsop and the natives' economic expectations of whites limited the number of social visits, there were nonetheless fairly regular meetings between the explorers and the Indians. Trading for objects made by native skill or gathered from the land or sea had always been a point of contact between Indians and Europeans. Even though both parties sometimes believed they were being shortchanged, the lure of furs and iron pots kept them coming back for more.

At Fort Mandan the corn trade had been essential for the expedition's survival. Establishing the war-axe forge had been a measure of how far Lewis and Clark were willing to stretch their diplomacy to ensure a reliable food supply. But at Fort Clatsop there was a conscious effort to achieve self-sufficiency. The south side of the Columbia was chosen as a wintering site because it was reported to have a plentiful game supply. Led by George Drouillard, hunters in the expedition were expected to provide staples for the winter diet. But the scarcity of game, its often poor quality, and the difficulty in preserving meat in a warm, damp climate made self-sufficiency an impossible goal. It was plain that the expedition's larders would be bare or at least its diet monotonous unless an Indian food trade was established.

As their closest neighbors, the Clatsops were most often the expedition's trading partners. Coboway's people soon realized that Lewis and Clark were not ordinary traders in search of fur. Quickly readjusting their own marketing strategies, the Indians were ready to provide produce, not pelts. Beginning in early December 1805, Indian canoes came up the Netul loaded with a wide variety of foodstuffs. Believing that the explorers' tastes were much like their own, native merchants brought quantities of wappato, fish, salal berry cakes, shannetahque (cured edible thistle root), and culhomo (seashore lupine root). Those same canoes also held stacks of hats, bags, mats, and an occasional dog. Sea otter and elk skins were usually offered for sale by traders not familiar with the market conditions. Shrewd dealers as they were, the Clatsops quickly grasped the expedition's needs and increasingly offered what would sell.

The Fort Clatsop market was never as busy or as noisy as the corn exchange at Fort Mandan. During the nearly four months the explorers lived on the coast, Indians came to trade on only twenty-four days. The fort was never a major market stop, something a party of Wahkiakums made plain when they refused to sell all their wappato there, preferring to vend it at the Clatsops for whale blubber.[11] If native sellers tried to cater to Fort Clatsop needs without abandoning traditional trade patterns, white buyers were equally selective in what they purchased. Prices too high or quality too low were sure grounds for no sale. On well over half of the trading days, goods offered by Indians were rejected or a partial purchase was made. Selective buying meant that Lewis and Clark obtained foodstuffs that were reasonably priced and of good quality while rejecting higher-priced items. In all this there must have been a great deal of haggling conducted by signs and an occasional phrase in the trade jargon.

It did not take Lewis and Clark long to learn that "those people ask generally double and tribble the value of what they have to sell, and never take less than the real value of the article in such things as is calculated to do them service." At that rate, the expedition's stock of merchandise was bound to diminish with alarming speed. Once lavish in their gifts to Indians along the Missouri, the explorers were reduced to a very short supply of trade goods. Gone were the calico shirts, brass combs, and "small cheap looking glasses" that so charmed the Indians up the big river and across the Great Divide. What remained was a motley collection of fish-hooks, brass wire and armbands, moccasin awls, worn files, and beads of various colors. By early January 1806, Lewis complained, "Our merchandize is reduced to a mear handfull." Despite an inventory that could fit into two handkerchiefs, trade continued. Throughout the dismal winter months, the expedition purchased roots, berries, and fish. The rain-shedding qualities of Chinookan hats so impressed Lewis and Clark that they had some made especially to their own head measurements. Unfortunately, the journals are silent on the price paid to Indian women for such custom-fitted articles. Wappato continued a major item, so important that Cobo-way made at least one special trip upriver just to locate a fresh supply of the roots.[12]

Even with the limited number of trade contacts, there were problems. Those difficulties were not so much disagreements about price or quality as misunder-standings over trading protocol and etiquette. Each partner had rules and believed they should be obeyed, even if his opposite number neither understood nor agreed to those rules. Lewis and Clark expected the Indians to follow the new orders about leaving the fort at sunset. Four Wahkiakums who had been trying to sell roots at rather high prices proved "very forward" and left the fort "with relictiance" when confronted with the new orders.[13] Perhaps the most memorable case of trade in-volved the Clatsop Cuscalar and his family. It was Cuscalar who welcomed Clark to "Dried Salmon" village in December 1805, and the two men soon struck up some-thing of a friendship. When the Indian was sick, Clark thoughtfully sent a piece of cinnamon to cheer him. On the day before Christmas 1805, Cuscalar, his younger brother, and two women appeared at the fort. Seated on the ground before the captains, the Indian ceremoniously laid out a supply of mats and roots. Whether this was a gift or goods offered for trade is not clear now and may not have been so to the explorers. Later in the evening Cuscalar asked for several metal files. If the mats and roots were gifts, then the Indian had every reason to think that a reciprocal present would be offered. Plainly confused by what was going on, Lewis and Clark announced that no files were available and abruptly returned Cuscalar's goods. Undaunted, the Indian then offered the captains the services of the two women in his party. When this gesture was rebuffed, Cuscalar was displeased and the women "highly disgusted."[14]

Whether or not sales were made, and cultural confusions aside, trading did provide the Indians and the explorers a small space of common ground in an other-wise suspicious atmosphere. The cultures of both groups shared many economic values and practices. Each placed great emphasis on acquiring material wealth and measured personal status by that wealth. Individuals who excelled as traders were praised for their skill and rewarded for their enterprise. Yankee capitalists, no less than Chinookans, expected every business contact to have an almost balletlike quality in which both buyer and seller spent hours dancing around each other offering price and counterprice. Lewis learned that lesson when he spent a full day dickering with an Indian over the relative values of a watch and some sea otter pelts, only to have the whole transaction come to naught. Like the New England shop-keeper or the backcountry merchant, the Chinookan trader knew when to hold his ground and when to sell quickly. Sea otter pelts that cost fathoms of blue beads one day might go the next for half a twist of tobacco or some castoff clothing. Had circumstances been different and the traders his own cultural kin, Lewis might have meant as praise his description of Indian merchants as "close dealers" who would "Stickle for a very little, never close a bargin except they think they have the advantage."[15]

Although Clark called Fort Clatsop "the most eligable Situation for our pur-poses," no expeditionary assignment proved harder to define or more elusive to execute than diplomatic relations with the coastal peoples. When the Corps of Discovery struggled up the Missouri and wintered at Fort Mandan its diplomatic agenda was very plain. It included proclaiming United States sovereignty, estab-lishing legal relations with native peoples, and surveying the northern and western boundaries of the Louisiana Purchase. Equally important was extending the St. Louis–based American trade empire, something essential in Jefferson's vision of a West more commercial than colonial. The tactics Lewis and Clark employed in pursuing those goals ranged from confronting Canadian traders and meeting with native leaders to forming, ever so slowly, an alliance of villagers against pro-British nomads. Flags, medals, presents, client chiefs, and full-dress parades—all this Lewis and Clark inherited from a long tradition of Indian-white diplomacy that stretched back to eastern forests.

But what seemed so clear on the Missouri and within the bounds of the newly purchased lands became less plain on the other side of the mountains. Despite Robert Gray's effective discovery of the Columbia River in 1792, the infant Ameri-can Republic had neither the power to proclaim sovereignty in the Northwest nor was this Jefferson's immediate intention. The president did explain to Lewis in 1803 his desire to shift control of the Pacific fur trade out of British hands at Nootka Sound to an American post near the headwaters of the Missouri.[16] On the Missouri, American efforts aimed at diminishing British influence involved complex attempts to rearrange Indian-trader alliances and recast tribal politics. Promoting peace among tribes, offering weapons and American military protection, promising to bring vast stores of trade goods—all were diplomatic strategies toward that end. But down the Columbia, American interests were less clear. Thinking that their Missouri River diplomacy had succeeded, Lewis and Clark may have attempted to create similar economic alliances on the coast. The effort to patch up quarrels between Sahaptian and Chinookan speakers at The Dalles suggests such diplomacy had not been entirely abandoned. But at Fort Clatsop, Lewis and Clark found no open tensions to resolve, nor were they certain of their own authority. And, of course, if most Indians did not think the writ of the young Republic ran even as far as the Mandans, it surely could not cross the mountains to touch the lives of the Chinooks and the Clatsops.

What passed for diplomacy during the winter among the Clatsops began even before the expedition settled along the Netul. Contacts with the Chinooks-proper started in mid-November 1805 on something less than a friendly note. Angered by an attempt to steal guns from the expedition, Clark bluntly informed the Indians that anyone seen near the baggage would be shot. Two days later, on November 17, a man identified only as "the principal chief of the Chinnooks" appeared at the American camp. Since neither the Chinooks nor any of their neighbors were tribes with unified political leadership but were autonomous villages, this man could have been any one of several headmen. The expedition's records are equally unhelpful in revealing what took place between the captains and their visitor except that the explorers now knew the Chinooks to be "noumerous" and "well armed with fusees."[17]

It was not until later in November, with the expedition still camped on the north side of the Columbia, that any recorded diplomatic exchanges with the Chinooks took place. On November 20, as Clark and his party returned from their Cape Disappointment reconnaissance, they found the Chinook chiefs Comcomly and Chillarlarwil with Lewis. There are no journal entries by Lewis for this period, so what passed between the explorer and the chiefs is not known. Clark reported only that the two Indians were given medals and one was additionally favored with a flag. Lewis and Clark usually linked such objects to accepting American sovereignty and the essentials of federal Indian policy. But neither at this meeting nor at any other during the winter did the explorers make any promises or require the Indians to submit to American control. Hindered by language problems and mutual wariness, diplomacy with the Chinooks proceeded at a glacial pace.[18]

Despite the fact that the Chinooks were the largest, best-armed, and most influential native group at the mouth of the Columbia, Lewis and Clark made no effort to build on their initial talks. They did not venture across the Columbia to visit Chinook villages, nor did they invite chiefs like Comcomly, Chillarlawil, or Taucum to council at Fort Clatsop. For explorer-diplomats who had been instructed to redirect the fur trade toward American posts, this was a strangely passive way to go about it.

Throughout the long winter on the coast there was only one other formal meeting with a Chinook chief. Near the end of February 1806, Fort Clatsop's routine was interrupted by the arrival of Taucum and some twenty-five Chinook men. This was the largest Indian delegation to come to the fort, and no doubt some in the expedition nervously fingered their weapons during their stay. Any fears about Taucum's

intentions, however, were quickly laid to rest. The Chinook chief had been dealing peacefully with white traders for more than a decade, and he was not about to
endanger such good relations or to attack well-armed men. Taucum evidently came
to the fort more out of curiosity than a serious interest in negotiation. There was,
after all, nothing to negotiate, nor were the white strangers real traders. Whatever
his motives, the chief made it plain that his was a friendly call. Impressed by his good
looks and taller-than-average stature, Lewis and Clark gave Taucum as warm an
official welcome as they ever offered any coastal chief. The Indian and his entou-
rage were fed and "plied plentifully with smoke." Throughout the afternoon Taucum
and his friends enjoyed food and tobacco but evidently had no interest in hearing
about the ideas of the "great chief of the Seventeen great nations." Almost as an
afterthought, Lewis and Clark presented the chief with a medal. Taucum "seemed
much gratified" but may have believed that it was no more than his just due. If the
Chinook thought the medal was a sign of the expedition's trust and good will, he
was quite mistaken. At sunset Taucum and his party were hustled unceremoniously
out of the fort as if they were an unwelcome set of traders selling rotten fish. As if to
justify such inhospitable conduct, Lewis wrote a long, vindictive journal entry
filled with frightening images of treacherous Indians lurking around the fort ready
to pounce on unsuspecting explorers. Fort Clatsop may have been secure that night,
but closing the gates at dusk was hardly a way to impress important and powerful
neighbors.[19]

If Lewis and Clark's diplomatic relations with neighbors across the Columbia
proved oddly inconclusive, much the same was the case in their dealings with the
nearby Clatsops. Those Indians, some four hundred strong living in three autonomous villages, had several chiefs, including Coboway, Shanoma, and Warhalott.
Coboway, known to the explorers as Comowooll or Conia, was the only Clatsop
chief who had any recorded contact with the expedition. Early in December, with
Fort Clatsop still under construction, Coboway led two canoes of his folk to pay a
call on the white newcomers. The chief exchanged some wappato, shannetahque,
and a small sea otter pelt for some fishhooks and a small sack of Shoshoni tobacco.
Despite the bustle of construction, Lewis and Clark treated the Clatsop delegation
"with as much attention as we could." Coboway was given a medal, but with trade
goods already in short supply, others in the delegation probably found American
hospitality somewhat meager on the material side. Coboway's visit predated the
regulations limiting overnight stays, so the chief spent the night with the explorers.[20]
From Coboway's point of view, the visit had mixed results. He must have been
pleased with the attention paid to him, but the evident poverty of the explorers was
disappointing. If Coboway thought he had scored a victory in having Fort Clatsop
on his side of the river, he never pressed that advantage, nor did the Chinooks see
the expedition's wintering place as a slight aimed at them. Lewis and Clark made no

promises to any chief and evidently sought nothing more than a friendly but distant relationship.

During the winter, the explorers were visited by two other delegations from nearby villages. In each case, the Indians took the initiative in making contact with the Americans. At the end of December, a young Wahkiakum chief and several people from his village came up the Netul for trade and talk. Once again, expedition records do not reveal what, if any, official words passed between the chief and the captains. The Wahkiakum was given a small medal and, like the Assiniboin band chief Chechank at Fort Mandan, a piece of ribbon to put on his hat.[21] Early in January, the Cathlamet chief Shahharwarcap and eleven men ventured to the fort. Lewis gave the chief a medal of the smallest size and in return received some wappato and tobacco. Following protocol, Lewis then offered some twine for a skimming net. After some time in trading, Shahharwarcap was escorted out of the fort at sunset and spent the night in the woods.[22] These contacts with Wahkiakum and Cathlamet chiefs hardly qualify as talks, but they did round out a network of reasonably friendly relations between Fort Clatsop and the surrounding villages.

Lewis and Clark's diplomacy at Fort Clatsop was characterized by modest goals and relative inaction. At Fort Mandan there had been a sense of urgency in talks with the Mandans and Hidatsas. The captains had had a clear picture of United States interests on the Missouri, even if their grasp of tribal politics had been less sure. But similar clarity was lacking at Fort Clatsop. American interests in the Pacific Northwest were as yet unformed. The trade empire Lewis and Clark represented was centered in the St. Louis of the Chouteau brothers and Manuel Lisa, not the New York of John Jacob Astor. Here the explorers were uncertain of and uninterested in village and band rivalries. It is revealing that Comcomly, the Chinook headman who emerged in the period after Lewis and Clark as the most powerful political leader in the area, never visited Fort Clatsop. Whatever diplomatic initiatives there were during the winter came from the Indians themselves. It was very rare for whites to winter in the region, and the natives' visits to the fort may be interpreted as an effort to determine the intentions of the expedition. If there was a network of "understandings" binding the Indians and the explorers, it was the result of action by the former. By the second winter, the explorers had expended not only the material substance of diplomacy but much of their intellectual capital as well. Perhaps it seemed enough to fulfill the forms of diplomacy with the few remaining flags and medals, leaving the substance to others.

If Lewis and Clark were reluctant traders and inactive diplomats, they better fulfilled their ethnographic responsibilities. The Fort Clatsop diaries are enlivened with a wealth of information on lower Chinookan life, including drawings of weapons, canoes, and the tools of daily life. At Fort Mandan, Lewis and Clark had used a wide variety of techniques to gather and preserve information about the

Indians: interviews, direct observation, participation in ceremonies, and collection of artifacts. The results of that considerable effort were recorded in journals, maps, and the impressive "Estimate of the Eastern Indians." Knowing what they did well and what was possible, the expedition's ethnographers centered on describing Indian material culture. If past experience meant anything, the expedition was admirably prepared to document the lives of the coastal people. That the Fort Clatsop ethnographic achievement proved somehow less major than expected was the result of a whole battery of information gathering problems, some beyond the expedition's control and others of its own making.

It has become a historical commonplace to describe the Chinookans encountered by Lewis and Clark as "a decadent stock." In a burst of rhetoric more colorful than accurate, Bernard De Voto branded the Chinooks and their kin as "dull-witted, thievish, lying, [and] rotten with gonorrhoea and the pox."[23] Although others have not written such powerful slander, students of the expedition have often assumed that Chinookan life was somehow a "culture in decline." This latter-day estimate would have astonished everyone from white traders and explorers to the Indians themselves. When Lewis and Clark came to the coast in 1805, they found a thriving people fully at one with a bountiful physical environment. Arguments about cultural decline to the contrary, the maritime fur trade had dramatically enhanced the wealth and power of the coastal people. As one story describing the advent of metal trade goods put it, "the people bought this and the Clatsop became rich."[24] Like those ingenious Mandans who dismantled a corn grinder to make tools more suited to their own needs, the Chinookans bought only certain European goods and then quickly made them part of native life. The assertion that the Chinookans were "dull-witted" would have brought looks of disbelief from white merchants who knew firsthand the talents of Indian traders. To be fair, it must be said also that there was probably no more venereal disease on the coast than at Fort Mandan. The expedition's experience suggests that more men had the ailment at Fort Mandan than at Fort Clatsop. And as for the charge that the Chinookans were liars, it is revealing that the only serious case of deception during the winter involved the expedition and not the natives. Coboway, Cuscalar, Taucum, and the women who worked for Delashelwilt's wife were neither noble nor savage. Their lives moved to a pattern often difficult for the explorers to discern. It was just as hard for the natives to comprehend the Lewis and Clark expedition.[25]

Lewis and Clark were always drawn to the characteristic objects of Indian life. Few items more fully symbolized native cultures on the Northwest Coast than the canoe. From the first time they saw such canoes on the Columbia, Lewis and Clark admired their way in the water and the skill of those who paddled them through heaving river swells. From the Tlingits of British Columbia down to the coastal Salish of Oregon, there were five distinctive canoe styles in use. Ranging south from British Columbia to the mouth of the Columbia River and then up to the Cascades, the Chinook or Nootka canoe was a dominant style. The Chinook canoe, typically twenty to thirty-five feet long with a flat bottom, was quickly recognizable by its separate wood piece fitted over an undercut prow and a sharp, vertical stern. The cutwater canoe, common among lower Chinookans, obtained its name from the use of a board cutwater placed on the prow. Cutwaters were often thirty to thirty-five feet long and carried ten to twelve persons and considerable cargo. Also widespread in coastal Washington and Oregon and on the lower Columbia was the shovel-nose canoe. This style was the only kind used above The Dalles. Shovel-noses could be recognized by their distinctive sharply undercut prow and stern. This canoe was usually some fifteen feet long and maneuvered by two or three paddlers. Perhaps the most impressive and certainly the most memorable canoe in lower Chinookan waters was the double cutwater style. This very large canoe, usually thirty-five feet or longer, had cutwater boards at both bow and stern. More important, both ends were decorated with large carved totem animals. Finally, there were several kinds of simple hunting canoes.[26]

In a long, illustrated journal entry dated February 1, 1806, both Lewis and Clark presented detailed descriptions of four of the five canoe styles of the Northwest Coast. The first canoe in the sequence of Lewis's drawings was the shovel-nose. Lewis and Clark had often seen the Cathlamets and Wahkiakums use these small canoes around the "marshey Islands" near their villages. Second in Lewis's illustrated entry was the Chinook, the sort of canoe that may have been frequently drawn up on the banks of the Netul. The third drawing depicted the cutwater canoe. Both explorers noted its use up to The Dalles as well as its unmistakable cutwater board. That feature of native naval design was something neither man had ever seen, and both admitted that on first sight they had confused the bow for the stern, perhaps thinking the board was a simple rudder. Like every outsider who ever saw the double cutwater, Lewis and Clark were impressed by its size and ornamentation. Lewis's drawing shows a large double cutwater with what may be a human figure on the prow and a carving, clearly of an animal, at the stern. When Clark visited the Tillamook-Clatsop village at present-day Seaside, Oregon, he measured a double cutwater but evidently either forgot or mislaid the figures when writing his entry.[27]

The explorers knew that there was more to say about canoes beyond simple physical characteristics. Like James G. Swan who spent three years among the Chinooks in the 1850s, they understood that "the manufacture of a canoe is a work of great moment with these Indians." A brief but accurate discussion of construction techniques and materials completed the captains' journal entry. Impressed by the canoes themselves, Lewis and Clark were even more taken with the skill of their builders. With a chisel made from a worn file embedded in a wooden handle, Indian

Interior of a Chinook Lodge, by Paul Kane. Courtesy of Stark Museum of Art,
Orange, Texas.

craftsmen made boats marked by easy handling and graceful lines. "A person would
suppose," wrote the captains, "that the forming of a large canoe like this was the
work of several years; but these people make them in several weeks." It was no
wonder that canoes were prized possessions not to be traded away except at the
highest prices.[28]

Some of the best of Lewis and Clark's ethnography responded to Jefferson's
requirement that they describe Indian "food, clothing, & domestic accomoda-
tions." Throughout its journey, the expedition took careful note of Indian architecture, recording the designs and construction principles of earth lodges, tepees,
brush wickiups, and on the Northwest Coast, plank houses. Lewis and Clark first
encountered plank houses around The Dalles and saw them with increasing fre-
quency downriver. Drawing on observations made during the winter, they were
able to describe in considerable detail the size, shape, and materials for a Chinookan
plank dwelling.

Although there was some variety in the plank house's size and shape, depending
on local circumstances and the status of the inhabitants, Lewis and Clark found a
common overall plan and structure. After finding a proper location with good

access to water and enough sunlight, Indian builders excavated a pit some three to five feet deep. When finished, the pit measured anywhere from fourteen by twenty to forty by one hundred feet on its sides. A strong framework of cedar timber posts and gables was then erected over the pit. Split cedar boards were then driven into the ground vertically so that the tops of these planks could be attached to the gable rafters and eave poles. Roofs were made with thin planks, sometimes laid in a double thickness. Oval door openings often provided a place for Chinookan craftsmen to demonstrate their considerable carving abilities. Entrances were made to appear as animal or human mouths. When Lewis and Clark visited the Cathlamet village on the return journey, they noted such designs, "some of these which represented human figures setting and supporting the burthen on their shoulders." [29]

The insides of those houses were filled with the domestic clutter of Chinookan daily life. Sleeping mats, bowls, knives, bags, digging sticks, and clothing were only some of the items in a typical coastal household inventory. It was not until the drawings and paintings of John Webber, an artist with Captain Cook at Nootka Sound, and Paul Kane, a nineteenth-century artist, became better known that there was visual confirmation of what Lewis and Clark first described. The explorers provided a catalog of the utensils that the Chinookans used every day. Their journals contain accurate descriptions of wooden bowls, reed mats, different sizes of woven rush bags, and "neet trenchers made of wood." There is a fine account of root-digging sticks with a simple sketch to illustrate the tool. Lewis also made drawings of several weapons, including clubs, swords, and the common double-bladed handknife. [30]

Food and clothing did not escape the ethnographer's eyes. In a long journal entry written on a dismal, rainy day in January, Lewis took pains to describe "the Culinary articles of the Indians in our neighbourhood." Handsomely carved bowls, water baskets that doubled as hats, and horn spoons were all duly noted, as was the proper way to roast fish on a skewer. Lewis and Clark would not have recognized the word *ethnobotany*, but their observations on the natives' use of plants as a major food source has no equal in the literature of early exploration. The captains were no less attentive to Chinookan clothing. Despite Lewis's ill-tempered outburst proclaiming Chinookan female dress and ornament as "the most disgusting sight I have ever beheld," the journals contain remarkably precise descriptions of native dress. At one point, Clark summarized: "All go litely dressed ware nothing below the waist in the coldest weather, a pice of fur around their bodies and a short robe composes the sum total of their dress, except a fiew hats, and beads about their necks arms and lets." [31]

Lewis and Clark were especially fascinated by the unique and skillfully made hats worn by Indians up and down the coast. Made of cedar and bear grass, these brimless, cone-shaped hats were often decorated with geometric or pictorial figures

Northwest Coast Indian Woven Hat. Courtesy of British Columbia Provincial Museum, Victoria, British Columbia.

woven into them. Clark saw a common Nootka design and described it as "faint representations of the whales, the Canoes, and the harpooners Strikeing them." Lewis was impressed with their practical design, writing, "They are nearly water-proof, light, and I am convinced are much more durable than either chip or straw." The explorers found such hats so well-suited to endless days of rain that they purchased several for themselves, drew four pictures of them, and took one back for Charles Willson Peale's Philadelphia museum.[32]

Lewis and Clark's ethnography was never an end in itself, but was always intended for the service of government policy or commercial expansion. When Jefferson instructed Lewis to learn about the "ordinary occupations" of native people, he had in mind the ways that Indian economic patterns might fit into an American trade system. Knowing that an essential part of their mission was to lay the foundations of future "commercial intercourse," the explorers paid special attention to Indian trade routes and the kinds of goods that passed along them. By the time Lewis and Clark got to The Dalles, they were experienced in analyzing trade networks and their potential for the eager merchants of St. Louis. The Northwest Coast contained an exchange system every bit as extensive as that at the Mandan villages. Had Lewis and Clark been farther north, they might have had a closer look at the maritime fur trade, but their location near the Columbia nonetheless provided a good place to watch a stream of brass tea kettles, blue beads, wappato, and pelts pass around a circle of Indian and white hands.[33]

Despite the fact that more than one hundred American ships had been engaged in fur operations on the Northwest Coast between 1788 and 1803, Lewis knew very little about the organization or the schedule of that trade. When he gathered his notes and began writing about coastal trade, he did not know whether traders who visited the Columbia came from Nootka Sound or made the river their first stop on voyages direct from England or the United States. Lewis was equally unsure about the existence of a trading post somewhere on the Pacific coast south of the Columbia. Strangely enough, the explorer did not even appear aware of the role of Hawaii as an important resupply point, although he speculated that "some island in the pacific ocean" was perhaps being used in the trade. From Indians, Lewis learned that traders came to the Columbia in April, anchored at Bakers Bay, and stayed some six or seven months. More important, he was able to learn what sort of goods the Indians were anxious to obtain. Those goods ranged from high quality two- and three-point blankets and coarse cloth to sheet copper and brassware. Also in demand were knives, fishhooks, pots, kettles, and firearms. The Chinookans enjoyed sporting European fashions, making castoff sailors' clothing an item for exchange. Of course, there was always a market for blue beads, known in the Chinook trade jargon as *tyee-kamosuk* or "chief beads." In return, the maritime traders obtained dressed and undressed elk skins, sea otter and beaver pelts, and so Lewis thought, dried salmon. Lewis knew that vast quantities of pounded fish came down from The Dalles market but frankly could not understand why white traders wanted it. Later he discovered that he had misinterpreted Indian information. The salmon was not meant for the sailors but was part of a large domestic trade of which the tall ships were only a small part.[34]

The extensive native trade network also got the expedition's attention. Lewis knew about the role of The Dalles as "the great mart for all the country." After further investigation, he better understood the flow of pounded salmon and European goods up and down the river. Typical of the exchanges that Lewis was able to trace were a variety of products from blubber and whale oil to wappato and beads. On one day in January, Lewis watched Cathlamet canoes loaded with upriver wappato destined for the Clatsop towns. At those towns the wappato would be traded for blubber and oil, items the Clatsops obtained from their Tillamook neighbors. The Clatsops, rich in European trade goods, paid for the whale products with beads and metal. "In this manner," explained Lewis, "is a trade continually carryed on by the natives of the river each trading some article or other with their neighbors above and below them; and thus articles which are vended by the whites at the enterence of this river, find their way to the most distant nations enhabiting its waters."[35]

Whenever Lewis and Clark ventured beyond describing objects to write about the "character" of an Indian group they ran afoul of powerful stereotypes that had long been a part of the Euro-American frontier experience. The explorers could and did have good relations with individual Indians, but when they tried to evaluate whole cultures, traditional attitudes and categories almost always came to the surface. Until they reached the Columbia, Lewis and Clark made do with two stereotypes for Indians. There were the Missouri River villagers, potential American customers and allies. In the explorers' eyes, these were the good Indians, sometimes childlike and potentially dangerous but good nonetheless. Baptized by reason of their trade potential, cultural salvation was extended to the Shoshonis, Flatheads, and Nez Perces. The Sioux and the Assiniboins formed a second image. These natives Lewis and Clark judged harshly, not necessarily because they were nomads but for their links to British traders. This negative evaluation was not unchangeable. If Black Buffalo's warriors abandoned their English friends, they might be redeemed and welcomed into the American congregation. Such attitudes were intellectually satisfying and practically useful; they provided quick reference points as the expedition moved through a maze of Indians in an unknown land. Facial features, treatment of women and the elderly, differing traditions of hospitality toward strangers, economies of hunting and farming, even the sounds of language—all of these could be put into familiar mental pictures that made the world comprehensible.

But in the Northwest those reassuring images were challenged in disturbing ways. Here were people who made graceful canoes but flattened the heads of their children, carved beautiful designs on wooden bowls but squatted like frogs, and bargained with Yankee skill but had a language that sounded like hens clucking. The Chinookans simply did not fit into any convenient mental category. They were villagers who did not farm and warriors who preferred trade to combat. How could they be "Indians" when they did not look or act like any "Indian" the expedition had yet encountered? Confronted with human beings and cultural patterns that did not conform to the familiar categories, Lewis and Clark fell back on intellectual positions prepared by previous generations of Indian-white contact. At a moment when it might have been possible to escape the thrall of perceptions that had held Europeans since the Age of Reconnaissance, Lewis and Clark chose to reassert the familiar themes of native treachery and brutality. Language more suited to the bloody engagements in the Ohio country of the 1790s was conferred on the coastal people. Lewis and Clark had a singular chance to see the Indians beyond stereotype; to see them as inventive, adaptable men and women living prosperous lives between the mountains and the sea. That the explorers failed to transcend their own past is a measure of how deeply rooted those mental categories had become for white Americans.

When Lewis and Clark offered negative evaluations of the Chinookans they usually focused on two features of coastal life, one physical and the other behavioral. There is no doubt that they found the shape of Columbia and coastal peoples unattractive. Like other Euro-Americans, the explorers were conditioned to admire tall, slender bodies. Thin lips, narrow noses, and small feet were all essential parts of the body beautiful. Although the plains and plateau Indians came close to that image, the river and coastal folk surely did not. Lewis and Clark repeatedly used the words "low," "illy formed," and "badly made" to describe Chinookan bodies. Lewis wrote, "They are low in stature, rather diminutive and illy shapen; possessing thick broad flat feet, thick ankles, crooked legs, wide mouths, thick lips, nose moderately large, fleshey, wide at the extremity with large nostrils, black eyes and black coarse hair."[36] Although its unflattering aspects were surely intended, this physical portrait is generally accurate. More important, it does not directly engage in the kinds of racial typing common later in the century, nor is its language as harsh as that used by later travelers to the coast. It is worth recalling that the most vindictive thing said about Indians in the extant journals—Lewis's cruel characterization of hungry men eating uncooked meat as savage brutes—described Shoshonis, not Chinookans.

But the behavior of some coastal Indians was hardly endearing. From The Dalles down to the coast, Lewis and Clark were troubled by repeated incidents of theft. Those thefts posed two quite distinct problems. Plainly the expedition could not afford to lose tools, weapons, and valuable trade goods. But on another level, the explorers found persistent theft a habit hard to understand. Differing concepts of property, notions of communal sharing, increased commercialization of native life, and theft as an attention-getting tactic were all explanations that did not occur to the ethnographers in the expedition. Instead, Lewis speculated that thievery was an irreducible part of the coastal Indians' psyche. "I therefore believe," he wrote, "this trait in their character proceeds from an avaricious all grasping disposition."[37]

The captains may not have liked their Fort Clatsop neighbors nor wanted their constant company, but at the same time, they said very positive things that must not be overlooked. Indeed, they had as many favorable things to say about the Chinookans as they had about plains or plateau Indians. For all the talk about "badly made," thievish natives, Lewis and Clark found Coboway and his kin "mild inoffensive people." Hospitality toward strangers was evident when Clark visited a Clatsop house and was treated with "extrodeanary friendship." The explorers were equally impressed with Chinookan family life, noting that "the greatest harmoney appears to exist among them." "Cheerful but never gay," possessed with "good memories," "very loquacious and inquisitive," the Chinookans may have sometimes seemed like transplanted Yankee peddlars—not a wholly flattering esti-mate, come to think of it, from men with Virginia and backcountry roots.[38]

By the time Lewis and Clark wintered at Fort Clatsop, they had settled on several ways to record ethnographic information. Journals, maps, vocabularies, artifacts, and tabular estimates were all familiar parts of their ethnography. At Fort Clatsop, the bulk of material about the Indians was written by Lewis in long journal entries. Each entry was a miniature essay on a particular aspect of Indian material culture or behavior. On subjects ranging from trade routes and hunting techniques to clothing styles and burial practices, Lewis's essays represent a substantial achievement in the history of ethnography. They reflect his keen powers of observation and a remark-able ability to bring objects alive with words.[39]

Although the journals of the captains hold much valuable information about the Indians, the same cannot be said of the diaries kept by Sergeants Ordway and Gass. Earlier in the voyage, Ordway often had recorded telling bits of native life. The look of an Arikara cornfield or the unique sound of the Salish language were things that he would not miss putting in his journal. Gass could be equally observant, especially about Indian houses. But during the winter on the coast, the sergeants' powers of observation declined. For reasons that are not clear, their journals are thin and without significant ethnographic value.

Perhaps the greatest advance in ethnographic recording at Fort Clatsop was the inclusion of illustrations in the journals. Drawings had appeared briefly when the party spent time with the Lemhi Shoshonis, but at Fort Clatsop the illustrative art flowered. Whatever the cause for the drawings, whether sheer boredom or genuine interest in new subjects, these visual records provide a new dimension to the expe-dition's ethnography. Sketches of North Coast hats, swords, clubs, knives, and arrows dot the journal pages, as do drawings of fishhooks, digging sticks, canoes, and paddles. These drawings continue to enliven our understanding of Chinookan life. Most striking is Clark's simple but powerful set of sketches depicting Chi-nookan heads and a head-flattening cradleboard.[40] The quality and perceptiveness in the Fort Clatsop drawings makes one wish that the captains had discovered their artistic gifts earlier and practiced them longer.

The comprehensive "Estimate of the Eastern Indians" had been the lasting ethno-graphic accomplishment to come out of Fort Mandan. At Fort Clatsop, Lewis and Clark attempted a similar estimate for western Indians but with far less success. Abandoning the interrogative and comparative structure that made the eastern estimate so valuable and remarkable, the explorers settled for a simple list of tribes, bands, and villages with populations given in numbers of lodges and persons. The "Estimate of Western Indians" was begun at Fort Clatsop, revised during the return journey, and further annotated by Clark when the expedition had ended. In organi-

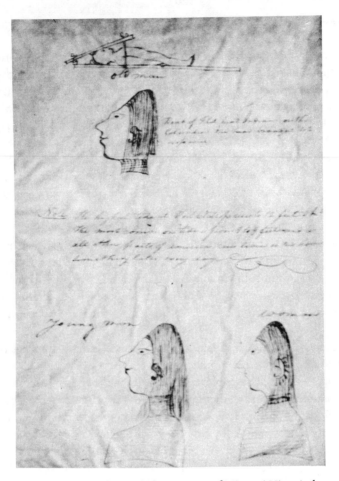

Heads of Clatsop Indians, by William Clark. Courtesy of Missouri Historical Society.

zation, the western estimate is a straightforward recital of native groups, moving from the Shoshonis, Flatheads, and several Nez Perce bands to the Yakimas, Wanapams, and Walulas encountered at the junction of the Snake and Columbia rivers. The estimate enumerates the Columbia River Sahaptians and Chinookans, reaching east to the Shahala or Cascade Indians. Then applying an unusual economic or botanical standard, the explorers list bands from the Cascades of the Columbia to the Cowlitz River as "wappato Indians." These include the Clatskanies, a number of groups living around Wappato or Sauvies Island, and the Skilloots. Moving to the coast, the estimate records the Wahkiakums, Cathlamets, Chinooks-proper, and Clatsops.

Because Lewis and Clark never traveled farther south along the Oregon coast than the Tillamook village of Necost, their information on groups much past Cape Lookout was very sketchy. The explorers knew the names and locations of the Tillamook towns around Tillamook Bay. Perhaps based on information gathered during Clark's visit, the estimate contains a list of Salish and Yakonan speakers south to Cape Blanco and the Rogue River. Lewis and Clark had even less information from the Chinooks-proper north along the coast. The few contacts with Chinooks during the winter made the estimate of those in the northern reaches meager indeed. Under one entry, Lewis and Clark listed a number of groups along the Washington coast as far north as the Quinaults on the Olympic Peninsula. When Clark made his brief reconnaissance up the Willamette River on the return journey, listings were added for bands and peoples commonly known as the Multnomahs. Also noted were groups of Sahaptian speakers living on the middle Columbia above the Snake-Columbia junction. For all the care Lewis and Clark took with it, the western estimate has a barebones quality. Whether it was a failure of energy, imagination, or information, the document did not meet the standard set at Fort Mandan.[41]

The weaknesses in the "Estimate of the Western Indians" reflect the deeper problems that made Fort Clatsop ethnography less successful than the studies undertaken a winter earlier. The explorers had not abandoned their commitment to "name the nations," nor had they suddenly lost their descriptive skills. At Fort Clatsop, Lewis and Clark were up against a battery of information-gathering problems, some of their own making and others simply beyond remedy.

Fort Mandan had been ideally situated for ethnographic field work. Two Mandan villages and three Hidatsa ones were close by. Because these villages were the center for northern plains trade, Lewis and Clark had access to Indian information far beyond the range of their own travels. If Fort Mandan was set at what geographer John Allen has aptly termed "the keystone of the upper Missouri region," Fort Clatsop was isolated in a cultural backwater.[42] Only one small Clatsop village was within easy walking distance. The Chinook villages on the north side of the Columbia seemed as remote as the Tillamook towns to the south.

Compounding the physical isolation at Fort Clatsop was the restrictive visiting policy discussed above. Unfortunately, the evening curfew was enforced in an atmosphere of fear and distrust. Then, too, the coastal Indians did not find the white men a novelty and were disappointed by their slim store of trading goods. The result was far fewer Indian visitors than there had been at Fort Mandan and a sketchier ethnographic record. Lewis and Clark may have felt more secure with fewer Indians about, but their cultural isolation yielded a written record long on objects and short on those who made and used them.[43]

That mental and physical distance from Indians meant fewer native informants. Even with Indians like Coboway, Cuscalar, and Delashelwilt—men who visited the fort fairly regularly—Lewis and Clark never developed the sort of rapport they had had with Black Cat, Sheheke, or many other Mandan Indians. Some of that difficulty was a matter of language. However difficult and time-consuming the translations at Fort Mandan, at least the words and sentences had been forthcoming. At Fort Clatsop, translation was much more difficult. No one in the party could speak the Chinookan language, and the explorers evidently picked up only a rudimentary knowledge of the trade jargon. Over and over, Lewis lamented: "I cannot understand them sufficiently to make any enquiries."[44]

During the winter at Fort Mandan, many of the gaps in Indian information could be filled by traders like Jusseaume, Charbonneau, and Heney. At Fort Clatsop, there was no comparable group of knowledgeable whites for Lewis and Clark to question. Already hemmed in by inhospitable weather, miserable food, and a strange language, the absence of helpful traders deepened the expedition's isolation and ignorance.

The winter at Fort Clatsop wore on in days of cold drizzle. The men habitually noted in their journals that "nothing worthy of notice occurred today." No sooner had the fort been built than the whole party began "counting the days which seperate us from the 1st of April and which bind us to fort Clatsop."[45] In the routine of hunting, cooking, mending, and salt-boiling, several incidents stand out to reveal the lights and shadows of personal relations between the explorers and the Indians. Some of these are no more than snapshots from the Fort Clatsop family album, but at least two might be short films on the subject of friendship betrayed.

At Fort Mandan, Indians and explorers had been allies in a struggle to survive a plains winter. But at Fort Clatsop their relationship was at best an armed truce. Yet there must have been moments, especially at trading times, when something like the atmosphere of that plains winter crept into the Fort Clatsop compound. The Chinooks were convivial folk who enjoyed storytelling and good company. Their zest for life was reflected in a delight with bargaining that went beyond business into the realm of sport. Lewis and Clark never recorded any of the arresting tales in coastal oral tradition, nor do their journals contain any hints of the actual words that passed between Indians and whites. But in a memorable entry written by Lewis, there is a hint of those brief times when neighbors shared trade and food. "With us," he recalled, "their conversation generally turns upon the subjects of trade, smoking, eating or their women; about the latter they speak without reserve in their presents, of their every part, and of the most formiliar connection."[46] In journal entries usually empty of an Indian presence, this is an especially vivid picture. Earthy talk, a sly wink or pointed finger, and the forceful way the Chinookans blew smoke from their lungs—all lent a flash of color to otherwise gray days.

Talk about that "most formiliar connection" is a reminder that sexual liaisons with Indian women had been part of the life of the expedition at least since the time at the Arikara villages. Lewis certainly was not surprised, and he wisely purchased the proper medical supplies in Philadelphia to cope with venereal disease. The captains simply accepted sexual relations as part of frontier life and were worried only if they endangered the expedition's health or security. It is probably safe to say that "Louis Veneris" was an unpaid, unenlisted, but ever-present member of the Corps of Discovery throughout its long voyage.

Clark once wrote that Chinook women were "lude and carry on sport publickly," and added that "the Clotsops and others appear deffident, and reserved."[47] His unflattering assessment of Chinook morals and the differences in behavior of women on either side of the Columbia brings us closer to understanding why sex was so freely offered to the Americans. With the coming of white traders in the mid-1790s, Chinook women began to play an increasingly important role in an expanding native economy. Trusted by whites who perhaps feared males, Chinook women soon became the principal intermediaries between fur merchants and their own kin. Women operated their own business canoes and were regularly consulted on trade matters by men on both sides of the counter. In a culture that frowned on sexual intercourse only if it involved incest, it was reasonable for these women to use their own sexual favors and those of others to make and seal trade agreements. Women who made personal and business alliances with traders enhanced the wealth of their own families. Certainly the Chinook who was reported to be "Mr. Haley's favorite woman" brought influence and material rewards to her family. The young woman who had "J. Bowmon" tattooed on her arm probably had a similar relationship with that trader. The plains people, concerned with acquiring spirit power, had used sex as one means to gain that end. The Chinookans, whose lives focused on trading and material wealth, saw sex as an equally valid way to amass the goods that signaled power and prestige.[48] In a telling set of remarks made in a speech to the Mercantile Library Association of Boston in 1846, one-time coastal trader William Sturgis observed, "Among a portion of the Indians, the management of trade is entrusted to the women. The reason given by the men was, that women could talk with white men *better* than they could, and were willing to talk *more*."[49]

Encounters with Chinook women began while the expedition was still on the north side of the Columbia. Toward evening on November 21, 1805, the wife of the Chinook chief Delashelwilt brought six women to the American camp. Their arrival prompted a brisk exchange of goods and services between young men and women who Clark admitted were "handsome." "The young women sport openly with our men" was Clark's understated way of reporting what must have been quite a romp. In fact, their men were giving away goods at such alarming speed that Lewis and Clark were forced to call a temporary halt to the good times. Finding a ready solution, the captains "divided some ribbon between the men of our party to bestow on their favorite Lasses, this plan to save the knives and more valuable articles."[50] These sexual contacts produced many venereal complaints, belatedly recorded by Lewis and Clark the following spring.

Just how often the Chinook woman, now known as "the old baud," brought her following to Fort Clatsop is not clear. Although Lewis and Clark remained silent on the subject, there are some clues to suggest that sexual contacts were fairly regular. Exchanging goods for sex may have led to the stern prohibition against selling "any tool or iron or steel instrument, arms, accoutrements or ammunicion," issued as part of the General Order dealing with Indian-expedition relations. More specific and less circumstantial is the evidence from Patrick Gass. The sergeant reported that "the old baud" and nine girls "frequently visited our quarters." He noted that sex was available at an "easy rate," and Nicholas Biddle later commented that payment rates were fixed on the basis of female appearance. Medical evidence for all this activity is not wanting. Lewis and Clark alluded to "many" venereal complaints after the initial Chinook meeting. Although there do not appear to have been as many cases at Fort Clatsop as at Fort Mandan, by January at least two men—Hugh McNeal and Silas Goodrich—had contracted the malady.[51]

McNeal's case of "the pox" was certainly uncomfortable, but his "connection" to one Chinook woman saved his life and probably rescued the expedition from involvement in a nasty confrontation. On the evening of January 9, Clark and several men were smoking with Indians at a cluster of Tillamook and Clatsop houses on the Necanicum River near the coast. At ten o'clock the quiet was shattered by loud calls from houses across the river. As many Indians rushed to investigate, Clark's Clatsop guide told him that rumor had it someone's throat had been cut. When Clark discovered that Hugh McNeal was missing, he quickly sent Sergeant Pryor and four armed men to find him. Pryor had no sooner set out than he met McNeal coming "in great haste." Regaining his composure, McNeal explained that he had been invited to one of the houses by a Tillamook man. After sampling some blubber at one lodge, the two men had gone on to another. McNeal did not know that the Indian was intent on killing him for his blanket and personal effects. A Chinook woman described only as "an old friend of McNeals" knew of the plot and seized the American by his blanket cape in an effort to thwart the scheme. Still unaware that his life was at risk, McNeal pushed the woman away. Undaunted, she then alerted the village. In the commotion that followed, McNeal's would-be assassin escaped. Clark provided a proper ending to the whole escapade when he dubbed the Necanicum "McNeal's Folly Creek."[52]

Sex sometimes had comic overtones. When a Clatsop man brought his sister as payment for medical attention, the offer was swiftly rejected. Not to be denied, the woman took up residence with the Charbonneau family. Once her presence was known, a number of men in the expedition came knocking on her door only to find their "solicitations" turned down. After two or three days of sulking around the fort, the woman finally realized that medical bills were easier to incur than to pay.[53] In mid-March, as the party prepared to leave Fort Clatsop, Delashelwilt, "the old baud," and six girls made camp outside the stockade and laid "close seige" to the expedition's affections. Fearing that the "winning graces" of the Chinooks might touch off another epidemic of venereal disease like that in November 1805 and endanger the return journey, the captains delivered a stiff lecture on the dangers that waited outside the fort. The lecture ended, at least so claimed Lewis and Clark, with the entire party giving "the vow of celibacy." In what must be the most inappropriate gesture in expedition history, Delashelwilt was then given a certificate of "good deportment." Lewis and Clark might as well have gone one step further and awarded his wife and her retinue a citation for meritorious service.[54]

Friendly talk and intimate encounters made a dismal winter bearable for at least some of the explorers. At those times the distances that separated explorer from Indian was, if not bridged, at least narrowed. But there was a darker side to Indian relations at Fort Clatsop, something that went beyond the indignity of the password "no Chinook" or the inhospitable treatment afforded visiting chiefs. During February and March, the expedition played out a particularly sordid tale of deception and friendship betrayed. It involved a premeditated theft of a Clatsop canoe in plain violation of Indian legal practice and expedition policy. Writers of detective fiction later in the century might have entitled it "The Case of the Purloined Canoe." Whatever the label, it proved a cautionary tale—one that revealed the brand of white morality confronted by the Indians in the grim years to come.

What later became a blot on the expedition's honor began simply enough in early February when some Clatsop Indians took six elk from George Drouillard's cache. Short on food, Lewis and Clark properly complained to Coboway about the theft. Following traditional practice, the chief sent a man to the fort on February 12 with three dogs to pay for the stolen meat. This well-intentioned and legally correct act went momentarily awry when the dogs bolted and ran off. But all was put right when Drouillard went to the Clatsop village and retrieved the animals. As far as the Indians were concerned, the case was now closed; proper restitution had been made and accepted. There was every reason to believe that the unpleasantness at the elk cache would be forgotten.[55]

But in March, with preparations underway for the journey home, the incident suddenly took on new life. Lewis and Clark knew they would need several Indian canoes to flesh out the expedition's flotilla. Drouillard was therefore sent to the Clatsop village to purchase what craft he could find. He returned with some Clatsops and an "indifferent" canoe; the Indians refused to part with it even when offered Lewis's fancy-dress uniform coat. Indians remained at the fort throughout the day but would not sell their canoes "at a price which it was in our power to give consistently with the state of our stock of merchandize." [56]

Stymied in their efforts to obtain the necessary canoes by honest trade, a plan surfaced that was at worst criminal and at best a terrible lapse of judgment. One of the interpreters—either Drouillard or Charbonneau—and several other men proposed the revival of the elk theft case as a pretext for taking a Clatsop canoe. As Lewis blandly put it, "We yet want another canoe, and as the Clatsops will not sell us one at a price which we can afford to give we will take one from them in lue of the six elk which they stole from us in the winter." Lewis and Clark were not up against the wall of survival, nor was this a food emergency. The captains were abandoning a two-year tradition of never stealing from the Indians. The essential honesty that distinguished Lewis and Clark from explorers like Hernando DeSoto and Francisco Pizarro had been tarnished. Expedition goods were in short supply, but experience always proved that patience in coastal trade usually yielded a satisfactory exchange. Unfortunately, patience was not the order of the day. [57]

On the next day, March 18, an unsuspecting Coboway spent the whole day at the fort. While the chief was there, four of Lewis and Clark's men slipped away toward his village. Knowing where the canoes were beached, they took one and brought it up near the fort. Because Coboway was still there, the thieves concealed their prize nearby until he left. It had been one thing for Lewis to trick Cameahwait into thinking that Clark's party was close at hand when the fate of the expedition hung in the balance at Shoshoni Cove. Even then Lewis admitted his deception "set a little awkward." It was another thing to cheat Coboway—a man Lewis described as "friendly and decent," "kind and hospitable"—and not even feel a pang of conscience. [58]

That singular betrayal of friendship begins to make sense when projected against remarks made by Lewis during the period between the stealing of the elk and the stealing of the canoe. After a visit on February 20 by Taucum and a large Chinook delegation, Lewis launched into a vitriolic attack on the natives. Dredging up language and images rooted in two centuries of white frontier experience, Lewis branded the Indians as treacherous savages beyond redemption. Brushing aside any thought that the two peoples might ever be linked in genuine friendship, the explorer maintained that kindness from whites had always been repaid with brutality from Indians. "The too great confidence of our countrymen in their sincerity and friendship," exclaimed Lewis, "has caused the destruction of many hundreds of us." Turning his attention to the expedition, Lewis admitted that long months of good relations with Indians made it difficult to believe the party could fall victim to attack. Against that general good feeling, Lewis charged that the Indians did not deserve the expedition's confidence, no matter how helpful they had been. About all Indians, he declared, there was something fundamentally treacherous. Lewis was determined to do everything in his power to undermine any favorable impression his men had of the Indians. The central theme of Indian treachery had to be drilled into their minds. The Corps of Discovery had to be taught to hate. In phrases reminiscent of Puritan fears of the howling wilderness and savage devils, Lewis repeated his conviction "that our preservation depends on never loosing sight of this trait [treachery] in their character, and being always prepared to meet it in whatever shape it may present itself."[59] With those words Lewis moved from common-sense vigilance of the sort required of every explorer to a dangerous flirtation with paranoia.

Lewis's ranting was not typical of either the language or the practice of the expedition. It was not even typical of events during the Clatsop winter. But those were powerful words that demand the historian's attention and explanation. A long way from home, the expedition felt hemmed in by a strange environment and seemingly unpredictable people. Isolation, loneliness, and fear—all extract a high price from even the strongest and most moral. Such conditions often release pent-up feelings of hostility toward outsiders. Fort Clatsop always had an atmosphere of "us versus them," unlike the "we" of Fort Mandan. Lewis and Clark were not the first Europeans who had their moral sensibilities challenged and then eroded by the new American land. Lewis's outburst and the theft of the canoe mark a low point in expedition-Indian relations.

The winter at Fort Clatsop ended as it had begun—with overcast skies and splatters of rain. On March 23, 1806, after giving Coboway possession of their winter quarters, Lewis and Clark "bid a final adieu to Fort Clatsop." Lewis claimed that with the exception of not meeting any white traders, all the expedition's goals had been achieved.[60] In most particulars his evaluation was accurate. Secured in carefully sewn elkskin bags was what amounted to a virtual catalog of western North America—its land, peoples, plants, and animals. The face of a vast portion of the continent now would be disclosed for all to see in journals, drawings, maps, vocabularies, botanical specimens, and artifacts. If Lewis and Clark were disturbed that their primary mission—finding a passage through the American garden—had not yielded the result Jefferson hoped for, they did not show it. For now there was only the hurry to sever those ties that for a winter had bound them to the North Coast.

Some eight years later there was a disquieting and sad postscript to the Fort

Clatsop winter. On May 21, 1814, Coboway brought to the North West Company trader Alexander Henry a piece of paper the chief had carefully preserved through all those damp winters. Dated March 19, 1806, it was a list of the members of the Corps of Discovery of the Northwest. Despite their ill treatment of him, the chief obviously cherished this reminder of those his people called *pâh-shish'-e-ooks,* the "cloth men." Coboway's rude introduction to the world of imperial rivalries came when Henry abruptly threw the document into a fire and then presented the chief with a British replacement.[61] Lewis and Clark had done their work well. Lured by what the captains saw, those eight years had brought a flood of Astorians, Nor'-Westers, and empire builders to the Northwest. And Coboway's world had been transformed in ways hard to understand and difficult to predict.

9

The Way Home

"Last evening the indians entertained us with seting the fir trees on fire. They have
a great number of dry lims near their bodies which when set on fire creates a very
suddon and immence blaze from bottom to top of those tall trees. They are a
beatifull object in this situation at night. This exhibition reminded me of a display
of fireworks. The natives told us that their object in seting those trees on fire was
to bring fair weather for our journey."
—MERIWETHER LEWIS, 1806

When Lewis and Clark left Fort Clatsop late in March 1806, their exploring duties
were far from over. Ahead loomed responsibilities every bit as challenging as those
that had driven the explorers up the Missouri and across the mountains nearly two
years before. During the winter, Lewis and Clark had heard from Indian sources
about a river that struck south from the Columbia and reached the "gulph of
California." Finding that river, known to both Indians and explorers as the Multnomah, raised the expedition's hopes for a trade connection into the Southwest.
Equally important were charting the northern course of the Marias River and exploring the Yellowstone. Finally, Lewis and Clark needed to verify Indian information concerning a shorter route between Travelers' Rest and the Great Falls of the
Missouri. All that exploring would demand skill and coordination in field operations beyond anything yet attempted by the Corps of Discovery.

But in all these intricate maneuvers, Indian matters were not forgotten. Promoting and encouraging intertribal peace as a requisite for trade was a goal from the
earliest days of the journey. On the return, Lewis and Clark needed to foster such
notions, often in the face of long-standing tradition. Equally important was the
complex matter of organizing delegations of Indians to visit federal officials in
Washington. Like intertribal peace, this accomplishment hinged on neutralizing
"the Sioux menace." Finally, there were ethnographic tasks yet undone. In their
hurry to reach the Pacific, Lewis and Clark had not carefully studied the Nez Perce
people. Time spent with those Indians would allow the American ethnographers to
record aspects of their life and culture.

Speed, timing, and survival were essential for success in all these efforts. Lewis
and Clark were determined to reach St. Louis in one season of travel, with careful
planning and good fortune. The explorers had to work their way back up a flood-
stage Columbia even more hazardous than before, avoid Indian complications at
the Cascades and The Dalles, and reach their horses at the Nez Perce villages before
those Indians left for summer hunts. Delays caused by snow on the Lolo Trail could
throw their schedules seriously off track. Finally, and no small matter, several field

parties had to be coordinated to reach the Upper Missouri before freeze-up. All told, the return journey presented challenges and opportunities as great as any the expedition had yet faced.

The cold, wet days of spring on the Columbia did nothing to boost the men's spirits as they struggled back upriver. And struggle they did, since the river ran higher and faster than in the fall of 1805. Although Lewis and Clark found friendly treatment at several Chinookan villages along the lower Columbia, there were already unsettling signs. The expedition was intent on finding the Multnomah River, but information from the Indians on the short, shallow character of the Quicksand (Sandy) and Seal (Washougal) rivers was troubling. A brief reconnaissance of those rivers by Sergeant Pryor verified those disappointing reports.

But that disappointment could not match the real concern produced by news from Indians coming downriver from The Dalles. Lewis and Clark had expected to supplement the expedition's food stores with pounded salmon purchased from Wishram and Wasco traders. Now that plan was in doubt as party after party told of scarcities of food and even starvation upriver. "This information," said Lewis with considerable understatement, "gave us much uneasiness with rispect to our future means of subsistence." Quickly rejecting a time-consuming wait at The Dalles for the first salmon run, Lewis and Clark decided to remain at their camp on the north side of the river while laying in a supply of dried meat sufficient for the journey to the Nez Perces. Such a halt would also afford Clark time to extend his search for the elusive Multnomah River.[1]

On April 2, with expeditionary hunters out on resupply missions, Clark resumed his quest for the Multnomah. That effort was materially advanced when several Watlala Indians came to camp to trade. With them were two young men from one of the bands living on the Willamette, the river Clark would eventually select as his Multnomah. From these men he obtained a sketch of the river and directions to find its mouth. Convinced this was the true object of his search, Clark hired an Indian pilot and took seven men to reconnoiter the Willamette. Before reaching the entrance of the river, blocked from earlier view by Sauvies Island, Clark landed at the large Neerchekioo village. As was so often the case with Lewis and Clark's ethnography, it is not clear whether this name refers to a location, a village, or a band. The captains further confused things by describing town residents as the Neerchekioo tribe of the Shahhala (Watlala) nation. The village site was dominated by a large plank house, with more than one hundred cutwater canoes "piled up and scattered in different directions about in the woods."

Exploring the Willamette was Clark's principal objective, but seeing so imposing a plank house piqued his curiosity. That there might be some wappato for exchange could not have been far from his mind as well. Plank houses of this size were usually partitioned into several "apartments." Clark entered one of the rooms and offered goods in trade for wappato. He met stony silence, "sulkey" faces, and a firm rejection of his offer. Clark's mood is hard to guess. What he did next may have been practical joking or the reflection of more hostile feelings. Taking a piece of cannon fuse from his pocket, the explorer tossed it into the fire. As the fuse sputtered and the fire changed color, Clark used a magnet on his inkstand to make a compass needle spin around the rose. "Astonished and alarmed," the Indian women pleaded for him to restore their "healthy" fire. They hastily put several parcels of wappato at his feet. Throughout this display of technological wizardry, an old blind shaman had been "speaking with great vehemunce," calling on spirit forces to protect the village. The drama ended when Clark belatedly paid the women for the wappato.[2]

For all its color and comic overtones, this incident at Neerchekioo does have a grimmer side. In light of the canoe-stealing episode in the last days at Fort Clatsop, Clark's actions in the plank house suggest an increasing willingness to bend the rules whenever it suited the expedition's needs. Frightening and intimidating women and an elderly blind man did little to enhance the honor or the reputation of men who had set a high standard of conduct for themselves and others.

By the second week of April, the expedition had moved farther up the Columbia and was now in position for its first major river challenge—the Cascades portage. That long and difficult carry was more than a dangerous trek around boiling rapids. As Lewis and Clark knew, the Watlala Indians of the Cascades resented the presence of any outsiders who even appeared to threaten their control at this place on the river trade system. Harrassment, hostility, and petty theft were all part of the toll Cascades folk extracted from all travelers. Lewis and Clark were not exempt from that tariff. As the Americans labored up the north shore, against swift current and over high boulders, they met Indians increasingly "sulky and illy disposed." Everything pointed to a portage physically taxing and emotionally trying. One false step could mean canoes and goods irretrievably lost; an overreaction to Indian provocation could have fatal results.[3]

Friday, April 11, proved the crucial day for the Cascades portage. Clark was in charge of the actual portaging operation while Lewis remained at a base camp at the lower end of the Cascades. The captains elected to guide empty canoes through the rapids by means of ropes from the shore. Goods had to be transported over a narrow, rough, and slippery path nearly three thousand yards long. Even without Indian troubles, it was a demanding and nerve-racking task. No sooner had the portage begun than the Watlalas commenced their delaying tactics. So many Indians crowded around the base camp that several extra men had to be assigned to guard duty. The harrassment increased when one particularly bold Indian began throwing stones down on two men in the portage party. John Shields, who had taken some extra time at the head of the Cascades to buy a dog, suddenly found himself the object of the Watlalas' attention. When several Indians attempted to take his future meal and push him off the portage path, Shields drew his knife in readiness for something more than a polite scuffle. Seeing his determined resistence, the native highwaymen fled. Even Lewis did not escape his share of trouble. Three Watlalas slipped into his camp at dusk, and before he could stop them, they had absconded with the dog Scannon. Absolutely furious, Lewis ordered three men to give chase and use all necessary force to rescue Scannon. Gunplay was fortunately avoided as the Indians released the dog when they saw armed explorers in hot pursuit. Not even the reassurances of a Watlala chief that these were the unsanctioned exploits of "two very bad men" and "not the wish of the nation" could mollify the Americans. Lewis and Clark ordered the sentries to shoot any Indian who dared steal the expedition's property. The Watlalas may have seen this all as a baiting game, but an edgy Lewis did not share that view. "I am convinced," he wrote, betraying both worry and belligerence, "that no other consideration but our number at this moment protects us."[4]

The following day there was less tension with Cascades natives. Guards armed with short rifles perhaps convinced them that their toll price was simply too high. But the rapids demanded its own fee as one American craft was caught in the current, slammed against a large rock, and sank. At the end of another cold, rainy day the expedition had passed the Cascades. Considering his anger earlier in the day, Lewis completed the portage quietly, taking a Watlala vocabulary and carefully noting some of the differences between upper and lower Chinookan dialects.[5]

In many ways the Cascades portage was a dress rehearsal for the tensions and troubles that lay ahead at The Dalles. Lewis and Clark knew from their westward journey that Indians at The Dalles might prove difficult. When last at the Narrows, the expedition had attracted relatively few curious Indians. Now in mid-April, with the first salmon run not far off, The Dalles was crowded with people. On April 15, after establishing Rock Fort Camp at the lower end of Long Narrows, the explorers settled in to pursue portage and trade duties. Convinced that an overland route to the Nez Perce villages would save considerable time, Lewis and Clark prepared to do some horse swapping. To speed that trade, it was decided that Clark would set up a temporary trading post on the north side of the Columbia. Lewis would remain to oversee packing and portaging operations from Rock Fort Camp.[6]

With those decisions made, Clark took Drouillard, Charbonneau, and nine other men across to the north shore. Horse trading had never been one of the expedition's strengths. Despite the fact that the frontiersmen knew good horseflesh when they saw it, they were usually at the mercy of native sellers who could set price and supply at will. The Indians who watched Clark's party make camp showed little or no interest in trade. Concerned at how poorly business was faring, Clark detailed

Charbonneau and Frazer to visit the Chilluckquittequaw village while Drouillard and Goodrich went to the Skilloots to drum up business.[7] These ventures produced scant results. Only Drouillard returned with any prospects, bringing a lame Skilloot chief who promised some trade. The chief's presence produced a few nibbles at Clark's merchandise, but the high price placed on horses made setting the hook nearly impossible. Faced with discouraging news, Clark cautiously accepted the Skilloot chief's invitation to visit his village. That night Clark's party was at the Skilloot camp. The explorers may have been pleased by the sight of so many fine horses. The whine of Cruzatte's fiddle and the stomp of dancing feet perhaps fostered hopes that The Dalles passage might not be so trying after all. But Clark experienced other and less favorable omens that night: he was bitten and chewed by "the mice and vermin with which this house abounded."[8]

Anticipation overcame the weariness of a restless night, and the next morning Clark eagerly laid out his goods on a nearby rock. They had been carefully packaged into individual parcels, one bundle offered for each horse. But his best efforts at creative merchandising went awry. Making and then promptly breaking agreements, the Indians "tenterlised" a frustrated William Clark. By the end of the day, he was worn out and ready to quit the Skilloots. Only word that more horses might be brought in convinced him to stay another day. And there was a second and more heartening piece of news. As the Skilloot trade languished during the afternoon, a chief and twenty people from the Sahaptian-speaking Eneeshur village appeared and promised good horses at low prices. For a man who had struggled all day to buy three horses, of which only one was a fit animal, the Eneeshurs' word was indeed welcome. Encouraged or not, Clark was willing to stay at the Skilloot village one more day in the hope that the winds of trade might shift.[9]

Horse trading on April 18 proved no better than on earlier days. Clark had pinned his hopes on the Eneeshurs now that Skilloot sellers persisted in demanding high prices. Those hopes received a sharp check early in the day when an Eneeshur party arrived and, to Clark's great "estonishment," announced that all trade understandings were off. Not about to give up, Clark fell back on his doctoring talents to change the market climate. He offered salve for the chief's sores, gave "some small things" to his children, and ministered camphor and warm flannel to the ailing back of the "sulky Bitch" who was the chief's wife. Just as medical skills had proved a powerful force in dealing with other Indians, Clark found the Eneeshurs' sales resistance lessening. But only two more horses were forthcoming. At prices double what Shoshoni and Flathead traders had asked, Lewis and Clark must have wondered if the expedition's corral would ever hold enough horses for the journey to the Nez Perces. Clark had not slept in two days; when he collapsed in exhaustion at Rock Fort Camp, his timetables were falling steadily behind.[10]

Throughout the next three days, expedition hands labored to drive packhorses and haul goods over The Dalles portage. Although that effort moved slowly, it was at least successful. The same could not be said for the continuing effort to swell the horse herd. Clark moved his trading post to the Eneeshur village above the Short Narrows and admitted that he used "every artifice decent and even false statements to enduce those pore devils to sell me horses." He unsuccessfully offered for each horse the full range of remaining trade items, including blankets, face paint, ribbon, beads, and brass. For a sweetener, Clark threw in his own large blue blanket, military coat, sword, and hat plume. All of that was to no avail because the canny Eneeshurs demanded cooking kettles for horses. In an outburst that revealed mounting frustration and worry, Lewis bitterly described the people of The Dalles as "poor, dirty, proud, haughty, inhospitable, parsimonious, and faithless in every rispect."[11]

As incidents of petty theft and harrassment increased, Lewis and Clark struggled to escape the grip of The Dalles. The last two days at the Narrows, April 21 and 22, held more unpleasantness with Indians than any comparable time in the history of the expedition. Determined to deny the Indians even castoff items, Lewis ordered canoes, poles, and paddles burned. When Lewis spotted an Indian taking one of the iron sockets from a canoe pole, the captain dealt him several blows and ordered the offender kicked out of camp. All the pent-up rage bred by days of trouble boiled over. "I now informed the Indians that I would shoot the first of them that attempted to steal an article from us; that we were not afraid to fight them, that I had it in my power at that moment to kill them all and set fire to their houses, but it was not my wish to treat them with severity provided they would let my property alone. That I would take their horses if I could find out the persons who had stolen the tommahawks but that I had rather lose the property altogether than take the horse of an innocent person." Just how much of this speech was understood is not clear. Lewis's exercise in spleen was perhaps more an index of the expedition's anxiety over homeward schedules than an overeager desire to burn and kill Indians. Punching one thief and shouting some ill-considered threats was not especially noble behavior, but there was sufficient provocation and confusion on both sides to make Lewis's words and deeds at least understandable.

Clark fared no better. Stuck at the Eneeshur village until Lewis's main party came up, he was surrounded by Indians who showed little regard for either his mission or his comfort. The captain's day was miserable as the Eneeshurs crowded around him, demanded tobacco, and made uncharitable remarks about his person. Clark's sole achievement was a chance meeting with a Nez Perce man who lent him a horse and promised to guide the party on their overland route to the Clearwater River.[12]

Lewis and Clark could not break free from The Dalles without one last incident. On April 22, as the expedition prepared to leave its camp at the mouth of the

Deschutes River and begin an overland trek, Charbonneau was caught in a final entanglement. The Frenchman's horse bolted, threw its rider, and ran off toward one of The Dalles villages. As the horse neared the village, Charbonneau's saddle and pad slid from the animal's back. The pad was evidently picked up by an Indian who then denied having it. This seemed the final insult, and Lewis quickly renewed his promise to put the torch to nearby mat lodges unless the robe was returned. On the ragged edge of exasperation and fatigue, Lewis declared, "They have vexed me in such a manner by such repeated acts of villany that I am quite disposed to treat them with every severyty, their defenseless state pleads forgiveness so far as respects their lives." [13] But once again the storm blew over and the captain's rhetoric was not translated into reality.

Finally beyond the reach of The Dalles, the expedition marched along the north side of the Columbia through rocky, sandy country. Guided by the Nez Perce who had earlier offered his services to Clark and aided by the presence of an additional Nez Perce family, the expedition headed toward the Walulas and their friendly chief Yelleppit. Progress was slowed by too few packhorses and, inevitably, the travelers' sore feet and twisted ankles. Such now-familiar hazards were soothed when they reached the camps of the convivial Klikitats and Pishquitpahs.[14] Those evenings with them were filled with fiddling, dancing, and the sort of good times the explorers had not experienced for a long time.

Four days after slipping free from The Dalles, Lewis and Clark finally met Yelleppit. Encountering the Walulas symbolized the end of the Columbia passage. It also meant that the mountains were ahead, and a time with the Nez Perces. Yelleppit's village of fifteen large mat lodges was currently on the north side of the Columbia some twelve miles below the Snake-Columbia confluence. Eager to show his pleasure at seeing the Americans, Yelleppit delivered a long speech enjoining his people to welcome the strangers. The chief then went about gathering food and fuel to set an example of hospitality. Firewood and roasted fish were valuable but even more precious was information offered by the Walulas on the best way to reach the Nez Perce camps on the Clearwater.[15]

On the westbound journey, Lewis and Clark had not been able to spend much time with Yelleppit's folk but had promised to be more neighborly on the return. The chief, interested in gaining a prominent place in the American trade system, was not about to let that promise go unfulfilled. Early on the morning of April 28, he arrived at the expedition's camp with "a very eligant white horse" as a gift for Clark. Like The Dalles traders, the chief had his eye on acquiring some kettles. Since the expedition was dangerously short on cooking pots, the Indian was offered instead Clark's sword, one hundred rounds of ammunition, and some trade goods.

If the captains thought this exchange would satisfy Yelleppit and the expedition might then cross the Columbia, they were mistaken.

The Walula chief was not ready to let Lewis and Clark slip so easily from his grasp. He was willing to provide horses, food, canoes, and information but his price called for the Americans to stay in camp for at least an extra day. Yelleppit artfully recalled the promise made a year ago. An extra day spent with him would hardly make any difference in travel plans. Just how much the presence of Lewis and Clark meant to Walula prestige became plain when Yelleppit revealed that he had invited a large party of Yakimas for a grand feast and dance. Once again, the explorers proved the greatest tourist attraction in western America. Sensing that it would be both impolitic and impolite to disappoint Yelleppit, Lewis and Clark agreed to spend a day before attempting a river crossing. Talks with the Walulas were simplified by the presence of a female Shoshoni prisoner who provided the necessary translation link between Sacagawea and the Sahaptian-speaking Walulas. "We conversed with them," wrote Lewis, "for several hours and fully satisfyed all their enquiries with rispect to ourselves and the objects of our pursuit." Throughout the day, Clark practiced medicine, "a great wonder" to the Walulas, as Ordway noted. The day ended as a group of one hundred Yakimas came for an evening of dancing and singing, much of it led by a Walula shaman who declared that communication with the moon spirit had enabled him to predict the arrival of the Americans. In the firelight and shadow of that festive night, the entire expedition may have set aside their knowledge that the Lolo Trail and the Bitterroots loomed ahead.[16]

In the last days of April, the explorers crossed the Columbia and began a northeastern trek toward the Snake-Clearwater junction. They were now blessed with twenty-three "excellent young horses," most of them from the Walulas. By the first of May, they were along the Touchet River near present-day Waitsburg, Washington. Two days later, up Pataha Creek east of present-day Pomeroy, Washington, the expedition met a Nez Perce known to them as Wearkkoomt. More properly named Apash Wyakaikt or Flint Necklace, he had heard that Lewis and Clark were on the way and was eager to greet them. Although their journals did not mention it at the time, Apash Wyakaikt had evidently gone by land ahead of the expedition in October 1805 to announce their arrival at the Snake-Columbia confluence. Lewis was convinced that those efforts were "very instrumental in procuring us a hospitable and friendly reception among those natives." Not even rain, snow, hail, and scanty rations could diminish what must have been the expedition's pleasure at knowing they would soon be with the Nez Perces on the Clearwater.[17]

The weather and the dog-meat rations did not improve as the explorers slowly made their way toward the Clearwater. In the hard going of steep and narrow paths, men and animals slipped and stumbled. One packhorse loaded with irreplaceable ammunition fell into a creek, but that mysterious Lewis and Clark luck held and neither horse nor load was damaged. In the afternoon of May 4, the party arrived at the lodges of another Nez Perce familiar from a year before. Tetoharsky, along with Twisted Hair, had provided invaluable help on the westward voyage. From Tetoharsky's kin, Lewis and Clark now learned that they should cross the Snake at this point and then follow the Clearwater on the northeast side to where Twisted Hair had pastured the expedition's herd of horses. Knowing that more horses were close by may have improved morale, dampened by a night so cold and disagreeable that the Nez Perces huddled around Lewis and Clark's fire "in great numbers insomuch that we could scarcely cook or keep ourselves warm."[18]

On the following day, May 5, the explorers plodded along the Clearwater. Their enquiries at Nez Perce mat lodges for food found the larders nearly bare. And many Nez Perces resented the way the strangers crowded into the lodges, disregarding both etiquette and their obvious poverty. But at one of the lodges Lewis and Clark found an unexpected ally. On the westbound journey, Clark had done a good deal of doctoring among the Nez Perces. One of those he had medicated had "never ceased to extol the virtues of our medicines and the skill of my friend Captain Clark as a phisician." Ointments and salves now proved powerful agents as dozens of ailing Nez Perces began to line up for consultations with "their favorite phisician." Lewis doubted the efficacy of Clark's medicine chest but justified "this deception for they will not give us any provision without compensation in merchandize and our stock is now reduced to a mere handfull."

Provisions, especially dog meat, were what the expedition desperately needed. The Nez Perces did not usually eat dog and found it amusing that the explorers relished it. That amusement very nearly sparked a serious argument when a Nez Perce prankster "very impertinently" threw a scrawny puppy toward Lewis. Angered by the act and the general laughter it provoked, Lewis caught the dog and threw it back at the Indian "with great violence." At the same time, the explorer brandished his tomahawk and made signs that if another dog grew wings the Indian would suffer for it. With undisguised arrogance, Lewis recorded that he then continued lunch "*on dog*" without further interruption.

Later that afternoon, the expedition reached a large mat lodge measuring 15 by 156 feet. Holding thirty families, this Nez Perce long house was home to many in the band of Neeshneparkkeook, or Cutnose, who had gotten his name as the result of a wound suffered in combat with the Shoshonis. Although not especially impressed with either his physique or his intelligence, Lewis and Clark gave Cutnose a small medal. Perhaps more important, the explorers met a Shoshoni taken prisoner by the Nez Perces. With this man as translator, it was now possible to have direct talks with the Nez Perces without relying on signs. The first piece of information that came from the Shoshoni translator was worrisome. He indicated that at least one Nez

Perce elder believed Lewis and Clark were "bad men and had come to kill them." Knowing that such rumors had to be squelched, the captains were pleased when Flint Necklace rejoined the party.[19]

For the next two days, the expedition traveled east along the Clearwater. As before, those were days of slim rations. Horses traded for Clark's eyewash were quickly butchered. Clark also had time to record accurate descriptions of Nez Perce clothing, burial practices, and hunting techniques. But just beneath that travel routine was some very disturbing news, something beyond horses or diplomacy. Everyone in the party could now see that the Bitterroots were covered with snow, an observation confirmed by several Nez Perces who reported, "The snow is yet so deep on the mountains that we shall not be able to pass them until after the next full moon or about the first of June." Describing this as "unwelcome intiligence," Lewis admitted that the diet of horsemeat and roots already had most of the expedition dreaming of those "fat plains of the Missouri" and home.[20]

It was not until the afternoon of May 8, some miles south of the Clearwater, that Lewis and Clark found lodges belonging to Twisted Hair. The captains expected to see not only him but horses as well. What greeted them instead was a long-simmering quarrel between Twisted Hair and Cutnose. No sooner had the explorers met Twisted Hair than he began to speak in a loud and angry voice. Cutnose's reply was equally heated. Lewis and Clark did not immediately understand the cause of the dispute but quickly realized that any delay in finding their horses might be serious. Moving to cut off the argument, the captains announced that they were going to march on to the first good water and bed down for the night. Hoping to reconcile them, they invited both Twisted Hair and Cutnose to come along.

Once at their evening camp, Lewis and Clark acted to mediate between the two quarrelling Indians. During the past several days, the explorers had heard rumors that their horses were scattered and the saddle and tack cache damaged. Putting Twisted Hair and Cutnose on good terms might clear the air and make rounding up the horses much easier. Because the young Shoshoni interpreter refused to take part in what he said was not his affair, Lewis and Clark had to rely on signs to mollify both parties. After Drouillard found Twisted Hair, the explorers listened first to his explanation. Twisted Hair claimed that no sooner had he taken possession of the expedition's horses than Cutnose and Tunnachemootoolt (Broken Arm) returned from a raid against the Shoshonis. Angry and jealous of the prestige Twisted Hair had gained by his association with the Americans, Cutnose and Broken Arm evidently had begun a long and wearing argument with the elderly Indian. Tired and upset by their complaints, Twisted Hair now admitted he had neglected the horses. Unsure how close to the truth his words were but unwilling to worsen a complex situation, Lewis and Clark reminded the Indian that his reward of two guns and ammunition was still available if he would locate the missing horses. The captains then sent Drouillard to fetch Cutnose. His story was predictably different. Cutnose charged that Twisted Hair was "a bad old man" who "woar two faces." According to Cutnose, Twisted Hair had allowed several young men to ride expedition horses hard enough to injure them. Cutnose insisted that he and Broken Arm had tried to protect the horses, but to no avail. Denied the services of their translator, Lewis and Clark could neither ascertain the full truth nor resolve the quarrel. Prudence suggested staying with Twisted Hair one day to allow him time to bring in the horses and then moving on to Broken Arm's lodge to pay him proper due.[21]

Letting each man tell his tale and giving at least surface credence to both was a happy compromise. On the following day, Twisted Hair sent two young men to bring in the expedition's horses. Although most were healthy, at least three showed signs of hard use. In the afternoon, Twisted Hair and Alexander Willard went out to recover saddles, tack, powder, and lead from a cache built the previous year. Happily, there were signs that the row between Twisted Hair and Cutnose had become a thing of the past. But against these good omens was the growing awareness that the expedition would be spending more time with the Nez Perces than first anticipated. Lewis and Clark's location on May 9 was unsuitable for a more permanent camp. Access to water, good pasture, and protection against weather and theft all required finding another site.

That the expedition had left Fort Clatsop too soon became painfully evident when the explorers set out on May 10 for Broken Arm's village. With eight inches of snow on the ground, horses slipped repeatedly along the hazardous trail. It was not until late in the afternoon that Lewis and Clark finally came down to Lawyer's Canon Creek and straggled into the Nez Perce settlement. Greeting them were an impressive Nez Perce chief and his people, framed by a large mat lodge and an American flag left behind the previous year. Cold and hungry, Lewis and Clark asked Broken Arm's help to restock the expedition's supplies. The chief responded by bringing roots and dried salmon, food that stirred memories of agonizing indigestion and dysentery. He then graciously promised as many horses as needed for fresh meat.

While all this menu-planning was going on, the stage was being set for preliminary talks with the Nez Perces. Those councils moved a step closer when an important chief Lewis and Clark called Hohastillpilp arrived at Broken Arm's village with a party of fifty mounted warriors. More properly known as Hohots Ilppilp or the Bloody Chief, his village was some six miles away near the Clearwater. With Broken Arm, Cutnose, and Hohots Ilppilp present, Lewis and Clark decided to begin serious talks. Broken Arm and Hohots Ilppilp were first given medals. Using their Shoshoni interpreter, the explorers explained "the design and the importance of medals in the estimation of the whites as well as the red men who had been taught their value." Impressed by all this, and with his eye on gaining things more precious than medals, Broken Arm led the explorers to a council tepee. With a crowd of Indians packed into the lodge, everyone spent the rest of the evening eating prime horsemeat, smoking friendly pipes, and talking in a mixture of phrases and signs that were hastily translated. This council seemed to promise the kind of diplomatic success that had so often eluded Lewis and Clark.[22]

Early talks with Nez Perce chiefs prepared the way for two days of serious diplomatic exchange on May 11 and 12. If Lewis and Clark were unsure of their agenda at Fort Clatsop, they were more certain of their negotiating priorities with the Nez Perces and other plateau peoples. Participation in the American trade system, intertribal peace, and delegations of notables destined for the president's reception room were all on the list of subjects to be broached with the Nez Perces. It was an agenda that Lewis and Clark believed applicable to every native group. That such diplomacy—especially the dangerous practice of promising arms to traditional enemies—might have unforeseen and unpleasant consequences had not yet become plain to the Corps of Discovery diplomats.

With the arrival of Yoomparkkartim (Five Big Hearts), "a chief of great note," all major Nez Perce headmen in the immediate area were present. Lewis and Clark never lacked a flair for the dramatic, no matter how understated their journal entries. Borrowing from native cartographic techniques, the captains began the grand council by drawing a map of the country with charcoal on a stretched hide. Smoking, gift-giving, and the mapping revealed just how much the explorers had learned of Indian protocol. If past experience proved any guide, Lewis was responsible for making the formal presentation. Although his remarks were short and uncomplicated, translations proved "tedious" as every word passed through English, French, Hidatsa, Shoshoni, and Nez Perce speakers. Half the day was taken up getting Lewis's message across to the patient chiefs. The American officer presented four closely related points. Establishing trading posts, instituting intertribal peace, and preparing delegations were a trio of themes that had been repeated since the earliest days on the Missouri. The issue of American sovereignty was an unspoken part of the talks, although what had been said the previous day about the design and meaning of medals suggests that thoughts of sovereignty were not far from the Americans' minds. But there was a final point in Lewis's presentation that was both spoken and demonstrated. Throughout their long voyage Lewis and Clark were always at pains to show as forcefully as possible the military prowess and technological strength of the new republic. Parades, keelboat curiosities, telescopes, mirrors, and the omnipresent airgun were all for that purpose. "After the council was over," wrote Lewis, "we amused ourselves with showing them the power of magnatism, the spy glass, compass, watch, air gun and sundry other articles equally novel and incomprehensible to them." When one young and important warrior told the captains that he had "opened his ears to our councils and that our words had made his heart glad," Lewis and Clark must have believed that a major diplomatic victory was in the offing.[23]

The captains understood enough Indian political and diplomatic practice to realize that no immediate answer to the American plans could be expected. There had to be time for talk and a ceremonial acceptance of a consensus that was ultimately binding on none. Throughout the morning of Monday, May 12, chiefs and elders spoke their minds in a council that eventually proved to have far-reaching consequences for the Nez Perce people. The Nez Perce leaders assembled at Broken Arm's village certainly understood what was at stake. By 1806 there were about four thousand Nez Perces living in several autonomous bands. The predictable rhythms of their lives were increasingly challenged by the flood of firearms falling into the hands of Blackfeet and Atsina warriors. The Nez Perce situation was similar to that of Cameahwait's Lemhi Shoshonis. Both peoples desperately needed a place in the American trade system, if only to obtain guns and ammunition. In a plains and plateau world undergoing profound change, links to American traders promised what must have seemed cheap security. Several hours of talk behind him, Broken Arm emerged and set in motion one of the most dramatic moments in expedition history. Taking flour made from cous roots, the chief made a thick mush and then ladled it into "the kettles and baskets of all his people." After a long speech in which he explained the decisions reached in council, Broken Arm called on all who accepted those decisions to eat the mush. In a colorful line, Lewis observed, "All swallowed their objections if any they had very cheerfully with their mush." This was done to a background of women crying and tearing their hair, perhaps sensing that links with the strangers might bring unequal measures of safety and danger.

With ritual acceptance of the council's decisions, it was time for the Indians to present formally their views to Lewis and Clark. Because so many Nez Perces required medical attention, the captains decided that Clark would spend the rest of the day doctoring while Lewis pursued his diplomacy. The official orator for the Nez Perces was the elderly father of Hohots Ilppilp, a man of considerable prestige and political skill. Declaring that the Nez Perces now spoke with one heart and one mind, the old speaker presented a perceptive, critical evaluation of American proposals and native needs. He agreed that peace with neighboring tribes had real advantages. As if to underscore the unity of American and Nez Perce policies, he reported that in the summer of 1805 a Nez Perce delegation had gone to parley with Shoshonis along the Snake River. But those emissaries had been killed by Shoshoni warriors and the resulting raid against the Snake River people had counted forty-two Shoshonis dead and only three Nez Perce casualties. The blood of the slain peacemakers had been properly revenged and peace was now possible. But whether the old man meant peace as Lewis and Clark understood it or a temporary truce remained unclear. As they had along the Missouri, the explorer-diplomats unthinkingly assumed that "peace" meant the same thing on both sides of the cultural divide.

As the Nez Perce leadership understood it, the real issue was trade and security. Access to guns symbolized their concern. Speaking to that complex matter, the Nez Perce orator declared that his people were willing to travel on to the Missouri plains for trade. However, no Nez Perce was prepared to make such a trading journey unless there were solid assurances that Blackfeet and Atsina warriors were not lying in ambush along the trail. All of this meant arming the Nez Perces and making peace with those plains warriors already well armed by Canadian traders. That these two objectives were mutually exclusive may have been evident to some Nez Perces but not to Lewis and Clark. The old speaker pledged everlasting friendship to the Americans, saying that although the bands were poor, "their hearts were good." There may have been plenty of "good hearts" in evidence, but what the Nez Perces really wanted were guns. As for a delegation to the Federal City, that issue was unresolved. If the Americans could deliver weapons, then perhaps a long journey to see the chief of the seventeen fires would be worth the trouble and danger.

Lewis and Clark's fullest day of diplomacy since talks with Cameahwait ended with a flurry of eating, singing, dancing, and gambling. Pipes were passed, more gifts exchanged, and Clark continued his medical ministrations. But in all this play and good feeling, there was one activity that especially fascinated many Nez Perce warriors. Firing rifles at targets drew their attention. The presence of native visitors on the weapons range was a clear indication of what lay behind so much of the talk during that day. When Lewis struck the mark twice from a range of 220 yards, those warriors could not help but be impressed with the weapons that might soon be in their hands.[24]

Lewis and Clark believed that their major diplomatic objectives with the Nez Perces had been accomplished. After the talks, they were increasingly concerned with the problem of deep snows in the Bitterroots. During the grand council, there were further reports that the Lolo Trail would not be passable for at least another month. Any hope of a quick passage over the mountains was now gone. A site had to be found for a camp among the Nez Perces, and arrangements had to be made for guides once the trail was open. Lewis and Clark hoped that by inviting Twisted Hair's family to live nearby, guides from his household might be hired. Following suggestions from several chiefs, they located a camping place along the north bank of the Clearwater River near modern-day Kamiah, Idaho. This was an especially favorable site, providing access to good hunting grounds, fine pasture for horses, and the river when the salmon finally ran. The expedition's baggage was stored in the center of a depression made by an abandoned winter pit lodge. Although the expedition spent nearly a month (May 14–June 10, 1806) at this spot, Lewis and Clark never gave the camp a formal name. Tradition has called it Camp Chopunnish, Long Camp, or Camp Kamiah. Clark placed his seal of approval on the location by declaring himself "perfectly satisfied with our position." [25]

Although Camp Chopunnish was never much more than a collection of leaky brush wickiups, luggage pens, and a makeshift horse corral, it was the center of busy activity. Day by day there were more Indians who found a welcome at Camp Chopunnish than at Fort Clatsop. Contacts with the Nez Perces ranged from trade and medicine to sport and sex. As they waited for snows to melt up in the Bitterroots, members of the expedition developed close ties with these Indians.

Despite the best efforts of expeditionary hunters led by George Drouillard, it was plain by early May that a reliable trade in foodstuffs had to be established with the Nez Perce villages. It was this trade that most often provided common ground for explorer and Indian. What to offer for stocks of camas and cous roots and the much-sought-after cous bread proved a serious problem. Nez Perce tastes in trade goods did not run to "baubles," as Lewis called them. Beads, armbands, and other luxury items failed to attract much attention. The practical Nez Perces sought knives, kettles, blankets, and moccasin awls. But the expedition's supplies of those tools and utensils were short, and if Lewis and Clark hoped to foster a dependable trade, canny substitutions had to be found. [26]

By mid-May, as the expedition's hunting fortunes further declined, Lewis and Clark organized trading parties to visit the Nez Perce villages. Typical of those ventures was the first mission to Broken Arm's village. Toussaint Charbonneau, John Thompson, Peter Wiser, John Potts, and Hugh Hall were given moccasin awls, knitting pins, and brass armbands to exchange for cous roots and bread. After a day of haggling, "our marketers" returned near dark with six bushels of roots and bread. On May 20, Frazer was sent on the second trade foray. He reported that the Nez Perces were apparently ready to depart from their usual utilitarian demands and might be wooed with brass uniform buttons. Buttons promptly vanished from the expedition's clothing as each man gathered what he could to make trade bargains. Lewis and Clark evidently feared that such a scramble might produce economic chaos and reduced morale. On May 21, the captains collected all the remaining goods and carefully parceled them out to each man. Every member of the Corps of Discovery was given one awl, one knitting pin, half an ounce of vermilion paint, two needles, a few skeins of thread, and one yard of ribbon. With this "slender stock," each man was to make any agreements he could to obtain the food necessary for the Lolo Trail passage. [27]

In the last days of May, small expedition parties made regular trips to Indian camps along the Clearwater. Trading was often difficult as Nez Perce folk soon learned that the laws of supply and demand favored them. Gass admitted that roots and bread could only be bought "at a very dear rate." Hardpressed to meet Nez Perce business demands, some men ingeniously fashioned moccasin awls from small links of a discarded chain. The Nez Perce trade was not only difficult but dangerous as well. When Charbonneau and Jean Baptiste Lepage went up the Clearwater to trade at a village some eight miles away, they experienced, in Lewis's words, "a broken voyage." Things began to go wrong for the two French traders when their packhorse slipped and fell into the Clearwater. Terrified, the horse bolted and swam across the river. An Indian on the opposite shore helpfully tried to drive the horse back toward the traders, but the pack cinches broke and precious cargo was lost. And to compound troubles, a raft loaded with roots destined for Charbonneau and Lapage struck a rock and capsized. "The river having fallen heir to both merchandize and roots," wrote Lewis laconically, "our traders returned with empty hands." The troubles experienced by Potts, Shannon, and John Collins were far more serious. While attempting to cross the Clearwater, their canoe caught the full force of the current and slammed into a tree. Potts was "an indifferent swimmer"; as he floundered in the river, the canoe quickly filled with water and sank. In the confusion three blankets, one blanket coat, and a supply of trade goods were lost. Efforts by Pryor and his men to raise the canoe and recover the goods failed. The loss of the blankets was indeed serious. As Gass explained, "The loss of these blankets is the greatest which hath happened to any individual since we began our voyage, as there are only three men in the party who have more than one blanket apiece." [28]

By the first days of June, the expedition's stocks of trade items were nearly gone. High prices, accidents, and continued poor hunting made business with the Nez Perces increasingly difficult and jeopardized the explorers along the Lolo Trail. "Having exhausted all our merchandize," wrote Lewis, "we are obliged to have recourse to every subterfuge in order to prepare in the most ample manner in our power to meet that wretched portion of our journey, the Rocky Mountains, where hungar and cold in their most rigorous forms assail the wearied traveller." Whether those "subterfuges" were the same as the tricks of trade employed by Clark along the Columbia is not plain in the journals. What is recorded is a desperate effort to find any objects that might attract the Indians' attention. Lewis and Clark cut the buttons from their own coats and made up measures of several medications. Those goods, along with some unused phials and tin boxes, were given to McNeal and York. When the two men returned bringing three bushels of roots and some cous bread, their success was "not much less pleasing to us than the return of a good cargo to an East India Merchant." [29] Less successful was a long trip undertaken by Ordway, Frazer, and Wiser to an Indian fishery at Wild Goose Rapids on the Snake River to trade for salmon. After a journey that lasted a week and covered some one hundred miles, Ordway's party returned with seventeen spoiled fish and a few cous roots. [30]

Throughout the first week of June, Lewis and Clark continued to pursue the Nez Perce trade. Believing that snows would be sufficiently melted within the next two weeks, the explorers redoubled their efforts to stockpile food for the mountain passage. But these efforts were hampered by few goods for trade and the failure of salmon to run on the Clearwater. Nothing could be done about the tardy fish, but many men in the party used considerable imagination to create "little notions" from bits and pieces of worn files, spare bullets, and tattered fish nets. These ventures in product design evidently paid off, much to Lewis and Clark's surprise. The captains, who had been so pessimistic a few days before, found that by June 6 the Corps had enough rations to dare the Lolo Trail.[31] The remaining trade centered on obtaining ropes for packsaddles, skin bags to hold provisions, and animal hair for saddle pads.

That the Nez Perces continued to have "good hearts" toward their Camp Chopunnish neighbors was the result of two expectations. Hope that ties to the Americans might bring a steady supply of trade goods, especially guns and ammunition, and some lessening of tensions with plains raiders clearly shaped the Indians' behavior. Only slightly less important for expedition–Nez Perce relations were the medical services Clark provided to countless Indian men, women, and children. Just how interested the Nez Perces were in his doctoring was evident even before Camp Chopunnish was established. As Clark explained it, cures accomplished during the westbound journey "raised my reputation and gives those nativs an exolted oppinion of my skill as a phisician." Quickly realizing that much of their future comfort and security depended on Nez Perce good will, the explorers were willing to continue the "deception" of Clark as the great healer. But Clark was not without scruples, and he maintained: "We take care to give them no article which can possibly injure them, and in many cases can administer and give such medicine and sirgical aid as will effectually restore them in simple cases."[32]

As the Nez Perces' "favorite phisician," Clark had a waiting room filled with eager patients. Throughout the days at Camp Chopunnish, he saw a wide variety of diseases and disorders. Most common were sore eyes, rheumatism, strained muscles, and abrasions. But there were also more demanding medical problems, including serious abscesses, mental depression, and "disorders intirely out of the power of Medison." Determined to do what he could for those "poor afflicted wretches," Clark utilized simple medications and common-sense therapies. Those included various salves, elixirs, pills, and large quantities of eyewash. Laudanum (tincture of opium) was the most potent drug in the expedition's medicine chest. Clark also administered back rubs and on at least one occasion performed minor surgery on a festering abscess. The fact that a party of Nez Perces once spent two days in the saddle to obtain some of Clark's famous eyewash is a reminder of how important his medical services were at Camp Chopunnish.[33]

Of all the Nez Perce cases seen by Clark, none was more dramatic or as well-documented as that of a paralyzed chief. This unnamed "chief of considerable note" first appeared at camp on May 11. With clinical precision, Lewis and Clark described the Indian's symptoms and speculated on the cause of his apparent paralysis. "This man is incapable of moveing a single limb but lies like a corps in whatever position he is placed, yet he eats hartily, dejests his food perfectly, enjoys his understanding. His pulse are good, and has retained his flesh almost perfectly; in short were it not that he appears a little pale from having been so long in the shade, he might well be taken for a man in good health. I suspect that their confinement to a diet of roots may give rise to all the disorders of the nativs of this quarter except the Rhumitsism and Sore eyes, and to the latter of those, the state of debility incident to a vegitable diet may measureably contribute." Although betraying a cultural preference for red meat in the diet, in every other way the diagnosis represents a skillful piece of physiological observation.[34]

With this case Lewis and Clark learned the difference between successful diagnosis and effective therapy. The explorers were especially eager to provide good care for the chief. Success in treatment would further insure Nez Perce hospitality and support. But in a case as complex as this, they were quite unsure how to proceed. Notions about diet as the root cause of the man's immobility offered slight guidance for a condition that had already lasted five years. Clark first prescribed "simple cooling medicenes" for the chief. When these failed and the chief's relatives persisted in hoping for a cure, he gave several doses of sulphur and cream of tartar and proposed a regimen of daily cold baths. But in all of this Clark admitted that he was "at a loss to deturmine what to do for this unfortunate man." In desperation, he suggested a few drops of laudanum and the expedition's version of chicken soup, a watery broth made from portable soup.[35]

A breakthrough of sorts came on May 24. After giving a powerful sweat bath to chronically ill William Bratton and seeing its positive results, the captains decided to try the treatment on the chief. But the sweating hole dug for Bratton proved too small for the chief. Stymied but not ready to admit defeat, Lewis and Clark urged relatives to take the chief to their larger sweat lodges. And reflecting current medical interest in the possible healing effects of electricity, Lewis declared that the chief "would be an excellent subject for electricity" and regretted that "I have it not in my power to supply it."[36]

Clark may have thought that, after his failure to sweat the chief, his advice to the anxious family might end the expedition's involvement. But Clark's reputation was too powerful for that, and when both patient and family lingered in camp, he was compelled to once again prescribe sulphur and cream of tartar and urge that the stricken chief be taken home. When the latter suggestion was strongly resisted, it was agreed to attempt a second sweat. On the following day, May 27, the chief's father carefully enlarged the sweat pit. The man was then lowered into the pit with ropes and, despite considerable pain, the therapy seemed promising.

In the days that followed, the heat treatments were repeated. To the surprise of all, the chief gradually recovered use of his arms and hands. By the end of May, the man was washing his face and was able to move his toes and legs. As the expedition prepared to leave Camp Chopunnish in early June, the chief continued to report progress. Whether his improvement was sustained is not known, but the efforts of Lewis and Clark in this difficult case reenforced the positive image of the explorers in the minds of many Nez Perces.[37]

Busy with trade, medicine, and the demands of daily life, Lewis and Clark still found time to record something about the lives of their Indian hosts. As had become the rule in their ethnography, the explorers paid most attention to Nez Perce material culture. In references scattered throughout the Camp Chopunnish entries, Lewis and Clark commented on a variety of topics. Eating habits, domestic architecture, hunting techniques, and the Nez Perce passion for fine horses all found a place in their records. Clothing, saddles, and weapons were duly noted and described. Attitudes about old age, the protocol of diplomacy, and the custom of sacrificing horses at the death of a prominent person made the Nez Perces come alive in the journals. And the explorers took time to set down one vivid aural impression of native life. "The noise of their women pounding roots reminds me of a nail factory," wrote Lewis.[38]

Camp Chopunnish was second only to Fort Mandan as a place where Indians and explorers could enjoy each other's company. Although records for this period are neither as full nor as explicit as those kept at Fort Mandan, there is evidence strongly suggesting that the Americans stood "at ease" among the Clearwater people. Finding much to admire in Nez Perce customs, hospitality, and physique, Lewis and Clark felt comfortable enough to relax and enjoy some breathing time before assaulting the dreaded Lolo Trail. There were times for fiddling, dancing, and singing. On several occasions, the expedition's hunters shared meat with hungry Indians. In return, the natives showed the Americans a remarkably infection-free method for gelding horses. Even at Fort Mandan there had been bumps and scrapes in Indian-expedition relations. But if such troubles drifted into Camp Chopunnish, they were so minor as to elude all journal keepers.[39]

Even more elusive are the facts about sexual relations between men in the expedition and Nez Perce women. Among the Nez Perces, there were no strong sanctions for or against sex with whites. These plateau people used sex neither to seal trade bargains nor to gain spiritual power. The expedition's records during the winters with the Mandans and the Clatsops are filled with the pleasures and troubles of native affairs. But the Camp Chopunnish entries in all journals are oddly silent on what was from the beginning an accepted part of the life of the expedition. There seems little doubt that contacts more intimate than trading for roots took place during those early spring days. Sex usually made for good copy in the journals when it involved disease, personal trouble, or cultural misunderstanding. Since relations with the Nez Perces were amiable, whatever personal encounters took place may well have been mutually satisfactory.

Perhaps the most intriguing piece of evidence to suggest the presence of such liaisons is a photograph taken by the noted western cameraman William H. Jackson. Before the 1877 Nez Perce War, Jackson encountered a Nez Perce band and was introduced to a blue-eyed, sandy-haired man claiming to be William Clark's son. Sufficiently impressed, Jackson photographed the man. The assertion that Clark left a son behind along the Clearwater persisted, and when Chief Joseph's band surrendered to General Nelson Miles in 1877, one of the Nez Perce prisoners was pointed out as Clark's son. Although in no way conclusive, the story does reveal the continued positive reputation of Lewis and Clark among the Nez Perces well into the nineteenth century. Whether this particular man was indeed Clark's son or the child of another white explorer is beyond the power of existing historical evidence either to verify or deny. At the same time, the persistence of the tale hints at one more part of the physical life at Camp Chopunnish.[40]

Far less difficult to document were times of boisterous fun and athletic competition in what might be aptly described as the Camp Chopunnish Olympics. The men of the expedition had been selected, at least in part, for their sound constitutions. Despite long months of travel and often irregular diets, most remained in good condition. Their frontier and military backgrounds were filled with demanding physical conditioning as well as a tradition of competitive sports. The Nez Perce men equally admired strong bodies and tests of skill and strength. Early in June, as the expedition prepared to leave camp, the explorers and Indians staged an impromptu series of athletic contests. There had already been some target shooting, and now foot races were added to the schedule. Matched against a Nez Perce team that Lewis admitted was "very active" were sprinters George Drouillard and Reuben Field. But Indian runners proved very swift, and at least one was as fast as the best the Corps of Discovery had to offer. Following the races was a game Lewis and Clark described as "prison base," an activity much like "keep away" or "running bases." These good-natured competitions provided yet another chance for all in camp to enjoy simple pleasures. For the captains there was an additional benefit. As Lewis explained it, with the mountain crossing drawing near, those men who had become "rather lazy and slouthfull" needed some rigorous exercise.[41]

As May slipped into June and the time grew closer to leave Camp Chopunnish, there were several diplomatic questions still unanswered. Although Lewis and Clark certainly believed that most of the American proposals had been accepted, some issues had not yet received formal Nez Perce replies. Those included the expedition's requests for guides beyond the mountains, a Nez Perce group to accompany Lewis at least partway in his journey to negotiate with Atsina and Blackfeet bands, and a delegation to visit President Jefferson.

On June 4, as Broken Arm and several other chiefs prepared to leave for their own villages, Lewis and Clark reminded them of earlier promises to aid the expedition. The chiefs' reply revealed not so much second thoughts about an American trade and military alliance as some caution about the powers and abilities of untested new friends. Broken Arm carefully declined the invitation for some young warriors to accompany Lewis beyond Travelers' Rest, declaring that his hunters would not venture beyond the Bitterroots until late in the summer. He hinted that there was little hope for a Nez Perce delegation to go with Lewis. Although none of the chief's replies spelled defeat for American diplomacy, they did reveal a certain prudent wariness. The Nez Perces wanted American guns and the security they promised, but there were always those cries of fearful women to counsel caution.[42]

Not about to accept Broken Arm's words as a final answer, the captains decided to send Clark and a small party to parley once again with the chief. Receiving the Americans with unfailing hospitality, Broken Arm told Clark of the presence of many headmen from small and more distant villages who had not been at the grand council in early May. Broken Arm had thoughtfully invited them and now asked Clark to repeat to them the American plans. If Clark hoped that a larger audience and a second chance to explain federal policy might change some minds, he was wrong. Broken Arm repeated what he had said two days before: no large number of Nez Perces were about to accompany the expedition. The request for some warrior-diplomats to foster intertribal peace on the Marias could not be decided until a larger council met.

But Broken Arm did not want Clark to think the whole notion of peace with neighbors was now in doubt. The chief explained that, as a result of recent contacts with Shoshonis who desired peace with Nez Perce and Cayuse bands, a Nez Perce delegation had been sent toward the Snake River to negotiate such an agreement. Broken Arm promised he would never break that peace and to emphasize his good intentions presented Clark two ceremonial pipes—one a traditional Nez Perce pipe for the explorers and the other a fancy plains pipe with silver inlays for the Shoshonis. Knowing the significance of those pipes, Clark decorated the one destined for the Shoshonis with blue ribbon and white wampum to symbolize a mutual desire for peace. As he made his way back to camp, Clark may well have noted that, although American policy now seemed on firmer ground, the immediate need for guides over the treacherous Lolo Trail was yet unmet.[43]

From the first days at Camp Chopunnish, Lewis and Clark had maintained a close watch on snow conditions in the Bitterroots. The expedition's timetables called for a quick journey over the mountains. A long stay with the Nez Perces, no matter how pleasant, seriously endangered the homeward voyage. By the middle of May, both captains were looking for any sign to prove that the Lolo Trail would soon be passable. Clark reported: "I frequently consult the nativs on the subject of passing this tremendious barrier which now present themselves to our view." Lewis anxiously eyed the level of the Clearwater River for some hint that snows were melting. In a moment of frustration, he lashed out at "that icy barrier which seperates me from my friends and Country, from all which makes life esteemable—patience, patience." Lewis might well have counseled patience for himself and the whole party. Both Nez Perce and expedition hunters reported deep snows that might not melt until at least mid-June.[44]

As mid-June approached, the entire expedition busied itself preparing for the Lolo assault. By June 6, Lewis and Clark felt certain that their food stocks were sufficient to meet any challenge on the trail. But two days later, all those hopes and plans suffered an unexpected setback. A Nez Perce reported that the trail beyond Weippe Prairie was still so deep with snow that any passage during June was courting disaster. As the Indian explained, "If we attempted it sooner our horses would be at least three days travel without food on the top of the mountain." Lewis admitted, "This information is disagreeable inasmuch as it causes some doubt as to the time at which it will be proper for us to set out." A hurried and anguished meeting to discuss tactics must have followed that unwelcome Nez Perce road report. When Lewis and Clark had held a similar talk in early June 1805 to decide whether the Marias River was the true Missouri channel, they had made the right choice. But in a rush to get home, and increasingly fearful of delay, the captains now blundered into the wrong decision. "As we have no time to loose we will wrisk the chanches and set out as early as the Indians generally think practicable or the middle of this month." Risking the chances was dangerous enough; without Indian guides, the expedition was moving toward a rendezvous with the Lolo that not even the old Lewis and Clark luck could overcome.[45]

The decision to leave Camp Chopunnish against Indian advice and without guides was dead wrong, but it was very popular with the rank and file in the Corps of Discovery. Lewis insisted that "our party seem much elated with the idea of moving on towards their friends and Country, they all seem alirt in their movements today." But as the day of departure approached, both captains began to have second thoughts. "Even now," said Clark, "I shudder with the expectation [of] great difficuelties in passing those Mountains." Lewis was typically more explicit in his appraisal of the situation.

> I am still apprehensive that the snow and the want of food for our
> horses will prove a serious imbarrassment to us as at least four days

journey of our rout in these mountains lies over hights and along a
ledge of mountains never intirely distitute of snow. Every body seems
anxious to be in motion, convinced that we have not now any time to
delay if the calculation is to reach the United States this season; this I
am detirmined to accomplish if within the compass of human power.[46]

That determination now brought Lewis and Clark to risk their chances on what all
remembered as a harsh, unforgiving trail.

On June 15, the explorers rode from Camp Chopunnish to Weippe Prairie. Even
that reasonably easy path proved hazardous as spring rains made the ground slippery. Fallen timber blocked much of the route and Lewis was forced to concede that
"our march [was] slow and extreemly laborious." On the following day, as the
expedition moved to higher elevations, the full impact of snowy conditions on the
trail became plain. Although the Lolo vanished in deep snow, the expedition was
determined to press on. But even Lewis began to question such foolhardy valor, and
at the end of an exhausting day wrote that the Bitterroot snow "augers but unfavorably with rispect to the practibility of passing the mountains."[47]

June 17 proved a day of decision and defeat. Floundering in drifts sometimes
twelve to fifteen feet deep, each member of the party must have recalled those
terrible days of September 1805 when it seemed the Lolo would be a cold grave.
With men near exhaustion and horses unable to breast the drifts, Lewis and Clark
held another hurried conference. Lewis made the choices and chances painfully
clear. "If we proceeded and should get bewildered in these mountains the certainty
was that we should loose all our horses and consequently our baggage, instruments
perhaps our papers and thus eminently wrisk the loss of the discoveries which we
had already made if we should be so fortunate as to escape with life." The needle on
the compass of human power had swung about and now counseled retreat. Bested
by the bitter snows, the expedition "a good deel dejected" turned around and
headed back toward Weippe Prairie, there to wait for Indian guides hired by
Drouillard and Shannon. Patrick Gass caught the mood at the end of the day when
he wrote that most in the party were "melancholy and disappointed." Camping
that night in a chill rain that edged toward sleet, Lewis could only recall, "This is the
first time since we have been on this long tour that we have ever been compelled to
retreat or make a retrograde march."[48]

After the difficult and depressing trek back to Weippe Prairie, the expedition's
fortunes took an upward turn. Drouillard brought three Nez Perce guides into
camp. In return for guns and ammunition, these men promised to direct the explorers
at least as far as Travelers' Rest. Lewis and Clark were told that a peace had been
arranged between Nez Perce, Walula, and Shoshoni bands. But news about fresh
engagements with Atsina warriors was troubling. The Nez Perce guides claimed

that hostile raiders had recently killed many Shoshonis and Flatheads. Those deaths added both danger and urgency to Lewis's diplomacy on the Marias.[49]

Led by experienced Nez Perces, the expedition made a safe and swift passage over those tremendous mountains. By June 29 the explorers were at the Lolo Hot Springs enjoying the recuperative powers of steaming water on aching muscles and bruised feet. Once at Travelers' Rest on July 1, Lewis and Clark put the final touches on an intricate plan that promised to fulfill many of their objectives and test their field skills.

The captains "consurted" the following strategy. Lewis would take a small party overland to the Great Falls of the Missouri "by the most direct route." Privates Thompson, Goodrich, and McNeal would remain at the falls to retrieve and refurbish equipment cached in 1805. In the meantime, Lewis would take a handful of volunteers up the Marias River to chart its northern course, explore the country, and contact the Blackfeet and Atsina Indians. After that dangerous reconnaissance, Lewis hoped to rejoin the Great Falls detachment on the Missouri for a grand reunion with Clark's party at the mouth of the Yellowstone.

Although Lewis's Blackfeet adventure on the Two Medicine River was more dramatic than anything Clark undertook, Clark's assignment was every bit as important. He was to proceed south from Travelers' Rest through the Bitterroot Valley and eventually cross the Great Divide to Three Forks. At the forks, Clark planned to take his party overland to find the Yellowstone and explore its course to the Missouri. At the same time, a group under Ordway would travel by canoe from Three Forks to Great Falls for a linkup with the men left by Lewis. Eventually the whole Corps of Discovery would reassemble at the Yellowstone-Missouri confluence.[50]

One last detail remained to be done that day at Travelers' Rest. Thinking about the complex diplomacy ahead with Missouri River villagers and Sioux bands, Lewis and Clark decided that the Nor'Wester Hugh Heney might prove a valuable ally in the struggle either to win or to cow the Sioux. In a long letter to Heney, the explorers offered him the office of Indian agent. More specifically, the captains wanted the trader to use his influence to wean Sioux chiefs away from British merchants like Murdoch Cameron and bring them into the St. Louis trade system. At the same time, they hoped Heney could organize a delegation of chiefs and elders for a journey to Washington. Reflecting Lewis's ideas on American trade along the Missouri, the letter urged Heney to employ every means to pacify or at least neutralize Teton power. So long as the Sioux choked traffic from St. Louis, the American fur trade would slowly die. Lewis and Clark explained to Heney that American Indian policy was based on peace and reconciliation. But the iron fist of coercion was undisguised in the letter. If the Sioux did not allow passage of American trade goods, Lewis and Clark were "positive that she [the United States] will not long suffer her citizens to be deprived of the free navigation of the Missouri by a fiew comparatively feeble bands of Savages who be so illy advised as to refuse her proffered friendship and continue their depridation on her citizens who may in future assend or decend the river." The captains' claims that Sioux warriors amounted to "comparatively feeble bands of Savages" would have surprised men like Black Buffalo and the Partisan who had effectively derailed American policy two years before. The letter suggests that when it came to understanding plains Indian politics, the explorers had still not learned the lessons of the Teton confrontation.[51]

One day after leaving Travelers' Rest, Lewis and his party were reminded of the dangers that lay ahead. Lewis knew that entering Blackfeet and Atsina territories was risky, but when his Nez Perce guides left him and warned that the "Pahkees" would "cut us off," the full weight of that danger came home. Two days later, when Lewis and his men were at the Big Blackfoot River, they saw so many abandoned lodges as to become "much on our guard both day and night." Lewis's concern was justified, but by the time his detachment reached the Great Falls of the Missouri on July 15, they still had seen no Indians. Once at the falls, Lewis selected Reuben and Joseph Field and George Drouillard to take part in what was to be the most violent Indian encounter in expedition history.[52]

Leaving Great Falls on July 17, the explorers rode northwest, believing this route would bring them to the Teton or Rose River and then on to the Marias. On Montana shortgrass plains as flat as "a well shaved bowling green," Lewis and his men maintained a "strict lookout" for any Indians. By July 21 a disappointed Lewis realized that the course of the Marias was not as northward as he had hoped. That unhappy discovery was overshadowed on the following days as the explorers found more signs that Indians were nearby. When the ever-watchful Drouillard located a cluster of eleven recently abandoned skin lodges, Lewis assumed that these were made by Atsina buffalo hunters camped along the main branch of the Marias. At Camp Disappointment on July 25, there were even more traces of recent native presence. As he had once before, Lewis wrote that he was "extreemly fortunate in not having met with these people."[53]

The captain's good fortune ran out the next day, July 27. Leaving Camp Disappointment, Lewis rode with the Field brothers while Drouillard scouted the Two Medicine River valley. At midafternoon, as Lewis forded Badger Creek and came up a sharp rise, he spotted to his far left some thirty horses, about half having saddles. The captain quickly drew out his small telescope for a closer look. He saw "a very unpleasant sight." Standing out against the afternoon sky were several Indians looking intently down toward the Two Medicine River valley and its cottonwood fringe. These Indians were so fixed on watching Drouillard that they did not appear to notice Lewis and his companions. Lewis immediately decided to make the best of an uncertain situation and proceeded to "approach them in a friendly way."[54]

To signal their intention, Lewis sent Joseph Field riding on ahead with an American flag. At that moment, the Indians saw the Lewis forces and became frightened. As Lewis later explained, they "appeared to run about in a very confused manner as if much allarmed." Plainly fearing an attack, several Indians came down toward the horses and drove them back up to the summit. If the Indians were fearful of hostilities, Lewis was equally concerned. He believed that there might be at least as many warriors as there were horses—surely a daunting thought. Lewis was also convinced that any attempt to escape from such a large, well-armed war party would invite disaster. Riding on, the Americans came to within a quarter of a mile of the warriors before the Indians made any move toward them.

Some hint of what was going on in the minds of the Piegan warriors comes from an interview conducted in the early 1900s by the ethnologist George Bird Grinnell with an elderly Piegan named Wolf Calf. Wolf Calf was the youngest member of the war party, and his recollections of that meeting with Lewis were still vivid and remarkably accurate. The Indian admitted that his companions were both surprised and frightened when they saw Lewis's men but decided to act in "a friendly fashion" for at least a short time. That decision was made plain when one Indian galloped toward Lewis at full tilt. Seeing this and understanding it was not a general charge, Lewis dismounted and extended his hand to the Piegan. The warrior eyed Lewis and then cantered his horse back to the main Blackfeet group. Whatever this scout said to his fellows was not recorded by Wolf Calf, but the fact that all eight soon came riding to meet the Americans perhaps suggests that the Indians were now confident of their own security.

As the Blackfeet neared Lewis and the Field brothers, the captain remained certain that additional warriors were still hiding close at hand. Claiming an expertise that was not really his, Lewis told Joseph and Reuben that these Indians were "Minnetarees of Fort de Prairie" or Atsinas. Using language filled with more swagger than wisdom, Lewis pronounced his willingness to "resist to the last extremity prefering death to that of being deprived of my papers instruments and gun." Lewis, once again on his horse, advanced slowly and met the one Indian who was ahead of the rest. Both men cautiously shook hands and then moved on to use the same welcome with those behind. This accomplished, Lewis dismounted. Perhaps thinking this signaled the beginning of a parley, the Indians asked for pipes and tobacco. Those supplies were with Drouillard who was still down along the Two Medicine. While one Indian joined Reuben Field to find Drouillard, Lewis tried his hand at some sign language. Inquiring as to what tribe these men belonged, Lewis understood their answer to be that they were Atsinas. Although unquestionably they were Piegans, there are two possible explanations for Lewis's faulty identification. Because the expedition's most skilled sign language interpreter was still down

Wolf Calf, a Piegan Warrior. Photograph by George B. Grinnell, from Olin D. Wheeler, *The Trail of Lewis and Clark.*

in the river valley, Lewis may have simply misunderstood what was being signed. It is equally possible that the Piegans, already thinking about stealing guns and horses, hoped to shift the blame on other Indians. Whatever the case, Lewis's attempt at conversation as well as his handing out of medals, flags, and handkerchiefs did little to calm the edgy Piegans. They seemed "more allarmed at this accedental interview than we were." Still worried about more warriors, and with evening approaching, Lewis suggested leaving high ground for a camp nearer the river. Guiding their horses down steep bluffs made more dangerous by loose, slippery gravel, the explorers and their nervous Blackfeet hosts made their way to three solitary cottonwood trees near the Two Medicine River.

At those trees which still stand near the river, the Blackfeet put up a makeshift shelter of buffalo skins. Then the Indians invited Lewis's party to join them. Lewis was anxious to learn as much as possible from the Piegans. Using Drouillard's signs, he conducted "much conversation" inside the hide wickiup that night. The Blackfeet said that they were part of a large band camped along the Marias. Lewis must have perked up when he heard that this band had a white trader in camp. He may well have urged Drouillard to press the Piegans for more details about Blackfeet-Canadian trade. What Lewis learned simply reenforced Jefferson's worst fears. Agents of the Hudson's Bay Company and the North West Company were firmly entrenched on the northern plains and were rapidly extending their influence throughout the region. The Blackfeet made regular visits to posts like Buckingham House and Rocky Mountain House along the North Saskatchewan River. Those Indians brought to the "Northern White Men" wolf and beaver pelts for guns, ammunition, and alcohol. Their loyalty to the Canadians made it clear that American fur traders would find this part of the northern plains a hard market to crack.[55]

Although what Lewis heard from the Piegans worried him, what he said frightened them. Explaining that he came from the east and had been beyond the mountains to the great ocean, Lewis unwittingly dropped a geo-political bombshell by declaring that the Blackfeet's traditional enemies—the Nez Perces, Shoshonis, and Kutenais—were now united by an American-inspired peace. Even more shocking to Piegan ears was word that these united tribes would be getting guns and supplies from Yankee traders. If Lewis thought the Blackfeet would receive such news with glad hearts and then join an American alliance, he gravely misjudged western realities. That night along the Two Medicine the explorer, in effect, announced the clash of empires had come to the Blackfeet. After more than twenty years of unchallenged power on the plains made possible by Canadian guns, the Blackfeet now faced a profound threat to their power and survival. Unaware that this was a frontal assault on Blackfeet influence, Lewis invited the warriors to help form a delegation of chiefs and elders for additional talks in Washington. To make that offer more attractive, he promised ten horses and much tobacco to those who ventured east to see the great chief of the seventeen fires. But all this naive talk did not hide the fact that Lewis and his men were among well-armed Piegans whose intentions were unclear. Had the captain known what young Wolf Calf knew that night—that a decision had been made to steal the expedition's guns—the explorer might have doubled the watch.[56]

In the chill dawn hours of July 27, Joseph Field struggled to fight back sleep and keep his watch. As soon as it was light, the Piegans were up and crowding around the fire. Intent on watching them, Field carelessly laid his gun behind him and close to his sleeping brother Reuben. One of the Indians, seeing the gun unguarded, slipped behind Joseph and quietly took the weapon. That act was a signal for other Indians to take guns belonging to Lewis and Drouillard. Still unnoticed, the Piegans then attempted to make good their escape with valuable booty. It was only then that Joseph Field saw what was happening and shouted to rouse his sleeping brother. Reuben, armed only with a broad-blade knife, gave angry chase. He proved a faster runner than a Piegan named Side Hill Calf. Field caught the Indian, pulled the guns away, and in a moment of fury thrust his knife into the man's chest. When an excited Reuben Field told John Ordway late the next day about the deed, he said that Side Hill Calf "drew but one breath [and] the wind of his breath followed the knife and he fell dead."

But Side Hill Calf's violent end was only the beginning of confusion and bloodletting around the lonely cottonwoods. Awakened by all the shouting, Drouillard saw an Indian making off with his rifle and shot pouch. Springing up, the Frenchman yelled, "Damn you let go my gun," and wrested it from the Piegan's hands. That shout awakened Lewis, who by his own admission had been in "a profound sleep." Still groggy, Lewis demanded to know what was going on. What he saw was explanation enough as Drouillard scuffled with the Indian. Going to aid the interpreter, Lewis reached for his rifle only to find it missing. He then drew his horse pistol and began to run after one of the fleeing Piegans. Quickly overtaking him, Lewis leveled his pistol at the Indian and demanded return of the rifle. The hapless thief was about to do as ordered when the Field brothers, still boiling with anger, came up and asked permission to shoot the Indian. Lewis wisely refused and allowed the Piegan to put down the rifle and walk quietly away. Lewis refused a similar request from Drouillard, who had now captured the would-be robber of his weapon.

It now appeared that the Piegan plan had been thwarted and the Blackfeet might quietly retire. If Lewis believed that, he was soon jolted back to a harsher reality. Once the Indians saw that the Americans had all their guns back, the Blackfeet turned their attention to the expedition's horses. Losing guns was serious enough, but without horses Lewis and his men would be stranded in a difficult country. For the Piegans, it seemed a last chance to rescue some honor and bring home valuable prizes. Now they threatened the survival of the American detachment and the ultimate success of the whole western venture. Understanding the stakes, Lewis ordered his men to open fire on any Indians trying to make off with horses. While the Field brothers and Drouillard pursued some Blackfeet, Lewis ran after two Piegans doing just that. Nearly out of breath from the long dash, Lewis called on the Indians to release the stolen horses or he would fire. One Indian hid behind some mushroom-shaped rocks and called to his friend, standing about thirty paces from Lewis. That armed Indian suddenly turned around and squarely faced Lewis. Certain he was about to be attacked, the captain shot his adversary through the stomach. Stunned by what was plainly a mortal wound, the warrior fell to his knees. Then suddenly he raised himself up on one elbow and fired a desperate shot at Lewis. But from his awkward position the dying man could not take clean aim and the ball went whistling just over the captain's head. "Being bearheaded," recalled Lewis, "I felt the wind of his bullet very distinctly."

As quickly as the Two Medicine fight had exploded in two deaths, it was over. Whatever the combatants on both sides felt about each other, all were united by a common desire—to escape as quickly as possible. Fleeing north, the six surviving Piegans must have feared that more armed whites were on the way. Lewis was equally fearful of Blackfeet revenge. He ordered the horses rounded up and decided to use the stronger Indian ones to make good a speedy escape. While Drouillard and the Field brothers prepared the horses, Lewis gathered up shields, bows, and arrows abandoned by the Piegans. He burned the weapons and in a final act of defiance put a peace medal around Side Hill Calf's neck so that "they might be informed who we were." As if to count coup on the Blackfeet, Lewis cut off the amulets from the shields and took them along as spoils of war.[57]

What remained now was to escape the Two Medicine killing ground. Ahead lay two full days of hard riding over broken ground to reach Ordway's party on the Missouri. When Lewis and his men finally reached the great river on the afternoon of July 28, they had "the unspeakable satisfaction to see our canoes coming down." Lewis and his tired companions left behind at the Two Medicine the seed of a myth that has long shaped popular understanding of the Blackfeet fight. That myth links the Two Medicine encounter with later Blackfeet-American hostilities. As the story goes, the violence directed against American fur traders in the years after Lewis and Clark was the result of Piegan revenge wreaked on the killers of Side Hill Calf and his unnamed fellow warrior. The death of George Drouillard at Three Forks in 1810 at the hands of a Blackfeet war party has been used to strengthen the claim for an undying Indian vengeance.

The Two Medicine myth was not the product of anything either the explorers or their contemporaries wrote about the fight or about later trapper troubles. Rather, the tale appears to have its genesis in the fertile imagination of Washington Irving. In his *Astoria*, Irving claimed that the Blackfeet had "conceived an implacable hostility to the white men, in consequence of one of their warriors having been killed by Captain Lewis, while attempting to steal horses." When David H. Coyner published his *The Lost Trappers* in 1847, he repeated Irving's claim and added, "The act created an implacable hatred for the whites from that day till this." By the time Elliott Coues produced his edition of Nicholas Biddle's *History* in 1893, the legend was in full bloom. Coues gave his stamp of approval to the tale in a footnote citing the Irving account and stories he heard on the northern Montana frontier in 1874. Although historians from Hiram Chittenden to more recent scholars have discredited this interpretation of native behavior and have suggested more persuasive explanations, the myth continues to be repeated in popular accounts of the expedition as well as in an occasional serious study.[58]

As Alvin Josephy, Jr., pointed out in 1965, the key to understanding Blackfeet actions toward American traders comes from something Lewis himself said that July night around the fire along the Two Medicine. After telling the Piegans that their traditional enemies had been united in a peace promoted by American diplomats, Lewis dropped the other shoe. Traders from St. Louis were going to sell guns to those united tribes, thus challenging the place of the Piegan, Blood, and Siksika peoples. All of that seemed to come terribly true in subsequent years. By 1807–1808, men working for St. Louis entrepreneurs were busy trading with Blackfeet rivals. When a former member of the expedition, John Colter, joined in an 1808 battle with Crow and Flathead warriors against the Blackfeet, the message was not lost on anyone. It may well have been that those merchants in places like Rocky Mountain House saw to it that the import of that message was fully understood. In the face of a massive assault on their plains empire, Blackfeet warriors hardly had time to think of avenging Side Hill Calf and his unfortunate companion. Lewis was unwittingly the prophet of events like the 1821 Immell-Jones massacre; he was not their cause. The bloody fray on the morning of July 27 provides a window into the ever-unstable balance of plains power. Although Blackfeet revenge against Americans for the deeds of Reuben Field and Meriwether Lewis may satisfy the modern writer's sense of historical symmetry, it was the more potent forces of guns and international trade that made the Blackfeet feared by a generation of American mountain men.[59]

It was not until noon on August 12, 1806, that the Corps of Discovery reassembled. Much had happened since those days at Travelers' Rest. Clark's party had explored the Yellowstone, the plan for Pryor to carry a letter to Hugh Heney had misfired when Crow Indians stole expedition horses, and Lewis had been wounded in a freak hunting accident. But now on the Missouri below the Yellowstone, the company was whole again. What remained of its Indian business was the same thorny problem that had occupied so much time during the winter with the Mandans. Establishing peace among Mandan, Hidatsa, and Arikara villagers and the consequences of that peace were at the heart of that problem. Lewis and Clark had not abandoned their commitment to a villager alliance aimed at eliminating or reducing Sioux influence. The explorers thought they had successfully planted the seeds of that policy during their first winter. In truth, the alliance and the tactics to execute it were no more realistic in 1806 than they had been in 1804. But realism had never been part of the expedition's Indian policy. As the explorer-diplomats began their final talks with the Indians, there was no reason to think that they might suddenly understand the Missouri facts of life.[60]

For three days beginning on August 14, William Clark carried on constant and sometimes difficult negotiations with Mandan and Hidatsa leaders. Neither cast nor lines had changed much since the explorers and the Indians had met during the winter of 1804–1805. The issues—trade, sovereignty, and the villager alliance—were the same. Black Cat, Sheheke, Black Moccasin, Little Raven, and Le Borgne were familiar faces from the earlier scene. Believing that the Mandan chief Black Cat was the key to American success, Clark quickly sought him out after paying brief calls at the villages of Metaharta and Mahawha. Black Cat greeted Clark with customary warmth, and together the two men shared a summer squash and smoked a friendly pipe.

Anxious to begin talks on the delegation issue as soon as possible, Clark detailed Charbonneau to call on Hidatsa chiefs while Drouillard was sent to Sheheke's village to hire René Jusseaume as council interpreter. When Jusseaume arrived at the expedition's camp just above Matootonha village, the talks began. Following a familiar agenda, Clark first renewed the invitation to visit Washington and speak with the president. Black Cat agreed that such a journey would be important but insisted that the price in danger exacted by Teton Sioux warriors was too high. It was just those kinds of fears that Clark sought to allay. Claiming more power than either the expedition or the United States actually had, he told Black Cat that the Americans "would not suffer those Indians [the Sioux] to hurt any of our red children who should think proper to accompany us." Bent on making promises even more difficult to keep, Clark offered continued federal military protection against hostile raiders after the chiefs returned home. To make American proposals more palatable, Clark reminded Black Cat that there would be lavish gifts for all who ventured so far from home.

This exchange was interrupted by the arrival of Le Borgne. If there was one man the explorers had failed to impress during the Mandan winter, it was this powerful and astute Hidatsa chief. That Le Borgne now came without much coaxing illustrated his recognition that some accommodation might be necessary with the persistent strangers from downriver. Knowing how important this moment was, Clark rounded up whatever other chiefs he could find and assembled them along the riverbank. With Jusseaume as interpreter, Clark once again repeated the familiar litany of American proposals. Delegations could see for themselves the wealth and power of the American nation. Clark encouraged quick action on the invitation, hinting that a prompt decision would hasten the arrival of quality trade goods at reasonable prices.

Le Borgne's reply was characterized by the kind of political acumen that marked so much of his diplomacy with both Indians and whites. He showed some passing interest in making the long trip to Washington but insisted that dangers posed by the Sioux made the journey far too hazardous. "The Sioux were in the road," he said, "and would most certainly kill him or any others who should go down." Suddenly turning the negotiating tables, the chief observed that the American claim to have brought peace to the Missouri was not true. Sioux warriors had recently killed eight

Hidatsas and taken some horses. And there had been renewed tension with the Arikaras. If Lewis and Clark were peacemakers of dubious repute, Le Borgne boasted that he had done much better. The chief had recently negotiated a complex trade agreement with the Cheyennes. When the Americans pacified the Teton Sioux, then Le Borgne might consider a visit to the federal father.[61]

Clark must have finally realized that Le Borgne was not a likely prospect for conversion to client-chief status. But there was always Black Cat. When he asked Clark to make a second visit to Rooptahee, the captain may have taken new hope that the delegation problem was nearing some solution. As the two men again shared a pipe, Black Cat broke the news Clark most feared. Because "the Sioux were still very troublesom," not a single prominent man was willing to risk a Missouri voyage. Black Cat tried to soften the blow by offering twelve bushels of corn from what had been a slim harvest. But that well-meaning gesture could not hide a serious failure of the expedition. Plainly disappointed, Clark urged the chief and his elders to "pitch on some man which they could rely and send him to see their great father." After more objections were aired, one young man stepped forward and agreed to go. But when George Gibson reported that the man had taken his knife, all fury broke loose. For all the comic overtones in a process that seemed to move two steps back for every one forward, Clark was justifiably angry. Tongue-lashed by Clark, the chief and elders hung their heads. Black Cat broke the painful silence and admitted that fear of Sioux ambushes and reprisal made it impossible for anyone to accompany the expedition. At last Clark seemed to grasp the depth of Mandan concern. To his credit, he gracefully accepted the inevitable and quietly spent more time smoking with Black Cat.

Later the same day, August 15, Jusseaume brought some startling news. The Frenchman claimed that Little Raven, second chief at Matootonha, had expressed a desire to go with the expedition. After so many false starts and setbacks, Clark was determined not to let this opportunity slip away. Taking Charbonneau with him, Clark hurried to the Mandan village for a talk with Little Raven. The chief acknowledged his interest in the journey but wanted to talk with friends and family before setting out on so dangerous a course. A pipe of tobacco moved that intention along and Clark returned to his camp thinking the delegation issue settled at last.

What Clark heard late that night made the need for any diplomatic success even more urgent. Since returning to the Mandan and Hidatsa villages, Charbonneau had spent some time at Metaharta, where he and Sacagawea had lived before joining the expedition. From those contacts he had learned that several Hidatsa war parties had gone out against Cameahwait's Lemhi Shoshonis and the Grand River Arikaras. Such news plainly demonstrated the fragile character of any villager alliance. Even more worrisome, continued Hidatsa forays against the Shoshonis and other potential American allies could only subvert and discredit diplomatic efforts made over the past two years. A symbolic gesture in the form of a Mandan-Hidatsa delegation could not change old patterns of warfare, but it might rescue the expedition's diplomatic reputation.[62]

On August 16, compelled by a sense of desperation, Clark made one last effort to fashion a respectable delegation. When Le Borgne and several other Hidatsa chiefs appeared uninvited at the American camp, he was given a rare opportunity. Here was a final chance to impress Le Borgne and perhaps bring him into the federal fold. Clark may have even dared to hope that at least one Hidatsa might join Little Raven to form a genuinely representative delegation. Pulling out all the ceremonial stops, the captains decided to give Le Borgne one of the swivel guns that had originally been on the keelboat. As Clark had the cannon loaded, he offered a double-barreled message. Raids against the "pore defenceless Snake Indians" had to stop, and such a potent weapon could always be used to defend American friends.

Although Le Borgne was plainly pleased with the gift, it was the elderly chief Caltarcota who now replied to Clark. The Hidatsa orator, who had so effectively challenged the expedition's diplomacy two years before, now repeated what must have been painfully familiar to all the explorers. The Hidatsas wanted to see the great father, but so long as the Sioux stood in the way such a trip was impossible. But Caltarcota had more to say and more than Clark wanted to hear. The Hidatsa chief had been opposed to an Arikara peace and lessening of tensions with the Teton Sioux in 1804, and nothing he had heard since had changed his mind. Raids against enemies were both strategically wise and culturally necessary. The Hidatsas were not about to alter old ways and endanger village security simply to please the seemingly odd whims of unpredictable strangers. There would be no Hidatsa representatives, nor would there be any promises of peace and cooperation. Le Borgne proudly took the cannon back to his village, but as was so often the case, the American diplomats were left with empty hands and empty promises.

For all the disappointment with the Hidatsas, Clark felt certain that he still had Little Raven as a token delegate. Later on the evening of August 16, Clark walked to Matootonha to keep up the chief's resolve. To his astonishment, Clark was bluntly told that Little Raven had changed his mind and would not accompany the expedition downriver. Not even a gift of a flag could change the Indian's mind. When Clark pressed Jusseaume to find reasons for this unwelcome change of heart, the interpreter reported that there had been a serious argument between Sheheke and Little Raven. Sheheke was evidently jealous of the prestige offered to Little Raven. At this point a frustrated Clark simply did not care who the delegate was so long as he was of sufficient rank and influence. Turning again to Jusseaume, Clark asked him to use his influence to enlist Sheheke in the expedition's ranks. The trader, a man always in search of the main chance, drove a hard bargain. He promised to deliver Sheheke if the Americans agreed to provide transportation and rations for the Sheheke and Jusseaume families. Worn down by days of fruitless talk and seeing no alternatives, Clark grudgingly agreed.[63]

Saturday, August 17, was a day to tie up loose ends. There were brief but inconclusive talks with some Hidatsa chiefs, financial settlements with Charbonneau and a fur trade–bound John Colter, and some poignant words from Clark about the future of Sacagawea's young Jean Baptiste Charbonneau, "a butifull promising child." By midmorning the expedition was at Matootonha to pick up the Sheheke and Jusseaume entourages. The explorers were already anticipating the joys of a festive homecoming, but when Clark came to Sheheke's lodge he saw what it meant for the Mandan chief to leave for an uncertain future. Grim-faced elders sat smoking farewell pipes while women wept. Despite Clark's efforts to reassure the villagers with gifts of powder and bullets, "maney of them cried out aloud" as Sheheke and his family went to the canoes. Tears and gunpowder were not the sort of legacy Lewis and Clark wanted to leave behind.[64]

Only one piece of Indian diplomacy was left before reaching St. Louis. The role of the Arikaras in Middle Missouri trade and politics had always eluded Lewis and Clark. The explorers simply could not comprehend the intricate relationship between Arikara farmers and Sioux hunters. In the eyes of the explorers, the Arikaras should have been willing recruits in the struggle against Teton power. That Sioux and Arikara warriors continued to carry out joint raids against Mandan and Hidatsa towns was bewildering. How could the Arikaras pursue a policy that further bound them to their Sioux oppressors? Lewis and Clark hoped that the earlier delegation sent under Joseph Gravelines, and now the presence of Sheheke, might at last end the raids that fueled endless hostilities.

By the morning of August 21, the expedition was at the Grand River and the Arikara villages. After exchanging volleys of shots in greeting, the Americans landed opposite the upper village of Waho-erha. While securing their canoes, the explorers could not miss the white skin lodges that dotted the hillsides above the Arikara towns. Those tepees belonged to Cheyennes who regularly traded for Arikara corn. Lewis and Clark had met individual Cheyennes during the Fort Mandan winter, but now there was a chance for serious talks with these important plains people. Once on shore, Clark was greeted by a crowd of friendly and inquisitive Arikaras and Cheyennes.

Without further ceremony, Clark decided to hold a council. Putting Sheheke to his left, he faced a semicircle of eager Indians. To symbolize the hoped-for peace between villages, Sheheke offered Mandan tobacco for all to smoke. Encouraged by the acceptance of that gift, Clark launched into a capsule history of the expedition, relating "where we had been, what we had done and said to the different nations." He was aided in that narrative by the presence of the trader and translator Joseph Garreau. As Clark surveyed the assembled dignitaries, he may have noticed a man of substantial importance who had not been seen in October 1804. That man was Grey Eyes, who had taken the place of Kakawissassa as principal chief and would lead defiance against American forces in 1823. After being introduced to Grey Eyes, Clark again emphasized the need for peace with neighbors and unity against the Sioux. The Arikara chief then delivered a "very animated" speech, filled with rhetorical sound and fury denouncing the Sioux as "bad people." But the sharp words were intended to please Clark and did not signify any change in Arikara policy. Grey Eyes certainly wished that the Sioux might be less troublesome at market times, but he was not about to alienate so strong and important a customer in order to please untested whites.

As the day grew hotter and the diplomacy less successful, Clark was grateful when a Cheyenne chief invited him to enjoy the shade of a tepee. Making little progress with the Arikaras, the captain hoped for better with the Cheyennes. After smoking with the chief, Clark offered him a small peace medal. It was an awkward moment when the frightened chief firmly rejected the gift. "He knew that the white people were all medecine," explained Clark, "and was afraid of the medal or anything that white people gave them." It was only with the greatest difficulty that Clark convinced the chief that flags and medals were signs of status and prestige, not carriers of disease and death. As things fell out, American diplomacy proved more successful with the Cheyennes than the Arikaras. Just before leaving the villages on August 22, Clark was approached by several Cheyenne chiefs who asked that American traders be sent among them to teach proper trapping techniques. That was the kind of request to gladden the heart of any St. Louis merchant.[65]

But Cheyenne requests were still in the future as Sheheke, who had accompanied Clark to the Cheyenne camp, offered a long discourse on villager tensions—a diatribe that contained more self-justification than serious analysis. The Mandan's torrent of invective was finally checked when the Cheyenne chief caustically observed that all the village folk shared a measure of blame. Never one to miss a chance to press the fundamentals of American Indian policy, Clark again insisted that "if they wished to be happy they must shake off all intimecy with the Sioux and unite themselves in a strong alliance and attend to what we had told them." But, as before, American proposals got no more than token assent.

Unnoticed throughout the day was the growing tension caused by the presence of Sheheke and his family. They were constant reminders of all the blows and strikes the Arikaras and the Mandans had exchanged over the years. Resentment finally exploded late in the evening. Sheheke found himself embroiled in an acrimonious shouting match with an Arikara chief named One Arm. Fearful that One Arm's "loud and threatening tone" might lead to violence, Clark stepped in and reminded the Arikaras that Sheheke was under American protection. Any harm done to him would bring a strong response from the expedition. That threat evidently worked since Clark finished the evening hearing One Arm and the other chiefs swear peace toward the Mandans and loyalty to the United States.[66]

But their solemn oaths meant little. The next morning, as the expedition prepared to make the final pull for St. Louis, Garreau reported that the Arikara chiefs had decided not to form another delegation until the first party had safely returned. And the Arikara leaders themselves again told Clark how dependent they were on the Sioux for guns and ammunition. Those were facts that not even the most adept diplomat could shape to fit an American mold. Except for the interest in the fur trade shown by the Cheyennes, the expedition left the Arikaras with little to call success.[67]

The next month saw Lewis and Clark sprint for home. Moving quickly with the Missouri current, the expedition often covered fifty or sixty miles in a day. Despite unending mosquito attacks, sudden rain squalls, and sore eyes from river glare, the men "ply'd their orers very well." But Black Buffalo and the Brulé Teton Sioux, those most redoubtable of expedition adversaries, were not about to allow Lewis and Clark to leave the river without one last set-to. At the end of August, as the Americans neared present-day Yankton, South Dakota, they spotted Black Buffalo and a large band of well-armed men along the river bank. What ensued was a nasty verbal exchange that pitted Clark and Jusseaume against Black Buffalo. The jeering and hooting so unnerved the explorers that when they came upon some friendly Yankton Sioux two days later there was nearly fatal gunfire.

But raw nerves were soothed in the days that followed. Edginess was replaced by excitement. Every day brought fresh signs that the great venture—what Lewis had once called "a darling project of mine"—was nearly done. New clothes, tobacco, and alcohol obtained from trader James Aird brought the men of the expedition one step closer to home and further from the life they had shared for so long. And then in the third week of September there were the familiar sights and faces of St. Louis and what had been the Corps of Discovery was about to escape into national history and myth.

The final scene in a drama that had so long bound together the lives of Indians and explorers was played out on September 23 at Fort Bellefontaine along the Missouri above St. Louis. Sentries on duty that cold, wet morning were perhaps the only audience as Clark escorted Sheheke to the "publick store" so that the Mandan chief could outfit himself and his family in the latest fashion.[68] As the Indian searched through stacks of calico shirts, fancy handkerchiefs, and colored beads, he symbolized the first fruits of the Lewis and Clark expedition. The explorers brought Indian America face to face with the Industrial Revolution and a rising American empire. Still ahead for people from the Missouri to the Columbia were more delegations, more talks, and more troubles. The calloused hands of the explorers had delivered the Indians into the finer fingers of agents, merchants, and bureaucrats. But, for now, none of that was clear to grizzled veterans or to anxious Indians. For Lewis and Clark, there was only the homecoming reserved to those once feared lost and now found. Men of the expedition were about to reenter a familiar world; Sheheke and his kin could not say the same. The Mandan chief, dressed in the best the young Republic could afford, did not know how much those explorers had forever changed his world.

Afterword

"We have been to the great lake of the west and are now on our return to my country. I have seen all my red children quite to that great lake and talked with them, and taken them by the hand in the name of their great father the Great Chief of all the white people."
—WILLIAM CLARK, 1806

On a cold, rainy day in mid-May 1806, Meriwether Lewis sat in camp along the Clearwater River and wondered where the Indians were. For the first time in many weeks no Nez Perces came to talk, trade, or stare at the bearded strangers.[1] It was almost two years to the day since the Lewis and Clark expedition had begun its western venture. Those years had been filled with a native presence that bound Indians and explorers together in a common struggle to survive. Formal conferences, personal friendships, and chance meetings all bridged the cultural divide. Indians were so much a part of the life of the expedition that their absence was worthy of note. When no Indians were present as actors and audience, Lewis and Clark felt strangely alone.

Whether written as simple fact or out of relief to be free from inquisitive neighbors, Lewis's observation reveals something fundamental about western exploration in general and Thomas Jefferson's Corps of Discovery in particular. Exploration was a cooperative endeavor requiring substantial information and support from the Indians. The Indians shaped the exploratory effort by their very presence on the land. They were people to be reckoned with, whether as potential sources of aid or as possible enemies. No latter-day Coronado or Champlain could ignore them. The anticipated behavior of the Indians was a decisive factor in the choice of equipment, personnel, routes, camp rules, and even ultimate destination. Whatever the official objectives, explorers carefully considered their presence.

But we need to measure more than explorer's reactions to a passive population. Indians were active participants in exploration, as the first comers to the land and, later, as guides for Euro-Americans. To a vast enterprise they lent their intelligence, skill, and nerve. Certainly the Lewis and Clark expedition benefited greatly from the Indians' knowledge and support. Maps, route information, food, horses, openhanded friendship—all gave the Corps of Discovery the edge that spelled the difference between success and failure. The presence of Sacagawea on the expedition's roster is only the barest hint of what Indian support meant to Lewis's "darling project." That roster should also include names like Sheheke, Cameahwait, Old Toby, Tetoharsky, Twisted Hair, and Flint Necklace. There needs to be a place for those unnamed Shoshoni women who carried expedition baggage over Lemhi Pass as well as for countless Indians who traded food and affection. As guides, packers, interpreters, and cartographers, native Americans were essential to Lewis and Clark's achievement.

Lewis and Clark left St. Louis filled with apprehension about encounters with hostile Indians. But what emerged over nearly two and a half years of western travel was an atmosphere of friendship and mutual trust between men and women who shared a common frontier life. Indians and explorers stood together in the rituals of hunting, holidays, and horse racing. Sex, sports, and music were simple pleasures that united strangers. Lewis admitted as much when he wrote, "So long have our men been accustomed to a friendly intercourse with the natives, that we find it difficult to impress on their minds the necessity of always being on guard with rispect to them."[2] The assertion that the Corps of Discovery acted like "a conquering army" of hungry imperialists does not square with either the Lewis and Clark record or the larger history of North American exploration.[3] Lewis and Clark neither enslaved Indians as did DeSoto nor pillaged pueblos as did Coronado. Stealing a canoe from Coboway and tricking Cameahwait stand out in the journal notes because they were exceptional acts, not typical of the captains and their crew.

The typical patterns of friendship and sharing that generally characterized Indian-expedition relations were not the result of any special nobility of character on either side of the cultural divide. Native hospitality was both genuine and useful as tribal people sought trade or attempted to manipulate the expedition for personal ends. For their part, Lewis and Clark recognized the necessity of Indian cooperation. There were undeniable moments of swagger, bluster, and arrogance, but more often than not good sense and patience won the day. Clark once bragged that he could have tomahawked terrified Umatillas, but he did not do the deed. Despite angry threats, no member of the expedition put the torch to mat lodges at The Dalles. And Lewis would not allow George Drouillard and the Field brothers to shoot unarmed Piegans in the heat of the Two Medicine fray. For most of the journey there was mutual respect born of expediency. That respect and friendship was genuine nonetheless. Lewis and Clark left behind among many Indians a legacy of nonviolent contact. Those who came later enjoyed that legacy and too often betrayed it.

If expedition-Indian personal relations were amiable, success did not come so easily when Lewis and Clark ventured into diplomatic waters. Clark claimed that the swivel gun he gave to the Hidatsa chief Le Borgne had spoken in thunder to "all the nations we had seen."[4] But what the gun said and how its report was answered depended on circumstances far beyond the expedition's control. Lewis and Clark believed that official diplomacy was a simple matter of rearranging Indian patterns to suit the needs of the new nation. Proclaiming American sovereignty, establishing trade connections, and constituting delegations to visit Jefferson all seemed goals within easy reach. Who could deny the rationality of intertribal peace or a united front against common enemies? But when the captains sought to implement those policies, they met the often unyielding realities of village and band politics. Lewis and Clark's ill-considered attempt to forge a villager alliance against the Teton Sioux illustrates the depth of their ignorance. The explorers comprehended neither river economics nor plains politics. In a world where "peace" meant "truce" and where warriors fought one day and traded the next, Lewis and Clark were simply unable and sometimes unwilling to face the facts of native life.

Lewis and Clark's Indian diplomacy failed in part because the explorers were blind to those western facts of life. But the failure of the villager alliance and the promises of intertribal peace extracted at so many councils came from something more fundamental than naive optimism. What seemed failure for the captains was often success for the chiefs. It was more than inept policy and cultural arrogance that kept federal goals just out of reach. When Lewis and Clark came into the West and Pacific Northwest, native political sovereignty and autonomy were still potent realities. Men like Le Borgne, Cameahwait, and Broken Arm enjoyed genuine power. They and their counselors could make decisions without bowing to the dictates of faraway white fathers. Despite Lewis and Clark's rhetoric, western Indians were not "our red children." Rather, they were mature adults with a substantial measure of freedom to choose those parts of the American program that best suited their own needs. Diplomacy during the journey was ceremony and talk among equals, even if Lewis and Clark did not always recognize that fact. If the captains failed to persuade the Indians to become children of a distant father, it was because the Indians still had the power to accept American guns while rejecting less useful gifts.

Bernard DeVoto once wrote that the records of the Lewis and Clark expedition amounted to "the first detailed account of whatever length, of the western tribes."[5] The ethnographic legacy has proven to be one of Lewis and Clark's most durable contributions, although its value was not plain at the time of the expedition. Guided by Jefferson's precise instructions and their own curiosity, expedition ethnographers amassed a virtual library of information about the Indians. Journal entries, vocabularies, drawings, maps, artifacts, population estimates—all hold priceless knowledge about Indian ways from the great river to the western sea. When Nicholas Biddle first examined that ethnographic data, he felt some reason to apologize for its inadequacies. "Those who first visit the ground," wrote the Philadelphian, "can only be expected to furnish sketches, rude and imperfect."[6] But Biddle's evaluation missed the mark. The expedition gathered far more than "rude and imperfect" records. In their writing, drawing, and collecting they managed to capture an essential part of American life on the edge of profound change.

In 1821 an obscure North West Company mariner named Peter Corney wrote,

"By the journey of Captains Lewis and Clark across the Rocky mountains to the Pacific Ocean, the whole of that western region is now laid open."[7] It was more than rivers and mountains that were laid open to view. Lewis and Clark were part of an expansionist movement that steadily brought traders, bureaucrats, ranchers, and farmers into Mandan, Shoshoni, Nez Perce, and Chinookan homelands. "We were happy when he [the white man] first came," explained the Flathead chief Charlot. "We first thought he came from the light; but he comes like the dusk of evening now, not like the dawn of morning. He comes like a day that has passed, and night enters our future with him."[8] But that night had not yet come in 1806. In tales repeated in lodge and tepee, in the faces of children paler than their brothers and sisters, in cherished flags and medals, and in individual memories now lost, Lewis and Clark seemed part of the dawn. They appeared as the Shoshonis described them—"children of the Great Spirit" who offered dazzling gifts. That the coming day would bring other, duller lights was a scene not yet revealed to William Clark and Meriwether Lewis, much less to men like Cameahwait and Yelleppit. Having shared a moment in history, each slipped away to wonder about the fate of the other.

Appendix
A Note on Sacagawea

Readers of this book will undoubtedly wonder why the most famous Indian associated with the Lewis and Clark expedition is mentioned so infrequently. Over the past century a powerful mythology has grown up, making extravagant claims for Sacagawea as expedition guide and American heroine. Writers from Eva Emery Dye and Grace R. Hebard to Donald Culross Peattie and Anna Lee Waldo have fashioned narratives that go far beyond what can be known from reputable historical sources. When evidence runs thin, many writers have been all too willing to pass off fabrication for fact. Thus the claims still persist that Sacagawea single-handedly guided the expedition through unknown lands to the Pacific and that she died an old woman at Wind River, Wyoming in 1884. Such myths diminish Sacagawea and make a balanced evaluation of her genuine contributions more difficult. More important, they draw our attention away from those native men and women who made more fundamental contributions to the expedition's success.

What is reliably known about Sacagawea makes for only a brief biographical sketch. Sometime in the fall of 1800, the young Lemhi Shoshoni girl, then perhaps twelve or thirteen years old, was camped at the Three Forks of the Missouri with others from her band. As so often happened to northern Shoshonis who ventured out on the plains to hunt buffalo, the party at Three Forks was attacked by Hidatsa raiders. In the fighting that followed, several Shoshonis were killed. Among the prisoners taken were four boys and several women, including Sacagawea. Sometime between 1800 and 1804, she and one other Shoshoni captive were purchased by Toussaint Charbonneau, a trader with ties to the North West Company. When Lewis and Clark met Charbonneau at Fort Mandan on November 4, 1804, the trader and his family were living at the Awatixa Hidatsa village of Metaharta. Sacagawea was already pregnant and on February 11, 1805, she gave birth to a son named Jean Baptiste. When Toussaint Charbonneau was finally hired by Lewis and Clark as an interpreter, Sacagawea and her child became part of the Corps of Discovery.

Three questions about Sacagawea have long fascinated Lewis and Clark scholars. The name of the Indian woman—its meaning and proper spelling—continues to spark considerable debate. Sacajawea, Sacagawea, and Sakakawea have all had their partisans. The concern about spelling is not just a quibble over orthography. If the woman's name was Sacajawea, the word might be Shoshoni, meaning "boat launch-er." However, if the spelling is more properly Sacagawea, the name would be Hidatsa and translate as "Bird Woman." The journal evidence from Lewis and Clark appears as to support a Hidatsa derivation. On May 20, 1805, Lewis wrote: "Sah ca gah we ah or bird woman's River" to name what is now Crooked Creek in north-central Montana. The most effective arguments for a Sacagawea spelling and a Hidatsa meaning are offered by Irving Anderson in his "Sacajawea, Sacagawea, Sakakawea?" (*South Dakota History* 8 [1978]: 303–11). Anderson summarizes the pre-vious literature and finds that the Sacagawea spelling best fits both the historical and linguistic evidence. However, it should be noted that an unpublished paper by Bob Saindon, " 'Sacajawea': The Origin and Meaning of a Name," does raise important questions about the whole matter. Both Anderson and Saindon rely heavily on the findings of professional linguists, who in turn differ considerably in their conclu-sions. Along with the historian Donald Jackson, I have found the Sacagawea spell-ing most acceptable.

Far more important than the spelling and meaning of Sacagawea's name is the nature and scope of her contributions to the expedition. Perhaps the most persistent Lewis and Clark myth is that Sacagawea "guided" the party to the Pacific. In countless statues, poems, paintings, and books she is depicted as a westward-point-ing pathfinder providing invaluable direction for bewildered explorers. In the interest of correction, there has been a tendency to underestimate Sacagawea's genuine achievements as a member of the Corps of Discovery. Not as important as George Drouillard or John Ordway, the young woman did make significant con-tributions to the expedition's success.

Those contributions can be discussed under four heads. When the expedition left Fort Mandan in April 1805, its most immediate need was to find the Shoshoni Indians and obtain horses for what was assumed would be an easy mountain portage to Pacific waters. Lewis and Clark certainly believed that Sacagawea would be of considerable value in the Shoshoni mission. They expected that she might recog-nize landmarks along the route and would provide general information about the location of Shoshoni camps. When Sacagawea became ill at the Great Falls of the Missouri, Lewis admitted, "This gave me some concern as well as for the poor object herself, than with the young child in her arms, as from the consideration of her being our only dependence for friendly negocition with the Snake Indians."[1] But just what the captains expected from her in those talks is not plain. For reasons that are now unclear, Sacagawea was not included in Lewis's advance party that finally made contact with the Shoshonis in August 1805. Good relations between the explorers and Cameahwait depended far more on promises of guns and trade than on any intercessions made by Sacagawea.

Sacagawea was not an expedition guide in the usual sense of the word. When Lewis and Clark needed to make a critical decision in early June 1805 about the true channel of the Missouri, she took no part in the process. Much later, when the expedition needed guides, men like Old Toby, Tetoharsky, and Twisted Hair were hired for that duty. Only twice did Sacagawea provide what might be termed guide services. In late July and early August 1805, she recognized important geographical features on the way to find Shoshoni camps. On the return journey in 1806, Sacagawea accompanied Clark's party and provided the explorer with valuable information on what has since been named Bozeman Pass. For most of the transcontinental journey, Sacagawea was seeing country as new to her as it was to the captains. That she was not in the lead making trail decisions does not diminish the fact that when she did recognize a landmark, "this piece of information cheered the spirits of the party."[2]

Success in many of the expedition's Indian missions depended on reliable communication and translation. Both diplomacy and the collection of ethnographic information demanded the sort of communication that George Drouillard's signs could not always provide. One of Sacagawea's most important roles in the expedition was that of translator, or as Clark quaintly put it, "interpretress with the Snake Indians." She often worked as part of a long and cumbersome translation chain that took each native word through many speakers before reaching the captains. Sacagawea was able to continue those duties west of the Continental Divide because of the presence of Shoshoni prisoners among groups that did not speak Shoshoni. Talks with the Flatheads at Ross's Hole were conducted through such a prisoner, as were those on the return journey with the Walulas and Nez Perces.

The expedition also benefited from the physical presence of Sacagawea and her child. Indians who might have thought the explorers part of a war party were evidently reassured when they saw a woman and an infant in the group. Clark said as much when he wrote, "The Wife of Shabono our interpreter We find reconsiles all the Indians, as to our friendly intentions. A woman with a party of men is a token of peace."[3]

If Sacagawea's life and accomplishments have been hotly debated, controversy has also swirled around the date and place of her death. When Grace R. Hebard published her *Sacajawea* in 1933, she claimed that the Indian woman had lived at Wind River, Wyoming, under the name Porivo until her death in 1884. As Irving Anderson points out in his closely argued "Probing the Riddle of the Bird Woman" (*Montana: The Magazine of Western History* 23 [1973]: 2–17), Hebard's book misinterpreted some evidence and neglected much more. Statements by William Clark and trader John C. Luttig make it plain that Sacagawea died on December 20, 1812, at Fort Manuel in present-day South Dakota. Most scholars now accept Clark's note in his Cash Book that Sacagawea was dead by the 1825–28 period and Luttig's note—"this Evening the wife of Charbonneau, a Snake Squaw, died of a putrid fever she was a good and the best woman in the fort, aged abt 25 years"—as substantial evidence for Sacagawea's early death.

From the time of the expedition itself, Sacagawea has prompted strong opinions. Lewis and Clark themselves wrote quite different evaluations of the woman and her place in expedition history. Lewis, evidently unimpressed with her, declared, "If she has enough to eat and a few trinkets I beleive she would be perfectly content anywhere."[4] Clark did not share what seems the ill-concealed contempt in those lines. He wrote to Toussaint Charbonneau after the journey was over, "Your woman who accompanied you that long dangerous and fatigueing rout to the Pacific Ocian and back diserved a greater reward for her attention and services on that rout than we had in our power to give her at the Mandans."[5] Clark's care for the Charbonneau children after the expedition is yet another measure of his esteem for their mother.

Readers in search of a balanced treatment of Sacagawea might begin with Irving Anderson, "Probing the Riddle of the Bird Woman," *Montana: The Magazine of Western History* 23 (1973): 2–17, and E. G. Chuinard, "The Bird Woman: Purposeful Member of the Corps or Casual 'Tag-Along,' " *Montana: The Magazine of Western History* 26 (1976): 18–29. Also of considerable value are Irving Anderson, "A Charbonneau Family Portrait," *American West* 17 (1980): 4–13, 63–64; C. S. Kingston, "Sacajawea as a Guide—The Evaluation of a Legend," *Pacific Northwest Quarterly* 35 (1944): 2–18; Blanche Schroer, "Boat-Pusher or Bird-Woman? Sacagawea or Sacajawea?" *Annals of Wyoming* 52 (1980): 46–54. The best book-length treatment is Harold P. Howard, *Sacajawea* (Norman: University of Oklahoma Press, 1971). Ella P. Clark and Margot Edmonds, *Sacagawea* (Berkeley: University of California Press, 1979) must be read with caution since it uncritically accepts the notion of a Sacagawea who lived into the 1880s. Recent novels about Sacagawea, including Anna Lee Waldo, *Sacajawea* (New York: Avon Books, 1979) must be read as fiction, not history. Their claims to historical accuracy are dubious at best and misleading at worst.

Notes

Abbreviations

BAE   Bureau of American Ethnology

Field Notes. Osgood, Ernest S., ed. *The Field Notes of Captain William Clark, 1803–1805.* New Haven: Yale University Press, 1964.

Gass, *Journal.* Gass, Patrick. *A Journal of the Voyages and Travels of a Corps of Discovery.* Edited by David McKeehan. 1807. Reprint, with preface by Earle R. Forrest. Minneapolis: Ross and Haines, 1958.

Ordway, *Journal.* Quaife, Milo M., ed. *The Journals of Captain Meriwether Lewis and Sergeant John Ordway.* Madison: Historical Society of Wisconsin, 1916.

Thw.   Thwaites, Reuben G., ed. *The Original Journals of the Lewis and Clark Expedition.* 8 vols. New York: Dodd, Mead & Co., 1904–1905.

Whitehouse, *Journal.* "The Journal of Private Joseph Whitehouse." In Thw. 7:29–190.

Chapter 1

1   Donald Jackson, *Thomas Jefferson and the Stony Mountains: Exploring the West from Monticello* (Urbana: University of Illinois Press, 1981), pp. 25–26.

2   Jefferson to Benjamin Smith Barton, February 27, 1803; Jefferson to Caspar Wistar, February 28, 1803; Jefferson to Benjamin Rush, February 28, 1803, Donald Jackson, ed., *The Letters of the Lewis and Clark Expedition with Related Documents, 1783–1854,* 2d ed., 2 vols. (Urbana: University of Illinois Press, 1978), 1:16–19.

3   Albert Gallatin to Jefferson, April 13, 1803, ibid. 1:32–34. This judgment must be modified if it can be determined that Gallatin had a major role in formulating some of the Indian questions William Clark copied in a long list sometime early in 1804. See Clark, "List of Questions," ibid. 1:157–61.

4   Levi Lincoln to Jefferson, April 17, 1803, ibid. 1:35.

5   Benjamin Rush, *Medical Inquiries and Observations* (Philadephia: Thomas Dobson, 1794), pp. 9–77. See also Stephen J. Kunitz, "Benjamin Rush on Savagism and Progress," *Ethnohistory* 17 (1970):31–42.

6   Rush, "Questions to Merryweather Lewis before he went up the Missouri, May 17,

262

1803," Jackson, ed., *Letters,* 1:50. This list was passed to Jefferson in a letter from Lewis dated May 29, 1803, ibid. 1:52.

7 Jefferson, "Message to Congress—Confidential, January 18, 1803," ibid. 1:10–13; Jefferson to André Micheau, [sic], April 30, 1793, ibid. 2:669–72, especially p. 670 where the language is clearly influential for the instructions to Lewis.

8 Jefferson, "Instructions to Lewis, June 20, 1803," ibid. 1:62–63. Jefferson's particular concern for Indian languages added a document to the instructions. He had printed for the expedition's use blank vocabulary sheets listing common English words with spaces for Indian equivalents. See Thw. 7:408–9.

9 Jefferson, "Instructions to Lewis," 1:62.

10 Jefferson to John Adams, June 11, 1812, Lester J. Cappon, ed., *The Adams-Jefferson Letters,* 2 vols. (Chapel Hill: University of North Carolina Press, 1959), 2:307.

11 Jefferson, "Instructions to Lewis," 1:63.

12 Ibid. 1:64. Jeffersonian Indian policy, as distinct from the theories used to rationalize that policy, is skillfully analyzed in Reginald Horsman, *Expansion and American Indian Policy, 1783–1812* (East Lansing: Michigan State University Press, 1967), chap. 7. Jefferson's own concise statement of federal goals can be found in a February 27, 1803, letter to William Henry Harrison, Jefferson Papers, Library of Congress.

13 Jefferson to Lewis, January 22, 1804, Jackson, ed., *Letters,* 1:165–66.

14 Charles Royster, *A Revolutionary People at War* (Chapel Hill: University of North Carolina Press, 1979), p. 93.

15 Lincoln to Jefferson, April 17, 1803, Jackson, ed., *Letters,* 1:35.

16 Lewis, "Estimate of Expenses," ibid. 1:9.

17 Lewis, "List of Requirements," ibid. 1:72–75.

18 Israel Whelan, "Recapitulation of Purchases by The Purveyor for Capt. Lewis," ibid. 1:94.

19 Clark to George Croghan, May 2, 1804, ibid. 1:178.

20 Lewis to Jefferson, December 28, 1803, ibid. 1:161–62.

21 *Field Notes,* p. 16.

22 Lewis to Jefferson, December 28, 1803, Jackson, ed., *Letters,* 1:154.

23 Ibid. 1:155.

24 James Mackay, "Journal," in A. P. Nasatir, ed., *Before Lewis and Clark: Documents Illustrating the History of the Missouri, 1785–1804,* 2 vols. (St. Louis: St. Louis Historical Documents Foundation, 1952), 2:493–94.

25 James Mackay, "Notes on Indian Tribes," Voorhis Collection, box 4, Missouri Historical Society, St. Louis.

26   Jefferson to Lewis, November 16, 1803, Jackson, ed., *Letters*, 1:138–39. Jefferson did
      not send direct quotations from the journal but a summary of the major points in
      Jean Baptiste Truteau's "Description of the Upper Missouri" and his "State of the
      Indian Nations." See Nasatir, ed., *Before Lewis and Clark*, 2:376–85. In his January
      22, 1804, letter to Lewis, Jefferson enclosed what he described as a full translation
      of the Truteau journal.

27   Lewis to Jefferson, December 28, 1803, Jackson, ed., *Letters*, 1:148. The English
      version of Soulard's map is in Gary E. Moulton, ed., *Atlas of the Lewis and Clark
      Expedition* (Lincoln: University of Nebraska Press, 1983), plate 4. The French
      version is in Sara J. Tucker and Wayne C. Temple, comps., *Atlas: Indian Villages of
      the Illinois Country* (Springfield: Illinois State Museum, 1942, 1975), plate 77. The
      Spanish rendering is in Carl I. Wheat, *Mapping the Transmississippi West*, 5 vols. (San
      Francisco: Institute of Historical Cartography, 1958–62), 1: plate 235a. Valuable
      notes on the Soulard map are in John L. Allen, *Passage through the Garden: Lewis
      and Clark and the Image of the American Northwest* (Urbana: University of Illinois
      Press, 1975), pp. 148–49; Aubrey Diller, "A New Map of the Missouri drawn
      in 1795," *Imago Mundi* 12 (1955): 175–80; Wheat, *Mapping the Transmississippi West*,
      1:157–60.

28   Allen, *Passage through the Garden*, pp. 141–42 and fig. 23.

29   W. Raymond Wood, "The John Evans 1796–97 Map of the Missouri River," *Great
      Plains Quarterly* 1 (1981): 39–53; quoted, 39.

30   *Field Notes*, pp. 35–36; Thw. 6:270–77.

31   Thw. 1:16.

32   *Field Notes*, p. 21.

33   Jefferson to Robert Patterson, March 2, 1803, Jackson, ed., *Letters*, 1:21.

34   Thw. 1:29.

35   Ordway, *Journal*, p. 85; Thw. 1:46–47.

36   Thw. 1:86. Indian history and culture for this part of the river is ably treated in R.
      David Edmunds, *The Otoe-Missouria People* (Phoenix: Indian Tribal Series, 1976);
      G. Hubert Smith, "Notes on Omaha Ethnohistory, 1763–1820," *Plains Anthropologist*
      18 (1973): 257–70; William Whitman, *The Oto*, Columbia University Contributions
      to Anthropology, 28 (New York, 1937): 1–32.

37   Gass, *Journal*, p. 26; Thw. 1:88–89.

38   Roy E. Appleman, *Lewis and Clark: Historic Places Associated with Their
      Transcontinental Exploration* (Washington, D.C: National Park Service, 1975), pp.
      336–37; Ordway, *Journal*, p. 102; Thw. 1:92–94.

39   Ordway, *Journal*, p. 104; Thw. 1:96.

40   Ibid. 1:97.

264

41   "Lewis and Clark to the Oto Indians," Jackson, ed., *Letters,* 1:203–8.

42   *Field Notes,* p. 8.

43   Thw. 1:36–37.

44   *Field Notes,* p. 95; Gass, *Journal,* p. 30; Ordway, *Journal,* p. 104; Thw. 1:97–99; Whitehouse, *Journal,* p. 48.

45   Smith, "Notes on Omaha Ethnohistory," pp. 264–69; Thw. 1:102, 106, 109–10.

46   Ibid. 1:111.

47   Ibid. 1:112; Whitehouse, *Journal,* p. 50.

48   *Field Notes,* pp. 109–10; Thw. 1:112–14.

49   Ibid. 1:126, 128.

50   Gass, *Journal,* p. 37; Ordway, *Journal,* pp. 119–20; Thw. 1:131.

51   *Field Notes,* pp. 125–26; Ordway, *Journal,* pp. 121–23; Thw. 1:131.

52   Although the expedition's attention at Calumet Bluff was focused on questions of diplomacy and progress upriver, William Clark did record valuable data about Yankton life. Clark noted Sioux dress, weapons, and musical instruments. He filled in a vocabulary form and wrote a long description of the important warrior societies that gave shape to the lives of Sioux males. From Pierre Dorion, Clark obtained a useful list of the Sioux bands. See Thw. 1:129–33.

Chapter 2

1   The Brulé territory at the time of Lewis and Clark was bounded by the North Platte River on the south and somewhat beyond the Missouri River on the east. The northern boundary was between the Bad and Cheyenne rivers. The Brulés hunted as far west as the Black Hills. John C. Ewers, *Teton Dakota Ethnology and History* (Berkeley, Calif.: Western Museum Laboratories, United States Department of the Interior, 1938), p. 9, map 4; Robin W. Wells, *Tribal Distribution Map Series, North America* (Toledo: University of Toledo Cartographic Services, n.d.), map for 1760–1810.

2   Ordway, *Journal,* pp. 394–95; Thw. 5:365–67.

3   Jean Baptiste Truteau, "Journal on the Missouri River, 1794–1795," in Nasatir, ed., *Before Lewis and Clark,* 1:269; Thw. 1:29. Something of the climate of opinion in St. Louis concerning the Sioux can be seen in: Lewis to Jefferson, December 28, 1803, Jackson, ed., *Letters,* 1:154–55; Lewis to Auguste Chouteau, January 4, 1804, ibid. 1:161–62; *Field Notes,* p. 16.

4   Thw. 1:162.

5   Gass, *Journal,* p. 50; Ordway, *Journal,* pp. 136–37; Thw. 1:162–63; Whitehouse, *Journal,* pp. 61–62.

6   Jefferson to Lewis, November 16, 1803, Jackson, ed., *Letters*, 1:138–39.

7   Jefferson to Robert Smith, July 13, 1804, Jefferson Papers, Library of Congress; Jefferson to Lewis, January 22, 1804, ibid. 1:166.

8   Annie H. Abel, ed., *Tabeau's Narrative of Loisel's Expedition to the Upper Missouri* (Norman: University of Oklahoma Press, 1939), pp. 121–23, 131; John C. Ewers, "The Indian Trade of the Upper Missouri before Lewis and Clark," Missouri Historical Society *Bulletin* 10 (1954): 429–46; Donald Jackson, ed., *The Journals of Zebulon Montgomery Pike with Letters and Related Documents*, 2 vols. (Norman: University of Oklahoma Press, 1966), 1:213–15, 221; Thw. 1:189, 6:45, 98; Truteau, "Journal," 1:301–2, 310; W. Raymond Wood, "Contrastive Features of Native North American Trade Systems," University of Oregon Anthropological Papers, No. 4 (Eugene, 1972), pp. 153–69. William Clark's 1810 map contains notations about the location and function of the Dakota Rendezvous. See Wheat, *Mapping the Transmississippi West*, 1: map 291. Lewis's incisive comments, made after the expedition, on the Missouri trade system are in Thw. 6:45–46.

9   Abel, ed., *Tabeau's Narrative*, pp. 108–9, 111–13. The Partisan may have been present at an Indian council held by Zebulon Pike at the confluence of the Minnesota and Mississippi rivers on September 23, 1805. He was surely at a conference arranged by Manuel Lisa at Prairie du Chien in July 1815. See Jackson, ed., *Journals of Zebulon Pike*, 1:37–38; Richard E. Oglesby, *Manuel Lisa and the Opening of the Missouri Fur Trade* (Norman: University of Oklahoma Press, 1963), p. 157.

10   Richard White, "The Winning of the West: The Expansion of the Western Sioux in the Eighteenth and Nineteenth Centuries," *Journal of American History* 65 (1978): 326.

11   Thw. 1:164.

12   Ibid. 1:129–33.

13   Ibid. 1:112–14, 129–33.

14   For a similar demand see "Report of Clamorgan and Reihle, St. Louis, July 8, 1795," Nasatir, ed., *Before Lewis and Clark*, 1:340.

15   Thw. 1:113.

16   This arresting claim is not in Clark's journal or in his field notes, but both Gass, *Journal*, p. 51, and Whitehouse, *Journal*, p. 63, record it.

17   *Field Notes*, p. 148; Ordway, *Journal*, pp. 138–39; Thw. 1:164–65.

18   Elliott Coues (*History of the Expedition under the Command of Lewis and Clark*, 4 vols. in 3 [1893; reprint, New York: Dover Publications, 1964], 1:137) notes that many of the Indians present on September 26 were Okandanda or Oglala Teton Sioux. This is possible but not recorded in any of the expedition's journals. The Elliott Coues edition of Nicholas Biddle's 1814 *History of the Expedition under the Command of Captains Lewis and Clark* is hereafter cited as Biddle-Coues, *History*.

19 Ewers, *Teton Dakota*, pp. 26–28; Ordway, *Journal*, pp. 139, 141.

20 Gass, *Journal*, pp. 51–52; Ordway, *Journal*, pp. 139–40.

21 Paul R. Cutright, *Lewis and Clark: Pioneering Naturalists* (Urbana: University of Illinois Press, 1969), p. 91; Ewers, *Teton Dakota*, pp. 16–18.

22 George Catlin, *Letters and Notes on the Manners, Customs, and Conditions of the North American Indians*, 2 vols. (1844; reprint, New York: Dover Publications, 1973), 1:245–46, plate 104; Frances Densmore, *Teton Sioux Music*, Smithsonian Institution, BAE Bulletin no. 61 (Washington, D.C., 1918), pp. 48–51, plates 38, 39, 46; Ewers, *Teton Dakota*, p. 65.

23 Ordway, *Journal*, p. 140.

24 Thw. 1:166–69; Whitehouse, *Journal*, pp. 63–64.

25 *Field Notes*, pp. 149–50; Thw. 1:189.

26 Ibid. 1:169–70.

27 Gass, *Journal*, pp. 52–54; Ordway, *Journal*, pp. 141–42; Whitehouse, *Journal*, p. 64.

28 Thw. 1:168.

29 Ibid. 1:169–70.

30 James A. Hanson, *Metal Weapons, Tools, and Ornaments of the Teton Dakota Indians* (Lincoln: University of Nebraska Press, 1975), pp. 14–17, 26, 45.

31 "Biddle Notes," Jackson, ed., *Letters*, 2:518.

32 Gass, *Journal*, p. 54; *Field Notes*, p. 151; Ordway, *Journal*, pp. 142–43; Thw. 1:170–71; Whitehouse, *Journal*, p. 65.

33 Thw. 1:171.

34 Jefferson, "Instructions to Lewis," 1:64.

35 Thw. 6:98.

36 Lewis to Jefferson, April 7, 1805, Jackson, ed., *Letters*, 1:233.

37 Bernard DeVoto, *The Course of Empire* (Boston: Houghton Mifflin Co., 1952), pp. 445, 448.

38 Clark to Hugh Heney, July 20, 1806, Jackson, ed., *Letters*, 1:310. This is Clark's copy of a letter that Lewis drafted in early July 1806.

Chapter 3

1 Truteau, "Description," 2:378–79; Thw. 1:172; Ordway, *Journal*, p. 142.

2 Thw. 1:174.

3 Ordway, *Journal*, p. 144; Thw. 1:175. The Arikara villages seen on September 29

and Octobcr 1, 1804, were evidently part of what archaeologists call the Black Widow Site (39ST25 and 39ST50) in present-day Stanley County, South Dakota. See Donald J. Lehmer and David T. Jones, *Arikara Archeology: The Bad River Phase*, Smithsonian Institution River Basin Surveys Publications in Salvage Archeology, no. 7 (Washington, D.C., 1968), p. 83.

4   *Field Notes*, p. 153; Thw. 1:175.

5   Gass, *Journal*, pp. 57–58; Thw. 1:177–78; Whitehouse, *Journal*, p. 66.

6   Abel, ed., *Tabeau's Narrative*, pp. 125, 127–28: Lehmer and Jones, *Arikara Archeology*, p. 93; Thw. 1:179.

7   Gass, *Journal*, p. 59; Lehmer and Jones, *Arikara Archeology*, p. 93; Ordway, *Journal*, p. 147; Thw. 1:181.

8   Lehmer and Jones, *Arikara Archeology*, p. 94; Ordway, *Journal*, p. 148; Thw. 1:182.

9   Both Lewis and Clark (Thw. 6:88) and John Bradbury, *Travels in the Interior of America* (Liverpool: Smith and Galway, 1817), p. 111, note Star-rah-he as the "primitive" name of the Arikaras. Douglas R. Parks, "Bands and Villages of the Arikara and Pawnee," *Nebraska History* 60 (1979): 224, finds that AxtaRAhi, the Pawnee word for the Arikaras, was probably the name of the largest band. See also Abel, ed., *Tabeau's Narrative*, pp. 124–25.

10   Ibid., pp. 125–26; Thw. 6:89.

11   Roger T. Grange, Jr., "An Archeological View of Pawnee Origins," *Nebraska History* 60 (1979): 134–60, especially p. 144; Donald J. Lehmer, *Introduction to Middle Missouri Archeology*, United States Department of the Interior, National Park Service, Anthropological Papers, no. 1 (Washington, D.C., 1971), pp. 124–28.

12   Lehmer, *Middle Missouri Archeology*, chaps. 4–5; Lehmer and Jones, *Arikara Archeology*, pp. 82–83; Roy W. Meyer, *The Village Indians of the Upper Missouri: The Mandans, Hidatsas, and Arikaras* (Lincoln: University of Nebraska Press, 1977), pp. 7–8.

13   Lehmer, *Middle Missouri Archeology*, p. 172.

14   Truteau, "Journal," 1:295–96.

15   Henry M. Brackenridge, *Views of Louisiana; Together with a Journal of a Voyage up the Missouri River, in 1811* (Pittsburgh: Cramer, Spear, and Eichbaum, 1814), p. 248; Bradbury, *Travels*, p. 110; Lehmer, *Middle Missouri Archeology*, p. 141.

16   Richard A. Krause, *The Leavenworth Site: Archaeology of an Historic Arikara Community*, University of Kansas Publications in Anthropology, no. 3 (Lawrence, 1972), pp. 23–40; Lehmer, *Middle Missouri Archeology*, pp. 106, 136–39.

17   Among the best descriptions of Arikara earth lodges are those in Abel, ed., *Tabeau's Narrative*, pp. 146–47, and Brackenridge, *Views of Louisiana*, p. 248.

18   Gass, *Journal*, pp. 60–61.

19   Waldo R. Wedel, *Archeological Materials from the Vicinity of Mobridge, South Dakota*, Smithsonian Institution, BAE Bulletin no. 157, *Anthropological Papers*, no. 45 (Washington, D.C., 1955), p. 75.

20   Edwin T. Denig, *Five Indian Tribes of the Upper Missouri: Sioux, Arickaras, Assiniboines, Crees, Crows*, ed. John C. Ewers (Norman: University of Oklahoma Press, 1961), pp. 44–45.

21   Edwin M. Betts, ed., *Thomas Jefferson's Garden Book, 1766–1824* (Philadelphia: American Philosophical Society, 1944), pp. 334, 339.

22   Thw. 1:181.

23   Gilbert L. Wilson, *Agriculture of the Hidatsa Indians: An Indian Interpretation*, University of Minnesota Studies in the Social Sciences, no. 9 (Minneapolis, 1917), pp. 68–81.

24   Gass, *Journal*, p. 61. A thorough discussion of Arikara plants is in Cutright, *Lewis and Clark: Pioneering Naturalists*, pp. 97–99.

25   Brackenridge, *Views of Louisiana*, p. 248; Denig, *Five Tribes*, pp. 44–45.

26   Abel, ed., *Tabeau's Narrative*, pp. 148–49. Thw. 1:188.

27   Abel, ed., *Tabeau's Narrative*, p. 149; Denig, *Five Tribes*, p. 46.

28   Abel, ed., *Tabeau's Narrative*, pp. 74, 132, 149; Brackenridge, *Views of Louisiana*, p. 255; Denig, *Five Tribes*, pp. 48, 61.

29   Thw. 6:89.

30   Ibid. 1:190.

31   Abel., ed., *Tabeau's Narrative*, pp. 130–31.

32   Ibid.; Thw. 1:189.

33   Lewis to Jefferson, April 7, 1805, Jackson, ed., *Letters*, 1:235–36.

34   Truteau, "Journal," 1:310.

35   Thw. 5:356.

36   Abel, ed., *Tabeau's Narrative*, pp. 151–52, 158; Brackenridge, *Views of Louisiana*, p. 251; Joseph Jablow, *The Cheyenne in Plains Indian Trade Relations, 1795–1840* (Seattle: University of Washington Press, 1950), pp. 51–58; Thw. 5:356, 6:89.

37   Abel, ed., *Tabeau's Narrative*, p. 162; Denig, *Five Tribes*, p. 47.

38   Abel, ed., *Tabeau's Narrative*, pp. 190–92, 216–17; Brackenridge, *Views of Louisiana*, pp. 256–57; Bradbury, *Travels*, p. 165.

39   Bradbury, *Travels*, pp. 165–66; Lehmer, *Middle Missouri Archeology*, pp. 139–40, figures 86, 87.

40   Preston Holder, *The Hoe and the Horse on the Plains: A Study of Cultural Development among North American Indians* (Lincoln: University of Nebraska Press, 1970), p. 30; George E. Hyde, "The Mystery of the Arikaras," *North Dakota History* 18 (1951):

204. Donald J. Lehmer quoted in W. Raymond Wood, "Northern Plains Village Cultures: Internal Stability and External Relationships," *Journal of Anthropological Research* 30 (1974): 9, offers a much lower pre-epidemic population estimate of 9,000 Arikaras in a total village population of 25,000.

41 Lehmer and Jones, *Arikara Archeology*, pp. 90–92; Truteau, "Journal," 1:299.

42 Abel, ed., *Tabeau's Narrative*, pp. 123–24; Donald J. Lehmer, "Epidemics among the Indians of the Upper Missouri," in *Selected Writings of Donald J. Lehmer*, ed. W. Raymond Wood (Lincoln, Nebr.: J & L Reprint Co., 1977), pp. 105–11; Thw. 6:89.

43 Truteau, "Journal," 1:299–303.

44 Abel, ed., *Tabeau's Narrative*, pp. 123–24, 129–37; Holder, *The Hoe and the Horse*, pp. 131–33.

45 "Biddle Notes," 2:537; Lehmer and Jones, *Arikara Archeology*, p. 93; Prince Maximilian reporting a conversation with Toussaint Charbonneau, in Reuben G. Thwaites, ed., *Early Western Travels*, 32 vols. (Cleveland: Arthur H. Clark Co., 1904–1906), 23:229–30.

46 "Biddle Notes," 2:537.

47 Abel, ed., *Tabeau's Narrative*, p. 125; Hyde, "Mystery of the Arikaras," pp. 52–53; Parks, "Arikara and Pawnee Bands," p. 218; Moulton, ed., *Atlas*, plate 10; Wood, "Evans Map," p. 47.

48 Thw. 1:189.

49 Ibid. 6:270.

50 Ibid. 1:183–84.

51 Ordway, *Journal*, pp. 148–49.

52 Truteau, "Journal," 1:296.

53 Horsman, *Expansion and American Indian Policy*, pp. 104–14; Abel, ed., *Tabeau's Narrative*, pp. 162–63; Thw. 1:184.

54 Abel, ed., *Tabeau's Narrative*, pp. 127–34, 204.

55 Bradbury, *Travels*, pp. 110, 122.

56 *Field Notes*, p. 158; Ordway, *Journal*, p. 149; Thw. 1:185.

57 Lewis and Clark do not make it clear why they decided to appoint Kakawissassa as First Chief. Nor is it plain why someone from Sawa-haini should take precedence over a chief from any of the other villages. Since Tabeau and Gravelines had close ties to Kakawita and Kakawissassa, it is possible that the Frenchmen influenced the decision.

58 "Lewis and Clark to the Oto Indians," Jackson, ed., *Letters*, 1:205.

59 *Field Notes*, p. 158. The presence of the Tetons is mentioned in no other expedition journal.

60 Abel, ed., *Tabeau's Narrative*, p. 171; Thw. 1:199, 6:151.

61 Ordway, *Journal*, pp. 150–51; Thw. 1:185–86.

62 Ordway, *Journal*, pp. 150–51.

63 Gass, *Journal*, pp. 60–61; Krause, *Leavenworth Site*, pp. 23–40.

64 Thw. 1:185–86.

65 *Field Notes*, p. 158; Holder, *The Hoe and the Horse*, pp. 47–48.

66 Thw. 7:303.

67 White, "The Winning of the West," p. 332.

68 Gass, *Journal*, p. 62; Ordway, *Journal*, p. 151; Thw. 1:186–87.

69 Gass, *Journal*, pp. 62–63; Ordway, *Journal*, pp. 151–52.

70 Thw. 1:188.

71 Ibid. 7:303–4.

72 "Biddle Notes," 2:537; Thw. 7:304–5.

73 Holder, *The Hoe and the Horse*, p. 58.

74 Truteau, "Journal," 1:258, 300.

75 Bradbury, *Travels*, pp. 124–25.

76 Ibid.

77 Ibid., p. 169; Thw. 1:189.

78 George Catlin, *O-Kee-Pa: A Religious Ceremony and other Customs of the Mandans*, ed. John C. Ewers (New Haven: Yale University Press, 1967), p. 8; Alice B. Kehoe, "The Function of Ceremonial Sexual Intercourse among the Northern Plains Indians," *Plains Anthropologist* 15 (1970): 99–103.

79 Thw. 7:370.

80 Gass, *Journal*, pp. 62–63; Abel, ed., *Tabeau's Narrative*, p. 174; Thw. 1:186; "Biddle Notes," 2:537.

81 Ibid. 2:503; Thw. 1:189, 194.

82 "Biddle Notes," 2:503; *Field Notes*, p. 158.

83 Brackenridge, *Views of Louisiana*, p. 258.

84 Ordway, *Journal*, p. 152; Thw. 1:193, 197.

85 Abel, ed., *Tabeau's Narrative*, pp. 200–1.

86 Thw. 1:188.

Chapter 4

1   Allen, *Passage through the Garden*, p. 207.

2   Thw. 1:208.

3   Frank H. Stewart, "Mandan and Hidatsa Villages in the Eighteenth and Nineteenth Centuries," *Plains Anthropologist* 19 (1974): 292–97; W. Raymond Wood, *The Origins of the Hidatsa Indians: A Review of Ethnohistorical and Traditional Data* (Lincoln: National Park Service, Midwest Archeological Center, 1980), pp. 8–11.

4   Elliott Coues, ed., *New Light on the Early History of the Greater Northwest: The Manuscript Journals of Alexander Henry the Younger and of David Thompson*, 2 vols. (1897; reprint, Minneapolis: Ross and Haines, 1965), 1:337–38.

5   Edward M. Bruner, "Mandan," *Perspectives in American Indian Culture Change*, ed. Edward H. Spicer (Chicago: University of Chicago Press, 1961), p. 221; W. Raymond Wood, *An Interpretation of Mandan Culture History*, Smithsonian Institution, BAE Bulletin no. 198 (Washington, D.C., 1967), p. 16.

6   Richard Glover, ed., *David Thompson's Narrative, 1784–1812* (Toronto: The Champlain Society, 1962), p. 173.

7   G. Hubert Smith, *The Explorations of the La Vérendryes*, ed. W. Raymond Wood (Lincoln: University of Nebraska Press, 1980), pp. 67–94.

8   Lehmer, *Middle Missouri Archeology*, p. 169.

9   Bruner, "Mandan," p. 199.

10 Lawrence J. Burpee, ed., *Journals and Letters of Pierre Gaultier De Verennes De La Vérendrye and His Sons* (Toronto: The Champlain Society, 1927), pp. 323–24; Jablow, *Cheyenne in Plains Trade*, pp. 39–50; Truteau, "Description," 2:381.

11 Thw. 1:231, 251.

12 Burpee, ed., *Journals and Letters of Vérendrye*, pp. 324, 332–33.

13 *Field Notes*, p. 164; Thw. 1:199, 201–3.

14 *Field Notes*, p. 164; Ordway, *Journal*, p. 158; Thw. 1:204.

15 *Field Notes*, p. 166; Thw. 1:204–5.

16 Ordway, *Journal*, p. 158; Thw. 1:206.

17 *Field Notes*, p. 169.

18 Thw. 1:208–9.

19 Ordway, *Journal*, p. 159; Thw. 1:209–10.

20 Thw. 6:177.

21 *Field Notes*, p. 169.

22   Thw. 1:230.

23   Gass, *Journal*, p. 70; Ordway, *Journal*, pp. 159–60; Thw. 1:210–13, 6:177, 257.

24   Alfred W. Bowers, *Hidatsa Social and Ceremonial Organization*, Smithsonian Institution, BAE Bulletin no. 194 (Washington, D.C., 1965), pp. 27–29.

25   Ordway, *Journal*, p. 160; Thw. 1:213, 7:305.

26   Thw. 7:305.

27   *Field Notes*, p. 172; Ordway, *Journal*, p. 160; Thw. 1:214–15, 7:306.

28   Ordway, *Journal*, p. 160; Thw. 1:125, 7:306.

29   Ibid. 7:69.

30   Ibid. 1:221–22.

31   Ibid. 1:221.

32   Ibid. 1:223.

33   Ibid. 1:224.

34   Charles Mackenzie, "The Mississouri Indians: A Narrative of Four Trading Expeditions to the Mississouri 1804–1805–1806," ed. L. R. Masson, *Les Bourgeois de la Compagnie du Nord-Ouest*, 2 vols. (1889–1890; reprint, New York: Antiquarian Press, 1960), 1:330–31.

35   Thw. 1:226.

36   Mackenzie, "Narrative," 1:330–31.

37   Coues, ed., *New Light*, 1:349–50; François Antoine Larocque, "The Missouri Journal, 1804–1805," Masson, ed., *Les Bourgeois*, 1:304–306; Mackenzie, "Narrative," Masson, ed., *Les Bourgeois*, 1:345, 385; Ordway, *Journal*, p. 167; Thw. 1:227, 3:29–30.

38   Thw. 1:228.

39   Larocque, "Missouri Journal," 1:304–6; Thw. 1:228–29.

40   Ordway, *Journal*, p. 168; Thw. 1:230–32.

41   Thw. 1:233.

42   Ibid. 1:240.

43   Ibid. 1:214.

44   Ordway, *Journal*, pp. 163, 164, 167.

45   Thw. 1:224.

46   Ordway, *Journal*, p. 186; Thw. 1:228, 233.

47   Ordway, *Journal*, pp. 169, 174, 176–77; Thw. 1:233, 240.

48   Ibid. 1:225, 255.

273

49   Ordway, *Journal*, pp. 172, 174; Thw. 1:240, 255, 272.

50   Ibid. 1:256.

51   Ordway, *Journal*, p. 174; Thw. 1:243.

52   Gass, *Journal*, pp. 79–80; Ordway, *Journal*, p. 175; Thw. 1:244.

53   Ordway, *Journal*, p. 160.

54   Thw. 1:216, 219, 223.

55   Ordway, *Journal*, p. 178; Thw. 1:241–42.

56   Ibid. 1:252.

57   Ordway, *Journal*, pp. 185–86, 353; Thw. 1:252, 255, 272.

58   Gass, *Journal*, p. 77; Ordway, *Journal*, p. 174; Thw. 1:239.

59   Coues, ed., *New Light*, 1:329.

60   Thw. 7:370.

61   Coues, ed., *New Light*, 1:349–50.

62   Biddle-Coues, *History*, 1:210–11; Ordway, *Journal*, pp. 170–71; Thw. 1:234–35.

63   Ibid. 1:239, 246–47, 251.

64   Ordway, *Journal*, p. 158.

65   Thw. 1:225.

66   Thw. 1:248, 250, 279; "Supplies from Private Vendors," Jackson, ed., *Letters*, 1:80.

67   Abel, ed., *Tabeau's Narrative*, pp. 196–97; *Field Notes*, p. 172; Mackenzie, "Narrative," 1:348.

68   Ordway, *Journal*, p. 177; Thw. 1:248.

69   Ordway, *Journal*, p. 177; Thw. 1:249.

70   Ordway, *Journal*, p. 181; Thw. 1:261–62.

71   Ordway, *Journal*, pp. 181–82.

72   Gass, *Journal*, p. 85; Ordway, *Journal*, pp. 184–85; Thw. 1:267.

73   Ibid. 1:247–48.

74   Brackenridge, *Views of Louisiana*, p. 261; Bradbury, *Travels*, p. 149; "Biddle Notes," 2:505; Coues, ed., *New Light*, 1:379–80, 387.

75   Ordway, *Journal*, p. 186; "Biddle Notes," 2:539; Thw. 1:270.

Chapter 5

1   Wendell H. Oswalt, *Other Peoples, Other Customs: World Ethnography and Its History* (New York: Holt, Rinehart, and Winston, 1972), pp. 1–73.

2   Gass, *Journal*, pp. 81–82.

3   Alfred W. Bowers, *Mandan Social and Ceremonial Organization* (Chicago: University of Chicago Press, 1950), p. 94.

4   Thw. 1:256.

5   Ibid. 1:224, 225.

6   Ibid. 1:212.

7   Ibid. 1:270–71. Several versions of Hidatsa migration stories are analyzed in Wood, *Origins of the Hidatsa Indians*, pp. 26–68, 78–86.

8   Thw. 6:111.

9   Ibid. 1:221, 233.

10   Mackenzie, "Narrative," 1:336–37.

11   Ibid., p. 336.

12   Larocque, "Missouri Journal," 1:308; Thw. 1:238. A fragment of a map based on Heney's information is in *Field Notes*, p. 324.

13   Thw. 1:209, 220.

14   Ibid. 1:209.

15   Ibid. 1:214–15.

16   See also Clark's description of the Mandan medicine stone and its role in decision making, Thw. 1:264.

17   "Biddle Notes," 2:519–20.

18   Bowers, *Hidatsa*, p. 26; Bowers, *Mandan*, pp. 33–36; Bruner, "Mandan," p. 226.

19   Ordway, *Journal*, p. 159. See also Catlin, *Letters and Notes*, 1:90–91, plate 48, and Prince Maximilian in Thwaites, ed., *Early Western Travels*, 23:360–62.

20   Ordway, *Journal*, pp. 160, 167; Wilson, *Hidatsa Agriculture*, pp. 87–96.

21   Ordway, *Journal*, p. 172. See also Biddle-Coues, *History*, 1:213–14, which Biddle took directly from Ordway's account but added the notion of a French billiard origin. The game is also described in Henry A. Boller, *Among the Indians: Eight Years in the Far West, 1858–1866*, ed. Milo M. Quaife (1868; reprint, Chicago: The Lakeside Press, 1959), pp. 165–66, and Prince Maximilian in Thwaites, ed., *Early Western Travels*, 23:298. There are drawings of the game by Karl Bodmer in Thwaites, ed., *Early Western Travels*, 25: plate 59 and Catlin, *Letters and Notes*, 1: plate 59. Fine Bodmer pencil sketches of playing sticks and hoops are in Davis Thomas and Karin Ronnefeldt, eds., *People of the First Man* (New York: E. P. Dutton, 1976), p. 200. The most thorough treatment of the game is in Stewart Culin, *Games of the North American Indians*, Smithsonian Institution, BAE 24th Annual Report [1902–1903] (Washington, D.C., 1907), pp. 420–527.

22   Jackson, *Thomas Jefferson and the Stony Mountains*, pp. 192–95.

23   Thw. 1:254–55. See also Catlin, *Letters and Notes*, 1: plates 63, 99.

24   Thw. 1:272–74. See also Krause, *Leavenworth Site*, p. 82, and Abel, ed., *Tabeau's Narrative*, p. 149.

25   Thw. 1:285.

26   Ibid. 1:256, 280–82; Waldo R. Wedel, *Observations on Some Nineteenth Century Pottery Vessels from the Upper Missouri*, Smithsonian Institution, BAE Bulletin no. 164 (Washington, D.C., 1957), pp. 91–114; Charles C. Willoughby, "A Few Ethnological Specimens Collected by Lewis and Clark," *American Anthropologist* 7 (1905): 633–41. References to Jefferson's experiments with Indian seeds are in Betts, ed., *Jefferson's Garden Book* and in letters between Jefferson and Bernard McMahon in Jackson, ed., *Letters*.

27   Thw. 1:234–35.

28   Ibid. 6:82–83. Similar questions were used in the reports made by Zebulon Pike. See Jackson, ed., *Journals of Pike*, 1:218–25, 2:39–42. When Clark sent a copy of the estimate to the Secretary of War, the explorer added what he termed "additional Remarks" focusing on the economic and political situations of the various tribes and bands.

29   Thw. 1:190, 238, 269.

30   "Biddle Notes," 2:503; Jefferson to José Corrèa da Serra, April 26, 1816, Jackson, ed., *Letters*, 2:611.

31   Thw. 7:408–9. The blank vocabularies printed at Jefferson's order contain 322 words. However, there are several duplicated terms, bringing the correct total to 315. See also Bob Saindon, "The Lost Vocabularies of the Lewis and Clark Expedition," *We Proceeded On* 3 (1977): 4–6.

32   Thw. 1:246; Allen, *Passage through the Garden*, p. 213; Herman R. Friis, "Cartographic and Geographic Activities of the Lewis and Clark Expedition," *Journal* of the Washington Academy of Sciences 44 (1954): 348.

33   Thw. 1:238, 245–46; Moulton, ed., *Atlas*, plates 31a and b.

34   Thw. 1:249; "Biddle Notes," 2:532; Allen, *Passage through the Garden*, p. 247; C. A. Burland, "American Indian Map Makers," *Geographical Magazine* 22 (1947): 285–92; G. Malcolm Lewis, "Indian Maps," *Old Trails and New Directions: Papers of the Third North American Fur Trade Conference*, eds. Carol M. Judd and Arthur J. Ray (Toronto: University of Toronto Press, 1980), pp. 9–23.

35   William Clark, "A Map of part of the Continent of North America" in Wheat, *Mapping the Transmississippi West*, 2: map 270.

36   Thw. 6:50–51, 55.

37   Ordway, *Journal*, pp. 160, 174–75; Thw. 1:240; Wilson, *Hidatsa Agriculture*, pp. 63–64.

38   Bruner, "Mandan," pp. 200–1; Jablow, *Cheyenne in Plains Trade*, p. 46.

39   Burpee, ed., *Journals and Letters of Vérendrye*, p. 331; "Biddle Notes," Jackson, ed., *Letters*, 2:502; Thw. 1:221–22.

40   "Biddle Notes," Jackson, ed., *Letters*, 2:531; Bowers, *Hidatsa*, pp. 166–68; Bowers, *Mandan*, p. 272; Thw. 1:239.

41   "Biddle Notes," 2:520–21; Gass, *Journal*, pp. 81–82.

42   Bowers, *Hidatsa*, pp. 54, 60, 307, 314; Bowers, *Mandan*, pp. 87–88.

43   "Biddle Notes," 2:538; Bowers, *Mandan*, pp. 283–86; Bruner, "Mandan," p. 217; Kehoe, "Functions of Ceremonial Sexual Intercourse," pp. 99–103; Meyer, *Village Indians*, pp. 79–80; *Field Notes*, p. 172; Thw. 1:245.

44   "Biddle Notes," 2:520.

Chapter 6

1   Thw. 1:284–85.

2   Lewis to Jefferson, April 7, 1805, Jackson, ed., *Letters*, 1:233.

3   Thw. 2:12, 6:105.

4   Lewis to Jefferson, April 7, 1805, Jackson, ed., *Letters*, 1:232; Thw. 1:284.

5   Thw. 1:302, 306, 313.

6   Ibid. 1:318.

7   Ibid. 1:360, 362, 365, 366.

8   Ibid. 2:12.

9   Ibid. 2:20. No other expedition diarist records this concern on May 10. Either Lewis and Clark kept their fears to themselves or those fears were somewhat exaggerated.

10   Thw. 2:88.

11   Ibid. 2:92–93; W. Raymond Wood, "Lewis and Clark and Middle Missouri Archaeology," *Quarterly Review of Archaeology* 3 (1982): 3–5.

12   Thw. 2:175.

13   Ibid. 2:234; Whitehouse, *Journal*, p. 115. Since northern Shoshonis like those in Cameahwait's band did not usually make their crossing to eastern hunting grounds until September, it is not clear who these Shoshonis were.

14   Thw. 2:244.

15   Ibid. 2:252, 254.

16   Ordway, *Journal*, p. 251; Thw. 2:260; Whitehouse, *Journal*, p. 119.

17   Ordway, *Journal*, p. 251; Thw. 2:271.

18   Ibid. 2:279.

19   Ordway, *Journal*, p. 254. This was the first recognition that Shoshonis might still be
      on the western side of the Great Divide.

20   Thw. 2:290.

21   Ibid. 2:313.

22   Ibid. 2:321.

23   Ibid. 2:323–27.

24   Ibid. 2:329–31.

25   The phrase "men with faces pale as ashes" comes from an oral tradition about the
      initial Shoshoni-expedition meeting. The account was collected by Thomas J.
      Farnham in 1839 at Brown's Hole. The information was given to Farnham by a
      Shoshoni who claimed to have been the man seen by Lewis on August 11. Much of
      this account does not square with events recorded by Lewis. Thomas J. Farnham,
      "Travels in the Great Western Prairies" (1843), Thwaites, ed., *Early Western Travels*,
      28:272–73. Because northern Shoshoni history and culture so pervades the
      following discussion, I have chosen to list all major sources in one note. Sven
      Liljeblad, *The Idaho Indians in Transition, 1805–1960* (Pocatello: Idaho State
      University Museum, 1972); Robert H. Lowie, *The Northern Shoshone*, Anthro-
      pological Papers of the American Museum of Natural History, vol. 2, pt. 2 (New
      York, 1909), pp. 169–306; Robert H. Lowie, *Notes on Shoshonean Ethnography*,
      Anthropological Papers of the American Museum of Natural History, vol. 22
      (New York, 1922), pp. 187–314; Brigham D. Madsen, *The Lemhi: Sacajawea's People*
      (Caldwell, Idaho: Caxton Press, 1979); John E. Rees, "The Shoshoni Contribution
      to Lewis and Clark," *Idaho Yesterdays* 2 (1958): 2–13; Julian H. Steward, "Culture
      Element Distributions: 23 Northern and Gosiute Shoshoni," *Anthropological Records*
      8, pt. 3 (1943): 263–392; Omer C. Stewart, "The Shoshoni: Their History and Social
      Organization," *Idaho Yesterdays* 9 (1965): 2–5, 28; Virginia C. Trenholm and
      Maurine Carley, *The Shoshonis: Sentinels of the Rockies* (Norman: University of
      Oklahoma Press, 1964).

26   Thw. 2:333–36.

27   Ibid. 2:337–43.

28   Clues about Shoshoni attitudes are scattered in Lewis's journal entries for August
      13–15, 1805. The most reliable Shoshoni oral account of the August 13 meeting and
      events through the 15th is in Warren A. Ferris, *Life in the Rocky Mountains*, ed. Paul
      C. Phillips (Denver: The Old West Publishing Co., 1940), pp. 90–93.

29   Thw. 2:347–48.

30   Ibid. 2:349–51.

31   Ibid. 2:354–58.

32   "Biddle Notes," 2:518–19; Ordway, *Journal*, pp. 267–69; Thw. 2:361–67.

278

33 The bulk of Lewis's Shoshoni ethnography is in his journal entries for August 19–21, and 23–24, 1805.

34 Lewis's almost photographic ability to portray Shoshoni clothing can be seen in his entries for August 19–21. A drawing of Lewis wearing his Shoshoni tippet by Charles B. J. F. de Saint-Mémin is in Paul R. Cutright, "Lewis and Clark Portraits and Portraitists," *Montana: The Magazine of Western History* 19 (1969): 43.

35 Thw. 3:20.

36 Ibid. 2:355, 358, 3:43.

37 Ibid. 2:370.

38 Ibid. 2:366.

39 The fullest account of this meeting is in Lewis's entry, Thw. 2:380–84. Clark's own entry contains only the barest outline of the conference.

40 Ordway, *Journal*, p. 272; Thw. 3:13–14.

41 Thw. 3:34–36. For Lewis's comments on Shoshoni hunger see Thw. 2:355, 3:14, 18, 41.

42 Ordway, *Journal*, p. 270; Thw. 2:367.

43 Thw. 3:27–28.

44 Ordway, *Journal*, pp. 275–76; Thw. 3:46–48.

45 Olin D. Wheeler, *The Trail of Lewis and Clark, 1804–1904*, 2 vols. (New York: G. P. Putnam's Sons, 1904), 2:65–66.

46 Ordway, *Journal*, p. 281; Thw. 3:53. Information on Flathead history and culture can be found in John Fahey, *The Flathead Indians* (Norman: University of Oklahoma Press, 1974); H. H. Turney-High, *The Flathead Indians of Montana*, Memoirs of the American Anthropological Association, vol. 48 (Menasha, Wisconsin, 1937), pp. 1–161; Verne F. Ray, *Cultural Relations in the Plateau of Northwestern America*, Publications of the Frederick Webb Hodge Fund, no. 3 (Los Angeles: Southwest Museum, 1939). Important aspects of Flathead life after Lewis and Clark but before substantial white contact can be found in missionary accounts by Gregory Mengarini, *Recollections of the Flathead Mission*, ed. Gloria R. Lothrop (Glendale: Arthur H. Clark Co., 1977) and Joseph P. Donnelly, trans., *Wilderness Kingdom: Indian Life in the Rocky Mountains, 1840–1847; The Journals and Paintings of Nicholas Point, S.J.* (New York: Holt, Rinehart and Winston, 1967).

47 "Biddle Notes," 2:519; Ordway, *Journal*, pp. 281–82; Thw. 3:53–54; Whitehouse, *Journal*, p. 150.

48 Thw. 3:54–55; Whitehouse, *Journal*, pp. 150–51.

49 Gass, *Journal*, p. 164.

50 The best treatments of the Lolo Trail segment of the journey are Appleman, *Lewis*

and Clark, pp. 171–75; DeVoto, *Course of Empire,* pp. 503–6; John J. Peebles, *Lewis and Clark in Idaho* (Boise: Idaho Historical Society, 1966), pp. 16–22 and folding maps; Ralph Space, *Lewis and Clark through Idaho* (Lewiston, Idaho: Tribune Publishing Co., 1964). The quote by Clark is from Thw. 3:69; the one by Gass is from his *Journal,* p. 164.

51   Alvin Josephy, Jr., *The Nez Perce Indians and the Opening of the Northwest* (New Haven: Yale University Press, 1965), pp. 645–46. Whether the Nez Perce Indians pierced their noses has long been a subject of heated controversy. There is no question that in 1806, on their return journey, Lewis and Clark saw some Nez Perces sporting shell ornaments in their noses. See Thw. 4:372, 5:30.

52   Ibid. 3:77–79.

53   Josephy, *Nez Perce,* pp. 37–38; Thw. 3:81–82.

54   Josephy, *Nez Perce,* p. 38; Thw. 5:22.

55   Ordway, *Journal,* p. 290; Thw. 3:84–85. The results of Clark's interviews with those Nez Perce "men of note" can be seen in several of his maps. See Thw. 3: between 118 and 119, 8: map 30, pt. 3.

56   Ordway, *Journal,* p. 290; Thw. 3:106; Whitehouse, *Journal,* p. 162.

57   Thw. 3:87.

58   Gass, *Journal,* p. 173; Thw. 3:93–94.

59   Gass, *Journal,* p. 175; Thw. 3:98–100.

60   Ordway, *Journal,* p. 296; Thw. 3:100–1.

Chapter 7

1   Thw. 3:159.

2   Donald W. Meinig, *The Great Columbia Plain: A Historical Geography, 1805–1910* (Seattle: University of Washington Press, 1968), pp. 3–20.

3   Thw. 3:113–16.

4   Ibid. 3:109.

5   Verne F. Ray, "Native Villages and Groupings of the Columbia Basin," *Pacific Northwest Quarterly* 27 (1936): 119; Robert H. Ruby and John A. Brown, *Indians of the Pacific Northwest: A History* (Norman: University of Oklahoma Press, 1981), p. 17; Thw. 3:116.

6   Gass, *Journal,* p. 181; Ordway, *Journal,* p. 299; Thw. 3: 119–20.

7   Thw. 3:124–27. Photographs of mat houses can be found in Ruby and Brown, *Indians of the Pacific Northwest,* p. 18.

8   Gass, *Journal,* p. 182; Thw. 3:128–32; Whitehouse, *Journal,* p. 175.

9   Thomas R. Garth, "Early Nineteenth Century Tribal Relations in the Columbia Plateau," *Southwestern Journal of Anthropology* 20 (1964): 45–48; Glover, ed., *Thompson's Narrative*, pp. 350–51; Thw. 3:134–35. Because the Walulas were dependent on Cayuse traders for their manufactured goods, it is possible that Yelleppit was searching for a source of supply that would make his people less dependent on the Cayuses.

10   "Biddle Notes," 2:529; Thw. 3:136–37.

11   Ordway, *Journal*, p. 301; Thw. 3:145.

12   Gass, *Journal*, p. 183; Thw. 3:138, 140.

13   "Biddle Notes," 2:527.

14   Alexander Ross, *Adventures of the First Settlers on the Oregon or Columbia River.* ed. Milo M. Quaife (1849; reprint, Chicago: The Lakeside Press, 1923), pp. 127–28.

15   Biddle-Coues, *History*, 2:785–90; "Biddle Notes," 2:499–500; Ross, *Adventures on the Oregon*, pp. 127–29; Thw. 4:289. For recent studies see David French, "Wasco-Wishram," Spicer, ed., *Perspectives in American Indian Culture Change*, pp. 343–52; Leslie Spier and Edward Sapir, *Wishram Ethnography*, University of Washington Publications in Anthropology, vol. 3 (Seattle, 1930), pp. 224–28; Wood, "Contrastive Features," pp. 153–66.

16   Ordway, *Journal*, p. 302; Thw. 3:148.

17   Ibid. 4:267–69, 302–9.

18   French, "Wasco-Wishram," pp. 352–53.

19   Ordway, *Journal*, p. 303; Thw. 3:150–51. Whitehouse, *Journal*, p. 179.

20   Garth, "Tribal Relations," pp. 51–55.

21   Gass, *Journal*, p. 186; Whitehouse, *Journal*, p. 180. For additional information on the Nixluidix site, see W. Duncan Strong, *Archaeology of the Dalles-Deschutes Region*, University of California Publications in American Archaeology and Ethnology, vol. 29 (Berkeley, 1930), pp. 1–16. Clark's detailed map of Indian villages in The Dalles region is in Thw. 3:158.

22   Gass, *Journal*, p. 187; Ordway, *Journal*, p. 304; Thw. 3: 158.

23   Joel V. Berreman, *Tribal Distributions in Oregon*, Memoirs of the American Anthropological Association, vol. 47 (Menasha, Wisconsin, 1937), p. 16; Thw. 6:117.

24   Ibid. 3:197–98.

25   Ordway, *Journal*, p. 308; Thw. 3:205, 207.

26   Thw. 3:216.

27   Ibid. 3:210.

28   "Biddle Notes," 2:541; Thw. 3:224–26, 243–44.

281

29   Ibid. 3:199.

30   Ibid. 3:253. See also 3:186, 244–45, 251.

31   Ibid. 3:311.

32   Ibid. 3:186, 239.

33   Ibid. 3:209, 217.

34   Ibid. 3:234.

Chapter 8

1   Thw. 3:270.

2   Ordway, *Journal*, pp. 317, 322, 326; Thw. 3:267, 285, 291.

3   Barry Gough, *Distant Dominion: Britain and the Northwest Coast of North America, 1579–1809* (Vancouver: University of British Columbia Press, 1980), pp. 116–34; Derek Pethick, *First Approaches to the Northwest Coast* (Vancouver: J. J. Douglas, 1976), pp. 77–133; Robert H. Ruby and John A. Brown, *The Chinook Indians: Traders of the Lower Columbia River* (Norman: University of Oklahoma Press, 1976), pp. 40–58. An important oral tradition relating the first Clatsop sighting of a European ship is in Franz Boas, ed., *Chinook Texts*, Smithsonian Institution, BAE Bulletin no. 20 (Washington, D.C., 1894), pp. 277–78. Lower Chinookan perceptions of Capt. Robert Gray can be found in Philip Ashton Rollins, ed., *The Discovery of the Oregon Trail: Robert Stuart's Narratives of His Overland Trip Eastward from Astoria in 1812–13* (New York: Edward Eberstadt and Sons, 1935), pp. 15–16.

4   Thw. 3:311.

5   T. C. Elliott, ed., "The Journal of the Ship *Ruby*," *Oregon Historical Quarterly* 28 (1927): 261–63.

6   Berreman, *Tribal Distribution in Oregon*, pp. 13–15; Verne F. Ray, *Lower Chinook Ethnographic Notes*, University of Washington Publications in Anthropology, vol. 7 (Seattle, 1938), pp. 37–41; Leslie Spier, *Tribal Distribution in Washington*, General Series in Anthropology, no. 3 (Menasha, Wisconsin, 1936), pp. 21–23, 42; John R. Swanton, *The Indian Tribes of North America*, Smithsonian Institution, BAE Bulletin no. 145 (Washington, D.C., 1952), pp. 414, 417–18, 458, 471–73; Thw. 3: map between 281–82, 294–95, 6:117. Lewis and Clark's spatial understanding of the Indians around them is portrayed in Clark's map in Moulton, ed., *Atlas*, plates 81–85.

7   Thw. 4:128.

8   Ordway, *Journal*, p. 316; Thw. 3:286, 362.

9   Thw. 3:315.

10   Ibid. 3:302–4.

282

11   Ibid. 3:296–97.

12   Ibid. 3:286, 316, 4:94–95.

13   Ibid. 3:299.

14   Ibid. 3:289

15   Ordway, *Journal*, p. 325; Thw. 3:245, 278, 289, 4:105.

16   Jefferson, "Instructions to Lewis," 1:65.

17   Thw. 3:226, 229–30.

18   Ibid. 3:238.

19   Ibid. 4:89–90. Taucum's earlier dealings with traders are traced in Elliott, ed., "Journal of the Ship *Ruby*," pp. 267–78. In the list of chiefs prepared early in the Fort Clatsop winter, Taucum is called Stock-home. See Thw. 3:294.

20   Thw. 3:278.

21   Ibid. 3:296.

22   Ibid. 3:332.

23   DeVoto, *Course of Empire*, pp. 508–9.

24   Boas, ed., *Chinook Texts*, p. 278.

25   Erna Gunther, *Indian Life on the Northwest Coast of North America* (Chicago: University of Chicago Press, 1972), pp. 55–90; Susan Kardas, " 'The People Bought This and the Clatsop Became Rich.' A View of Nineteenth-Century Fur Trade Relationships on the Lower Columbia between Chinookan Speakers, Whites, and Kanakas" (Ph.D. diss., Bryn Mawr College, 1971), chap. 2; Ray, *Lower Chinook Ethnographic Notes, passim;* Verne F. Ray, "The Chinook Indians in the Early 1800s," in *The Western Shore: Oregon Country Essays Honoring the American Revolution,* ed. Thomas Vaughan (Portland: Oregon Historical Society, 1976), pp. 138–39.

26   Philip Drucker, *Indians of the Northwest Coast* (New York: McGraw-Hill Co., 1955), pp. 63–67; Ronald L. Olson, *Adze, Canoe, and House Types of the Northwest Coast,* University of Washington Publications in Anthropology, no. 2 (Seattle, 1927), pp. 18–23; Ray, *Lower Chinook Ethnographic Notes,* pp. 101–6.

27   Clark's entry, Thw. 4:35, has five canoe drawings. The first two are both shovel-noses of different sizes. The succeeding drawings follow the same sequence as in the Lewis entry. Clark also has drawings of two different canoe paddles, the pointed type used exclusively with shovel-nose canoes and the more common notched style.

28   James G. Swan, *The Northwest Coast, or, Three Years' Residence in Washington Territory* (1857; reprint, Seattle: University of Washington Press, 1969), p. 80; Thw. 4:30–36. See also Gabriel Franchère, *A Voyage to the Northwest Coast of America,* ed. Milo

283

Quaife (1854; reprint, Chicago: The Lakeside Press, 1954), pp. 186–87; Ross, *Adventures on the Oregon*, pp. 72–74.

29   Thw. 3:356–57, 4:198–99. See also Franchère, *Voyage to the Northwest Coast*, pp. 187–88; Ray, *Lower Chinook Ethnographic Notes*, pp. 124–26; Swan, *Northwest Coast*, pp. 110–11, 339.

30   Thw. 3:274, 288, drawings between 326 and 327, 4:9, 24; J. Russell Harper, ed., *Paul Kane's Frontier* (Austin: University of Texas Press, 1971), plate 37, figs. 158, 192, 194; John Webber, "Interior of a house at Yuquot, Nootka Sound, 1778," J. C. Beaglehole, ed., *The Voyage of the Resolution and Discovery, 1776–1780* (Cambridge: The Hakluyt Society, 1967), plate 38.

31   Thw. 3:297; 4:185–87. Cutright, *Lewis and Clark: Pioneering Naturalists*, pp. 264–71 has a superb treatment of Lewis and Clark ethnobotany at Fort Clatsop.

32   Thw. 3:294, 296, 360, 4:23, 94–95. Hats identical to those described in the journals can be seen in Drucker, *Indians of the Northwest Coast*, p. 75, and J. C. H. King, "The Nootka of Vancouver Island," in *Cook's Voyages and the Peoples of the Pacific*, ed. Hugh Cobbe (London: British Museum Publications, 1979), p. 94.

33   Lewis and Clark did record in both words and pictures Indian hunting and fishing techniques but along with Jefferson tended to define "ordinary occupations" in a way most suited to American business interests. See Thw. 3:346–47, 350.

34   Thw. 3:327–28. See also Frederic W. Howay, *A List of Trading Vessels in the Maritime Fur Trade, 1785–1825* (Kingston, Ontario: Limestone Press, 1973), pp. 1–57. On several occasions Indians gave the expedition detailed information about ships and traders on the Columbia. Those names were probably garbled in transmission since only one, Capt. Hugh Moore of the *Phoenix*, can be identified from Howay's master list. See Thw. 3:306–7, 4:200.

35   Thw. 3:338, 343. Lewis and Clark never suggested building a permanent post on the Columbia, although Lewis noted the good location of Bakers Bay as an anchorage, Thw. 3:340–41.

36   Thw. 4:184.

37   Ibid. 3:311.

38   Ibid. 3:274, 311, 315, 360. Practices such as head flattening and ankle binding, which were certainly beyond the experience of the explorers, were given remarkably value-free descriptions in the journals.

39   Perhaps the best of the Lewis essays written during the winter at Fort Clatsop: a comparison of the treatment of the elderly in the coastal and plains culture areas, Thw. 3:315; coastal burial practices, Thw. 3:326–27; hunting techniques, Thw. 3:346–47; house construction, Thw. 3:356–57; canoes, Thw. 4:30–36; clothing and physical appearance, Thw. 4:183–88.

40   Thw. 4: between 10 and 11. See also Harper, ed., *Paul Kane's Frontier*, figs. 170, 171.

284

41   Thw. 6:114–20. Early attempts at listing western Indians can be seen in Thw. 3:294–95 and Clark's "A List of the Nations and Tribes of Indians residing West of the Rocky Mountains," Clark Papers, Missouri Historical Society, box 5. Clark's map of the Pacific coast from Cape Disappointment to Cape Lookout in Moulton, ed., *Atlas,* plates 81–85, gives some spatial dimension to the western estimate as does his 1810 map. See also Berreman, *Tribal Distribution in Oregon,* fig. 1; Sapir, *Tribal Distribution in Washington,* map at p. 42; Swanton, *Indian Tribes of North America,* map facing p. 186.

42   Allen, *Passage through the Garden,* p. 207.

43   Ordway, *Journal,* p. 174; Thw. 3:302–4.

44   Thw. 3:327, 4:74. In Lewis's entry for April 11, 1806, there is an interline note reporting that the explorers learned some jargon during the winter. Such words and phrases would have been enough to carry on trade talks but insufficient for a discussion of social beliefs and practices.

45   Ibid. 4:128.

46   Ibid. 3:315.

47   Ibid. 3:294.

48   "Biddle Notes," 2:504; Coues, ed., *New Light,* 2:837–38, 859; Ruby and Brown, *Chinooks,* pp. 64–66; Swan, *Northwest Coast,* p. 154.

49   Ruby and Brown, *Chinooks,* p. 75.

50   Thw. 3:339–41.

51   Biddle-Coues, *History,* 2:779; Gass, *Journal,* p. 229; Thw. 3:304, 4:16, 27. McNeal and Goodrich continued to suffer the effects of their sexual adventures as late as July, 1806. See Thw. 5:255.

52   Ordway, *Journal,* p. 321; Thw. 3:328–29.

53   Biddle-Coues, *History,* 2:779; "Biddle Notes," 2:503.

54   Thw. 4:170, 176, 180.

55   Ibid. 4:39, 45, 61, 94, 102.

56   Ibid. 4:162, 168, 173.

57   Ibid. 4:177, 179.

58   Ordway, *Journal,* p. 329; Thw. 4:138, 195. Ordway was the only expedition member to record details of the theft.

59   Thw. 4:89–90.

60   Ibid. 4:197. R. G. Thwaites and others have claimed that Indians, especially "the crafty Chinook Concomly," knowingly kept from the expedition knowledge of the presence of the brig *Lydia.* See Thw. 3:328n. John Jewitt, a sailor rescued by the

285

Lydia from captivity at Nootka Sound, indicates that the ship entered the Columbia at an unspecified date and its crew learned that Lewis and Clark had left Fort Clatsop some two weeks before. Thwaites believed that the *Lydia* was on the Columbia before mid-March 1806, an assumption not based on any evidence in Jewitt's account, which is very unclear on dates. However, there seems no reason to doubt Jewitt's two-week information. Equally significant, there is no reason for the Chinookans to keep this sort of information from Lewis and Clark. See Robert F. Heizer, ed., *Narrative of the Adventures and Sufferings of John R. Jewitt* (1820; reprint, Ramona, Calif.: Ballena Press, 1975), p. 88.

61   Coues, ed., *New Light,* 2:915; Thw. 4:185, 188.

Chapter 9

1   Thw. 4:227–28.

2   Ibid. 4:235–39.

3   Ibid. 4:259–60.

4   Ibid. 4:266–68.

5   Ibid. 4:273.

6   Ibid. 4:284.

7   Although the Skilloot villages were usually clustered around the Cowlitz River, during the spring salmon runs many Skilloots built temporary mat lodges at The Dalles.

8   Thw. 4:288–90.

9   Ibid. 4:292–94.

10   Ibid. 4:296, 298–300.

11   Ibid. 4:306–7.

12   Ibid. 4:308–12.

13   Ibid. 4:313.

14   Ordway, *Journal,* p. 347; Thw. 4:317, 319, 321. The identity of Lewis and Clark's Pishquitpahs remains unclear. They were certainly not Salish-speaking Pishquows as Thwaites claimed, Thw. 3:137. It seems more likely that they were Sahaptin speakers and a band of either Cayuses or Umatillas.

15   Thw. 4:328–29.

16   "Biddle Notes," 2:532; Ordway, *Journal,* p. 348; Thw. 4:331–32.

17   Josephy, *Nez Perce,* p. 11; Thw. 4:351–52.

18   Thw. 4:354–55.

19   Ibid. 4:357–60.

20   Ibid. 4:371.

21   Ibid. 5:4–9.

22   Ibid. 5:14–16.

23   Ordway, *Journal*, p. 356; Thw. 5:18–20.

24   Josephy, *Nez Perce*, pp. 11–14; Verne F. Ray, *Lewis and Clark and the Nez Perce Indians* (Washington, D.C.: The Westerners, 1971), pp. 11–14; Thw. 5:23–27.

25   Appleman, *Lewis and Clark,* pp. 272–73; Peebles, *Lewis and Clark in Idaho*, p. 30; Thw. 5:33–35.

26   Thw. 5:30.

27   Ibid. 5:52–53. What remains unclear in this arrangement is whether all food obtained by trade was put in a common stockpile or if each mess or individual was responsible for his own rations.

28   Gass, *Journal*, pp. 265–66; Thw. 5:86, 95.

29   Thw. 5:98.

30   Ordway, *Journal*, pp. 360–63; Thw. 5:99–100.

31   Thw. 5:113.

32   Ibid. 5:360–61.

33   Thw. 4:359, 365, 5:27, 48, 50.

34   Thw. 5:22. Modern medical opinion suggests that the chief was suffering from a variety of polymyositis. C. L. Thomas, ed., *Taber's Cyclopedic Medical Dictionary,* 13th ed. (Philadelphia: F. A. Davis Co., 1977), Ibid. 112, and personal communication with Charles McGowen, MD.

35   Thw. 5:27, 62–63.

36   Ibid. 5:63.

37   Ibid. 5:67, 72.

38   Ibid. 5:4, 11, 16, 29–31, 72.

39   Ibid. 5:35, 49, 58, 68.

40   Josephy, *Nez Perce*, p. 14.

41   Thw. 5:117.

42   Ibid. 5:105–6.

43   Ibid. 5:112–13.

44   Ibid. 5:43, 46, 51, 53.

45   Ibid. 5:95, 103, 113–14, 118. Although the journals do not offer a clear explanation

287

for the lack of Nez Perce guides, Clark told Nicholas Biddle, "The reason of our having no guide was that the Indians had declared that the hills were impassable. One of them had attempted and returned we met him." "Biddle Notes," 2:544.

46   Thw. 5:134–35.

47   Ibid. 5:135, 137.

48   Gass, *Journal*, p. 273; Thw. 5:141–42.

49   Thw. 5:153, 156–58.

50   Ibid. 5:175–80.

51   Clark to Heney, July 20, 1806, Jackson, ed., *Letters*, 1:309–13. Donald Jackson's view that the July 20 draft is Clark's copy of a document composed by Lewis, probably on July 1, fits what is known about Lewis's Indian policy.

52   Thw. 5:188, 192, 203. The word "Pahkee" specifically referred to the Siksikas or Blackfeet-proper but was often used by Shoshonis and Nez Perces to mean any plains enemy.

53   Ibid. 5:207–208, 212, 215–17.

54   The Indians that Lewis saw were Piegans. Bloods, Piegans, and Siksikas or Blackfeet-proper were the three constituent tribes of the Blackfeet confederacy. The tribes were politically independent but united by a common language, common customs, and common enemies. See John C. Ewers, *The Blackfeet: Raiders on the Northwestern Plains* (Norman: University of Oklahoma Press, 1958), pp. 3–18.

55   For the rise and growth of the Blackfeet trade, see Ewers, *Blackfeet*, pp. 19–44 and E. E. Rich, *The Fur Trade and the Northwest to 1857* (Toronto: McClelland and Stewart, 1967), pp. 122–29.

56   Thw. 5:219–23. Wolf Calf's talk with Grinnell is recorded in Wheeler, *Trail of Lewis and Clark*, 2:311–12. A second and less accurate account from Blackfeet tradition can be found in James H. Bradley, "The Bradley Manuscript," Montana Historical Society *Contributions* 8 (1917): 135.

57   Ordway, *Journal*, p. 383; Thw. 5:223–27; "Peale's Memorandum of Specimens and Artifacts," Jackson, ed., *Letters*, 2:477. My understanding of both Camp Disappointment and the Two Medicine River fight site was greatly enhanced by Wilbur Werner, who guided me over both locations in the summer of 1981.

58   Biddle-Coues, *History*, 3:1105n; David H. Coyner, *The Lost Trapper*, ed. David J. Weber (1847; reprint, Albuquerque: University of New Mexico Press, 1970), p. 55; Washington Irving, *Astoria; or, Anecdotes of an Enterprise Beyond the Rocky Mountains*, ed. Edgeley W. Todd (1836; reprint, Norman: University of Oklahoma Press, 1964), p. 147.

59   Josephy, *Nez Perce*, pp. 651–53. Josephy's conclusions were somewhat anticipated

288

by Ewers, *Blackfeet,* p. 48, and Dale L. Morgan, *The West of William H. Ashley, 1822–1838* (Denver: The Old West Publishing Co., 1964), p. xxxv.

60 The councils with Missouri River Indians in 1806 were conducted by William Clark since Lewis's painful wound limited his active participation in expedition affairs.

61 Le Borgne's diplomatic achievements are recorded in Coues, ed., *New Light,* 1:367–97.

62 Thw. 5:337–42.

63 Ibid. 5:342–43.

64 Ibid. 5:344–46.

65 Ibid. 5:347.

66 Ibid. 5:350–53.

67 Ibid. 5:355–56.

68 Ibid. 5:393–94.

Afterword

1 Thw. 5:44.

2 Ibid. 4:89–90.

3 William Nichols, "Lewis and Clark Probe the Heart of Darkness," *American Scholar* 49 (1979–80): 97.

4 Thw. 5:343.

5 Bernard DeVoto, ed., *The Journals of Lewis and Clark* (Boston: Houghton Mifflin Co., 1953), p. lii.

6 Biddle-Coues, *History,* 2:762.

7 Peter Corney, *Voyages in the Northern Pacific, 1813–1818* (1821; reprint, Fairfield, Washington: Ye Galleon Press, 1965), p. 91.

8 Frederick W. Turner III, ed., *The Portable North American Indian Reader* (New York: Viking Press, 1974), pp. 253–54.

Appendix

1 Thw 2:162–63.

2 Ibid. 2:260.

3 Ibid. 3:111.

4 Ibid. 2:283.

5 Clark to Charbonneau, August 20, 1806, Jackson, ed., *Letters,* 1:315.

Bibliography

Primary Sources

Abel, Annie Heloise, ed. *Tabeau's Narrative of Loisel's Expedition to the Upper Missouri.* Norman: University of Oklahoma Press, 1939.

Beaglehole, J. C., ed. *The Voyage of the Resolution and Discovery, 1776–1780.* Cambridge: The Hakluyt Society, 1967.

Beckwith, Martha W., ed. *Mandan-Hidatsa Myths and Ceremonies.* Memoirs of the American Folk-Lore Society, vol. 32. New York: J. J. Augustin, 1938.

Betts, Edwin M., ed. *Thomas Jefferson's Garden Book, 1766–1824.* Philadelphia: American Philosophical Society, 1944.

Boas, Franz, ed. *Chinook Texts.* Smithsonian Institution, Bureau of American Ethnology Bulletin no. 20 (1894).

Boller, Henry A. *Among the Indians: Eight Years in the Far West, 1858–1866.* 1868. Reprint edited by Milo M. Quaife. Chicago: Lakeside Press, 1959.

Brackenridge, Henry M. *Views of Louisiana, Together with a Journal of a Voyage up the Missouri River, in 1811.* Pittsburgh: Cramer, Spear and Eichbaum, 1814.

Bradbury, John. *Travels in the Interior of America in the Years 1809, 1810, and 1811.* Liverpool: Smith and Galway, 1817.

Bradley, James H. "The Bradley Manuscript," Montana Historical Society *Contributions,* vol. 8 (1917).

Burpee, Lawrence J., ed. *Journals and Letters of Pierre Gaultier de Varennes de La Vérendrye and His Sons.* Toronto: Champlain Society, 1927.

Cappon, Lester J., ed. *The Adams-Jefferson Letters.* 2 vols. Chapel Hill: University of North Carolina Press, 1959.

Catlin, George. *Letters and Notes on the Manners, Customs, and Conditions of the North American Indians.* 2 vols. 1844. Reprint. New York: Dover Publications, 1973.

———. *O-Kee-Pa: A Religious Ceremony and Other Customs of the Mandans.* Edited by John C. Ewers. New Haven: Yale University Press, 1967.

Corney, Peter. *Voyages in the Northern Pacific, 1813–1818.* 1821. Reprint. Fairfield, Washington: Ye Galleon Press, 1965.

Coues, Elliott, ed. *History of the Expedition under the Command of Lewis and Clark.* 4

vols. in 3. 1893. Reprint. New York: Dover Publications, 1964.

————. ed. *New Light on the Early History of the Greater Northwest: The Manuscript Journals of Alexander Henry the Younger and of David Thompson*. 3 vols. in 2. 1897. Reprint. Minneapolis: Ross and Haines, 1965.

Coyner, David H. *The Lost Trappers*. 1847. Reprint edited by David J. Weber. Albuquerque: University of New Mexico Press, 1970.

Cutright, Paul R., ed. "The Journal of Private Joseph Whitehouse: A Soldier with Lewis and Clark," *Bulletin* of the Missouri Historical Society, 27 (1972): 143–61.

Denig, Edwin T. *Five Indian Tribes of the Upper Missouri: Sioux, Arickaras, Assiniboines, Crees, Crows*. Edited by John C. Ewers. Norman: University of Oklahoma Press, 1961.

DeVoto, Bernard, ed. *The Journals of Lewis and Clark*. Boston: Houghton Mifflin Co., 1953.

Donnelly, Joseph P., trans. *Wilderness Kingdom: Indian Life in the Rocky Mountains, 1840–1847; The Journals and Paintings of Nicholas Point, S.J.* New York: Holt, Rinehart and Winston, 1967.

Elliott, T. C., ed. "The Journal of the Ship *Ruby.*" *Oregon Historical Quarterly* 28 (1927): 258–80; 29 (1928): 337–46.

Farnham, Thomas J. "Travels in the Great Western Prairies" (1843). In *Early Western Travels*. Edited by Reuben G. Thwaites, vol. 28. Cleveland: Arthur H. Clark Co., 1904–1906.

Ferris, Warren A. *Life in the Rocky Mountains*. Edited by Paul C. Phillips. Denver: Old West Publishing Co., 1940.

Franchère, Gabriel. *A Voyage to the Northwest Coast of America*. 1854. Reprint edited by Milo M. Quaife. Chicago: Lakeside Press, 1954.

Gass, Patrick. *A Journal of the Voyages and Travels of a Corps of Discovery*. Edited by David McKeehan. 1807. Reprint. Minneapolis: Ross and Haines, 1958.

Glover, Richard, ed. *David Thompson's Narrative 1784–1812*. Toronto: Champlain Society, 1962.

Harper, J. Russell, ed. *Paul Kane's Frontier*. Austin: University of Texas Press, 1971.

Heizer, Robert F., ed. *Narrative of the Adventures and Sufferings of John R. Jewitt*. 1820. Reprint. Ramona, Calif.: Ballena Press, 1975.

Irving, Washington. *Astoria; or, Anecdotes of an Enterprise Beyond the Rocky Mountains*. 1836. Reprint edited by Edgeley W. Todd. Norman: University of Oklahoma Press, 1964.

Jackson, Donald, ed. *The Journals of Zebulon Montgomery Pike with Letters and Related Documents*. 2 vols. Norman: University of Oklahoma Press, 1966.

————, ed. *Letters of the Lewis and Clark Expedition with Related Documents, 1783–1854*. 2d ed. 2 vols. Urbana: University of Illinois Press, 1978.

Jefferson, Thomas. "A Statistical View of the Indian Nations." *American State Papers,* class 2, Indian Affairs (Washington, D.C., 1806), 1: 705–43.

Lamb, W. Kaye, ed. *The Journals and Letters of Sir Alexander Mackenzie*. Cambridge: Hakluyt Society, 1970.

Larocque, François Antoine. "The Missouri Journal, 1804–1805." In *Les Bourgeois de la Compagnie du Nord-Ouest*. Edited by L. R. Masson, vol. 1: 299–313. 1889–90. Reprint. New York: Antiquarian Press, 1960.

Luttig, John C. *Journal of a Fur-Trading Expedition on the Upper Missouri, 1812–1813*. Edited by Stella M. Drumm. Rev. ed. with new preface by A. P. Nasatir. 1920. Reprint. New York: Argosy-Antiquarian Press, 1964.

Mackenzie, Charles. "The Mississouri Indians: A Narrative of Four Trading Expeditions to the Mississouri 1804–1805–1806." In *Les Bourgeois de la Compagnie du Nord-Ouest*. Edited by L. R. Masson, vol. 1:327–93. 1889–90. Reprint. New York: Antiquarian Press, 1960.

Mengarini, Gregory. *Recollections of the Flathead Mission*. Edited by Gloria R. Lothrop. Glendale, Calif.: Arthur H. Clark Co., 1977.

Morgan, Dale L., ed. *The West of William H. Ashley, 1822–1838*. Denver: Old West Publishing Co., 1964.

Moulton, Gary E., ed. *Atlas of the Lewis and Clark Expedition*. Lincoln: University of Nebraska Press, 1983.

Nasatir, A. P., ed. *Before Lewis and Clark: Documents Illustrating the History of the Missouri, 1785–1804*. 2 vols. St. Louis: St. Louis Historical Documents Foundation, 1952.

————, ed. *John Evans: Explorer and Surveyor*. St. Louis: Missouri Historical Society, 1931.

Osgood, Ernest S., ed. *The Field Notes of Captain William Clark, 1803–1805*. New Haven: Yale University Press, 1964.

Quaife, Milo M., ed. *The Journals of Captain Meriwether Lewis and Sergeant John Ordway*. Madison: Historical Society of Wisconsin, 1916.

Rollins, Philip Ashton, ed. *The Discovery of the Oregon Trail: Robert Stuart's Narratives of His Overland Trip Eastward from Astoria in 1812–13*. New York: Edward Eberstadt, 1935.

Ross, Alexander. *Adventures of the First Settlers on the Oregon or Columbia River*. 1849. Reprint edited by Milo M. Quaife. Chicago: Lakeside Press, 1922.

Rush, Benjamin. *Medical Inquiries and Observations*. Philadelphia: Thomas Dobson, 1794.

Swan, James G. *The Northwest Coast, or, Three Years' Residence in Washington Territory*. 1857. Reprint. Seattle: University of Washington Press, 1969.

Thomas, Davis and Karin Ronnefeldt, eds. *People of the First Man*. New York: E. P. Dutton, 1976.

Thwaites, Reuben G., ed. *The Original Journals of the Lewis and Clark Expedition*. 8 vols. New York: Dodd, Mead and Co., 1904–1905.

Tucker, Sara J. and Wayne C. Temple, comps. *Atlas: Indian Villages of the Illinois Country.* Springfield: Illinois State Museum, 1942; Suppl. 1975.

Turner, Frederick W. III, ed. *The Portable North American Indian Reader.* New York: Viking Press, 1974.

Wheat, Carl I. *Mapping the Transmississippi West.* 5 vols. San Francisco: Institute of Historical Cartography, 1958–62.

Secondary Sources—Books

Allen, John L. *Passage through the Garden: Lewis and Clark and the Image of the American Northwest.* Urbana: University of Illinois Press, 1975.

Appleman, Roy E. *Lewis and Clark: Historic places Associated with Their Transcontinental Exploration.* Washington, D.C.: National Park Service, 1975.

Axtell, James. *The European and the Indian: Essays in the Ethnohistory of Colonial North America.* New York: Oxford University Press, 1981.

Bakeless, John. *Lewis and Clark: Partners in Discovery.* New York: William Morrow and Co., 1947.

Bass, William M., David R. Evans, and Richard L. Jantz. *The Leavenworth Site Cemetery: Archaeology and Physical Anthropology.* University of Kansas Publications in Anthropology, no. 2, 1971.

Bowers, Alfred W. *Hidatsa Social and Ceremonial Organization.* Smithsonian Institution, Bureau of American Ethnology Bulletin no. 194, 1965.

————. *Mandan Social and Ceremonial Organization.* Chicago: University of Chicago Press, 1950.

Brebner, John B. *The Explorers of North America 1492–1806.* New York: Macmillan, 1933.

Chuinard, Eldon G. *Only One Man Died: The Medical Aspects of the Lewis and Clark Expedition.* Glendale: Arthur H. Clark Co., 1979.

Cook, Warren L. *Flood Tide of Empire: Spain and the Pacific Northwest, 1543–1819.* New Haven: Yale University Press, 1973.

Criswell, Elijah H. *Lewis and Clark: Linguistic Pioneers.* Columbia: University of Missouri Press, 1940.

Culin, Stewart. *Games of the North American Indians.* Smithsonian Institution, Bureau of American Ethnology Annual Report no. 24, 1907.

Cutright, Paul R. *Lewis and Clark: Pioneering Naturalists.* Urbana: University of Illinois Press, 1969.

Densmore, Frances. *Teton Sioux Music.* Smithsonian Institution, Bureau of American Ethnology Bulletin no. 61, 1918.

DeVoto, Bernard. *The Course of Empire.* Boston: Houghton Mifflin Co., 1952.

Drucker, Philip. *Indians of the Northwest Coast.* New York: McGraw-Hill, 1955.

Edmunds, R. David. *The Otoe-Missouria People*. Phoenix: Indian Tribal Series, 1976.

Eide, Ingvard. *American Odyssey: The Journey of Lewis and Clark*. Chicago: Rand, McNally and Co., 1969.

Ewers, John C. *The Blackfeet: Raiders on the Northwestern Plains*. Norman: University of Oklahoma Press, 1958.

————. *Teton Dakota Ethnology and History*. Berkeley, Calif.: National Park Service, Western Museum Laboratories, 1938.

Fahey, John. *The Flathead Indians*. Norman: University of Oklahoma Press, 1974.

Gilmore, Melvin R. *The Uses of Plants by the Indians of the Missouri River Region*. 1919. Reprint. Lincoln: University of Nebraska Press, 1977.

Goetzmann, William. *Exploration and Empire: The Explorer and the Scientist in the Winning of the American West*. New York: Alfred A. Knopf, 1966.

Gough, Barry. *Distant Dominion: Britain and the Northwest Coast of North America, 1579–1809*. Vancouver: University of British Columbia Press, 1980.

Gunther, Erna. *Indian Life on the Northwest Coast of North America*. Chicago: University of Chicago Press, 1972.

Haines, Francis. *The Nez Percés: Tribesmen of the Columbia Plateau*. Norman: University of Oklahoma Press, 1955.

Hanson, James A. *Metal Weapons, Tools, and Ornaments of the Teton Dakota Indians*. Lincoln: University of Nebraska Press, 1975.

Holder, Preston. *The Hoe and the Horse on the Plains: A Study of Cultural Development among North American Indians*. Lincoln: University of Nebraska Press, 1970.

Horsman, Reginald. *Expansion and American Indian Policy, 1783–1812*. East Lansing: Michigan State University Press, 1967.

Howay, Frederic W. *A List of Trading Vessels in the Maritime Fur Trade, 1785–1825*. Kingston, Ontario: Limestone Press, 1973.

Jablow, Joseph. *The Cheyenne in Plains Indian Trade Relations, 1795–1840*. Seattle: University of Washington Press, 1950.

Jackson, Donald. *Thomas Jefferson and the Stony Mountains: Exploring the West from Monticello*. Urbana: University of Illinois Press, 1981.

Josephy, Alvin M., Jr. *The Nez Perce Indians and the Opening of the Northwest*. New Haven: Yale University Press, 1965.

Koch, Ronald P. *Dress Clothing of the Plains Indians*. Norman: University of Oklahoma Press, 1977.

Krause, Richard A. *The Leavenworth Site: Archaeology of an Historic Arikara Community*. University of Kansas Publications in Anthropology, no. 3. (1972).

Lehmer, Donald J. *Introduction to Middle Missouri Archeology*. U.S. Department of the Interior, National Park Service, Anthropological Papers no. 1, Lincoln, Nebr., 1971.

————. and David T. Jones. *Arikara Archeology: The Bad River Phase*. Smithsonian

Institution, River Basin Surveys Publications in Salvage Archeology no. 7, Lincoln, Nebr., 1968.

Liljeblad, Sven. *Idaho Indians in Transition, 1805–1960*. Pocatello: Idaho State University Museum, 1972.

Madsen, Brigham D. *The Lemhi: Sacajawea's People*. Caldwell, Idaho: Caxton Printers, 1979.

Meinig, Donald W. *The Great Columbia Plain: A Historical Geography, 1805–1910*. Seattle: University of Washington Press, 1968.

Meyer, Roy W. *The Village Indians of the Upper Missouri: The Mandans, Hidatsas, and Arikaras*. Lincoln: University of Nebraska Press, 1977.

Oglesby, Richard E. *Manuel Lisa and the Opening of the Missouri Fur Trade*. Norman: University of Oklahoma Press, 1963.

Oswalt, Wendell H. *Other Peoples, Other Customs: World Ethnography and Its History*. New York: Holt, Rinehart and Winston, 1972.

Peebles, John J. *Lewis and Clark in Idaho*. Boise: Idaho Historical Society, 1966.

Pethick, Derek. *First Approaches to the Northwest Coast*. Vancouver: J. J. Douglas, 1976.

Prucha, Francis P. *American Indian Policy in the Formative Years*. 1962. Reprint. Lincoln: University of Nebraska Press, 1970.

Ray, Verne F. *Cultural Relations in the Plateau of Northwestern America*. Los Angeles: The Southwest Museum, 1939.

_____ . *Lewis and Clark and the Nez Perce Indians*. Washington, D.C.: The Westerners, 1971.

Rich, E. E. *The Fur Trade and the Northwest to 1857*. Toronto: McClelland and Stewart, 1967.

Royster, Charles. *A Revolutionary People at War*. Chapel Hill: University of North Carolina Press, 1979.

Ruby, Robert H. and John A. Brown. *The Chinook Indians: Traders of the Lower Columbia River*. Norman: University of Oklahoma Press, 1976.

_____ . *Indians of the Pacific Northwest: A History*. Norman: University of Oklahoma Press, 1981.

Sauter, John and Bruce Johnson. *Tillamook Indians of the Oregon Coast*. Portland: Binfords and Mort, 1974.

Sheehan, Bernard W. *Seeds of Extinction: Jeffersonian Philanthropy and the American Indian*. Chapel Hill: University of North Carolina Press, 1973.

Space, Ralph. *Lewis and Clark through Idaho*. Lewiston, Idaho: Tribune Publishing Co., 1964.

Spier, Leslie. *Tribal Distribution in Washington*. General Series in Anthropology, no. 3. Menasha, Wisconsin: George Banta, 1936.

Smith, G. Hubert. *The Explorations of the La Vérendryes in the Northern Plains, 1738–1743*. Edited by W. Raymond Wood. Lincoln: University of Nebraska Press, 1980.

Stewart, Hilary. *Indian Fishing: Early Methods on the Northwest Coast*. Seattle: University of Washington Press, 1977.

Strong, W. Duncan, et. al. *Archaeology of the Dalles-Deschutes Region*. Berkeley: University of California Publications in American Archaeology and Ethnology, vol. 29 (1930).

Swanton, John R. *The Indian Tribes of North America*. Smithsonian Institution, Bureau of American Ethnology Bulletin no. 145, 1952.

Thomas, C. L., ed. *Taber's Cyclopedic Medical Dictionary*. 13th ed. Philadelphia: F. A. Davis, 1977.

Trenholm, Virginia and Maurine Carley. *The Shoshonis: Sentinels of the Rockies*. Norman: University of Oklahoma Press, 1964.

Wedel, Waldo. *Archeological Materials from the Vicinity of Mobridge, South Dakota*. Smithsonian Institution, Bureau of American Ethnology Bulletin no. 157, 1955.

———. *Observations on Some Nineteenth Century Pottery Vessels from the Upper Missouri*. Smithsonian Institution, Bureau of American Ethnology Bulletin no. 164, 1957.

Wheeler, Olin D. *The Trail of Lewis and Clark, 1804–1904*. 2 vols. New York: G. P. Putnam's Sons, 1904.

Whitman, William. *The Oto*. Columbia University Contributions to Anthropology, no. 28 (1937): 1–32.

Wilson, Gilbert L. *Agriculture of the Hidatsa Indians: An Indian Interpretation*. Minneapolis: University of Minnesota Studies in the Social Sciences, no. 9, 1917.

Wishart, David J. *The Fur Trade of the American West, 1807–1840: A Geographic Synthesis*. Lincoln: University of Nebraska Press, 1979.

Wood, W. Raymond. *An Interpretation of Mandan Culture History*. Smithsonian Institution, Bureau of American Ethnology Bulletin no. 198. 1967.

——— and Jeffrey R. Hanson. *The Origins of the Hidatsa Indians: A Review of Ethnohistorical and Traditional Data*. Lincoln: National Park Service, Midwest Archeological Center, 1980.

——— and Margot Liberty, eds. *Anthropology on the Great Plains*. Lincoln: University of Nebraska Press, 1980.

Secondary Sources—Articles

Allen, John L. "An Analysis of the Exploratory Process: The Lewis and Clark Expedition of 1804–1806." *Geographical Review* 62 (1972): 13–39.

Alwin, John A. "Pelts, Provisions, and Perceptions: The Hudson's Bay Company Mandan Indian Trade, 1795–1815." *Montana, the Magazine of Western History* 29 (1979): 16–27.

Anderson, Irving W. "Probing the Riddle of the Bird Woman." *Montana, the Magazine of Western History* 23 (1973): 2–17.

Berreman, Joel V. "Tribal Distribution in Oregon." *Memoirs* of the American Anthropological Association 47 (1937): 1–67.

Bruner, Edward M. "Mandan." In *Perspectives in American Indian Culture Change.* Edited by Edward H. Spicer, pp. 187–277. Chicago: University of Chicago Press, 1961.

Burland, C. A. "American Indian Map Makers." *Geographical Magazine* 22 (1947): 285–92.

Calloway, Colin G. "The Inter-tribal Balance of Power on the Great Plains, 1760–1850." *Journal of American Studies* 16 (1982): 25–47.

Cressman, L. S. "Cultural Sequences at The Dalles, Oregon: A Contribution to Pacific Northwest Prehistory." American Philosophical Society, *Transactions* 50 (1960): 1–108.

Cutright, Paul R. "Lewis and Clark Indian Peace Medals." *Bulletin* of the Missouri Historical Society 24 (1968): 160–67.

———. "Lewis and Clark: Portraits and Portraitists." *Montana, the Magazine of Western History* 19 (1969): 37–53.

Diller, Aubrey. "A New Map of the Missouri River drawn in 1795." *Imago Mundi* 12 (1955): 175–80.

Ewers, John C. "The Indian Trade of the Upper Missouri before Lewis and Clark." *Bulletin* of the Missouri Historical Society 10 (1954): 429–46.

Fisher, Robin. "Cook and the Nootka." In *Captain James Cook and His Times.* Edited by Robin Fisher and Hugh Johnston, pp. 81–98. Seattle: University of Washington Press, 1979.

French, David. "Wasco-Wishram." In *Perspectives in American Indian Culture Change.* Edited by Edward H. Spicer, pp. 337–430. Chicago: University of Chicago Press, 1961.

Friis, Herman R. "Cartographic and Geographic Activities of the Lewis and Clark Expedition." *Journal* of the Washington Academy of Sciences 44 (1954): 338–51.

Garth, Thomas R. "Early Nineteenth Century Tribal Relations in the Columbia Plateau." *Southwestern Journal of Anthropology* 20 (1964): 43–57.

Grange, Roger T., Jr. "An Archeological View of Pawnee Origins." *Nebraska History* 60 (1979): 134–60.

Hyde, George E. "The Mystery of the Arikaras." *North Dakota History* 18 (1951): 187–218; 19 (1952): 25–58.

Jackson, Donald. "Some Books Carried by Lewis and Clark." *Bulletin* of the Missouri Historical Society 16 (1959): 3–13.

Kehoe, Alice B. "The Function of Ceremonial Sexual Intercourse among the Northern Plains Indians." *Plains Anthropologist* 15 (1970): 99–103.

King, J. C. H. "The Nootka of Vancouver Island." In *Cook's Voyages and the Peoples of the Pacific.* Edited by Hugh Cobbe, pp. 89–108. London: British Museum Publications, 1979.

Kunitz, Stephen. "Benjamin Rush on Savagism and Progress." *Ethnohistory* 17 (1970): 31–40.

Lehmer, Donald J. "Epidemics among the Indians of the Upper Missouri." In *Selected Writings of Donald J. Lehmer.* Edited by W. Raymond Wood, pp. 105–11. Lincoln, Nebr.: J & L Reprint Co., 1977.

Lewis, G. Malcolm. "Indian Maps." In *Old Trails and New Directions: Papers of the Third North American Fur Trade Conference.* Edited by Carol M. Judd and Arthur J. Ray, pp. 9–23. Toronto: University of Toronto Press, 1980.

Lowie, Robert H. "The Northern Shoshone." American Museum of Natural History, *Anthropological Papers* 2, pt. 2 (1909): 169–306.

————. "Notes on Shoshonean Ethnography." American Museum of Natural History, *Anthropological Papers* 22 (1924): 187–314.

Nasatir, A. P. "Jacques D'Eglise on the Upper Missouri, 1791–1795." *Mississippi Valley Historical Review* 14 (1927): 47–71.

Nichols, William. "Lewis and Clark Probe the Heart of Darkness." *American Scholar* 49 (1979–80): 94–101.

Nute, Grace L. "Posts in the Minnesota Fur-Trading Area, 1660–1855." *Minnesota History* 11 (1930): 353–85.

Olson, Ronald L. "Adze, Canoe, and House Types of the Northwest Coast." University of Washington *Publications in Anthropology* 2 (1927): 1–38.

Parks, Douglas R. "Bands and Villages of the Arikara and Pawnee." *Nebraska History* 60 (1979): 214–39.

Ray, Verne F. "The Chinook Indians in the Early 1800s." In *The Western Shore: Oregon Country Essays Honoring the American Revolution.* Edited by Thomas Vaughan, pp. 121–50. Portland: Oregon Historical Society, 1976.

————. "The Historical Position of the Lower Chinook in the Native Culture of the Northwest." *Pacific Northwest Quarterly* 28 (1937): 363–72.

————. "Lower Chinook Ethnographic Notes." University of Washington *Publications in Anthropology* 7 (1938): 29–165.

————. "Native Villages and Groupings of the Columbia Basin." *Pacific Northwest Quarterly* 27 (1936): 99–152.

————. "Tribal Distribution in Eastern Oregon and Adjacent Regions." *American Anthropologist* 40 (1938): 384–415.

———— and Nancy O. Lurie. "The Contributions of Lewis and Clark to Ethnography." *Journal* of the Washington Academy of Sciences 44 (1954): 358–70.

Rees, John E. "The Shoshoni Contribution to Lewis and Clark." *Idaho Yesterdays* 2 (1958): 2–13.

Saindon, Bob. "The Lost Vocabularies of the Lewis and Clark Expedition." *We Proceeded On* 3 (1977): 4–6.

Smith, G. Hubert. "Notes on Omaha Ethnohistory, 1763–1820." *Plains Anthropologist* 18 (1973): 257–70.

Spier, Leslie, and Edward Sapir. "Wishram Ethnography." University of Washington *Publications in Anthropology* 3 (1930): 151–300.

Steward, Julian H. "Culture Element Distributions: 23 Northern and Gosiute Shoshoni." *Anthropological Records* 8 (1943): 263–392.

Stewart, Frank H. "Mandan and Hidatsa Villages in the Eighteenth and Nineteenth Centuries." *Plains Anthropologist* 19 (1974): 287–302.

Stewart, Omer. "The Shoshoni: Their History and Social Organization." *Idaho Yesterdays* 9 (1965): 2–5, 28.

Turney-High, H. H. "The Flathead Indians of Montana." *Memoirs* of the American Anthropological Association 48 (1937): 1–161.

Wedel, Wildred M. and Raymond J. Demallie. "The Ethnohistorical Approach in Plains Area Studies." In *Anthropology on the Great Plains.* Edited by W. Raymond Wood and Margot Liberty, pp. 110–28. Lincoln: University of Nebraska Press, 1980.

White, Richard. "The Winning of the West: The Expansion of the Western Sioux in the Eighteenth and Nineteenth Centuries." *Journal of American History* 65 (1978): 319–43.

Willoughby, Charles C. "A Few Ethnological Specimens Collected by Lewis and Clark." *American Anthropologist* 7 (1905): 633–41.

Wood, W. Raymond. "Contrastive Features of Native North American Trade Systems." University of Oregon *Anthropological Papers* 4 (1972): 153–69.

————. "David Thompson at the Mandan-Hidatsa Villages, 1797–1798: The Original Journals." *Ethnohistory* 24 (1977): 329–42.

————. "The John Evans 1796–1797 Map of the Missouri River." *Great Plains Quarterly* 1 (1981): 39–53.

————. "Lewis and Clark and Middle Missouri Archaeology." *Quarterly Review of Archaeology* 3 (1982): 3–5.

————. "Northern Plains Village Cultures: Internal Stability and External Relationships." *Journal of Anthropological Research* 30 (1974): 1–16.

———— and Gary E. Moulton. "Prince Maximilian and New Maps of the Missouri and Yellowstone Rivers by William Clark." *Western Historical Quarterly* 12 (1981): 372–86.

Dissertations and Unpublished Materials

Kardas, Susan. " 'The People Bought This and the Clatsop Became Rich.' A View of Nineteenth Century Fur Trade Relationships on the Lower Columbia Between Chinookan Speakers, Whites, and Kanakas." Ph.D. diss. Bryn Mawr College, 1971.

Wells, Robin W. *Tribal Distribution Map Series, North America.* Toledo: University of Toledo Cartographic Services, n.d.

Wood, W. Raymond. "Notes on the Historical Cartography of the Upper Knife-Heart Region." Lincoln: National Park Service, Midwest Archeological Center, 1978.

Index

"I have proposed many quiries under sundry heads."
— MERIWETHER LEWIS, 1803

Abbreviations used in the index

LC: Lewis and Clark
LCE: Lewis and Clark Expedition
ML: Meriwether Lewis
TJ: Thomas Jefferson
WC: William Clark